Alpha
Teach Yourself

Estate
Planning

in 24 hours

ALPHA

A Pearson Education Company

Alpha Teach Yourself Estate Planning in 24 Hours

Copyright © 2002 by Keith R. Lyman

International Standard Book Number: 0-02-864197-3
Library of Congress Catalog Card Number: 2001091099

Printed in the United States of America

First printing: 2002

04   03   02   4   3   2   1

Note: This publication contains the opinions and ideas of its author. It is intended to provide helpful and informative material on the subject matter covered. It is sold with the understanding that the author and publisher are not engaged in rendering professional services in the book. If the reader requires personal assistance or advice, a competent professional should be consulted.

Trademarks

ACQUISITIONS EDITOR
Mike Sanders

DEVELOPMENT EDITOR
Suzanne Levert

PRODUCTION EDITOR
Billy Fields

COPY EDITOR
Rachel Lopez

INDEXER
Brad Herriman

PRODUCTION
Angela Calvert
Svetlana Dominguez

COVER DESIGNER
Alan Clements

BOOK DESIGNER
Gary Adair

MANAGING EDITOR
Jennifer Chisholm

PRODUCT MANAGER
Phil Kitchel

PUBLISHER
Marie Butler-Knight

Overview

Introduction   xvi

PART I Understanding the Basics

    HOUR 1 The Estate Planning Process   3

    HOUR 2 Inheritance and the Laws of Intestate Succession   17

    HOUR 3 What Is an Estate?   25

    HOUR 4 Defining Types of Assets   39

PART II Understanding Taxes

    HOUR 5 Income Taxes and Inheritance Taxes   55

    HOUR 6 Federal Estate Taxes   71

PART III Administering Estates

    HOUR 7 Dealing with Lifetime Issues   95

    HOUR 8 Probate   103

PART IV Using the Primary Estate Planning Tools

    HOUR 9 Wills   125

    HOUR 10 Revocable Living Trusts   137

    HOUR 11 Wills and Trusts: Important Provisions   163

    HOUR 12 Powers of Attorney, Health Care Representative Appointments, and Living Wills   181

PART V Special Assets

    HOUR 13 Life Insurance   193

    HOUR 14 Retirement Plans   205

    HOUR 15 Business Entities   221

PART VI Tax Saving Techniques

    HOUR 16 Credit Shelter Trusts   241

    HOUR 17 Irrevocable Life Insurance Trusts   251

    HOUR 18 Minor's Trusts and Education Planning   263

    HOUR 19 Charitable Trusts   275

    HOUR 20 Marital Trusts and Disclaimer Planning   301

    HOUR 21 Gifting of Assets   311

    HOUR 22 Planning for Non-Residents   327

PART VII Putting It All Together

    HOUR 23 Case Study 1: Single Individuals   335

    HOUR 24 Case Study 2: Married Couples   347

PART VIII Appendixes

    APPENDIX A Answers to Quiz Questions   357

    APPENDIX B Lady Di's Will   359

    APPENDIX C Last Will and Testament of Richard M. Nixon   367

    APPENDIX D References and Further Readings   383

    APPENDIX E Glossary   387

    Index   403

Contents

Introduction   **xvi**

PART I Understanding the Basics

HOUR 1 The Estate Planning Process   3

Why Plan? 4

What Is an Estate Plan? 4

The Estate Planning Process 5

     Calculating Estate Value 7

     Determining Your Estate's Tax Liability 7

     Understanding Your Lifetime Financial Needs 7

     Assessing Your Property 8

     Title to Property Included in Your Estate 8

     Considering Beneficiary Competency 9

     Determining Your Marginal Income Tax Bracket 9

     Understanding Your State Law 10

Estate Planning: The Failure to Plan 12

Estate Planning: Determining Your Need 13

Hour's Up! 15

HOUR 2 Inheritance and the Laws of Intestate Succession   17

The Nature of Property Ownership 17

     Identifying the Heirs 18

Modern Inheritance 19

     The Uniform Probate Code 20

Per Stirpes and Per Capita 21

     How It Works: Per Stirpes 22

     How It Works: Per Capita 23

Hour's Up! 23

HOUR 3 What Is an Estate?   25

Different Types of Property 25

     Real Property 26

     Personal Property 26

Probate and Non-Probate Estates Compared 28
    Your Probate Property 29
    Your Non-Probate Property..29
    Your Non-Taxable Estate 29
    Your Taxable Estate: Obvious Assets 30
    The Importance of Title 31
    Your Taxable Estate: Less Obvious Assets 32
    Even Less Obvious Assets 32
Hour's Up!..36

HOUR 4 Defining Types of Assets   39
    Single Ownership 39
    Joint Tenancy with Right of Survivorship 40
    Bank Accounts 42
    Tenancy in Common..43
    Tenancy by the Entirety 45
Understanding Contractual Assets 48
    Life Insurance Contracts..48
    Retirement Accounts 49
    Annuities..49
    Payable on Death Accounts 49
Community Property 50
Hour's Up!..52

PART II Understanding Taxes

HOUR 5 Income Taxes and Inheritance Taxes   55
    Blindsided by Tax Deferral 56
    Qualified Retirement Accounts 56
    Savings Bonds 57
The Decedent's Final Return 58
The Fiduciary Taxes 60
Allowable Deductions 63
    Filing the Return..64
Inheritance Taxes vs. Estate Taxes..64
    The Relationship Connection 66
Avoiding Inheritance Taxes 68
Hour's Up!..69

HOUR 6 Federal Estate Taxes   71
The Gift Tax..74
Estate Taxes vs. Inheritance Taxes..75

What to Include in the Gross Estate 75
   Real Estate 77
   Personal Property...77
   Cash...77
   Bank Accounts 77
   Money Market Accounts 78
   Certificates of Deposit...78
   U.S. Savings Bonds 78
   Treasury Bills, Notes, and Bonds...79
   Brokerage Accounts 79
   Retirement Accounts 80
   Annuities...80
   Life Insurance Proceeds..80
   Stocks and Securities..81
   Interests in Family-Owned Businesses 82
   Retained Life Estates...82
   Transfers Taking Effect at Death..82
   Revocable Transfers...83
   Joint Interests 83
   General Powers of Appointment 83
   The Valuation Date..84
Special Valuations 84
Understanding Deductions 85
   Administrative and Funeral Expenses 85
   Claims Against the Estate..85
   Casualty and Theft Loss 85
   Marital Deduction..85
   Charitable Deductions 86
Figuring Tax Rates 86
How the Unified Credit Works 88
   Allowable Credits 88
   Tax Day! 90
Hour's Up!...90

Part III Administering Estates

Hour 7 Dealing with Lifetime Issues   95

Legal Considerations 96
Types of Guardianships...97
   Minors 97
   Adults 98
Problems with Guardianships...99

Bypassing the Guardianship Process 100
Hour's Up!..101

HOUR 8 Probate   **103**

History of Probate...103
Probate Property 104
Functions of Probate...104
    Will Validity 105
    Who's in Charge? 105
    What to Do If There Is No Will..105
    Letters Testamentary 107
    Notice to Creditors 107
    Inventory 107
    Will Contests..109
    Duties of the Personal Representative 109
    Posting Bond 109
    Sale of Assets...109
    Getting the Appraisal 111
    Estate Property Insurance 111
    Taxes, Taxes, Taxes 111
    Income Taxes...111
    Inheritance Taxes 112
    Federal Estate Taxes 112
    Fiduciary Taxes 112
Alternate Probate Procedures..114
    Simplified Administration 114
    No Administration 114
Advantages of Probate Administration 114
    Protecting Personal Representatives...115
    Protecting Creditors 115
    Protecting Heirs...115
    Resolving Disputes 116
    Determining Heirship 116
Disadvantages of Probate Administration 116
    Attorneys, Personal Representatives, and Their Fees 116
    Probate Delays...120
    Mandatory Claims Period 120
    Valuation Issues...120
    Will Contests and Claims 120
    Ancillary Administration 120
    Public Proceedings..121
Hour's Up!...121

PART IV Using the Primary Estate Planning Tools

HOUR 9 Wills   125

Types of Wills 125
How Do Wills Work? 126
    Execution Requirements 127
    Self-Proving Declaration...128
Important Will Provisions 129
    Designating the Personal Representative 129
    Making Specific Gifts 130
    Designation of Guardians 131
Revocation of Wills 131
    Revocation by Written Declaration or Subsequent Will..........131
    Revocation by Destruction 132
    The Last Valid Will Prevails 132
Amending the Will 132
Updating Your Will 133
What a Will Can and Cannot Do for You......................................133
Wills of the Famous 134
Hour's Up!..135

HOUR 10 Revocable Living Trusts   137

What Is a Trust? 137
What Is a Living Trust? 138
The Mechanics of a Trust 138
    Control of a Trust 139
    Avoiding Probate 139
Comparing Wills and Trusts 140
Execution Requirements...140
    Having the Capacity 141
    Expressing the Intention...141
    Designating a Beneficiary 141
Important Trust Provisions 142
    Purpose of the Trust..142
    Identification of Trust Property..142
    Trust Funding...143
    Assignment of Personal Property 143
    Assets You Do Not Want In Your Trust 144
    Name of Trust 145
    Identification of the Trustee 145
    Discretionary Distributions 148
Issues of Institutional Trustees 148

Designation of Co-Trustees 150
Trustee Provisions 150
  Succession 150
  Resignation 151
  Compensation 151
  How Much Is Enough? 151
  Bond of Trustees 152
  Accounting Requirements 152
  Trustee Powers and Duties 153
Provisions for Revocation, Amendment, and Transfer 154
Further Thoughts on Incapacity..155
Protecting the Trust 156
  Spendthrift Provisions...156
  In Terrorem Provisions 157
Common Myths Concerning Living Trusts 157
Hour's Up!...160

HOUR 11 Wills and Trusts: Important Provisions   163
  Survivorship Provisions..164
  Simultaneous Death 165
  Distributing the Residue 166
Paying Back Debt 167
Disinheritance..170
  Who Can You Disinherit 171
  How to Disinherit 172
Identification of Beneficiaries 173
Specific Gifts..173
  How to Make Specific Gifts 173
Distribution Provisions...175
Hour's Up!...178

**HOUR 12 Powers of Attorney, Health Care Representative Appointments,
          and Living Wills   181**
  General Power of Attorney...181
  Special or Limited Power of Attorney 182
  Durable Power of Attorney..182
  Springing Durable Power of Attorney 183
  Termination at Death 184
Requirements for Execution 185
  Compensation and Reimbursement 185
  Recordation Requirements 185
  Revocation...185
  Advantages 186

Health Care Representative Appointment 186
Living Wills 188
    Execution Requirements 188
Hour's Up!...189

Part V Special Assets

Hour 13 Life Insurance   193

Life Insurance Policies – A Closer Look 194
    Term Insurance 194
Whole Life Insurance 196
Universal Life Insurance..198
Variable Life Insurance..198
Variable Universal Life Insurance 199
Survivorship Life Insurance 199
First to Die Life Insurance 200
Taxation of Death Benefits..200
The Value of Life Insurance 201
    Advantages of Life Insurance 202
Hour's Up!...203

Hour 14 Retirement Plans   205

Taxability of Retirement Accounts 206
    Income Taxation 206
    Federal Estate Tax 206
    State Inheritance Taxes..207
Non-Qualified Plans..207
    Annuities..208
    Variable Life Products 209
Qualified Plans for Individuals..210
    The Traditional IRA 210
    Roth IRA..210
Qualified Plans for Businesses 211
    Simplified Employee Pension (SEP)..211
    Savings Incentive Match Plan for Employees (SIMPLE) 212
    403(b)(7) Plan..212
    401(k) Plan 213
Penalty-Free Distributions 213
Minimum Required Distributions 214
Spousal Rollovers 218
Hour's Up!...219

HOUR 15 Business Entities   **221**

Sole Proprietorship 221
   Legal Documents Needed 222
   Liability Issues 222
   Taxation..222
   Advantages 222
   Disadvantages 222
The General Partnership 223
   Legal Documents Needed 223
   Liability 224
   Taxation..225
   Advantages 225
   Disadvantages 227
The Limited Partnership 227
   Legal Documents Needed 227
   Tax Requirements 227
   Advantages 228
   Disadvantages 228
The Corporation...228
   Legal Documents Needed 229
   Taxation of Corporations 230
   Advantages 234
   Disadvantages 235
Some Other Business Entities 235
Hour's Up!..237

PART VI Tax Saving Techniques

HOUR 16 Credit Shelter Trusts   **241**

Setting Up a Credit Shelter Trust 243
Formula Marital Deduction 244
Providing for Your Surviving Spouse 245
   Proving Income 245
   The Five and Five Power 246
   Limited Power of Appointment 247
   The Ascertainable Standard 247
Choosing the Trustee 248
Hour's Up!..249

HOUR 17 Irrevocable Life Insurance Trusts   **251**

Understanding the Plan 252
   Choosing the Right Policy 252

The Irrevocable Life Insurance Trust 253
    Who's in Charge? 254
    What Happens After the Trust Is Created? 254
    Paying the Premiums 255
Trust Fundamentals 256
    Exploring Beneficiary Tax Implications 257
Some Alternatives to an Irrevocable Life Insurance Trusts 258
Applying the Death Benefit 258
Other Twists and Turns 259
    The Standby Trust 259
Advantages of an Irrevocable Life Insurance Trust 260
Hour's Up! 260

HOUR 18 Minor's Trusts and Education Planning   **263**

Section 2503(c) Trust 263
    Tax Implications 264
    Additional Strategies 265
    Disadvantages 265
Section 2503(b) Trust 266
    Tax Implications 266
    Strategy 267
    Taxation 267
Educational Trusts 267
    Education IRAs 267
    Qualified State Tuition Programs 269
    Roth IRA Accounts 272
Prepaid Tuition Programs 272
Hour's Up! 273

HOUR 19 Charitable Trusts   **275**

Charitable Remainder Trusts 275
    Charitable Remainder Unitrust 276
    Charitable Remainder Annuity Trusts 280
    Makeup Provisions 285
    Charitable Lead Trust 285
    Charitable Lead Annuity Trust 290
Types of Charities 294
    I.R.C. Section 170(b)(1)(A) Organizations 294
    I.R.C. Section 2055(a) Organizations 294
    I.R.C. Section 2522(a) Organizations 295
    I.R.C. Section 509(a) Private Foundations 295

Pooled Income Fund 295
Advantages and Disadvantages...295
Hour's Up!...298

HOUR 20 Marital Trusts and Disclaimer Planning   301

The Unlimited Marital Deduction..301
Power of Appointment Trust 301
QTIP Trust..303
Using Disclaimers 304
The Qualified Disclaimer 305
Effect of a Disclaimer 305
Why Disclaim at All?...306
The Non-Qualified Disclaimer..307
The Disclaimer Trust 307
Hour's Up!..308

HOUR 21 Gifting of Assets   311

Valuation of Gifts 312
Non-Tax Advantages of Gifting..313
Income Tax Benefits 313
Estate Tax Benefits 315
Community Property Considerations..315
Annual Gift Exclusion 316
Future Interest Gifts 316
Gift Splitting 319
Unlimited Marital Deduction 321
Comparing Gift and Estate Taxes 321
More on Gifts and Taxes 322
Timing of Gifts 322
Tax Impact on Recipient 323
Stepped-Up Basis...323
Qualified Transfers 324
Hour's Up!..325

HOUR 22 Planning for Non-Residents   327

The Taxable Estate of the Alien 327
Marital Deduction for Aliens..328
United States Treaties 328
Unified Credit for Aliens..329
Availability of the Gift Tax Annual Exclusion 329
Qualified Domestic Trust (QDOT) 330
Hour's Up!..331

Part VII Putting It All Together

Hour 23 Case Study 1: Single Individuals   335

Analysis 339
Alternative 1: Projecting Future Growth 340
Analysis and Suggestions 340
Alternative 2 343
Analysis of Plan Implementation 344
Hour's Up! 345

Hour 24 Case Study 2: Married Couples   347

Example 1—All to Spouse 347
Example 2—Use of Credit Shelter Trusts 349
Example 3—Use of Irrevocable Life Insurance Trust 351
Hour's Up! 353

Part VIII Appendixes

Appendix A Answers to Quiz Questions   357

Appendix B Lady Di's Will   359

Appendix C Last Will and Testament of Richard M. Nixon   367

Appendix D References and Further Reading   383

Appendix E Glossary   387

Index   403

Introduction

WELCOME! You have now joined a select group of individuals who have recognized the importance of planning their estates. If you think this is not a real accomplishment, consider that thousands of individuals die each year with no will or trust. Many of these individuals had spouses and children, but without a will or trust, there was, in effect, no plan.

Whenever you fail to create a plan of your own, state law is there with its own plan. These laws direct who your beneficiaries will be and what portion of your estate they will receive. Do you know the laws of your state? Do you know what will happen if you should die today, before you create your plan?

Some people understand the need for planning, but simply put off the decision to go forward. That great enemy, procrastination, is there to stop even the most determined. That is why you have joined a very select group of people who have made the decision to control the destiny of their estates.

You probably were attracted to the title of this book, thinking that in 24 hours, you will have all of the information you need to plan your estate. You will be partially correct. If you take the time to digest each chapter, one day at a time, until you complete all 24 chapters, you will have been exposed to more information than most people, even many attorneys!

What matters most is what you do with your newly acquired knowledge. You are reading about a legal topic that is taught to law students over a period of two and one-half to three years. Law students take courses in *Estate Taxation, Wills and Probate, Estate Planning, Advanced Estate Planning, Corporations,* and *Partnerships,* to name but a few.

There are also financial issues to understand. Certified Financial Planners are trained in *Income Taxation, Fiduciary Taxation, Estate Planning, Charitable Gifting, Life Insurance, Annuities, Qualified Retirement Planning, Gifting Techniques,* and *Estate Taxation.*

Estate planning is a hybrid between these two professions. Law students are not taught all there is to know about financial planning. Likewise, financial planners are not taught all there is to know about law, nor are they licensed to give legal advice.

So what exactly is your responsibility? First, read this book. Move along at your own pace until you finish. DO NOT STOP! It is your obligation to complete the book and the process that you have begun. Then you must find an estate planning attorney and a financial planner to assist you with details.

You may be asking yourself why you should read this book if you are simply going to hire a professional to create your plan anyway. The reason is that you need to understand your choices and the ramifications of your choices. By reading this book, you will gain insight into how the entire estate planning process works that others simply do not have. You will not be forced to blindly take the advice of a professional who tells you what you need.

This book is about intelligent decision-making. You have the most important role in the estate planning process. All decisions are eventually yours to make. Estate-planning attorneys are to provide you with legal advice, but you must make the decisions. Financial planners are to provide you with the financial advice you need, but ultimately the decision is yours to make.

The estate planning process is all about preserving and protecting your assets, assets that you have spent an entire lifetime accumulating. The process is also about your family and your beneficiaries. It may be your spouse for whom you are planning, it may be your small children, it may be your elderly parents, or it may be someone suffering from physical or mental disability. Your estate planning lawyer and your financial advisor rely upon you to convey to them your personal goals and objectives. Their job is to implement the appropriate plan.

Above anything else, do not assume that you can prepare your own legal documents and implement your plan based upon the information contained in this book. To begin with, laws do change from time to time. This can make some of this material outdated rather quickly. Secondly, laws vary from state to state. It is difficult to make assumptions about the laws in every state. This book discusses general law except where indicated. You must learn from a professional what the laws are in your state.

My goal is to educate you and enable you to make informed decisions about your plan. I want you to understand what probate is before you tell your lawyer that you want to avoid it. I want you to be able to identify what property passes through probate. I want you to understand that certain decisions have tax consequences and learn what those consequences are. I want you to know the difference between a will and a trust and why you may choose one over the other. I want you to know how to reduce the taxation of your estate.

There is probably a better way to title your assets than the way you have them currently titled. There is probably a better way to save taxes than your current plan allows. Read, make notes as you go, take the quizzes, and all the while think about your situation and how it relates to what you are reading. When you are done, write down your objectives along with possible tools to utilize in achieving those objectives. Then contact a qualified estate planning lawyer and certified financial planner to give you the detailed advice you need to implement your plan.

Above all else, ENJOY THE PROCESS!

Last but not least, this book has a lot of miscellaneous cross-references, tips, shortcuts, and warning sidebar boxes. Here's how they stack up:

GO TO ▶
This sidebar gives you a cross-references to another chapter or section in the book to learn more about a particular topic.

JUST A MINUTE

 "Just a Minute" sidebars offer advice or teach an easier way to do something.

TIME SAVER

 "Time Saver" sidebars give you a faster way to do something.

STRICTLY DEFINED

"Strictly Defined" boxes offer definitions of words you may not know.

PROCEED WITH CAUTION

 "Proceed with Caution" boxes are warnings. They warn you about potential problems and help you steer clear of trouble.

About the Author

Keith R. Lyman, J.D., CFP, graduated from Washburn University School of Law in Topeka, Kansas, in 1978, and is a member of the American Bar Association, Indiana Bar Association, Probate, Trust, and Real Property section of the Indiana Bar Association, Terre Haute Bar Association, National Association of Estate Planners and Councils, and the National Academy of Elder Law Attorneys. Mr. Lyman has spoken twice for the Indiana Continuing Legal Education Forum on the topics of "Drafting Your First Trust Under $650,000" and "Drafting Your First Trust Under $675,000."

Mr. Lyman is licensed to practice law in both Indiana and Kansas and is also a certified financial planner, having received his designation through the College for Financial Planning in Denver, Colorado. His firm, Lyman-Kincaid, PC, handles estate planning and planning for long-term care, and is located at 401 Ohio St. #10, Terre Haute, Indiana 47807.

Acknowledgments

I would first like to thank Mike Sanders, acquisitions editor, for providing me with this opportunity to assemble my knowledge of estate planning concepts, tools, and techniques into this book. I also wish to acknowledge everyone at Alpha Books, including the development editor, Suzanne LeVert; project editor, Billy Fields; and copy editor Rachel Lopez, all of whom worked hard behind the scenes to get this book to press.

I also would like to offer a personal note to Tonya J. Davidson Kincaid. My thanks go to her for managing our firm's many clients during the months that it took to write this book. I also thank her for agreeing to study the manuscript and suggest technical changes.

My thanks also to Analiza M. Butterman, my paralegal, and Robin L. Winniski, my legal secretary, for reviewing the manuscript, making suggestions, and tolerating my unusual sense of humor while I worked on this project.

In addition, I thank Sean Drummond, financial planner with Capital Planning Systems, Inc., who read some of the more technical financial topics, offered his suggestions, and provided me with many helpful resources.

Above all, I thank my wife Janet for handling the many challenging responsibilities of home and children, while at the same time managing her own teaching career at Indiana State University. Also, a very special thank you goes to my two children, Matthew and Brooke, who were both very patient with my continued absence while writing this book.

Of course, thanks to you, the reader. Without you, there would be no point in writing.

Disclaimer

PART I

Understanding the Basics

HOUR 1   The Estate Planning Process

HOUR 2   Inheritance and the Laws of
Intestate Succession

HOUR 3   What Is an Estate?

HOUR 4   Defining Types of Assets

HOUR 1

The Estate Planning Process

W ithin the last 10 years, estate planning has emerged as one of the most rapidly evolving areas of practice in the legal community. In addition, the financial services industry now offers "estate planning" services to many of its clientele as well, which emphasizes the importance of this area of law.

The reason for this boom in estate planning is that the baby-boom generation is not only one of the largest segments of society, it is also one of the wealthiest. Thanks to market growth and rising salaries, many people in their 40s and 50s have far more wealth than their own parents ever dreamed of having during their lifetimes. Even with recurrent market adjustments and downturns, the overall growth of the market in recent years has vastly increased the wealth of this generation.

But the need to plan is not limited to the baby-boom generation. Many people of all ages who've invested money in company-sponsored 401(k) plans, individual retirement accounts, and other qualified plans have now reached the age of retirement but don't know how best to handle their newly found wealth. Most of these retiring individuals are shocked at how much their investments have grown over the past ten years. With the recent unprecedented boom in the stock market, those whose retirement accounts were valued at $300,000 in 1995 may find their accounts to be worth over $1,000,000 today.

CHAPTER SUMMARY

LESSON PLAN:

You deserve congratulations for taking the most difficult step in the estate planning process: beginning! The single biggest deterrent to properly planning your estate is procrastination. Nobody gets very excited about planning for his or her own demise or potential incapacity. Sometimes known as "the dark corner of financial planning," estate planning is difficult because, for one thing, it's hard to become motivated to plan and protect your estate for your family and other loved ones.

But now, just by picking up this book, you've taken the first big step on your estate planning journey. In this hour, you'll gain an understanding of the importance of planning your own estate. You'll see how setting goals is critical to your plan and learn the important factors involved in examining your estate. The basic background offered here will allow you to proceed in subsequent hours to develop the type of plan you need and your family deserves. You will learn ...

- The tax impact on planning decisions.
- The relationship between financial planning and estate planning.
- The basic steps involved in estate planning.
- The major estate planning considerations.
- How to determine the need for planning.

WHY PLAN?

Everyone needs to plan. Otherwise death taxes, such as the federal estate tax and state inheritance tax, will take huge chunks out of retirement funds and other assets that have taken years to accumulate. In addition, income taxes will take a toll on the accumulated but untaxed monies within *qualified plans* when withdrawn.

STRICTLY DEFINED

A **qualified retirement account** is an account that allows for special tax treatment of contributions, deferral of taxes on income and capital gains, but which is subject to minimum distribution rules.

Attorneys will also be taking their fair share out of the *probate estates* of decedents who die with no plan or who utilize wills and must require probate.

STRICTLY DEFINED

A **probate estate** consists of assets owned by a person that must pass through the probate court system to eventually reach the heirs.

Although no one denies the need for planning, the average person doesn't have a clue about where to begin. In many ways estate planning is a strange and complicated area and it's become increasingly difficult for average people to plan their own estates. This book provides you with a general overview of the process, but the need for outside legal and financial advice is now essential.

WHAT IS AN ESTATE PLAN?

The only sure way to reach your goals is to develop a plan. Without a plan, you'll be like a pilot who takes off without knowing where he's going and won't know where he is until he lands.

Like everyone else, you have your own set of unique goals and objectives, which means you require a specific plan to meet them. The tools you'll use to create that plan come from a toolbox shared by everyone who plans an estate. Some tools are appropriate to solve particular problems while some are better suited for other situations. Some tools will help you accomplish your goals whereas others may only create additional problems for you.

Planning your estate requires that you understand the uses of the tools in the toolbox so you'll know when and how to use a particular tool. Obviously, before you use a tool you must know what you're working on and what you're trying to achieve.

When planning your estate you'll need to consider many different issues—particularly the laws concerning wills, taxes, insurance, property, trusts, and lifetime gifting programs.

Most financial planners view wealth accumulation as the primary objective of most of their clients. However, concentrating only on accumulating wealth could fail to meet many clients' needs and goals if, upon disability or death, those assets are lost or simply misused. For that reason, estate planning is one of the most important aspects of financial planning.

THE ESTATE PLANNING PROCESS

Estate planning is a goal-oriented activity designed to provide the greatest possible financial security for both the individual and his or her beneficiaries. Effective estate planning should consider two primary areas: lifetime incapacity and post-death transfers of property. Later in the book, you'll learn which tools to use to accomplish the goals in your plan, and that will help you to intelligently discuss these objectives with your estate planning attorney.

There are many steps involved in the estate planning process. They include the following:

- Determining what assets your estate includes
- Establishing your various goals and objectives
- Prioritizing your goals
- Selecting an estate planning attorney
- Working with a qualified financial planner

TIME SAVER

 It is a good idea to determine your assets and prioritize your goals and objectives before meeting with your attorney. Doing so will make your meeting far more productive.

JUST A MINUTE

Locate an attorney that specializes in estate planning. An attorney that devotes his or her time to this single area of law is likely to be more informed about estate planning ideas and the use of the estate planning tools introduced to you in this book.

JUST A MINUTE

Try to find a financial planner that has experience working with clients on estate planning issues. You should also be aware that some planners have earned the designation of "certified financial planner." You can learn more about the significance of this designation by visiting the Web site for the Certified Financial Planner Board of Standards, www.cfp-board.org/.

- Explaining your goals and objectives to your planner and your attorney.
- Suggesting appropriate tools to achieve your objectives.
- Studying and evaluating your attorney's and your planner's advice.
- Determining the costs for implementation of your plan.

TIME SAVER

When you contact estate planning attorneys in your area, inquire up front about their fees. Does the attorney charge hourly? Does the attorney have pre-set fees for certain types of plans? Will the size of your estate affect the fees charged? Will there be recurring fees charged? Chances are, you'll need to amend your documents, so find out the fee schedule for doing so.

- Determining a time frame for completion of your initial plan.
- Approving an appropriate plan utilizing tools and techniques. Make sure you receive and review a draft of your estate planning documents.
- Monitoring the plan on a regular basis.
- Making appropriate revisions as needed.

FYI

Expect to review your plan on a regular basis. A good rule of thumb is to go over your plan with your attorney once a year. The advantage of doing so is that you will become "reacquainted" with your document and understand it better after each review. You will also have an opportunity to make changes based upon your needs and goals as they change over time.

Let's take a closer look at some of the important factors that might affect your selection of a particular estate planning technique.

CALCULATING ESTATE VALUE

Determining the value of your estate allows you to evaluate whether any death taxes are likely to be assessed. Death taxes are those taxes imposed following the death of an individual on property passing to beneficiaries of the decedent's estate. The two primary transfer taxes are federal estate taxes and state inheritance taxes. These will all be discussed in later hours. This evaluation includes federal estate taxes and state inheritance taxes. For purposes of this calculation, use the *taxable estate*. For more information about the difference between a taxable estate and a probate estate, see Hour 3, "What Is an Estate?"

STRICTLY DEFINED

Taxable estate includes all assets over which the person has a specified degree of control and which are subject to taxation.

DETERMINING YOUR ESTATE'S TAX LIABILITY

Once you've completed the valuation of your estate, you should calculate the impact of any federal estate or inheritance taxes due. Doing so requires you to make a reasonable estimate of future growth of assets. Since transfer taxes (estate, inheritance) are due at death, you'll need to make some reasonable estimate of when your death may occur. That way, you'll be able to approximate your future estate value. You'll need these future value estimates in order to determine which estate planning tools you should be considering.

Although you can use mortality tables to make these calculations, they do not take into account family longevity or specific health concerns. There are software programs available that will make these future value calculations for you. You can also find online sources that will help with these future value calculations. However, you might also require the services of a qualified financial planner.

GO TO ▶
Some excellent programs that can assist with future value calculations include: ZCALC Software (www.zcalc. com/), Visual Estate Plus, by ProBATE Software (www.probate-software. com/), and Quicken software (www. quicken.com/).

UNDERSTANDING YOUR LIFETIME FINANCIAL NEEDS

It would be shortsighted to plan your estate based upon present values. Planning for the future requires that you make a good faith estimate of what the value of your estate might be when you pass on. To do this accurately, you must ascertain both your spending habits and your future needs, which might result in a re-evaluation of your estate. Your projected future value actually might increase if your current income covers your expenses and you live a frugal lifestyle. On the other hand, your predicted future value might decrease if you have certain anticipated expenses such as college education, medical expenses, or travel or if you simply a desire a lavish lifestyle during your retirement years.

TIME SAVER

 If you feel that future value is something you want to include in your estate plan, you may wish to see a financial planner before seeing your estate planning attorney. Doing so will allow you to have future value calculations ready at the time of your initial meeting with your attorney, which will answer many questions up front.

Assessing Your Property

Generally speaking, you should include any asset you own in your estate, including real estate, household goods and furnishings, jewelry, automobiles, bank accounts, investment accounts, brokerage accounts, retirement accounts, government bonds, corporate bonds, money market funds, annuities, and stock, to name just a few.

GO TO ▶
Go to Hour 3 to learn more about the types of assets that people may own and how they are treated for tax purposes and probate purposes.

Having sufficient *liquid assets* to pay taxes and administrative expenses at the time of death is extremely important. If an estate consists of farmland, for example, it is difficult to liquidate farmland in order to come up with the cash necessary to pay taxes due at death. At the same time, an estate consisting largely of retirement accounts creates an expensive fund for the payment of taxes since withdrawal of funds from these accounts creates an income tax liability. Also, if a major estate asset is a family-run business, it may not be possible to find the necessary cash when needed.

STRICTLY DEFINED

Liquid assets are assets that can be used to pay administrative expenses and debts without forcing the sale of property.

Title to Property Included in Your Estate

Title is always the most crucial of all factors because this determines what assets will be a part of your estate. Even joint assets that pass to a surviving joint owner are subject to estate taxes. Retirement accounts payable to a non-spouse also are likely to incur a tax at death.

GO TO ▶

Advance to Hour 4, "Defining Types of Assets," for a detailed examination of different types of titles to property. Also, in Hour 6, "Federal Estate Taxes," you will find a comprehensive discussion of how assets are valued for federal estate tax purposes, as well as for state inheritance tax purposes. The unlimited marital deduction is explained further in that hour where deductions are discussed.

JUST A MINUTE

Although joint assets that pass to a surviving spouse are also subject to estate taxation, you will soon learn about the unlimited marital deduction that defers taxation on any transfers from a decedent to a surviving spouse.

Take the time now to review the title to your assets. Make a list of everything you own and indicate whether it is owned in single name, joint with right to survivorship, tenancy in common, and so on.

CONSIDERING BENEFICIARY COMPETENCY

An incompetent beneficiary might not be able to handle assets without the appointment of a guardian. For example, minor children named as beneficiaries must have either a court-appointed guardian or a guardian nominated by you in your legal documents. Beneficiaries receiving government assistance under certain programs might be disqualified from that assistance when they receive an inheritance. However, there are many techniques to solve these problems, so talk to your attorney or estate planner.

DETERMINING YOUR MARGINAL INCOME TAX BRACKET

Determining your *marginal income tax bracket*—the amount of income tax you're subject to based on your taxable income—is quite important when it comes to deciding who should be the recipient of income from your estate. For example, if you establish a trust for a beneficiary, the trust could be taxed at a rate as high as 39.6% on income not distributed over certain amounts. Distributing the income to a taxpayer in a lower tax bracket will result in significant income tax savings because the tax bracket for most individuals is lower than the tax bracket for trusts. As a result, the beneficiary will lose a smaller amount to taxes based upon lower individual tax rates. The use of charitable split-interest gifts can also reduce the income tax burden of many high-income taxpayers. (You'll learn more about the most common charitable planning techniques in Hour 19, "Charitable Trusts.")

STRICTLY DEFINED

The **marginal income tax bracket** refers to the amount of income tax you are subject to based upon your taxable income. Your bracket is found in I.R.S. tax tables, which are based in part on filing status (married filing jointly, married filing separately, single, etc.) and partially based upon taxable income.

UNDERSTANDING YOUR STATE LAW

There are important state law issues that you must take into account when planning your estate. Throughout the hours to follow, you will find many references to state law. As you develop your plan, please be certain to obtain the advice of a professional who can answer your questions about what your state laws dictate.

- **Execution requirements for a *will*** The way you create and administer a legal and binding will are matters of state law. If you don't comply with the law, your will can be declared void. However, most states do have agreements with other states for cases in which a will was prepared in another jurisdiction.

STRICTLY DEFINED

A **will** is a legal document made in anticipation of death in which a person directs the disposition of his or her property at death. It also contains instructions for payment of debts and taxes and nominates guardians for minor children and a personal representative for the estate.

- **Execution requirements for a trust** Although a requirement of state law, most states have very lenient execution requirements for trusts. In the majority of states, the only requirement is that the trust be a signed, written document. Some states do not even require notarization.
- **Execution requirements for a *living will*** These requirements vary significantly from state to state. An individual who changes residency should update his or her documents to comply with the requirements of the new state of residence.

STRICTLY DEFINED

A **living will** is a document that sets forth wishes with regard to the provision of artificial life support and artificially supplied nutrition and hydration.

- **Execution requirements for a *power of attorney*** These requirements also vary significantly from state to state. An individual who changes residency should update his or her documents to comply with the requirements of the new state of residence.

A **power of attorney** is a written document appointing someone to act on behalf of the drafter and which contains specific powers conveyed by the document to the individual appointed.

- **Execution requirements for the appointment of a *health care representative*** These requirements also vary significantly from state to state. An individual who changes residency should be certain to update his or her documents to comply with the requirements of the new state of residence.

A **health care representative appointment** is a legal document authorizing an individual to make health care decisions on behalf of the principal.

- **Rights of a surviving spouse to inherit a share of the deceased spouse's estate** State law provides this right. State *intestate law* (which governs the inheritance of property for cases in which there is no will or trust) usually allows a surviving spouse a certain percentage of the decedent's estate. If the decedent failed to provide for his or her spouse in an amount at least comparable to that allowed by state law, the surviving spouse may choose to take what the state law provides and ignore provisions for the surviving spouse, if any, that are contained in the will. Clearly, such a law might impact on the ability of a will or a trust to carry out the decedent's intent.

  GO TO ▶
  See Hour 11, "Wills and Trusts: Important Provisions," where you will find a more detailed explanation of the spousal allowance.

- **State inheritance taxes** Although the biggest tax bite comes from the federal estate tax, smaller estates not subject to the federal tax might be subject to a state inheritance tax. Although this tax is usually much smaller, it can be significant. However, not all states have inheritance taxes.

  GO TO ▶
  See Hour 5, "Income Taxes and Inheritance Taxes," for a discussion of income taxes and state inheritance taxes.

- **State property tax exemptions** Frequently overlooked in the planning process, transfers of property, particularly land, can impact the ability of the property owner to claim state property tax exemptions. For example, in Indiana, transferring a home to a revocable trust will cause the property to be ineligible for certain real estate or property tax exemptions and deductions unless special language is inserted in the deed.

ESTATE PLANNING: THE FAILURE TO PLAN

It is an unhappy fact that many people simply do not take the time to plan their estates. Unfortunately, the result of failing to plan is itself a plan, although not one consciously preferred by the individual. For people who don't plan, the default plan is whatever the law of the individual's state of residence says, taking into account the type of property owned by that individual and the manner in which such property is titled.

There are many reasons why people fail to plan their estates, including the fact that they simply find the topic of death unpleasant. Many people figure that what happens to their property after they pass away is up to their heirs. They might even sport bumper stickers that say, "I'm spending my children's inheritance."

A second reason for failing to plan an estate is the potential for major family problems that could arise from a plan, such as will contests, arguments over assets, disputes over professional fees, etc. Fears of family disruption can immobilize a person and prevent him or her from making even a simple estate plan.

A third reason for failing to plan an estate is that people are busier now than they have ever been, and simply do not feel that they have the time to plan. Even if they take the time to develop a plan, they may be stymied by an inability to answer some questions, including "Who will take care of my children when I'm gone?" or "Who will run my business if I'm incapable of running it myself?" As a result, no plan is forthcoming simply because the perfect answers to some select issues are not readily available.

Finally, there are those who simply procrastinate for any of a number of reasons, including some listed above. They keep putting off planning their estate until they become incapacitated, hospitalized, or otherwise are in a condition that does not allow them to think clearly, if at all, about their estate. To make matters worse, at this point, there's very little time to plan.

Regardless of the reasons for not planning your estate, it is important to remember that the failure to plan will result in a plan that you may not like. Therefore, even if you don't have the time or inclination to perfect a plan, you should pay attention to creating the best plan for you and your family. The sooner you get something workable down on paper, the more time you'll have to make changes if new circumstances arise.

The following are some of the reasons you might want to have an estate plan:

- To ensure that minor children receive proper care, both from a financial point of view and from the standpoint of providing for their physical and emotional welfare.

- To reduce or even eliminate estate taxes.

- To make provisions for the orderly transfer of ownership and management of a family-operated business. Failure to make such provisions could easily result in transferring business interests to others who have no experience and/or desire to continue the operation of the business.

- To provide for estate liquidity, which means having sufficient assets readily available to pay debts and final expenses. This will help you avoid the forced sale of assets at less than fair market value to pay bills and taxes.

- To reduce the likelihood of intra-family squabbles. Contrary to popular belief, by carefully constructing an estate plan you can reduce the possibility that an heir will feel he or she has received inadequate provisions.

- To provide for your needs should you become incapacitated.

ESTATE PLANNING: DETERMINING YOUR NEED

At this point, you can see that planning involves many factors. You should also be able to realize by now that failing to plan can have significant tax and non-tax implications for you and your heirs.

Please take the time to ask yourself the following questions. These questions are designed to call your attention to matters that affect your overall estate plan.

- Has it been more than one year since you last reviewed your estate, including your will or trust?

- Has it been more than one year since you last reviewed your life insurance policies?

- Are you unclear about what would happen to your property if you or your spouse passed away today?

- Do you have minor children?

- Do any of your beneficiaries have disabilities or special needs?

- Do you own property jointly with anyone?

- Do your loved ones and health care professionals really understand your health care wishes?
- Is your estate the beneficiary of any of your life insurance policies, retirement accounts, or annuities?
- Do you have any life insurance policies or retirement accounts or annuities with no beneficiary listed?
- Do you have any idea who your beneficiaries are on your retirement accounts, annuities, and life insurance?
- Do you or your spouse have children by a previous marriage?
- Do you wish to disinherit a spouse or child in your estate plan?
- Does your farm or business expose you to liability?
- Do you wish to avoid probate of your estate?
- If, upon your death, court approval is needed to operate your business, will this be disruptive to your business?
- Does the total value of your estate including life insurance, pensions, and retirement plans exceed $675,000 (in 2001)?
- Considering inflation and capital growth, is it possible that your estate might exceed $675,000 within the next few years?
- Have you made any gifts to others or do you plan on gifting property in the near future?
- Are any members of your family unsure about their economic future in a family business?
- Do you own any property that has substantially increased in value since you acquired it?

If you answered "yes" to any of the preceding questions, you have identified a potential problem with taxes, probate costs, delays, or simply a personal concern that has not yet been properly addressed. Estate planning tools and techniques are available to solve these problems or others that might become apparent during the planning process.

PROCEED WITH CAUTION

 Be certain to consult an estate planning attorney before implementing any of the techniques discussed in this book. The failure to obtain professional advice could result in additional expenses for administering your estate and could result in additional and unnecessary taxation of your estate. Additionally, the failure to properly prepare documents according to applicable law may render the documents useless.

Hour's Up!

Now it's time to see how much you have learned and retained from this lesson. Try to take the following quiz without referring back to this hour's materials.

1. The following is an important factor in the valuation of your estate:

    a. Historical returns on your investments

    b. Your current gross income

    c. Your itemized deductions

    d. Projected future value of your estate

2. One important reason to plan your estate is ...

    a. To reduce current taxable income

    b. To determine the need for additional medical insurance

    c. To reduce inheritance and estate taxes

    d. Your attorney needs your business

3. One of the most common reasons people fail to plan their estates is ...

    a. Procrastination

    b. A general dislike for attorneys

    c. A negative self-image

    d. The cost of planning

4. You should consider your health and the health of your family when planning because ...

    a. You might die before they do

    b. They might die before you do

    c. It might impact the future value of your estate

    d. All of the above

5. Proper estate planning should include the following considerations:

    a. The internal rate of return on your investments

    b. Future incapacity

    c. What your friends are doing

    d. Risk tolerance

HOUR 2

Inheritance and the Laws of Intestate Succession

CHAPTER SUMMARY

LESSON PLAN:

In this hour, we'll review the history of inheritance and conclude with a discussion of how individual states determine who your heirs will be. You will learn some legal terminology that should help you understand your planning options. You also will learn ...

- The historic importance of property ownership

- The history of intestate succession, which is the process of determining who inherits when the decedent leaves no valid will or trust.

- The basic provisions of the Uniform Probate Code—proposed statues recommended and available for adoption by every state—as they pertain to inheritance.

- How to designate your estate's distribution in the event an heir dies before you do.

Sometimes a little history lesson can help put complicated legal terminology into perspective. The history of intestate succession is interesting and helps to explain current statutory law. You will find many correlations to historical practices in current legislation.

THE NATURE OF PROPERTY OWNERSHIP

As one looks back over the history of inheritance laws and practices, it becomes clear that the nature of property ownership has played an important role in the development of laws governing inheritance.

In very primitive times, group ownership of property was relatively common. In those cultures, the death of a person was not particularly significant in terms of transfer of property because other owners were still alive. Since individuals did not own much property of their own, the issue of where property went after an individual's death was relatively non-existent.

Land, in particular, was owned by groups of people associated by genetics (clans) or by social groupings. Upon the death of one member of the group, the remaining members of the group continued to enjoy ownership of the land. This is similar to the concept of joint property ownership, as well as ownership by legal entities other than individuals, such as partnerships and corporations.

GO TO ▶
In Hour 4,
"Defining Types
of Assets," we'll
review the various
types of ownership
of property, includ-
ing single owner-
ship and joint
ownership.

In the majority of countries, group ownership of property has been sup-planted by the current notion of individually owned property. When indi-viduals own property, the burden is placed on them to designate who the successors-in-ownership will be.

The easiest way to do this is to allow the person to make his or her wishes known in a written document, known as a testament. When a testament was prepared, it was an easy matter to determine who would be authorized by law to own the property. This process is known as *inheritance*.

STRICTLY DEFINED

The term **inherit** is used to describe the transfer of ownership from a decedent to a beneficiary.

If a decedent left no testament, then the government or community needed another means to specify inheritance. Otherwise, the government could take control of all such property, a process called *escheating* to the state. The ulti-mate result would be that individuals would own nothing and the govern-ment would eventually own all property.

STRICTLY DEFINED

The term used to indicate the passing of a title from a decedent to the government is **escheat.** An estate will escheat to the state only if there are no living beneficiaries of a will or a trust, or if there are no living heirs at law according to state law.

To avoid this result, governments have developed laws that allow for the transfer of property from *decedents* to *descendants* in cases where there is no testament. Modern inheritance law has developed from these principles.

STRICTLY DEFINED

Don't confuse the terms **decedent** and **descendant.** The term "descendant" refers to a child, grandchild, or great grandchild or further down the ancestral line. A "dece-dent" is a deceased individual.

IDENTIFYING THE HEIRS

The next great debate focused on those individuals who should be allowed to inherit a decedent's property. Historically, societies and ancient cultures have viewed inheritance as an entitlement, earned only by those descending by blood from the decedent. This process, by definition, ruled out the spouse as an heir, which means husbands and wives could never inherit. The ancient Romans developed a very specific set of rules that passed on a decedent's property to those who were subject to the decedent's reign. Interestingly, in Roman society, since slaves were subject to the reign of the decedent, they could inherit by this rule as could blood descendants, but wives could not inherit unless there were no other available heirs.

Eventually, this system gave way to a system known as "The Twelve Tables." Under this system, when the head of the family, called the "house chief" died, the estate passed to those who were freed by his power. If no one succeeded on this basis, the estate would pass to the nearest male relative. Next in line for inheritance would have been a defined group of descendants.

As this system became increasingly complicated to administer, the government demanded that all citizens prepare a testament, outlining the path of succession. When the individual failed to create his or her own testament, the government had a system to determine heirship. This statutory scheme of succession is where the phrase *intestate succession* came from.

STRICTLY DEFINED

Intestate succession refers to the process of determining heirship when the decedent leaves no valid will or trust. A will or trust contains instructions on whom shall inherit his or her property. To die intestate means to die without a will or trust.

In England, those entitled to inherit from a decedent extends no further than grandparents, uncles, and aunts of the deceased. In the former Soviet Union, intestate succession failed to extend beyond descendants, the surviving spouse, grandparents, brothers, sisters, and incapacitated dependent persons.

Another method governments use to limit those who are entitled to inherit is to impose an inheritance tax that increases in proportion to the remoteness of the relationship with the decedent. This is the very basis for state inheritance tax law in the United States.

MODERN INHERITANCE

Modern legislation is quite different from ancient laws. For example, now a spouse has a right to share in the estate of a decedent—and that right might

GO TO ▶
For a more detailed discussion of state inheritance taxes go to Hour 5, "Income Taxes and Inheritance Taxes." There you will find a comprehensive discussion of how inheritance taxes are imposed and how they differ from the federal estate tax.

GO TO ▶
You can learn more about community property in Hour 4.

even be paramount to the rights of a child or other relative. *Community property* also is a reflection of the growing awareness of spousal rights to inheritance.

STRICTLY DEFINED

Community property is a form of ownership between husband and wife in which each spouse has a separate, undivided interest in property acquired during marriage. Only certain states follow the law of community property.

THE UNIFORM PROBATE CODE

In 1969 the National Conference of Commissioners on Uniform State Laws and the American Bar Association created a *uniform law* pertaining to intestate succession. The Uniform Probate Code sets forth the following rights of a surviving spouse when the decedent fails to leave a valid will or trust with instructions on the disposition of his or her property.

STRICTLY DEFINED

A **uniform law** is a proposed statute recommended and available for adoption by any state. By adopting the proposed language as law, states become uniform in the administration of that law. No state is obligated to adopt the law; if the legislature chooses to adopt a model law, it may make any modifications to the law it feels appropriate.

These rights are as follows:

- If there is no surviving *issue* or parent of the decedent, the surviving spouse inherits the entire intestate estate.
- If there is no surviving *issue* but the decedent is survived by a parent or parents, the surviving spouse inherits the first $50,000, plus one-half of the balance of the intestate estate.
- If there are surviving *issue*, all of whom also are *issue* of the surviving spouse, the spouse inherits the first $50,000 plus one half of the balance of the intestate estate.
- If there are surviving issue, one or more of whom are not *issue* of the surviving spouse, the spouse receives one half of the intestate estate.

STRICTLY DEFINED

Legally, when reference is made to children or descendants of children (grandchildren, great-grandchildren, etc.) the term used is **issue.**

For that portion of the estate that does not pass to a surviving spouse the Uniform Code provides for distribution to the heirs as follows. This inheritance includes all of the estate if there is no surviving spouse:

- To the children of the decedent.
- To his parent or parents equally if there are no surviving children.
- To the brothers and sisters and the children of each deceased brother or sister *by representation* if there are no surviving children or parents.

STRICTLY DEFINED

The term **by representation** refers to a manner of distribution whereby the bene-ficiaries receive the same share that would have been received by a deceased ancestor.

- Half of the estate passes to the paternal grandparents and the other half passes to the maternal relatives.

PROCEED WITH CAUTION

The reference above to the Uniform Probate Code is simplified to assist with read-ability. The full text contains additional information that is not repeated here.

I know these details are difficult to follow. In fact, the reason for describing this model law is to make you aware of the complicated nature of state inheritance law. As was true in ancient times, you are now duty-bound to create your own "testament" and provide for the passing of your assets according to your own plan.

At last count, this Uniform Probate Code has been adopted—at least in part—by eighteen states including Alaska, Arizona, Colorado, Florida, Hawaii, Idaho, Maine, Michigan, Minnesota, Montana, Nebraska, New Mexico, North Dakota, South Carolina, South Dakota, and Utah. Although each state is allowed to adopt its own law regarding intestate succession, to some extent all of them follow this general principal: The closer the relation, the more likely the person is to inherit. The more distant relatives are likely to take less or nothing at all, depending on the family genealogy.

PER STIRPES AND PER CAPITA

In the context of intestate succession, *per stirpes* is the modus operandi for determining heirship. The term "per stirpes" means to take by representation. The term "per capita" means to take by head count. The term "per stirpes" only applies when a primary beneficiary is deceased, or if the amount a beneficiary is to receive is measured by what an ancestor would have received if living.

For example, Tom is unmarried and has three living children. Tom dies without a will. Distribution "per stirpes" will dictate that Tom's three children inherit Tom's estate equally.

Let's review another example.

Ann has three children: Bob, Carl, and Dolly. Bob has one living child, Carl has two living children, and Dolly has three living children and one deceased child, who left two children surviving him. Let's see what happens under per stirpes and per capita terms.

How It Works: Per Stirpes

Ann's will states that she leaves all of her property to her three children, by representation ("per stirpes"). If all three children are living at Ann's death, each of the three inherit $1/3$. The language "per stirpes" has no bearing on this distribution since all of the primary beneficiaries are living.

Suppose, however, that Bob dies before Ann. Since Ann's will says "per stirpes," Bob's $1/3$ share will pass to those who inherit his share, which in this case is his only child. Carl and Dolly will still get their $1/3$ share each. Since a primary beneficiary is deceased, the use of the term "per stirpes" becomes appropriate.

Suppose now that both Bob and Carl predecease Ann. We have already established that Bob's $1/3$ will pass to his child. Carl's $1/3$ will likewise pass to Carl's two living children in equal shares. They will therefore inherit $1/6$ of the total estate each. Dolly will get $1/3$. Again, since a primary beneficiary is deceased, the use of the term "per stirpes" is appropriate.

Now suppose that all three of Ann's children predecease her. Bob's $1/3$ will pass to his child; Carl's $1/3$ will be divided equally between his two children, $1/6$ each. Dolly's $1/3$ will be divided as follows: $1/12$ will pass to each of her three living children ($1/4$ of her $1/3$ interest). The final $1/4$ share will be divided equally between the two surviving children of her deceased child, $1/8$ each. Again, the term "per stirpes" is used to reflect that the shares received by the grandchildren is based upon what the parent would have received, if living.

How It Works: Per Capita

Now let's change Ann's will to provide for a distribution to her three children "per capita." Assume that Dolly predeceases Ann. Ann's estate will be divided among the following people: Bob, Carl, each of the three surviving children of Dolly, and the two children of Dolly's predeceased child. This makes a total of 7 people. Each will therefore inherit $1/7$ of Ann's estate.

Fortunately, most state laws provide a presumption that distribution shall be per stirpes, at least as it pertains to children and other *lineal descendants*. Nevertheless, it is a good practice to specify in a will or trust how the property is to be distributed in the event of the death of a primary heir.

STRICTLY DEFINED

Lineal descendants are those in a direct line from an ancestor. This would include children, grandchildren, great-grandchildren, and so on.

PROCEED WITH CAUTION

Be certain to consult an estate planning attorney before implementing any of the techniques discussed in this book. The failure to obtain professional advice could result in additional expenses for administering your estate and could result in additional and unnecessary taxation of your estate. Additionally, the failure to properly prepare documents according to applicable law may render the documents useless.

Hour's Up!

Now it's time to see how much you have learned and retained from this lesson. Try to take the following quiz without referring back to the hourly materials.

1. When property escheats, it does what?

    a. It is destroyed.

    b. It passes to charity.

    c. It is subject to your will.

    d. It passes to the state.

QUIZ

2. Intestate succession refers to:
    a. The plan of distribution contained in your will
    b. The plan of distribution contained in state law
    c. The transfer of property to an incapacitated individual
    d. The repeated taxation of property at death

3. The Uniform Probate Code is …
    a. The law in all 50 states
    b. A federal law
    c. A proposed model law
    d. The law used in ancient Rome

4. When a decedent intends for property to pass equally to all living children who survive the decedent, it is said to pass:
    a. Per stirpes
    b. Per capita
    c. Per forma
    d. None of the above

5. When a decedent intends for property to pass to the children of a deceased child by representation, it is said to pass:
    a. Per stirpes
    b. Per capita
    c. Per forma
    d. None of the above

Hour 3
What Is an Estate?

Chapter Summary

LESSON PLAN:

Most of us do not consider the various types of property we own. Even the term "property" means different things to different people. To some, it refers to land; to others it refers to personal belongings such as household goods, furnishings, jewelry and other like things.

In this hour, you'll learn about how property is classified and understand the significance of these classifications. The classification of property will make the estate planning task much easier. You will also learn ...

- The difference between real and personal property.
- The difference between tangible and intangible personal property.
- The difference between probate and non-probate property.
- What constitutes your taxable estate.

In the most simplified form, an estate consists of either property or interests in property. An interest in property means some right or privilege relating to the property, such as the right to receive rent or the right to reside on the property for life. If you understand clearly what "property" means, you should be well on the way to planning your estate.

Most people become confused before they even begin planning their estates. The problem stems from the use of technical terms they don't fully understand. For example, if you were asked what property you owned, your response most likely would include bank accounts, certificates of deposit and retirement accounts. Did you think to include your real property, such as your home, your farmland, or rental properties? How about your interest in your uncle's trust? And did you forget the most commonly omitted asset, your life insurance?

Different Types of Property

There are several categories of property you'll need to assess in order to determine the worth of your estate. They include real property and several types of personal property. Below we will discuss each in more detail so that you will have a better grasp on what these terms mean to you.

FYI An estate consists of property. Property can be real or personal, tangible or intangible.

REAL PROPERTY

Your home is a prime example of real property. Not only is the land upon which the home is built on considered real property, but so is the home itself. This is because the home cannot be separated from the lot without incurring substantial damage or a decrease in value of the home.

Sometimes people think of the home and the land on which it sits as separate. When people purchase an empty lot, they are purchasing the land. They will obtain a deed showing that they are the owners of the land. If they eventually build a house on the land, they do not get a new deed. The law considers the house to be part of the land itself and therefore real property.

Farmland also falls into the category of real property. And, just like in the case of a house, any outbuildings or fencing constructed on the land is considered part of the land; thus, real property. Apartment buildings, office buildings, shopping malls, or similar income-producing structures built on land also are considered to be real property.

JUST A MINUTE

 Understanding what constitutes real property will help you evaluate the worth of your home when it comes time to sell it. Keep in mind that anything that will damage or decrease the value of your home if removed is considered part of the home, including furnaces, hot water heaters, built-in light fixtures and kitchen cabinets. The value of these fixtures, therefore, should be included when determining the value of your home.

PERSONAL PROPERTY

Personal property normally is identified as an object that is moveable. Although this description is partially correct, it does not encompass all personal property. Thus, the definition of property is broken down into two categories: *tangible* and *intangible*.

Tangible personal property consists of items of personal property that can be touched or physically possessed. Even though some of these objects would be difficult to move, they are still categorized as tangible (can be touched) personal property (can be moved). Examples of tangible personal property include the following:

- Household goods and furnishings
- Personal effects (such as jewelry and clothing)
- Office furnishings
- Automobiles
- Boats
- Trucks
- Helicopters
- Airplanes

Intangible personal property consists of items that have no *intrinsic value* but represent something of value. The best examples of intangible personal property are your personal checking and savings account.

Have you ever gone to the bank and asked the teller for permission to *See* your account to verify what is on deposit? Obviously, this cannot be done. Yet you still own the items that are "on deposit" in your account, which represents what's called an interest in intangible personal property.

STRICTLY DEFINED

The term **intrinsic value** refers to the actual, universally recognized, value of some thing.

Another example of intangible personal property is stock. If you own stock in XYZ Corp., your proof of ownership is the stock certificate. This stock certificate, however, represents your investment in the corporation, and so does your brokerage statement. Stock held by a brokerage firm is referred to as held in "street name," meaning you own the stock but do not have physical possession of the certificate.

Here is an example of how important the distinction between tangible and intangible property can be. A state statute provided that a creditor to whom you owe money may not take from you the following property to satisfy the debt:

- Tangible personal property worth $4,000 or less
- Intangible personal property worth $100 or less

A judgment creditor (someone who has obtained a court order declaring that you owe him or her money) is attempting to collect a debt in court. The defendant debtor comes to court with $4,000 cash in his pocket. The debtor thinks all the cash will be exempt as tangible personal property.

However, the judge allows the defendant debtor to keep only $100 and orders the debtor to turn over the remaining $3,900 to the creditor, ruling that cash is an intangible asset.

THE CHAMELEON EFFECT

Sometimes an item can change from a tangible asset to an intangible asset; for example, consider a chair in a classroom. A chair is an item of tangible personal property because you can move it from place to place without decreasing the value of the school building. However, some schools have chosen to secure chairs (and sometimes desks) to the floor. Once secured, those chairs become real property attached to the school building, which is attached to the land upon which the school sits.

To sum up, your estate consists not only of cash but also of the following forms of property:

- Real property
- Tangible personal property
- Intangible personal property

You now need to categorize all of your property as belonging to one of two types of estates: your *probate estate* and/or your taxable estate. Be aware that a person's probate estate and taxable estate frequently overlap. They are not mutually exclusive. A taxable asset may or may not be a probate asset, whereas a probate asset is usually taxable.

STRICTLY DEFINED

A person's **probate estate** consists only of assets owned by the person that must pass through the probate court system to eventually reach his or her heirs.

PROBATE AND NON-PROBATE ESTATES COMPARED

When planning your estate, you need to be mindful of which assets will be passing at your death through the *probate court* system and which will pass directly to some other person without court involvement. These two categories, probate and non-probate, are of fundamental importance in estate planning. The following definitions and examples will help you see the difference between these two categories of property.

YOUR PROBATE PROPERTY

Probate is a process created by state law that determines heirship, provides a means for paying creditors, and provides for an orderly distribution of assets. A person's probate estate consists only of assets owned by the person that must pass through the probate court system to eventually reach the heirs. The assets included in this system include property that is …

- Individually owned.
- Owned jointly as tenants in common, which is property held by two or more owners without rights to survivorship.
- An asset payable to no designated beneficiary.
- An asset payable to the owner's estate.

You'll read more about these various types of assets in subsequent hours. What they all have in common is that you haven't designated anyone to inherit the asset or designated a joint owner and thus you've left it to the probate process to determine ownership after your death.

GO TO ▶
For a more detailed discussion of probate, go to Hour 8, "Probate." There you will find a detailed discussion of what probate is and how it works.

YOUR NON-PROBATE PROPERTY

By contrast, non-probate property consists of everything else, including the following:

- Assets held as joint tenancy with right of survivorship, which is a form of ownership in which, upon the death of one co-owner, the surviving named co-owner(s) shall become full owner(s) of the asset.
- Assets payable to a named beneficiary other than the estate. Many people are confused because they think the term "estate" refers to both probate and non-probate. They also think it describes both a *taxable* and *non-taxable* estate. As you'll come to understand, each term refers to a different category of property.

YOUR NON-TAXABLE ESTATE

A person's non-taxable estate consists of assets over which the decedent had no control at death. This includes assets transferred before death, with the exception of life insurance policies transferred within three years of death.

As you will learn in the following section of this hour, your taxable estate is a broader category than your non-taxable estate. Basically, the only assets that would be included in your non-taxable estate would be those assets exempt from taxation by either state or federal law.

Sometimes life insurance death benefits are not taxable for state inheritance tax purposes if payable to someone other than your estate. Indiana has a statute that makes this provision for inheritance tax purposes.

Another example is property transferred less than three years before your death. Federal law will not count property as part of your taxable estate for estate tax purposes unless the property transferred is a life insurance policy (unless you retained some interest in the property as discussed in more detail in Hour 6, "Federal Estate Taxes"). Indiana, however, will include the value of assets transferred within one year of death for purposes of Indiana inheritance taxation.

YOUR TAXABLE ESTATE: OBVIOUS ASSETS

GO TO ▶
For more on the unlimited marital deduction, see Hour 6.

A person's taxable estate consists of assets over which the decedent had a specific degree of control. Whatever property you control or have a degree of control over is part of your taxable estate. Let's look at these examples:

- If a husband owns a home in his name alone, the home is probate property, because he has not designated a beneficiary on the title and a probate court will have to determine who becomes the beneficiary. The house also will be a part of the husband's taxable estate to the extent of 100 percent of the house value, because the husband owned 100 percent of the house.

- If a husband and wife jointly own the home, the home is not considered probate property because the surviving spouse will own the property when the other dies. The house will be included in the taxable estate of the first to die to the extent of just 50% of the house value because the surviving spouse owns the other 50%.

FYI As a result of the unlimited marital deduction, however, this transfer will be tax-deferred.

Notice how the title to the house is the controlling factor when it comes to deciding whether or not the house is in the taxable estate of the owner and whether it is in the owner's probate estate.

THE IMPORTANCE OF TITLE

How you own property controls everything from whether the asset is a probate asset to whether the asset will be included in your taxable estate.

JUST A MINUTE

Your first step in estate planning is to determine how you own each and every one of your assets. Remember: Nothing is more important than title. The manner in which you own an asset has priority over any direction contained in your will or trust.

Title to an asset usually is determined by the actual title document, referred to as *documents of title*. The following are examples of documents of title:

- Deeds to real estate
- Signature cards on bank accounts
- Certificates of deposit
- Savings bonds
- Brokerage account application forms
- Stock certificates
- Life insurance declaration pages
- Annuity declaration pages

However, keep in mind that not every asset has a document of title. For instance, personal belongings don't have documents showing ownership, nor do most household goods unless you consider sales receipts to be documents of title. If a piece of property does not have a document of title, title (ownership) usually is determined by possession, which is where the saying "Possession is nine-tenths of the law" comes from. However, possession is not always conclusive. If assets are borrowed or taken without their owner's permission, the person who took them does not have legal possession or title.

FYI Sales receipts do not represent ownership of an asset, unless the receipt clearly identifies the item and the owner's name.

What you must remember is that title to an asset will dictate how you should handle that asset in your estate plan. Indeed, title is more important than the nature of the asset itself. Therefore, to figure out whether an asset is a probate asset or a taxable asset, look not to the type of asset (real estate, personal property, bank account, certificate of deposit, and so forth); instead look to the document of title to that asset. This is where you'll find the answer.

Your estate consists of everything that you own, including the obvious—your home, real estate, bank accounts, investments, stocks, bonds and certificates of deposit. However, this also includes the less obvious, such as retirement accounts, life insurance, and annuities.

YOUR TAXABLE ESTATE: LESS OBVIOUS ASSETS

GO TO ▶
For a more detailed discussion of insurance, go to Hour 13, "Life Insurance." There you will find a detailed discussion of insurance products and how they differ.

There are several other assets that many people creating an estate plan fail to consider. The most commonly overlooked asset included in a person's estate is life insurance, perhaps because the value of that insurance is not realized until after death. However, even though the death benefits are payable only upon your death, if you have life insurance, you must include its value in your estate for tax purposes. If that doesn't seem logical to you, think of it this way: You could make your death benefits payable to your own estate. This would make them subject to your own debts, taxes, and expenses of administration.

EVEN LESS OBVIOUS ASSETS

Aside from the obvious and less obvious things people own, there are other assets not readily identifiable as part of a person's estate, including what are known as retained interests, contingent interests, and reversionary interests.

RETAINED INTERESTS—LIFE ESTATES

Retained interests are "strings of ownership" that still attach to property that is titled in another's name. The most common example of this type of interest is a *life estate*.

STRICTLY DEFINED

A **life estate** is the right of the original owner to live on and enjoy real estate for his or her entire life, even though the real estate has been deeded to another owner.

Putting real estate into a life estate often is used as a means of avoiding probate. For example, Bob and his wife Mary own their home. They have one child, Susan. As Bob and Mary get older, they become increasingly concerned that upon their deaths their home might be sold to pay for estate expenses, nursing home care, or taxes.

Bob and Mary meet with their lawyer and subsequently deed all of their ownership interest in the home to their daughter, Susan. Susan now owns the property. However, Bob and Mary do not wish to be at the mercy of Susan or her creditors. Therefore they state in the deed to Susan that they retain the right to remain living in the home for their natural lives, which is called "reserving a life estate."

Although this type of conveyance changes ownership, it does not transfer control. Bob and Mary have the exclusive right to live on the property for so long as either of them lives. There is nothing that Susan can do to evict them from the home. Even if Susan sold the home to another, she cannot remove Bob and Mary from the home without their consent—and neither can the new owner.

Because title will always control disposition of the asset at death—and neither Bob nor Mary owns the property—neither of them include the home in the probate estate. However, because Bob and Mary retained the right to live on this property until death, they have a retained life estate on this property, which means that the entire value of the home will be included in their taxable estates at death.

 FYI To legally remove any interest in the property held by Bob and Mary as life tenants, they would both be required to sign a deed conveying their life estates.

Since title will always control disposition of the asset at death, the home will not be included in the probate estate of either Bob or Mary since neither of them owns the property. However, since Bob and Mary retained the right to live on this property until death, they have a "retained life estate" on this property, which means that the entire value of the home will be included in their taxable estates at death for federal estate tax puposes.

GO TO ▶
See Hour 21, "Gifting of Assets," for more information on gifting and the tax implications of making a gift.

PROCEED WITH CAUTION

 When making a transfer to a child as described above, this constitutes a taxable gift. As a result, the cost basis for Bob and Mary is transferred to Susan, which will result in the property being subject to capital gains tax upon the sale of the property.

Contingent Interests

A *contingent interest* is one that may cause the property to revert back to the original owner when a specified event occurs. For example, Bob deeds property to Tom for as long as Tom uses the property for commercial purposes. If and when Tom ceases to use the property commercially, ownership of the property will revert to Bob. However, if Tom continues to use the property for commercial purposes, the contingent interest might never revert to Bob.

STRICTLY DEFINED

A **contingent interest** may revert to the original owner when some specific and specified event occurs.

REVERSIONARY INTERESTS

A *reversionary interest* is one that will cause the property to revert back to the original owner at a specified time. No conditions must be met for a reversionary interest to return title to the original owner. The eventual return of title to the owner is absolute. A conveyance for a term of years is a reversionary interest. For example, Sue conveys her real property to Betty for a term of 50 years, at which time the title will revert back to Sue.

RETAINED INTEREST—REVOCABLE TRANSFERS

GO TO ▶
For a more detailed discussion of trusts, go to Hour 10, "Revocable Living Trusts."

A revocable transfer is one in which the original owner reserves the right to amend, alter, revoke, or terminate the transfer at a later date. Revocable transfers are most commonly found in transfers to a trust. The popular living trust is one that allows the grantor to change the provisions of the trust at a future time. The grantor typically can alter the provisions, revoke any provision of the trust, or terminate the trust entirely. As a direct result of these provisions, any asset transferred to a revocable living trust is a revocable transfer; those assets will be included in the owner's taxable estate upon death.

 Grantor trust rules are found in the Internal Revenue Code in sections 671–679. Any asset fitting the definitions contained in those sections will be included as an estate asset.

POWERS OF APPOINTMENT

A power of appointment conveys authority to transfer a property interest owned by another. This also includes a grant of authority to choose those who may receive property from an estate. Most commonly found in trusts, powers of appointment can be either *limited* or *general*.

GENERAL POWERS OF APPOINTMENT

A *general* power of appointment is a grant of authority to transfer a property interest owned by another to anyone, including the person having this power. For example, Bob died leaving property in trust for the benefit of his wife, Mary. Upon Mary's death, the property will pass to their children. In this trust, Bob gives Mary the privilege of giving away or transferring any trust property from the trust to anyone she chooses, including herself. She has the discretion to transfer some assets to her children, some to her church, some to her neighbor and some to herself whenever she feels the urge. This privilege of transfer is called a *general* power of appointment. She does not own the property, yet she can direct to whom it shall go. Upon Mary's death, all of the trust property subject to this power will be considered hers for tax purposes (included in her taxable estate.)

JUST A MINUTE

Note that Mary's estate includes all of the property subject to her lifetime power, regardless of whether or not she exercised this power during her lifetime.

Here's another example: Suppose the value of Bob's trust is $500,000 and Mary has a general power of appointment. Further suppose that Mary uses only $20,000 of this trust to donate to charity during her lifetime. At Mary's death, she will be deemed the owner (for tax purposes only) of $480,000 even though she didn't use the power of appointment over that $480,000. It is the power over the property that is relevant, not the exercise of the power.

LIMITED POWERS OF APPOINTMENT

On the other hand, a limited power of appointment is a grant of authority to transfer a property interest to anyone except the one with the power, or his or her estate or creditors. This complicated statement simply means that if you have the ability to transfer the property to yourself (or your estate at death), the value of the property will be considered to be yours, and shall be a part of your estate.

The value of the property subject to the limited power cannot be considered to be yours (the person holding the power) nor can it be considered to be a part of your estate at death. An additional limitation is that the property cannot be transferred to a creditor. Creditors are mentioned because the use of the trust property to satisfy a debt is an indirect use of the asset to satisfy a potential estate claim. The property would be subject to creditor claims if it was transferred to the holder of the power during lifetime or if, at death, it was transferred to the holder's estate. Therefore, the ability to pay a creditor from these assets during lifetime will result in these assets being counted as part of the taxable estate.

For example: Bob died leaving property in trust for the benefit of his wife, Mary. Upon Mary's death, the property will pass to their children. In this trust, Bob gives Mary the privilege of giving away or transferring any trust property from the trust to anyone she chooses, with the exception of herself, her estate, or her creditors or the creditors of her estate. This privilege of transfer is called a *limited* power of appointment because Mary does not own the property, yet she can direct to whom it shall go, so long as it does not go to her (or her estate, etc.). Upon Mary's death, none of the trust property subject to this power will be considered hers for tax purposes (it will not be included in her taxable estate.)

PROCEED WITH CAUTION

As with all of the material in this book, be certain to consult an estate planning attorney before implementing any of the techniques discussed in this book. The failure to obtain professional advice could result in additional expenses for administering your estate and could result in additional and unnecessary taxation of your estate. Additionally, the failure to properly prepare documents according to applicable law may render the documents useless.

HOUR'S UP!

Now it's time to see how much you have learned and retained from this lesson. Try to take the following quiz without referring back to the hourly materials.

1. The following are examples of real property except:

    a. Your home

    b. The fence around your home

    c. Your refrigerator

    d. Your swimming pool

2. The following is an example of intangible personal property:

    a. Your car

    b. Your clothing

    c. Your television

    d. Your checking account

3. The following are included in your probate estate:

    a. Life insurance payable to your estate

    b. Annuities payable to your spouse

    c. Brokerage account held as joint tenancy with right to survivorship

    d. A gift of collectibles made just days before death

4. A limited power of appointment includes which of the following:

    a. A power to give away another's assets, but not to yourself

    b. A power to give away another's assets to yourself

    c. A power to give away your own assets

    d. A power to designate a guardian over your property

5. An example of a revocable transfer is ...

    a. A transfer of property by gift to another

    b. A completed transfer to a charity

    c. A transfer of property to an irrevocable trust

    d. A transfer of property to a revocable trust

QUIZ

Hour 4
Defining Types of Assets

There are several different ways individuals can own property. The following sections describe each category of property ownership, along with their identifying characteristics, functional characteristics, and risks of ownership.

Single Ownership

This form of ownership certainly is the easiest to establish and identify.

- **Identifying characteristics**   Only one name will appear on this type of asset—for example, "Tom R. Planner, owner."

- **Functional characteristics**   Unless he or she becomes incapacitated and an authorized person is appointed, only the owner can control this asset. This is a probate asset because the owner does not identify someone to take the property upon his or her death. With the exception of certain small estates, an estate with this type of property will usually require probate to determine heirship. This asset also will be included in the decedent's taxable estate for federal estate, state inheritance, and federal and state income tax calculations.

Unless exempted by federal or state law, assets in single ownership will be subject to the owner's creditors during his or her lifetime and after death. In the event of incapacity, there are only a few designated people who

Chapter Summary

LESSON PLAN:

In this hour, you'll learn about the different ways people own property. As discussed in the last hour, the determination of who owns the title to a piece of property is the most important consideration when planning your estate. You also learned how important it is to properly classify the type of property you own. Indeed, even the most sophisticated planning documents will fail if the titles to your assets are not consistent with how you list them in those documents.

In this hour, you'll learn that assets may be defined as either titled assets or contractual assets. Titled assets are those assets with a document of title indicating ownership of that asset. Contractual assets are those assets containing beneficiary designations, such as life insurance, retirement accounts, and annuities. Later in this hour, I'll show you the significance of each form of ownership as it applies to planning your estate. In addition, you'll learn ...

- The significance of single-owned property.
- The significance of joint ownership with rights of survivorship.
- The significance of tenancy in common.
- The meaning of tenancy by the entirety.
- The meaning of community property.
- The difference between titled assets and contractual assets.

GO TO ▶
For more information on powers of attorney, see Hour 12, "Powers of Attorney, Health Care Representative Appointments, and Living Wills."

are allowed to exert control, including a court-appointed guardian or an attorney-in-fact designated in a durable power of attorney. This type of power of attorney endures even if the principal becomes incapacitated.

If the asset is a bank account, there may be an *authorized signer*, designated by the owner, who will have authority to sign checks and make withdrawals from the account. Generally speaking, only a court-appointed personal representative will have power over these assets after the death of the owner.

STRICTLY DEFINED

An **authorized signer** is one who is authorized by the owner of an account to sign checks and make withdrawals from the account, but who has no ownership interest in the account during the lifetime or following the death of the owner.

 Neither an authorized signer nor an attorney in fact has any authority or control over the account of a deceased owner.

JOINT TENANCY WITH RIGHT OF SURVIVORSHIP

Most often established between a husband and wife, joint tenancy with right of survivorship (JTWROS) probably is the most common kind of ownership among two or more people.

Two or more names will appear on the title of this type of asset. In addition, most states require language similar to the following that specifically identifies the ownership type: "JTWROS" (joint tenancy with right of survivorship). Example: *"Tom R. Planner and John H. Smith, JTWROS."*

 Generally speaking, if the title does not have language specifying the right to survivorship, the asset will be categorized as tenancy in common. One exception to this general rule is property held between spouses, which is presumed by many states to have a right of survivorship, even if not specifically set forth in the title.

- **Functional characteristics** Either owner can control an asset of this type. If one of the owners becomes incapacitated, the other owner has access and control over the asset. If either owner has appointed an attorney-in-fact through a power of attorney, that agent will be able to access the asset to the same extent as the co-owner(s). This type of ownership specifies that when one co-owner dies, the surviving named co-owner(s) will fully own the asset until there is only one owner remaining, in which case the asset becomes a single-owner asset. A JTWROS asset is not a probate asset so long as there remains a surviving co-owner; therefore it will not require probate to determine heirship. It will be included, at least in part, in the decedent's final taxable estate for federal estate, state inheritance, and federal and state income tax calculations.

JUST A MINUTE

According to Internal Revenue Code section 2040(a), except as for joint tenants who are husband and wife, the full value of the jointly held properties will be included in the estate of the first to die. An exception occurs if the survivor is able to establish ownership of some part of that property before the joint tenancy was created. To fit within this exception, you must maintain accurate record keeping to establish prior ownership, such as cancelled checks, tax statements, bank records, or tax returns.

- **Risks of ownership** Unless exempted by federal or state law, this property will be subject to the creditors of any owner during lifetime as well as at death. Therefore, if your joint owner owes money to a creditor, that creditor could use judicial process to take the property, sell it, and apply a portion of the proceeds to satisfy the debt. Property can still be sold by a joint owner or encumbered by a lien on the property to secure a debt of the joint owner (such as a mortgage).

Another problem with the use of joint tenancy with right of survivorship concerns unanticipated state inheritance tax implications. For example, Mary, Susan, and Marge are sisters who are widows in their 90s, and they all wish to avoid probate. To do this, each of them will add the other two names to their bank accounts, with rights of survivorship, so that when any one of them dies, the other two will inherit.

Mary dies and her probate avoidance plan works like clockwork. Each account now has the remaining two siblings on the title to the account. There is only one problem: Because each account has Mary's name on the title—thus making her joint owner—all of the accounts are considered Mary's for state inheritance tax purposes. This means that even though the money from the siblings' accounts belonged to that respective sibling, the inheritance tax law treats all of that same money as belonging to Mary. Not only will the state and federal government take taxes from Mary's account; the siblings have to pay inheritance tax on their own money!

Fortunately, most state laws allow each surviving owner to present documentation of account activity to prove that the money in their separate accounts actually was their own money. For instance, showing that the deposits into the respective accounts generally were direct-deposited Social Security checks likely will be sufficient proof. Also helpful would be documentation that each separate account was under the social security number of the respective sibling.

PROCEED WITH CAUTION

 Although beyond the scope of this book, beware of joint ownership when considering eligibility for some needs-based government assistance programs, such as Medicaid. The entire value of jointly owned assets may be included in the eligibility determination. They are also subject to creditor claims against any of the owners.

BANK ACCOUNTS

Every state has laws that detail exactly how owners can handle joint accounts. The problem with joint bank accounts is that a person may wish to add another's name to the account "as a matter of convenience" so that person can sign checks, make deposits, etc. if the owner is unable to do so. This creates what is frequently called an "agency account." With an agency account, the additional person is not a joint owner and the property will not pass to that additional person at the owner's death. Unfortunately, however, if you're not careful, the additional name may be added as a "joint owner." Although this may not have been the owner's intent, the proceeds will pass to the "joint owner" when the original owner dies. This is precisely why you should title your assets with care and understand the function of those titles when you plan your estate.

PROCEED WITH CAUTION

 Each state has its own specific laws on the issue of joint bank accounts. Be certain to consult with an estate planning attorney to learn about the laws in your own state.

For example, a state law in New York presumes that a bank account with multiple names creates a right of survivorship. Additionally, when you create a joint bank account, most states will allow a joint owner to withdraw all of the funds from the account.

In other states, the rule provides that a joint bank account owner may withdraw only what he or she contributes to the account. For instance, Indiana's multi-party account law provides that "A joint account belongs, during the lifetime of all parties, to the parties in proportion to the net contributions by each to the sums on deposit, unless there is clear and convincing evidence of a different intent." (Indiana Code Section 32=4-1.5-3)

TENANCY IN COMMON

Most people acquire property as tenancy in common when they inherit property along with other people. This type of ownership is a creation of state law and does not require any special action on the part of the owners to create this type of title.

- **Identifying characteristics**   Two or more names will appear on the title to this type of asset. However, unlike joint tenancy with right of survivorship, the document will not indicate who inherits.

 As mentioned earlier, an exception to this general rule is property held between spouses (tenancy by the entireties), which is presumed by many states to have a right of survivorship, even if not specifically set forth in the title.

 Occasionally, property will be titled between two individuals with the conjunction "and/or." Depending upon state law, this language may authorize the surviving owners to acquire the share of the deceased owner automatically, by operation of law.

- **Functional characteristics**   Each owner controls his or her proportionate interest in the property. No single owner can transfer or dispose of the interest of another owner without his or her explicit permission. If one owner is incapacitated, the other owner(s) will still have the ability to control his or her own interest in the property. If any owner has appointed an attorney-in-fact through a power of attorney, that agent may access the proportionate interest of the incapacitated owner. This type of ownership specifies that upon the death of one co-owner, the interest of the deceased co-owner passes to the heirs of that decedent. Therefore, the surviving owners do not inherit the property simply because their names are on the title. If they happen to be the heirs of the deceased owner, they might inherit the decedent's interest through the decedent's will, trust, or through the operation of state law. This type of asset is a probate asset with regard to the proportionate interest the decedent had in the property, which means that it will require probate to determine heirship. The interest of the decedent in the asset will be included in his or her taxable estate for federal estate, state inheritance, and federal and state income tax calculations.

- **Risks of ownership** Unless exempted by federal or state law, this type of asset is subject to the creditors of any owner during lifetime and at death. Also, if any one co-owner is incapacitated, the surviving joint owner will not control the interest of the one incapacitated.

Let's take a look at an example of tenancy in common at work. Gertrude, a widow, has three children, all of whom are living. Gertrude is 98 years old and wants to transfer her 100-acre farm to her three children: Larry, Harry, and Barry. She makes out a will and names the three children as beneficiaries. Two years later, Gertrude dies. The property passes to the three children.

The children own the property as tenants in common. There is no survivorship feature; they all own an undivided one-third interest in the entire property. Five years later, Larry dies. Larry is a widower and has five children, A, B, C, D, and E, who are his sole heirs. Now the owners of the property are as follows:

Harry	$\frac{1}{3}$
Barry	$\frac{1}{3}$
A	$\frac{1}{15}$
B	$\frac{1}{15}$
C	$\frac{1}{15}$
D	$\frac{1}{15}$
E	$\frac{1}{15}$

Imagine what it must be like managing the farm operations among these seven owners. But it will only get worse. Two years later, Harry dies in a farming accident. Harry's surviving heirs include his wife Mabel and three children, F, G, and H. A fourth child, I, died years ago and has three surviving children, J, K, and L. Now let's see who owns this property. Assume that under the state law of Harry's residence, a surviving spouse inherits one half and the other one half passes to his surviving heirs.

Barry	$\frac{1}{3}$
A	$\frac{1}{15}$
B	$\frac{1}{15}$
C	$\frac{1}{15}$
D	$\frac{1}{15}$
E	$\frac{1}{15}$
Mabel	$\frac{1}{6}$
F	$\frac{1}{24}$
G	$\frac{1}{24}$

H	$1/_{24}$
J	$1/_{72}$
K	$1/_{72}$
L	$1/_{72}$

How is that for an estate plan? Of course, any one of the owners can seek a partition of the entire property. A partition results in a sale of the entire farm followed by the division of the proceeds among the owners according to their respective interests.

 An action to partition property might be filed to force the sale of the property, but each owner is still entitled to his or her respective interest in the proceeds.

TENANCY BY THE ENTIRETY

A tenancy by the entirety is a specific form of ownership between spouses similar to joint tenancy with right of survivorship. This type of ownership is created by state statute. It is an automatic form of ownership in that property owned by a married couple is automatically considered to be tenancy by the entirety, unless otherwise stated.

- **Identifying characteristics** In a tenancy by the entirety, the property will appear in the joint names of husband and wife. Some states require a statement indicating either that the owners are in fact husband and wife or a statement that the property is held as tenants by the entireties. An example is "Chuck R. Smith and Gertrude M. Smith, husband and wife."

- **Functional characteristics** Unlike joint tenancy with rights of survivorship, tenancy by the entirety allows neither spouse the ability to encumber or transfer the asset without the consent of the other spouse, even if that spouse is incapacitated. If the incapacitated spouse has a duly authorized attorney-in-fact through a durable power of attorney, that agent will be able to act on behalf of the incapacitated spouse. Without an attorney-in-fact, a court-appointed guardian will be required to act on behalf of the incapacitated spouse. Upon the death of one spouse, the surviving spouse shall become the complete owner of the asset. At that time the property becomes a single-name asset. Property owned as tenancy by the entirety is not a probate asset during the lifetime of both spouses, and it will not require probate to determine heirship at the death of the first spouse to die since the surviving spouse is automatically the owner. But this will become a probate asset upon the death of both spouses because there will no longer be a surviving owner. For property acquired after 1981, only one half of the value of this asset will be included in the decedent's taxable estate for federal estate, state inheritance, and federal and state income tax calculations.

Because it is so important to your estate to properly title your property, you should consult an attorney before creating or changing title to any deed, particularly real estate. You'll see why when you read and look (in the following figure) at the following example of a poorly drafted real estate deed.

Mildred is an elderly widow with one child, Wallace. Wallace is an adult on disability and is unmarried. Mildred owns 40 acres of land in single-name ownership. Wallace is living with Mildred and he suggests that she add his name to the title so that she can benefit from his property tax exemptions as a result of his disability. Mildred and Wallace intend to own the house jointly with right to survivorship so that upon the death of either of them, the other will own the property outright.

Wallace, who is a self-starter, goes to the local office supply store and buys a model deed. He fills it out and has Mildred sign it. He has the deed notarized and files it with the recorder's office.

Eventually, Wallace dies. Mildred thinks she owns the property, until Wallace's son, Bob, comes along and claims that he is the owner of the property. How can that be? Let's look at the deed drafted by Wallace.

Note that the deed was signed over by Mildred to "Wallace, with right to survivorship." Does this create a joint tenancy with right to survivorship? If so, who is the joint tenant with Wallace? Is it Mildred? Is it someone else?

In order to determine this point, the judge was asked to evaluate several possibilities. The language could be considered a deed to Wallace, with no other owners. In this case, Mildred would not own the property at all, but it would pass to Bob as Wallace's only beneficiary under his will. It could be considered to be a tenancy in common between Mildred and Wallace. If this were true, Wallace's one-half interest would pass to Bob at Wallace's death, leaving Mildred a one-half owner with Bob. But what about the unmistakable language that says "… with rights to survivorship"? Remember, the intent was for Mildred to own the property with Wallace, jointly with rights to survivorship.

Duly entered for taxation this _____
day of AUG _____ 19 92   **Quit Claim Deed**   Received for record this __ __ day of
                                                 Aug 19 92 at 10:00
92 12244 Auditors book   o'clock a M. and recorded in Book
Jennith R Thomas   Judith Anderson
Auditor VIGO _____ County   THIS INDENTURE WITNESSETH: Recorder Vigo County

That Mildred G. Pierson _____

Honey Creek Township _____ of _Vigo_ _____ County, in the State of Indiana
RELEASE AND QUIT CLAIM to _Wallace_ Pierson (With Right to survivorship)

Honey Creek Township _____ of _____ Vigo _____ County, in the State of Indiana
for and in consideration of the sum of $ 1.00 _____ Dollars,
the receipt whereof is hereby acknowledged, the following described Real Estate in Vigo
County in the State of Indiana, to-wit:

PRT W SIDE

D- 345/363-2
24-11-9 10.63 AC

INDEXED

IN WITNESS WHEREOF, The said Mrs. Mildred C. Pierson

hereunto set HER hand and seal, this 14th day of August 19 92
Mildred C. Pierson _____ (Seal)   _____ (Seal)
Mildred C. Pierson _____ (Seal)   _____ (Seal)
                         _____ (Seal)

STATE OF INDIANA, _____   COUNTY, ss:
Before me, the undersigned, a Notary Public, in and for said County and State, this _____ day of
_____ A.D. 19__, personally appeared the within named Mrs. Mildred C. Pierson
Widow

the above conveyance, and acknowledged the execution of the same to be _____ voluntary act and deed.
IN WITNESS WHEREOF, I have hereunto subscribed my name and affixed my official seal.
Commission expires June 8 19 96   Dorothy O Mars

How NOT to pre-
pare a quit claim
deed.

The court ruled this to be an error caused by the drafter of the deed (known as a scrivener's—or writer's—error) and held the property to be jointly owned between Mildred and Wallace with rights to survivorship. At Wallace's death, the property became the sole property of Mildred.

UNDERSTANDING CONTRACTUAL ASSETS

Contractual assets differ from titled assets in that the owner designates a specific beneficiary in a contract between the issuing company—an insurance carrier or a retirement fund, for example—and the owner. In this sense, the contract is the title document. Following are some of the most common contractual assets.

LIFE INSURANCE CONTRACTS

Life insurance contracts, although not easily understood by most people, are the most commonly owned contractual assets. There are three primary components of a life insurance contract:

- Owner
- Insured
- Beneficiary

The owner of a life insurance contract has power over the contract including the power to change owners, change beneficiaries, pay premiums, borrow from the contract, or terminate the contract. For tax purposes, ownership determines whether the policy is a taxable item in an estate valuation. The insured is the person upon whose life the policy is issued. If the owner and the insured are the same person, a life insurance policy will be included in the estate of the owner/insured. Otherwise, the policy will normally not be included in the estate of the insured.

GO TO ▶
Proceed to Hour 6, "Federal Estate Taxes," for the discussion of federal estate taxes and how those taxes are paid.

Obviously, the beneficiary of the life insurance policy is the individual who will receive the death benefit upon the death of the insured. In most cases, the beneficiary does not have to pay taxes on death benefits he or she receives. However, when the beneficiary dies, whatever remains of the death benefit is included as part of the beneficiary's estate.

As long as a life insurance policy has a designated beneficiary, the policy will not become a probate asset, unless the policy designates "the estate" as the beneficiary. Life insurance policies are included in the taxable estate for federal estate tax purposes but typically are not included in the taxable estate for state inheritance tax purposes.

PROCEED WITH CAUTION

Each state has its own specific laws regarding insurance policies. Be certain to consult with an estate planning attorney to learn about the laws in your own state.

RETIREMENT ACCOUNTS

Retirement accounts are the next most common contractual assets owned by individuals. These contracts have two primary components: the owner and the beneficiary. Although retirement accounts are included in the taxable estate of the owner, they are not included in the probate estate of the owner so long as there is a designated beneficiary other than the owner's estate.

ANNUITIES

Annuities are treated the same as retirement accounts. They are included in the taxable estate of the owner but not included in the probate estate unless the estate is the designated beneficiary.

STRICTLY DEFINED

An **annuity** is an investment contract in which the owner deposits a sum of money, either as a lump sum or in periodic installments, which accumulates tax-deferred, and in which the owner agrees to certain restrictions on the right of withdrawal.

PAYABLE ON DEATH ACCOUNTS

Payable on death accounts, also known as *transfer on death accounts*, are accounts that designate a beneficiary who will receive the balance in the account upon the death of the owner(s). Most states now allow property to be owned in individual name along with a designation of a beneficiary. This is unique in that beneficiary designations historically have been provided only on life insurance, retirement accounts, or annuities. These accounts now are available for checking accounts, savings accounts, certificates of deposit, savings bonds, and brokerage accounts.

FYI A "transfer on death" account is the same as a "payable on death" account. The terms are used interchangeably.

Kansas has an uncommon statute that allows for a transfer on death designation to appear on a real estate deed. Real estate can be titled this way by preparing, signing and recording a deed with specific wording indicating the intent to make the title one that will transfer ownership upon the death of the owner(s) to a designated beneficiary.

The advantage of a transfer on death account is that the asset can be owned in one name during lifetime and still avoid probate as a result of the designation of beneficiary on the account. Unlike the joint account, this account has no additional owners during the lifetime of the original owner. During the owner's lifetime, the property is treated the same as a single-owner account. Although this type of account will avoid probate, it will still be included in the taxable estate of the owner.

Another advantage to this type of ownership is that the property is not subject to the creditors of the beneficiary during the lifetime of the owner, unlike a joint account.

COMMUNITY PROPERTY

Some states have enacted laws that provide for ownership of property between spouses as community property. Understanding community property begins with an analysis of when the property in question was acquired. If one spouse acquired property prior to the marriage, it will retain its status as separate property, unless the parties agree otherwise through a written agreement. Any property acquired by the spouses during the marriage will be treated as community property.

In community property states, each spouse owns and controls an undivided one half interest in the community assets. However, each state has different laws that dictate how community property is to be treated in particular circumstances. Upon the death of one spouse, his or her estate shall be considered the owner of one half of the community assets for tax and probate purposes; the surviving spouse will own the other half. This is very similar to tenancy in common.

FYI An undivided interest in property means that all owners share a percentage of the ownership of the entire property. In other words, no boundary can be drawn around each owner's separate share. Every part of the property is owned jointly. To divide the interest is called a partition, allowing for boundaries to be established.

The nine community property states are as follows:

- Arizona
- California
- Idaho
- Louisiana
- Nevada
- New Mexico
- Texas
- Washington
- Wisconsin

PROCEED WITH CAUTION

The laws of any state may have changed by the time you read this book. Be certain to seek the advice of an estate planning attorney in your state to determine if your state follows community property laws.

The parties are allowed to enter into an agreement to classify property in a manner different from what is provided by community property statutes. In community property states, if either spouse inherits property during the marriage, that property is considered to be the separate property of that particular spouse.

It is very important that people who live in a community property state keep clear and accurate records regarding the origin and acquisition dates of their properties. They might even enter into an agreement that outlines who owns what property. Therefore, any transaction involving community property must be reviewed with an attorney in that particular state.

PROCEED WITH CAUTION

As with all of the material in this book, be certain to consult an estate planning attorney before implementing any of the techniques discussed in this book. The failure to obtain professional advice could result in additional expenses for administering your estate and could result in additional and unnecessary taxation of your estate. Additionally, the failure to properly prepare documents according to applicable law may render the documents useless.

QUIZ

HOUR'S UP!

Now it's time to see how much you have learned and retained from this lesson. Try to take the following quiz without referring back to the hourly materials.

1. An account designated as "transfer on death":

   a. Avoids probate

   b. Is payable on death of the owner to a designee

   c. Both of the above

   d. None of the above

2. One of the biggest drawbacks to jointly owned property is:

   a. It always avoids probate

   b. It is subject to creditors of all owners

   c. It is governed by your will

   d. You have no control over the asset

3. Tenancy by the entirety is similar to which of the following:

   a. Transfer on death accounts

   b. Tenancy in partnership

   c. Tenancy in common

   d. Joint tenancy with right of survivorship

4. In community property states, each spouse owns:

   a. Individual property acquired before the marriage

   b. Individual property inherited during the marriage

   c. One-half of property acquired during the marriage

   d. All of the above

5. Life insurance is included in the taxable estate of:

   a. The beneficiary for income tax purposes at the time of receipt and is reportable as income during the year received

   b. The owner for federal estate tax purposes

   c. The insured for all purposes

   d. None of the above

PART II
Understanding Taxes

HOUR 5 Income Taxes and Inheritance Taxes

HOUR 6 Federal Estate Taxes

HOUR 5

Income Taxes and Inheritance Taxes

CHAPTER SUMMARY

LESSON PLAN:

In this hour, you will learn how income taxes and inheritance taxes can impact the administration of an estate. With this knowledge, you will gain an understanding of the significance these taxes have on your estate at death. The focus of this hour will be on two taxes: income and inheritance. Aside from estate taxes, which will be discussed in the next hour, these two taxes can affect your planning significantly. You will also learn …

- The dangers of deferring taxes.
- The assets that contain hidden tax traps.
- The need to file the decedent's final income tax return.
- The importance of reporting estate income.
- The states that impose inheritance taxes.
- The impact of state inheritance taxes on planning.

Everyone knows what income taxes are, especially as April 15 approaches every year. In the context of estate planning, income taxes frequently are overlooked. Most planners and planning guides focus on the federal estate tax, which of course is a major issue for planning purposes.

Even though the federal estate tax is a major consideration when you plan your estate, a comprehensive estate plan will provide for all taxes that might be payable upon death. Income taxes can be one of the most significant of the *transfer taxes*—those taxes imposed because of the transfer of ownership of property—but because most people don't know how estates are taxed, often income taxes are overlooked.

STRICTLY DEFINED

A **transfer tax** is a tax imposed because of the transfer of ownership of property, either by gift during lifetime or by testamentary transfer at death. Examples of transfer taxes are inheritance taxes, estate taxes, and income taxes.

Many planners do not address the issue of income taxes in the estate planning context because accountants usually handle this aspect of a person's finances. Accountants are usually well trained to calculate income tax returns for trusts and estates, while estate planners tend to concentrate on techniques to avoid or reduce federal estate taxes. Estate planners receive less exposure to income tax planning in trade journals or in computerized planning programs.

Hour 6, "Federal Estate Taxes," goes into detail about the federal estate tax and the importance of planning to minimize that tax.

Let's take a closer look at the different contexts in which income taxes take their toll on a decedent's estate.

BLINDSIDED BY TAX DEFERRAL

There are several different ways that income taxes take a toll on an estate. We will now review the assets that pose the greatest risk of income tax and why it is so easy to overlook the tax aspects of these assets. Careful planning on your part can dramatically reduce the affect of these taxes on your overall plan.

QUALIFIED RETIREMENT ACCOUNTS

Qualified retirement accounts are accounts that allow for special tax treatment of contributions, deferral of taxes on income and capital gains, and which are subject to minimum distribution rules. Examples include individual retirement accounts, 401(k) plans, 403(b) plans, profit-sharing plans and pension plans.

GO TO ▶
For a more detailed discussion of qualified retirement accounts and the tax advantages associated with the different types of accounts, see Hour 14, "Retirement Plans."

When Individual Retirement Accounts (IRAs) were authorized in 1974, one of the greatest selling points was that all income taxes would be deferred until the owner of the account withdrew the funds. This meant that gains would not be offset by taxes until the money was allowed to grow for a period of years. In 1981, the law was expanded to allow contributions of up to $2,000 per year. Individuals who were already enrolled as employees in company pension plans were now allowed to contribute to individual retirement accounts, where unprecedented money was then deposited.

IRAs have increased in popularity for a few reasons. First, you're allowed to deduct from your yearly income the amount you invest in an IRA that year. Second, there is an advantage to compounding your savings without having those assets taxed immediately. Assets grow exponentially during your working years.

However, you must eventually pay the piper. When it comes time to withdraw those funds at retirement, many people are shocked at how much money they've actually been able to save—and at how much Uncle Sam is about to take. Additionally, not only are their IRAs larger than they anticipated, they also have a greater income from other sources. That means that they're in a higher income tax bracket than they had originally planned. That's when many people run to a financial planner for advice about estate planning.

The perceived "beauty" of deferred taxation has some parallels with the alarming rise in the use of credit. Instant gratification is achieved with credit cards because you don't have to pay for the items until another day. Although there is no doubt that tax deferral creates greater wealth, it also creates greater taxation at withdrawal time. Although it is clear that tax deferral is not the same as paying finance charges, the concept of paying taxes later has a familiar ring to those who use credit and pay for it later.

You also might owe taxes on other deferred income. Various qualified pension plans, including profit sharing plans, money purchase plans, simplified employee pension plans, and 401(k) and 403(b) plans have proliferated. The average retired individual is now paying income taxes on the minimum required distributions, which are based on rules issued by the Internal Revenue Service that govern the amount and timing of mandatory distributions from qualified retirement accounts.

GO TO ▶
See suggestions for proper planning with deferred tax accounts in Hour 14.

So what does all of this have to do with estate planning? Well, unfortunately, everyone eventually dies, and when they do their heirs are left to inherit these tax-deferred retirement plans. Unless the owner of these deferred-income accounts plans properly, their heirs might face punishing income taxation. To avoid this you must designate appropriate beneficiaries.

SAVINGS BONDS

As you'll discover, the series of bond you own determines how much your heirs will pay in taxes. For instance, if you own Series I, E, or EE bond, either your estate or your heirs will pay taxes on the accumulated income, depending on when the bonds are cashed in. This income technically is referred to as *income in respect of a decedent*.

Income in respect of a decedent refers to amounts of income earned by a decedent but not included in the decedent's taxable income in the year of his or her death. Examples include payment for services rendered before death and payment made under a deferred compensation agreement.

 An appreciated asset that is inherited is entitled to a "stepped up basis." This means that the date of death value becomes the beneficiary's basis for determining capital gains upon sale of the asset. Some assets do not get a stepped up basis. Savings Bonds are one such asset. Although the value is higher at death than when purchased, it is due to untaxed, accumulated income. This income is taxable upon sale of the asset.

THE DECEDENT'S FINAL RETURN

Your estate will be responsible for filing your final income tax after you die. Your personal representative files it at the time you normally would have filed your individual tax returns, unless you're survived by a spouse. In that case your surviving spouse should file a joint return for the calendar year in which your death occurs, even if that's on the last taxable day of the year. If the return clearly indicates the date of death and the word "deceased," the surviving spouse will receive any refund directly. If you and your spouse always file separate returns, the IRS requires that the filer submit a Form 1310, Statement of Claimant to Refund Due Deceased Taxpayer along with the return.

 If the court has appointed an executor or administrator, who is someone other than your surviving spouse, that person is the one who signs the final tax return. If not, your surviving spouse signs.

Hour 8, "Probate," will delve into the topic of probate and explain to you more about the personal representative, what probate administration is, and what powers the personal representative has.

Form **1310**
(Rev. March 1995)
Department of the Treasury
Internal Revenue Service

Statement of Person Claiming
Refund Due a Deceased Taxpayer

▶ **See instructions below and on back.**

OMB No. 1545-0073

Attachment
Sequence No. **87**

Tax year decedent was due a refund:

Calendar year _____ , or other tax year beginning _____ , 19 ____ , and ending _____ , 19 ____

Name of decedent	Date of death	Decedent's social security number

Please type or print

Name of person claiming refund

Home address (number and street). If you have a P.O. box, see instructions. | Apt. no.

City, town or post office, state, and ZIP code. If you have a foreign address, see instructions.

Part I   **Check the box that applies to you.** Check only one box. **Be sure to complete Part III below.**

A ☐ Surviving spouse requesting reissuance of a refund check. See instructions.

B ☐ Court-appointed or certified personal representative. You may have to attach a court certificate showing your appointment. See instructions.

C ☐ Person, **other** than A or B, claiming refund for the decedent's estate. Also, complete Part II. You may have to attach a copy of the proof of death. See instructions.

Part II   **Complete this part only if you checked the box on line C above.**

		Yes	No
1	Did the decedent leave a will?		
2a	Has a court appointed a personal representative for the estate of the decedent?		
b	If you answered "**No**" to 2a, will one be appointed?		
	If you answered "**Yes**" to 2a or 2b, the personal representative must file for the refund.		
3	As the person claiming the refund for the decedent's estate, will you pay out the refund according to the laws of the state where the decedent was a legal resident?		
	If you answered "**No**" to 3, a refund cannot be made until you submit a court certificate showing your appointment as personal representative or other evidence that you are entitled under state law to receive the refund.		

Part III   **Signature and verification. All filers must complete this part.**

I request a refund of taxes overpaid by or on behalf of the decedent. Under penalties of perjury, I declare that I have examined this claim, and to the best of my knowledge and belief, it is true, correct, and complete.

Signature of person claiming refund ▶   Date ▶

Paperwork Reduction Act Notice

We ask for the information on this form to carry out the Internal Revenue laws of the United States. You are required to give us the information. We need it to ensure that you are complying with these laws and to allow us to figure and collect the right amount of tax.

The time needed to complete and file this form will vary depending on individual circumstances. The estimated average time is:

Recordkeeping . . . . 7 min.
**Learning about the
law or the form** . . . . 3 min.
Preparing the form . . . . 16 min.
**Copying, assembling,
and sending the
form to the IRS** . . . . 17 min.

If you have comments concerning the accuracy of these time estimates or suggestions for making this form simpler, we would be happy to hear from you. You can write to the **Internal Revenue Service,** Attention: Tax Forms Committee, PC:FP, Washington, DC 20224. **DO NOT** send the form to this address.

General Instructions

Purpose of Form

Use Form 1310 to claim a refund on behalf of a deceased taxpayer.

Who Must File

If you are claiming a refund on behalf of a deceased taxpayer, you must file Form 1310 unless **either** of the following applies:

• You are a surviving spouse filing an original or amended joint return with the decedent, OR

• You are a personal representative (see back of form) filing an original Form 1040, Form 1040A, Form 1040EZ, or Form 1040NR for the decedent and a court certificate showing your appointment is attached to the return.

Example. Assume Mr. Green died on January 4 before filing his tax return. On April 3 of the same year, you were appointed by the court as the personal representative for Mr. Green's estate and you file Form 1040 for Mr. Green. You do not need to file Form 1310 to claim the refund on Mr. Green's tax return. However, you must attach to his return a copy of the court certificate showing your appointment.

Cat. No. 11566B   Form **1310** (Rev. 3-95)

Use this form to claim a refund due from a deceased taxpayer.

THE FIDUCIARY TAXES

Under the law, an estate is considered a separate legal entity, much the same as an individual or a corporation. Accordingly, as a legal entity, it must have a taxpayer identification number so that taxable income and capital gains can be reported to the IRS in order to pay fiduciary taxes, or those taxes incurred by a trust or estate during its administration. The *personal representative* of the estate should apply for this TIN by filing IRS Form SS-4 with the appropriate IRS office.

STRICTLY DEFINED

A **personal representative** is an individual who is in charge of a decedent's estate, whether or not there is a will to administer.

During the administration of a probate estate or the administration of a trust, the estate assets will continue to earn income. If this income is reported under the decedent's social security number, it will become necessary to continue filing tax returns for the decedent. For this reason, the personal representative should be certain to remove the decedent's Social Security number from all assets and replace it with the newly assigned identification number for the estate. Any *successor trustee*, a person who takes over the duties of the original trustee, should do likewise.

STRICTLY DEFINED

A **successor trustee** is a trustee of a trust that assumes the responsibilities of trustee only after a prior trustee resigns or is no longer able to serve as trustee.

The estate will either pay taxes on taxable income or will distribute the income to the beneficiaries during the taxable year. The personal representative distributes income by using an IRS Schedule K-1 (Form 1041). Income distributed in this manner is taxed only to the beneficiary. There is no double taxation. Typically, it's better to distribute taxable income than to have the estate pay the tax because of the estate's high income tax bracket.

Form **SS-4**	**Application for Employer Identification Number**	EIN	
(Rev. April 2000) Department of the Treasury Internal Revenue Service	(For use by employers, corporations, partnerships, trusts, estates, churches, government agencies, certain individuals, and others. See instructions.) ▶ Keep a copy for your records.	OMB No. 1545-0003	

1 Name of applicant (legal name) (see instructions)

2 Trade name of business (if different from name on line 1) | **3** Executor, trustee, "care of" name

4a Mailing address (street address) (room, apt., or suite no.) | **5a** Business address (if different from address on lines 4a and 4b)

4b City, state, and ZIP code | **5b** City, state, and ZIP code

6 County and state where principal business is located

7 Name of principal officer, general partner, grantor, owner, or trustor—SSN or ITIN may be required (see instructions) ▶

(left margin: Please type or print clearly.)

8a Type of entity (Check only one box.) (see instructions)

Caution: *If applicant is a limited liability company, see the instructions for line 8a.*

☐ Sole proprietor (SSN) _____ ☐ Estate (SSN of decedent) _____
☐ Partnership ☐ Personal service corp. ☐ Plan administrator (SSN) _____
☐ REMIC ☐ National Guard ☐ Other corporation (specify) ▶ _____
☐ State/local government ☐ Farmers' cooperative ☐ Trust
☐ Church or church-controlled organization ☐ Federal government/military
☐ Other nonprofit organization (specify) ▶ _____ (enter GEN if applicable) _____
☐ Other (specify) ▶

8b If a corporation, name the state or foreign country (if applicable) where incorporated | State | Foreign country

9 Reason for applying (Check only one box.) (see instructions) ☐ Banking purpose (specify purpose) ▶ _____
☐ Started new business (specify type) ▶ _____ ☐ Changed type of organization (specify new type) ▶ _____
☐ Purchased going business
☐ Hired employees (Check the box and see line 12.) ☐ Created a trust (specify type) ▶ _____
☐ Created a pension plan (specify type) ▶ ☐ Other (specify) ▶

10 Date business started or acquired (month, day, year) (see instructions) | **11** Closing month of accounting year (see instructions)

12 First date wages or annuities were paid or will be paid (month, day, year). **Note:** *If applicant is a withholding agent, enter date income will first be paid to nonresident alien. (month, day, year)* . . . . ▶

13 Highest number of employees expected in the next 12 months. **Note:** *If the applicant does not expect to have any employees during the period, enter -0-. (see instructions)* . . . . . ▶ | Nonagricultural | Agricultural | Household

14 Principal activity (see instructions) ▶

15 Is the principal business activity manufacturing? . . . . ☐ Yes ☐ No
If "Yes," principal product and raw material used ▶

16 To whom are most of the products or services sold? Please check one box. | ☐ Business (wholesale)
☐ Public (retail) ☐ Other (specify) ▶ | ☐ N/A

17a Has the applicant ever applied for an employer identification number for this or any other business? . . . . . ☐ Yes ☐ No
Note: *If "Yes," please complete lines 17b and 17c.*

17b If you checked "Yes" on line 17a, give applicant's legal name and trade name shown on prior application, if different from line 1 or 2 above.
Legal name ▶ | Trade name ▶

17c Approximate date when and city and state where the application was filed. Enter previous employer identification number if known.
Approximate date when filed (mo., day, year) | City and state where filed | Previous EIN

Under penalties of perjury, I declare that I have examined this application, and to the best of my knowledge and belief, it is true, correct, and complete. | Business telephone number (include area code)
( )
| Fax telephone number (include area code)
( )
Name and title (Please type or print clearly.) ▶

Signature ▶ | Date ▶

Note: *Do not write below this line. For official use only.*

Please leave blank ▶	Geo.	Ind.	Class	Size	Reason for applying

For Privacy Act and Paperwork Reduction Act Notice, see page 4. | Cat. No. 16055N | Form **SS-4** (Rev. 4-2000)

(right margin: Use this form to obtain your employer identification number.)

Use this form to distribute income from an estate or trust to a beneficiary.

SCHEDULE K-1 (Form 1041)
Department of the Treasury
Internal Revenue Service

Beneficiary's Share of Income, Deductions, Credits, etc.
for the calendar year 2000, or fiscal year
beginning .... , 2000, ending .... , 20 ....
► Complete a separate Schedule K-1 for each beneficiary.

OMB No. 1545-0092

2000

Name of trust or decedent's estate

☐ Amended K-1
☐ Final K-1

Beneficiary's identifying number ►

Estate's or trust's EIN ►

Beneficiary's name, address, and ZIP code

Fiduciary's name, address, and ZIP code

	(a) Allocable share item		(b) Amount	(c) Calendar year 2000 Form 1040 filers enter the amounts in column (b) on:
1	Interest	1		Schedule B, Part I, line 1
2	Ordinary dividends	2		Schedule B, Part II, line 5
3	Net short-term capital gain	3		Schedule D, line 5
4	Net long-term capital gain: **a** 28% rate gain	4a		Schedule D, line 12, column (g)
	b Unrecaptured section 1250 gain	4b		Line 11 of the worksheet for Schedule D, line 25
	c Total for year	4c		Schedule D, line 12, column (f)
5a	Annuities, royalties, and other nonpassive income before directly apportioned deductions	5a		Schedule E, Part III, column (f)
	b Depreciation	5b		⎫ Include on the applicable line of the appropriate tax form
	c Depletion	5c		
	d Amortization	5d		⎭
6a	Trade or business, rental real estate, and other rental income before directly apportioned deductions (see instructions)	6a		Schedule E, Part III
	b Depreciation	6b		⎫ Include on the applicable line of the appropriate tax form
	c Depletion	6c		
	d Amortization	6d		⎭
7	Income for minimum tax purposes	7		
8	Income for regular tax purposes (add lines 1, 2, 3, 4c, 5a, and 6a)	8		
9	Adjustment for minimum tax purposes (subtract line 8 from line 7)	9		Form 6251, line 12
10	Estate tax deduction (including certain generation-skipping transfer taxes)	10		Schedule A, line 27
11	Foreign taxes	11		Form 1116 or Schedule A (Form 1040), line 8
12	Adjustments and tax preference items (itemize):			
	a Accelerated depreciation	12a		⎫ Include on the applicable line of Form 6251
	b Depletion	12b		
	c Amortization	12c		⎭
	d Exclusion items	12d		2001 Form 8801
13	Deductions in the final year of trust or decedent's estate:			
	a Excess deductions on termination (see instructions)	13a		Schedule A, line 22
	b Short-term capital loss carryover	13b	( )	Schedule D, line 5
	c Long-term capital loss carryover	13c	( )	Schedule D, line 12, columns (f) and (g)
	d Net operating loss (NOL) carryover for regular tax purposes	13d	( )	Form 1040, line 21
	e NOL carryover for minimum tax purposes	13e		See the instructions for Form 6251, line 20
	f	13f		⎫ Include on the applicable line of the appropriate tax form
	g	13g		⎭
14	Other (itemize):			
	a Payments of estimated taxes credited to you	14a		Form 1040, line 59
	b Tax-exempt interest	14b		Form 1040, line 8b
	c	14c		⎫
	d	14d		
	e	14e		Include on the applicable line of the appropriate tax form
	f	14f		
	g	14g		
	h	14h		⎭

For Paperwork Reduction Act Notice, see the Instructions for Form 1041.   Cat. No. 11380D   **Schedule K-1 (Form 1041) 2000**

Income Tax

Trusts and Estates (2001)

Taxable Income	Tax on Column 1	Rate on Excess
$0	$0	15%
$1800	$270	28%
$4250	$956	31%
$6500	$1654	36%
$8900	$2518	39.6%

The personal representative has some choices to make that can impact the extent of taxation on the decedent's estate. For example, some tax deductions must be taken on the decedent's individual income tax return, some must be taken on the federal estate tax return, and some can be taken on either of the returns.

PROCEED WITH CAUTION

Be certain to obtain advice from a tax professional or an estate planning attorney when making these tax decisions.

ALLOWABLE DEDUCTIONS

Believe it or not, you'll probably earn some legitimate tax deductions even after your death. These deductions might include the following:

- **Income distributions** As mentioned in the preceding text, the estate might distribute income to the beneficiaries; if so, it can deduct this amount from its taxable income.

- **Funeral expenses** These expenses normally are taken on the federal estate tax return if one is filed. These expenses are not allowed as a deduction on the estate income tax return, Form 1041.

JUST A MINUTE

It may be possible to take a deduction for funeral expenses on the state inheritance tax return, depending on state law. Be certain to consult local law.

- **Administrative expenses** These expenses include the various costs of administering a decedent's estate. Included in this category are attorney fees, personal representative fees, appraisal fees, filing fees, court costs, publication fees, and so forth. The personal representative can choose whether to deduct these expenses on the federal estate tax return or the estate income tax return, Form 1041.

- **Estate income exemption** The Internal Revenue Code does allow an estate to exempt from taxation up to $600 of income per taxable year.

Filing the Return

The personal representative must file the fiduciary tax return (Form 1041) in a timely manner. It is not necessary to attach a copy of the will or trust agreement to the return. When the estate is terminated (all assets distributed to the beneficiaries and all taxes and legitimate debts and expenses paid), the personal representative must notify the IRS by filing Form 56, Notice Concerning Fiduciary Relationship.

Inheritance Taxes vs. Estate Taxes

Of all the taxes on the transfer of wealth in the United States, the federal estate tax gets most of the attention. It certainly should grab the attention of most people, with effective rates beginning at 37 percent and going as high as 55 percent. There is, however, another tax you will have to consider: the state *inheritance tax*. Most people are confused by the differences between the federal and state estate taxes and how they operate. We will now discuss the state inheritance tax and how this might affect your planning.

STRICTLY DEFINED

An **inheritance tax** is a state tax accessed by the state against an heir based upon the value of the property transferred to the heir and the relationship of the heir to the decedent.

Three factors influence how much the state takes in inheritance taxes: the value of the property transferred to an heir, the relationship of the heir to the decedent, and the state of residence of the decedent. These taxes are not federal; they are imposed at the state level. At last count, 19 states still impose some type of inheritance tax. This count may change at any time due to legislative initiative to reduce or even eliminate these taxes.

Form **56**
(Rev. August 1997)

Department of the Treasury
Internal Revenue Service

Notice Concerning Fiduciary Relationship

(Internal Revenue Code sections 6036 and 6903)

OMB No. 1545-0013

Part I   Identification

Name of person for whom you are acting (as shown on the tax return)	Identifying number	Decedent's social security no.

Address of person for whom you are acting (number, street, and room or suite no.)

City or town, state, and ZIP code (If a foreign address, see instructions.)

Fiduciary's name

Address of fiduciary (number, street, and room or suite no.)

City or town, state, and ZIP code	Telephone number (optional) ( )

Part II   Authority

1   Authority for fiduciary relationship. Check applicable box:

a(1) ☐   Will and codicils or court order appointing fiduciary. Attach certified copy   . .   (2) Date of death ....

b(1) ☐   Court order appointing fiduciary. Attach certified copy   . . . .   (2) Date (see instructions) ....

c   ☐   Valid trust instrument and amendments. Attach copy

d   ☐   Other. Describe ▶ ....

Part III   Tax Notices

Send to the fiduciary listed in Part I all notices and other written communications involving the following tax matters:

2   Type of tax (estate, gift, generation-skipping transfer, income, excise, etc.) ▶ ....

3   Federal tax form number (706, 1040, 1041, 1120, etc.) ▶ ....

4   Year(s) or period(s) (if estate tax, date of death) ▶

Part IV   Revocation or Termination of Notice

Section A—Total Revocation or Termination

5   Check this box if you are revoking or terminating all prior notices concerning fiduciary relationships on file with the Internal Revenue Service for the same tax matters and years or periods covered by this notice concerning fiduciary relationship   .   ▶ ☐

Reason for termination of fiduciary relationship. Check applicable box:

a   ☐   Court order revoking fiduciary authority. Attach certified copy.

b   ☐   Certificate of dissolution or termination of a business entity. Attach copy.

c   ☐   Other. Describe ▶

Section B—Partial Revocation

6a   Check this box if you are revoking earlier notices concerning fiduciary relationships on file with the Internal Revenue Service for the same tax matters and years or periods covered by this notice concerning fiduciary relationship   .   .   .   .   ▶ ☐

b   Specify to whom granted, date, and address, including ZIP code, or refer to attached copies of earlier notices and authorizations

▶ ....

Section C—Substitute Fiduciary

7   Check this box if a new fiduciary or fiduciaries have been or will be substituted for the revoking or terminating fiduciary(ies) and specify the name(s) and address(es), including ZIP code(s), of the new fiduciary(ies)   .   .   .   .   ▶ ☐

Part V   Court and Administrative Proceedings

Name of court (if other than a court proceeding, identify the type of proceeding and name of agency)	Date proceeding initiated			
Address of court	Docket number of proceeding			
City or town, state, and ZIP code	Date	Time	a.m. p.m.	Place of other proceedings

Please Sign Here

I certify that I have the authority to execute this notice concerning fiduciary relationship on behalf of the taxpayer.

▶ Fiduciary's signature	Title, if applicable	Date
▶ Fiduciary's signature	Title, if applicable	Date

For Paperwork Reduction Act and Privacy Act Notice, see back page.   Cat. No. 16375I   Form **56** (Rev. 8-97)

File this form when an estate is terminated.

GO TO ▶
You may wish to review Hour 3, "What Is an Estate?" where the taxable estate is defined and discussed.

The focus of an inheritance tax is different from the focus of the federal estate tax. The federal tax is assessed on the total value of the decedent's taxable estate. It is a transfer tax based upon total accumulation of assets. It is not based on either of the following:

- The value of property passing to a particular beneficiary
- The relationship of the decedent to the beneficiary

By contrast, the state inheritance tax focuses on both of these issues.

THE RELATIONSHIP CONNECTION

Historically, property was intended to pass only to those of close lineal ancestry to the decedent. Accordingly, the tax on the amount inherited by those bearing closer ancestry was less than the tax imposed on more distant relatives. This pattern continues in the laws of states that still impose this tax. For example, let's review the provisions of the Indiana Inheritance Tax. These provisions are similar to those found in other states:

- **Class A Transferee**   A lineal ancestor or lineal descendant of the transferor, such as a child, grandchild, or great-grandchild.
- **Class B Transferee**   A brother or sister of the transferor, or a descendant of a brother or sister of the transferor, or a spouse, widow, or widower of a child of a transferor.
- **Class C Transferee**   A transferee who is not a Class A or Class B transferee (other than a spouse), such as a neighbor, caregiver, or friend.

Class A

Taxable Estate	Tax Due
<$25,001	1%
$25,001–$50,000	$250 + 2% over $25,000
$50,001–$200,000	$750 + 3% over $50,000
$200,001–$300,000	$5,250 + 4% over $200,000
$300,000–$500,000	$9,250 + 5% over $300,000
$500,001–$700,000	$19,250 + 6% over $500,000
$700,001–$1,000,000	$31,250 + 7% over $700,000
$1,000,001–$1,500,000	$52,250 + 8% over $1,000,000
Over $1,500,000	$92,250 + 10% over $1,500,000

Class B

Taxable Estate	Tax Due
<$100,001	7%
$100,001–$500,000	$7,000 + 10% over $100,000
$500,001–$1,000,000	$47,000 + 12% over $500,000
Over $1,000,000	$107,000 + 15% over $1,000,000

Class C

Taxable Estate	Tax Due
<$100,001	10%
$100,001–$1,000,000	$10,000 + 15% over $100,000
Over $1,000,000	$145,000 + 20% over $1,000,000

The first item you should notice is that the beneficiaries are categorized according to three classes. Class A beneficiaries include children, grandchildren, great-grandchildren, and so forth. Because these beneficiaries are the most closely related to the decedent by blood, they receive the largest exemption available, $100,000. This means the first $100,000 in value inherited by a Class A beneficiary is exempt from taxation. Only amounts inherited in excess of this amount are calculated according to the tax schedule.

Class B beneficiaries include brothers, sisters, children of brothers and sisters, and spouse, widow, or widower of a child of a transferor. Because this category is more remote than a Class A beneficiary, the exemption is much lower: $500. Also note that the tax rate for Class B, 7–15 percent, is higher than for Class A beneficiaries, 1–10 percent.

Finally, Class C transferees are defined as anybody not covered by Class A or Class B. Because this group of beneficiaries is more remote than the other classes, the exemption allowed is only $100. The tax rate also is much higher: 10–20 percent.

The example does not specify the classification of a surviving spouse. According to the Indiana statute, amounts that pass to a surviving spouse are totally exempt from inheritance tax, regardless of the amount inherited.

Many states have made modifications to their inheritance tax laws. For example, Connecticut exempts from inheritance taxation the entire estate passing to parents, grandparents, adoptive parents, and any natural or adopted descendants for all decedents dying on or after January 1, 2001. Surviving spouses are already exempt in Connecticut.

Louisiana has enacted provisions that gradually reduce the tax rates. For Louisiana decedents dying between June 30, 2001 and June 30, 2002, the statutory rates are reduced by 40 percent. For those dying between June 30, 2002 and June 30, 2003, the statutory rates are reduced by 60 percent. If death occurs after June 30, 2003, the rates are reduced by 80 percent.

Virginia has a unique statutory provision imposing a tax on the probate of wills. This tax is equivalent to 10 cents for every $100 (.0010) of value on estates valued in excess of $5,000.

PROCEED WITH CAUTION

The information appearing above may have changed by the time you read this. Please be certain to contact your estate planning attorney, financial planner, or representative of the appropriate state government office who can advise you about the inheritance tax laws in your state of residence.

AVOIDING INHERITANCE TAXES

If you own any property at the time of your death, your estate and/or heirs will have to pay any inheritance taxes assessed by your home state. In Indiana, for example, if you transferred property within one year of your death, your estate and/or your heirs will owe the same amount of taxes as they would have had the transfer not been made.

As you can see, it's a bit tricky to avoid paying inheritance tax. From a planning perspective, it is primarily important to recognize that the tax exists in select states and factor this tax into the planning process.

 You will find in Hour 16, "Credit Shelter Trusts," that through the use of a "credit shelter trust" a married couple may double the federal credit shelter amount by separating ownership between the spouses into separate names and using two credit shelter trusts, one for each spouse. This same technique also allows the married couple to double the current state exemptions for state inheritance tax purposes. Since a child will inherit from both parents separately, rather than from the surviving parent only, the state exemption for inheritance tax calculations will be used twice, once at each parent's death.

Hour's Up!

QUIZ

Now it's time to see how much you have learned and retained from this lesson. Try to take the following quiz without referring back to the hourly materials.

1. Accumulations in qualified retirement accounts are taxable ...
   a. Upon withdrawal
   b. Immediately upon death
   c. Never
   d. Only when actually spent

2. Savings bonds require special consideration when planning because ...
   a. They are outstanding investments
   b. They are tax-free investments
   c. They are not included in the decedent's taxable estate
   d. They have untaxed income due upon redemption

3. Income earned during administration of an estate ...
   a. Can be distributed to the beneficiaries
   b. Is taxed both to the estate and to the beneficiaries
   c. Is deductible on the decedent's final income tax return
   d. Is taxable to the personal representative

4. The inheritance tax is imposed on ...
   a. The total value of the decedent's estate
   b. The value of property passing to the heirs
   c. One-half of all of the decedent's property interests
   d. Property passing only to non-lineal descendants

5. In general, the closer the relationship to the decedent, the ...
   a. Greater the inheritance tax will be
   b. More likely to be disinherited
   c. Less the inheritance tax will be
   d. Higher the federal estate tax will be

Hour 6

Federal Estate Taxes

CHAPTER SUMMARY

LESSON PLAN:

In this hour, you will learn why federal estate taxes have attracted the attention of the legislature and the concern of everyone subject to the tax. This burdensome assessment on wealth, with tax rates ranging from 37% to 55%, has the potential to destroy the best-laid plans for the accumulation of wealth in this country. This hour discusses valuation of an estate for federal estate tax purposes. This will be either date of death value or an alternate value. You will also learn ...

- What to include in your gross estate.
- How to value your estate.
- How to calculate the tax.
- The pros and cons of tax reform.

Both the gift and estate tax have a long history, in both the United States and elsewhere. Great Britain implemented a sweeping death tax in 1889. The first such tax in the United States was instituted in 1898 to help finance the Spanish War. That tax, known as the Spanish War Tax, was imposed only on personal property in estates worth more than $10,000. The next major legislation, known as the Revenue Act of 1916, made the maximum tax rate only 10%, with an exemption amount of $50,000.

Periodic legislation followed, increasing the maximum rate to as much as 40% in 1924. Two years later, the Revenue Act of 1926 repealed the 1924 estate tax rate, lowering the rate to 20% and increasing the estate tax exemption to $100,000.

In 1932, the legislature combined the gift and estate taxes to become one tax on lifetime (gift) and death transfers (estate) of property. The relief provided by the 1924 Act was eliminated and in its place, a whopping 45% estate/gift tax was established, while at the same time reducing the exemption to $50,000, only one half of the 1924 level.

The upward spiral continued with the maximum estate/gift tax rate rising to an incredible 70% in 1935. In that same year, the estate/gift tax exemption was reduced from $50,000 to $40,000.

Finally, in 1948, a safe haven was created for transfers between spouses. This type of transfer was called the marital deduction. Under this legislation, only one half of the total value of property transferring from a deceased spouse to the surviving spouse was subject to taxation. This represented a major break-through in the imposition of estate taxes, and created a substantial deferral opportunity for married couples.

Until 1954, when Congress established the Internal Revenue Code, various revisions were made to the estate and gift tax laws, with a tendency to tax more property than before. The Internal Revenue Code of 1954 then raised the estate tax exemption to $60,000 and lowered gift tax rates.

Not much happened legislatively between 1954 and 1976 with regard to the estate and gift taxes. The Tax Reform Act of 1976, however, ushered in a wide range of new taxes and revisions to existing taxes. This was the year, for example, that Congress decided to impose special taxes on anyone who transferred property at death to beneficiaries at least two generations removed from the decedent (such as parent to grandchild, great grandchild, and so on). This tax is called the Generation Skipping Tax. Congress also tackled the marital deduction, by placing a cap on the amount passing to a surviving spouse free from estate taxation.

PROCEED WITH CAUTION

Anyone who is contemplating a gift to a person at least one generation removed must be extremely careful. The Generation Skipping tax imposes a whopping 55% tax on transfers that skip at least one generation. The only good news is that there is a $1,000,000 exemption per donor. Seek competent advice if you wish to skip generations when planning your estate.

The Tax Reform Act of 1976 also created a single taxation scheme for both gift and estate taxes. The separate exemptions for estate tax ($60,000) and gift taxes ($30,000) were eliminated in favor of a single *unified credit* to be phased in between 1977 and 1981. These new unified rates ranged between 18% and 70%.

STRICTLY DEFINED

The **unified credit** is a specific amount that is allowed to each taxpayer that can be applied against the gift tax and/or the estate tax. In 2001, the amount of the unified credit is $220,550, equating to a taxable estate of $675,000 (the equivalent exclusion amount).

Then, in 1980, another significant piece of legislation was passed, called the Tax Reform Act of 1980, which provided for an increase in the basis of property inherited from a decedent called a stepped up basis.

GO TO ▶
For a more detailed discussion of step-up rules, see Hour 21, "Gifting of Assets."

The Economic Recovery Act of 1981 was enacted at the urging of President Reagan, and finally providing total tax relief for transfers between a deceased spouse and the surviving spouse. This is called the *unlimited marital deduction*. Additionally, this legislation gave a deduction for transfers for the benefit of a surviving spouse if the transfer met the requirements of a Qualified Terminable Interest Property Trust, more commonly known as a QTIP trust.

GO TO ▶
For a more detailed discussion of QTIP Trusts, see Hour 20, "Marital Trusts and Disclaimer Planning."

The unified credit was to be increased over a five-year period between 1982 and 1987. In 1982, the unified credit was $62,800. By 1987, the unified credit increased to $192,800, creating an equivalent exclusion amount of $600,000.

Unified Credit and Applicable Exclusion Amounts Between 1982 and 1987

Year	Applicable Credit Amount	Applicable Exclusion Amount
1982	$62,800	$225,000
1983	$79,300	$275,000
1984	$96,300	$325,000
1985	$121,800	$400,000
1986	$155,800	$500,000
1987	$192,800	$600,000

The legislation provided that the 70% estate tax rate was to be reduced gradually to 50% between 1982 and 1985. In 1984, The Retirement Equity Act extended this period to 1988 (before the 50% rate would be applicable). Then, in 1987, the Omnibus Budget Reconciliation Act (OBRA) again extended this period until 1993. This law also eliminated the marital deduction for non-citizen spouses unless a specialized trust (QDOT) is used. Go to Hour 22, "Planning for Non-Residents," where planning for aliens is discussed in more detail.

GO TO ▶
The Economic Recovery Act also had a significant impact on qualified retirement plans. For more discussion of retirement plans, see Hour 14, "Retirement Plans."

Finally, in 1993, President Clinton set the maximum rate at 55% through the Revenue Reconciliation Act, where it remains set today.

The Gift Tax

Confused enough yet? Well, there's more. In this section, we'll straighten out the differences between the various taxes on estates, starting with gift taxes. As discussed, the gift and estate tax became intertwined in 1932. During that year, the *annual gift exclusion* was established at $5,000 per beneficiary.

STRICTLY DEFINED

The **annual gift exclusion** is the amount allowed by federal law that can be given to another without the imposition of a gift tax (currently $10,000 per person, per year).

Then, in the Revenue Act of 1942, this annual gift exclusion was reduced to only $3,000 per beneficiary. When the Internal Revenue Code was first enacted in 1954, a new $30,000 cumulative lifetime gift tax exemption was created. Furthermore, within the major legislation of 1976 was a marital deduction on gifts between spouses.

Before 1976, the law provided what's called a "rebuttable presumption" that if a person made a gift of money within three years of his or her death, he or she did so "in contemplation of death." If the estate could not prove otherwise, the gift was taxed as if it were part of the decedent's estate. Now, with some exceptions, most notably life insurance, any gift made within three years of a person' death is not taxed as part of his or her estate.

JUST A MINUTE

Be certain that you are aware that if you give away a life insurance policy within three years of your death, the value of the policy will be included in your taxable estate at death for federal estate tax purposes. Read on in this hour to learn more.

Furthermore, as a part of the 1981 Economic Recovery Act, the $3,000 annual per beneficiary gift tax exclusion was increased to $10,000 per beneficiary. This means that a person was allowed to give up to $10,000 per year per beneficiary without being taxed on the amount of the gift. Additionally, the unlimited marital deduction on death transfers between spouses applied also to lifetime transfers between spouses. This meant that property of any value could be exchanged between spouses during lifetime without any tax implications.

JUST A MINUTE

The annual exclusion in 2001 for gifts remains at $10,000 per year per recipient.

For example, Husband and Wife can give $10,000 each to Child 1, $10,000 each to Child 2, and $10,000 each to Child 3 in any one calendar year. Each child would end up with $20,000. This could be repeated in each subsequent calendar year.

If only Husband wanted to make the gift, he could give out of his own money the same amount per child, so long as his wife consented to "split" the gift. Splitting the gift results in the treatment of the gift as if each spouse made the gift. Without this spousal consent, Husband could only give $10,000 to each of his three children.

GO TO ▶
Hour 21 goes into more detail about gifting and gift splitting.

ESTATE TAXES VS. INHERITANCE TAXES

In addition to being confused about gift taxes, people also find it difficult to differentiate between estate taxes and inheritance taxes. An estate tax is a federal tax imposed on the value of the decedent's estate, regardless of who the beneficiaries may be (with the exception of spouse beneficiaries and charitable beneficiaries, which are both exempt from the transfer tax). The inheritance taxes are state taxes imposed on the amounts transferred to beneficiaries, with a focus on the relationship of the beneficiary to the decedent.

GO TO ▶
Review Hour 5, "Income Taxes and Inheritance Taxes," which goes into more detail on the subject of state inheritance taxes.

WHAT TO INCLUDE IN THE GROSS ESTATE

In Hour 3, "What Is an Estate?" you learned that property is classified as taxable or non-taxable, probate or non-probate, and tangible or intangible. This hour concerns taxation, or how to identify what property you own is subject to taxation.

Recall that title is the most important factor when it comes to estate planning. To determine what assets to include in your taxable estate, you must review all of the titles to your property. What you will be looking for is whether the property is titled in single name, joint tenancy with right of survivorship, tenancy in common, payable on death, or whether there is a beneficiary designation on your life insurance, retirement accounts, and annuities. The following list may help you see what assets are included in your taxable estate.

- Real property
- Personal property
- Cash
- Bank accounts (checking and savings)
- Money market accounts
- Certificates of deposit
- Savings bonds
- Treasury bills, notes, and bonds
- Brokerage accounts
- Retirement accounts
- Annuities
- Life insurance proceeds
- Stock
- Interests in family-owned businesses
- Retained life estates
- Transfers taking effect at death
- Revocable transfers
- Joint interests
- General powers of appointment

Earlier in Hour 5, we discussed briefly the subject of valuation. While planning your estate, you must make some reasonable estimate of the value of your assets.

TIME SAVER

 Don't worry about getting appraisals of your property when planning your estate. You don't need exact numbers. Just use a good faith estimate of value. This is also true of other assets; simply make your best educated guess and go with that. After death, valuation becomes more specific because date of death values (unless alternate valuation is used) must be ascertained according to the rules of the Internal Revenue Service. The valuation rules in this hour pertain to how one values an estate after the death of the owner.

In this hour, we will go into more detail about how some assets are valued at death. Let's begin our exploration by first reviewing only assets in the individual name of a decedent. In other words, we will look at jointly owned property and some other assets included in the estate later in this section.

REAL ESTATE

The value of real estate is determined by appraisal. Any licensed appraiser can value the property at fair market value and submit a written valuation to the personal representative or trustee.

PERSONAL PROPERTY

Personal property also is valued by appraisal. Most real estate appraisers are able to place a value on household goods and furnishings. However, remember that the actual value is not what the items are worth to the heirs but rather what the items would bring at an auction or garage sale. Sentimental value means nothing.

The personal representative or trustee must be certain to secure all personal property immediately upon appointment to prevent loss. Jewelry and other family heirlooms have a funny way of disappearing and the personal representative, trustee, or successor trustee could be personally liable for the loss. This can best be done by locking the house and changing locks if necessary; keeping track of all keys to the house, the safety deposit box, and automobiles; removing from the house valuable items and securing them in a safe place, such as a safe deposit box.

CASH

Cash is the easiest asset to value, since its value is ordinarily face value, unless you have collectibles such as old vintage coins having a special value because of age, condition, or number of coins in circulation. The person in charge of the estate or trust should obtain a fair market value appraisal of these collectibles.

BANK ACCOUNTS

Your bank account's value is how much money is in it on the day that you die, less any checks you wrote before your death that haven't yet cleared. In some jurisdictions, financial institutions must report the value of investments in the name of a decedent to a government official.

MONEY MARKET ACCOUNTS

A money market account is simply an account paying a specified rate of interest on the amount deposited. Valuation is easy because the value is simply the amount on deposit, including interest, on the date of death.

CERTIFICATES OF DEPOSIT

When CDs are issued, the investor has the option of receiving the interest directly or having the interest reinvested. A CD that does not accumulate interest will remain at face value, making this a no-brainer for valuation purposes. If interest has accumulated, the bank will have to supply the value of the CD plus interest on the date of death.

U.S. SAVINGS BONDS

There are several types of savings bonds, each with a different rate of return.

I-BONDS

I-Bonds are a new type of bond that earn a guaranteed rate of return. They are sold at face value ($100 for a $100 bond) and they grow in value with inflation-indexed earnings for up to 30 years. (This refers to a rate of interest that is adjusted up or down in response to inflation rates.) Interest is added to the bond monthly and paid when the bond is cashed. These must be valued as of date of death by using a savings bond calculator such as the one made available on the website for the Bureau of Public Debt, www. savingsbonds.gov. I-Bonds cannot be redeemed for a period of six months from the date of purchase.

E AND EE BONDS

Series E and EE bonds also accrue interest. The original value of the bond increases as interest is added on. For example, a $100 E Bond is sold for $50. If held to maturity, the bond is worth its face value, $100. The increase in value from $50 to $100 is the interest earned on the bond.

Redemption value or date of death value must be determined by using a savings bond calculator at the website mentioned above. Both E and EE Bonds cannot be redeemed for a period of six months from the date of purchase.

H and HH Bonds

H and HH bonds are issued at face value, meaning you pay $50 for a $50 bond. They do not increase in value. They do, however, pay current income directly to you every six months. The date of death value will always be the face amount of the bond.

PROCEED WITH CAUTION

Bonds that accumulate interest earnings are taxable upon cashing. This means that if the personal representative cashes in the decedent's bonds, there will be taxable income to the estate. The tax must either be paid by the estate or passed on to the heirs utilizing a Form K-1 to include on their own personal income tax return. (See Hour 5.) This can be a tax time bomb for the unsuspecting personal representative who cashes out large numbers of bonds, makes distribution of the proceeds, and then finds out later that the estate owes the IRS income taxes. The personal representative must always estimate the amount of tax owing on these bonds and decide whether it is best to distribute the bonds to the beneficiaries or cash them in prior to distribution. Always consult a tax specialist to help evaluate these issues.

Treasury Bills, Notes, and Bonds

Aside from U.S. Savings Bonds, there are three basic securities issued by the Department of the Treasury: Treasury bills, Treasury notes, and Treasury bonds. When these are purchased, you are, in effect, loaning your money to the government in return for a promise to repay your money at a future date, with interest. This is why these securities are called debt instruments. These debt instruments are purchased at less than face value, gradually increasing in value until maturity when the value of the bill equals its face value. The difference between the purchase price and the face value is the interest on the bill. The value of the bill on date of death is not the face value, unless it has already matured. Treasury bills, notes, and bonds are transferable and can be exchanged on the securities markets. To determine date of death values, contact the U.S. Treasury Dept. or a local bank.

Brokerage Accounts

Brokerage accounts usually contain a hybrid of all of the different types of investments mentioned in this section. Therefore, the key to valuing a brokerage account is simply to value the component investments separately and add them together. Another option is to contact your broker and ask them to provide you with a date of death value. When planning your estate, you can simply use your most recent brokerage statement to value your investment.

RETIREMENT ACCOUNTS

GO TO ▶
Hour 14 covers retirement accounts and annuities in more detail.

Retirement accounts are valued in the same way a brokerage account is valued. Retirement accounts can consist of nearly all of the various investments outlined here. The custodian of the retirement funds will provide a date of death value upon request.

ANNUITIES

There are many different types of annuities. A typical annuity earns a fixed rate of return, tax-deferred. There now are variable annuities that invest in equities (stock investments). The best way to obtain a value on any annuity is to ask the insurance company that issues the annuity to provide a date of death value.

LIFE INSURANCE PROCEEDS

GO TO ▶
Go to Hour 13, "Life Insurance," for a comprehensive discussion of life insurance.

One of the most common misconceptions about life insurance is that it is non-taxable. This notion may have stemmed from a misunderstanding of the type of tax under discussion. It may also have stemmed from miscommunication by the insurance sales agent to the insured. When discussing life insurance, it is accurately stated that life insurance death benefits are not subject to income tax. However, when the discussion turns to estate taxes, it is not just the *cash value* that is included for tax purposes, but the actual value of the death benefit proceeds as well. The following are the various types of life insurance that are includable in the decedent's estate.

- **Insurance on decedent's life** Your taxable estate will include all the life insurance you hold on your life (if you are the owner of the policy), including proceeds from any car insurance policy that are paid to your estate.

STRICTLY DEFINED

The **cash value** of a life insurance policy is the portion that represents accumulated premiums remaining after policy expenses have been deducted.

- **Insurance received by estate**   All life insurance received by your estate as beneficiary also is included in your taxable estate, even if you didn't own the policy.

- **Incidents of ownership by decedent**   Whenever you possess any *incident of ownership* in a life insurance policy, the proceeds from that policy will be included in your estate.

STRICTLY DEFINED

An **incident of ownership** is a term used concerning life insurance that will result in the inclusion of the policy in the taxable estate of the individual found to have a necessary degree of control over the policy as defined by the Internal Revenue Service.

- **Corporate-owned life insurance**   You include this type of insurance in the stockholder's estate if the insured is the sole or controlling stockholder, even though the corporation is the owner of the policy.

- **Insurance transferred within three years of death**   If you transfer your life insurance to another person, you still must include it in your taxable estate if the transfer takes place within three years of your death.

- **Travel insurance**   If you carry travel insurance when you die, it becomes part of your estate when you die if you possessed the power to change beneficiaries on the policy. Travel insurance was held to be part of the estate of an insured traveler who purchased flight insurance even though it was found to be impossible for the insured to change beneficiaries while the plane was in flight.

- **Valuation of life insurance**   The value of any life insurance is the full face value of the policy at the time of death with some adjustments.

STOCKS AND SECURITIES

The valuation of stock and securities is a bit tricky. The actual date of death value of a traded security is the average price of the security as it traded on the decedent's date of death. This would actually be the mid-point between the day's high and the day's low. Technically speaking, the value is the mean (mid-point) between its highest and lowest selling prices quoted on the valuation date. If death occurs on a weekend or holiday, the value is determined by the last trading day before the decedent's death.

Interests in Family-Owned Businesses

GO TO ▶
See Hour 15, "Business Entities," which contains a detailed review of various business entities.

The closely held (non-publicly traded) corporation or unincorporated business can be one of the most difficult assets to value. Several factors enter into the picture including inventory, cash on hand, accounts receivable, accounts payable, and good will. The other problem with valuing these businesses is the lack of marketability. This is especially true of personal service businesses that will not be able to carry on successfully after the death of the primary business owner.

JUST A MINUTE

Marketability simply refers to the ability to sell something on the open market. An item is not marketable if it cannot be sold to the public, which might be the case if the asset was owned by a partnership that contains restrictions on the ability of a partner to sell an asset. This inability to freely sell an asset to the public reduces its fair market value.

Your estate will need to hire a qualified business appraiser or certified public accountant to make an appropriate valuation of a business. Because of the myriad of formulas available to the appraiser, the value derived may vary significantly from appraiser to appraiser. For this reason, (and others) the Internal Revenue Service frequently questions the values utilized and may ascertain the value of the business using its own valuation methods.

Retained Life Estates

Retained interests in property include the reservation of a right to live on real estate deeded to another. Any other asset in which the owner reserves the use, possession or other enjoyment of the property transferred for life will be fully taxed to the owner of the retained interest at his or her death. For example, the estate of the owner of closely held stock (which is stock in a company that isn't publicly traded) is taxed on the full value even though it was transferred to children, where the owner retained his or her voting rights.

Transfers Taking Effect at Death

Suppose that a husband creates a trust and transfers property to the trust. The terms of the trust provide for the payment of income to his spouse for life. Upon the death of his wife, the principal reverts back to him if he survives, or to his children if he predeceases his wife. Suppose the husband dies before his wife. Will any portion of the trust be includable in his estate for federal estate tax purposes?

The answer is a conditional yes. By specific language inserted in the trust agreement, husband retained the right to have the property returned to him if he survived his wife. To escape inclusion in his taxable estate, his reversionary interest (an interest in property that will cause the property to revert back to the original owner at a specified time) must be less than 5% of the value of the trust.

REVOCABLE TRANSFERS

Whenever a person transfers property to another and retains the right to alter, amend, revoke, or terminate the transfer, the IRS will conclude that the property belongs to the original owner of the property for tax purposes. The most common illustration of this is the creation of a revocable living trust. These trusts are fully revocable and amendable during the life of the person creating the trust (grantor). The assets in the trust are therefore included in the grantor's taxable estate.

JOINT INTERESTS

There are two rules applicable here, depending upon who the joint owner is. If the joint owner is the decedent's spouse, one half of the value of the property will be included in the decedent spouse's estate. However, if the joint owner is someone other than the decedent's spouse, the full value of the property will be included in the decedent's estate.

There is an opportunity for the estate to prove that the other non-spouse joint owner actually contributed to the property, thus reducing the taxable value to the estate. This proof must be by clear evidence with records to substantiate any contribution by the joint owner.

GENERAL POWERS OF APPOINTMENT

All property over which the decedent had the power at death to direct for his or her benefit, estate, creditors, or the creditors of his or her estate becomes part of the decedent's estate. Any power that excludes these uses is a limited power and thus will not be included in the estate.

THE VALUATION DATE

For federal estate tax purposes, the estate is valued as of the decedent's date of death. There is, however, an option for the executor or administrator to choose what is called an "alternate valuation" date, which is basically the value of the entire estate six months following the decedent's death. The executor or administrator is not allowed to "pick and choose" assets to which the alternate valuation will apply; it will apply, if elected, to all of the decedent's taxable assets.

SPECIAL VALUATIONS

If you're a farmer, you might be able to take advantage of some special estate tax breaks set up by the Internal Revenue Code. Property is normally valued at its "highest and best use." Rather than impose this standard, which tends to result in a high valuation of property, certain types of real property can be valued on the basis of its "actual use" which can be used when this would result in a lower value. Qualified real property is real property devoted to a qualified use by the decedent or a member of the decedent's family on the date of the decedent's death.

To qualify for this special valuation, the following conditions must be met:

- The adjusted value of the real and personal property used in the farming operation must constitute at least one half of the adjusted value of the property included in the gross taxable estate.
- At least one fourth of the adjusted value of the gross taxable estate must be qualified real property.
- The property must pass from the decedent to a qualified heir, generally a member of the decedent's family.
- The real property must have been owned by the decedent or a member of his or her family and used for a qualified purpose by these same people for at least five of the eight years prior to the decedent's death.
- There must have been material participation by the decedent or a member of his or her family for five of the eight years before the decedent's death, or the date the decedent became disabled or began receiving Social Security benefits.

These special valuation rules, especially the "material participation" requirements, go far beyond the scope of this book. Do not try to figure it all out on your own; you will be wasting your time. Consult a tax advisor or your attorney.

The problem with these special valuation rules is that the tax benefits are recaptured (taken away, resulting in tax owing) if any of the qualified real property is sold or transferred within 10 years to someone other than a member of the decedent's family.

UNDERSTANDING DEDUCTIONS

The total value of the gross estate can be reduced by specific deductions. Those allowable deductions are set forth below.

ADMINISTRATIVE AND FUNERAL EXPENSES

These expenses include attorney, personal representative, accountant, and appraisal fees; court costs; expenses incurred by selling estate property; funeral expenses; and medical expenses.

CLAIMS AGAINST THE ESTATE

Debts of the decedent are deductible including unpaid property taxes, income taxes, and gift taxes. Also deductible are unpaid mortgages and liens on property of the estate.

CASUALTY AND THEFT LOSS

In the event the estate incurs loss to estate property caused by fire, storm, or theft, these losses are deductible for estate tax purposes to the extent they are not reimbursed by insurance.

MARITAL DEDUCTION

In our discussion of the history of the estate tax, I mentioned the unlimited marital deduction. This deduction applies to all property interests transferred from the decedent to the surviving spouse, regardless of value. To obtain this deduction, the property must be fully available to the spouse as an outright gift. If there is a possibility that the property will revert back to the original owner, which is called a *reversionary interest*, then the transfer will not qualify for the marital deduction.

STRICTLY DEFINED

Reversionary interests are interests in property that will cause the property to revert back to the original owner at a specified time.

GO TO ▶
For a more detailed discussion of QTIP Trusts, see Hour 20, "Marital Trusts and Disclaimer Planning."

The only type of interest passing to a spouse that is not outright and still obtains the benefit of the unlimited marital deduction is a transfer to a Qualified Terminable Interest Trust. A QTIP trust must be created to conform to strict IRS rules. In general, to qualify for the unlimited marital deduction, property transferred to a QTIP trust must allow the spouse the absolute right to all income from the trust, with no such rights extending to anyone else except the spouse. There may be other provisions allowing the spouse access to principal that conform to IRS rules. The spouse-beneficiary of a QTIP trust does not have the power to change beneficiaries of the trust.

CHARITABLE DEDUCTIONS

Any transfer of property at death to a qualified charity qualifies for the unlimited charitable deduction. A qualified charity is one listed as such in IRS publications as a charitable, religious, educational, or governmental organization.

JUST A MINUTE

 If you need help figuring out what organizations the Internal Revenue considers qualified charitable institutions, order Publication 78 through an IRS Area Distribution Center.

FIGURING TAX RATES

The following table outlines the current Federal Gift and Estate Tax Rates in effect as of the beginning of 2001.

Gift and Estate Tax Schedule

Value of Estate			
From	**To**	**Tax on Col. 1**	**Rate on Excess**
$0	$10,000	$0	18%
$10,000	$20,000	$1,800	20%

Value of Estate

From	To	Tax on Col. 1	Rate on Excess
$20,000	$40,000	$3,800	22%
$40,000	$60,000	$8,200	24%
$60,000	$80,000	$13,000	26%
$80,000	$100,000	$18,200	28%
$100,000	$150,000	$23,800	30%
$150,000	$250,000	$38,800	32%
$250,000	$500,000	$70,800	34%
$500,000	$750,000	$155,800	37%
$750,000	$1,000,000	$248,300	39%
$1,000,000	$1,250,000	$345,800	41%
$1,250,000	$1,500,000	$448,300	43%
$1,500,000	$2,000,000	$555,800	45%
$2,000,000	$2,500,000	$780,800	49%
$2,500,000	$3,000,000	$1,025,800	53%
$3,000,000		$1,290,800	55%

As you can see from the rates in the preceding table, the federal estate tax actually begins on a taxable estate up to $10,000 at an 18% rate. A credit against this tax will effectively wipe out taxes on estates of less than $675,000. Following is the table showing the applicable credit amount.

Unified Credit and Applicable Exclusion Amounts

Year	Applicable Credit Amounts	Applicable Exclusion Amount
1987–1997	$192,800	$600,000
1998	$202,050	$625,000
1999	$211,300	$650,000
2000 and 2001	$220,550	$675,000
2002 and 2003	$229,800	$700,000
2004	$287,300	$850,000
2005	$326,300	$950,000
2006 and after	$345,800	$1,000,000

How the Unified Credit Works

The tax rates and the unified credits can seem confusing at first glance. Actually, the computations are quite similar. The confusion arises from how you view the tables. For example, the straightforward approach is to look at the tax rate table and calculate the tax based upon the value of the taxable estate. Following this calculation, you subtract from that tax the applicable credit amount from the unified credit table. The result is the amount of tax due. (Of course, you must include other factors in the calculation but this is sufficient for the purposes of this book.)

PROCEED WITH CAUTION

 Be certain to consult with an estate-planning attorney licensed in your state who can advise you properly on the application of the unified credit and the federal estate tax.

Another shorthand method of figuring the estate tax is to look at the applicable exclusion amount and subtract that from the value of the taxable estate. This method will tell you the *approximate* amount subject to tax. Although not scientific nor technically correct, this is a convenient method to *estimate* the impact of estate taxes and allows for a quick calculation of the approximate tax by multiplying the amount subject to tax by *at least* 37%.

PROCEED WITH CAUTION

 The shorthand approach only gives an approximation of the tax due. Never rely on this approach to give you a correct figure. Consult your attorney, financial planner, or accountant and ask them to calculate the tax for you. They should prepare the tax return, as well.

Allowable Credits

One of the principal credits against the estate tax is the credit for taxes paid to a state for death taxes. This is referred to as the credit for state taxes paid. On the federal estate tax return, there is a set amount that is allowed as a credit against the federal estate tax. A portion of that table is shown in the following table.

Computation of Maximum Credit for State Death Taxes

Adjusted Taxable Estate Equal to or More Than	Adjusted Taxable Estate Less Than	Credit on Amount in Column 1	Rate of Credit on Excess Over Amount in Column 1
$0	$40,000	$0	none
$40,000	$90,000	$0	0.8%
$90,000	$140,000	$400	1.6%
$140,000	$240,000	$1,200	2.4%
$240,000	$440,000	$3,600	3.2%
$440,000	$640,000	$10,000	4.0%
$640,000	$840,000	$18,000	4.8%
$840,000	$1,040,000	$27,600	5.6%
$1,040,000	$1,540,000	$38,800	6.4%
$1,540,000	$2,040,000	$70,800	7.2%

Suppose an individual's adjusted taxable estate (taxable estate after allowable deductions, such as contributions to individual retirement accounts) is $840,000. The tax on that estate would be $283,400 ($840,000 − $750,000 = $90,000 × .39 = $35,100 + $248,300 = $283,400). The credit against this tax is $220,550 assuming the death occurred in the year 2000 or 2001. The remaining tax owed would be $62,850. The state death tax credit would be $27,600 as seen on the State Death Tax Credit Table for a taxable estate of $840,000. The remaining tax owed would therefore be $35,250 ($62,850 − $27,600). If the actual tax owing to the state were less than this credit of $27,600, the difference would be paid to the state. Therefore, if the state inheritance tax were $15,000, the difference ($27,600 − $15,000 = $12,600) would be owing to the state. In other words, the credit applied on the federal estate tax return cannot exceed the amount paid to the state.

GO TO ▶
See Hour 5, which goes into more detail on the subject of state inheritance taxes.

The shortcut method of estimating this tax would be to take the gross taxable estate of $840,000 and subtract the unified credit equivalent amount for the year of death. In 2001, the unified credit equivalent amount is $675,000. $840,000 − $675,000 = $165,000. At a 39% tax rate the estimated federal tax would be $64,350. Compare this to the actual calculation of $62,850.

TAX DAY!

The federal estate tax is due and payable within nine months of the decedent's death. In general, no return is required if the taxable estate of the decedent is less than the exclusion amount. In 2001, that amount is $675,000.

PROCEED WITH CAUTION

As with all of the material in this book, be certain to consult an estate-planning attorney before implementing any of the techniques discussed in this book. The failure to obtain professional advice could result in additional expenses for administering your estate and could result in additional and unnecessary taxation of your estate. Additionally, the failure to properly prepare documents according to applicable law may render the documents useless.

HOUR'S UP!

QUIZ

Now it's time to see how much you have learned and retained from this lesson. Try to take the following quiz without referring back to the hourly materials.

1. The current annual exclusion for gifts is …
   a. $10,000 per person per year
   b. $20,000 per person per year
   c. $40,000 per year
   d. $10,000 per year

2. One spouse may split the gift made by the other spouse, so that the total gifts in one year to one person could be as much as …
   a. $100,000
   b. $675,00
   c. $50,000
   d. $20,000

3. In 2001, the federal credit shelter exemption equivalent amount is …
   a. $20,000
   b. $650,000
   c. $675,000
   d. $1,350,000

4. The most a single person can give to a single individual in one year without having to pay a gift tax is ...

    a. $10,000

    b. $20,000

    c. $685,000

    d. $675,000

5. Transfers at death to which of the following are fully deductible for federal estate tax purposes:

    a. Spouse

    b. Children

    c. Charity

    d. Two of the above

QUIZ

PART III

Administering Estates

HOUR 7   Dealing with Lifetime Issues

HOUR 8   Probate

HOUR 7

Dealing with Lifetime Issues

CHAPTER SUMMARY

LESSON PLAN:
In this hour, you'll learn that estate planning encompasses far more than what happens to your estate after death. Do not think that estate planning only benefits your family after you're gone. Planning should focus on issues that arise during your lifetime as well. Incapacity is an issue that must not be overlooked. These issues are usually ignored to your detriment. This hour begins with an overview of the guardianship process. Near the end of this hour, we will explore ways that you can bypass the guardianship process. You will also learn ...

- The different types of guardianships.
- What is involved in a guardianship.
- How to avoid guardianships.

Most of your estate planning will be focused on the administration of your estate after death. The need to plan for this time is obvious: If you don't plan, your state government will implement its own plan for you.

Most of us rarely see the need for lifetime planning, either because we have a good grasp on our affairs or because it's an easy subject to avoid. Disability, however, can strike all of us. According to the National Center for Health Statistics, information for the year 1995, 14.7% of the population suffered physical limitations due to chronic conditions. In 1990, for instance, 1,564,000 people were using wheelchairs. The National Center for Chronic Disease Prevention and Health Promotion reports that more than 90 million Americans live with chronic illnesses, defined as illnesses that are prolonged, do not resolve spontaneously, and are rarely cured completely. These same chronic diseases are estimated to account for 70% of all deaths in the United States.

The Chartbook on Disability in the United States for 1996 published by the National Institute on Disability and Rehabilitation Research estimates that:

- 10.9 million people between the ages of 18 and 69 are unable to work (6.6%) and 8.1 million are limited in work activity (5%). (This data came from the National Health Interview Survey.)

- Over 4.7 million children under the age of 18 have some limitation on activity (6.7% of all children) .
- Estimates are that nearly one in five people have a disability, with almost one half of those people considered to have a severe disability.
- Estimates are that 15% of non-institutionalized U.S. residents (37.7 million) have an activity limitation, with 11.5 million people unable to perform major activities.

With these statistics in mind, it would be careless not to consider disability planning as a part of your overall estate plan.

LEGAL CONSIDERATIONS

The legal considerations of disability involve determining how an individual with disabilities can handle his or her own affairs. Both physical and mental disabilities enter into the equation. A person with severe physical or mental limitations will be unlikely to be able to obtain substantial gainful employment or care for him or herself very well. The disabled individual will need the assistance of family and, in more severe cases, professional assistance from home practitioners, nurses, and home health care agencies. In the case of severe mental disability, financial and other decision-making is likewise hampered.

PROCEED WITH CAUTION

The law of your state may have provisions that differ from the information contained in this discussion. Be certain to consult with your estate planning attorney.

The solution provided by our legal system to such situations is known as *guardianship*. Guardianship is a creation of state law; therefore it varies from state to state, and both local court rules and state laws apply.

STRICTLY DEFINED

Guardianship is a process of determining the mental and physical capacity of an individual to care for themselves.

Guardians are individuals (or institutions) appointed by the court and given the responsibility of caring for an incapacitated person. Those who may be the subject of guardianship include those who are incapacitated due to mental or physical limitations due to illness, disease, or accident. Minor children are also subject to court guardianship proceedings because of their legal status as a minor. State law defines minority. Some states establish age 18 as the age of majority, others age 21. Because of limitations on the ability of a minor to own property or enter into contracts with others, there is a need for a guardianship whenever a natural parent is unable to provide those services.

TYPES OF GUARDIANSHIPS

There are different types of guardianships. Some people need assistance with their physical needs, while others might need assistance with only financial affairs. Unfortunately, some might need both.

The Uniform Guardianship and Protective Proceedings Act provides a statutory framework for guardianships and *conservatorships*. This Uniform Act maintains the distinction between a guardian for the person and a conservator for the property of the incapacitated person. Under the provisions of this act, no adult may be subjected to a guardianship or conservatorship without a judicial determination of incapacity and an opportunity to be heard in court.

STRICTLY DEFINED

A **conservatorship** is a guardianship over a person's property.

 Most state laws provide that a court may appoint an attorney or other representative called a *guardian ad litem* to protect the interests of the incapacitated person.

Once appointed, a guardian has specific responsibilities and duties to the incapacitated person as well as specific powers to carry out those responsibilities.

MINORS

The court may appoint a guardian over a minor child if the court finds that the appointment is in the best interest of the child, and any of the following:

- The parents consent to the appointment.
- All parental rights have been terminated.
- The parents are unwilling or unable to exercise their parental rights.

The Uniform Act preserves the right of the natural parent to appoint a guardian for a minor child by making an appropriate designation of guardian in the parent's will.

PROCEED WITH CAUTION

When drafting an appointment of guardian for your children, be careful to follow state law. If you fail to do so, your appointment might be unenforceable. Traditionally, the designation of a guardian must be made in the parent's will. Some states have expanded this to include any "other signed writing," which would include powers of attorney and health care appointments.

According to The Uniform Guardianship and Protective Proceedings Act, a guardian for a minor child should do the following:

- Become or remain personally acquainted with the child
- Take reasonable care of the child's personal effects
- Spend the child's money that has been received by the guardian for the child's current needs
- Conserve any excess money of the child for the child's future needs
- Keep the court advised as to the health and welfare of the child and account for the child's assets and expenditures made for the child as ordered by the court

The guardian of a minor child may also do such things as:

- Consent to medical or other care, treatment, or service for the child
- Consent to the marriage of the child

Interestingly, the court may even specifically authorize the guardian to consent to the adoption of the child, where appropriate.

ADULTS

When it comes to obtaining a guardianship over an adult incompetent, more procedural safeguards exist within the code. For one thing, the petition for guardianship must contain very specific information about the proposed ward and his or her assets. There must be a clear statement explaining why the guardianship is needed and a general statement estimating the value of the proposed ward's assets.

Usually, a physician's statement is submitted along with the petition for guardianship that establishes sufficient legal grounds for the establishment of the guardianship. In the vast majority of cases, the proposed ward is clearly incapacitated and the physician's statement becomes conclusive evidence of that fact at the hearing. Unless someone appears to object to the appointment, the court will enter the order approving the guardianship.

The court may appoint an attorney to represent the proposed ward if the court sees a need for the appointment. This may occur when the proposed ward is a minor child or when there are significant assets to safeguard. Notice is given to the proposed ward, the administrator of the institution where the proposed ward resides, and other interested parties, including next of kin.

The choice of who may be guardian is outlined in most state statutes. The Uniform Code sets forth the following priority for appointing a guardian:

- An existing guardian for the person, if any
- A person nominated as guardian in a durable power of attorney
- An agent appointed under a durable power of attorney for health care
- The spouse of the person appointing a guardian
- An adult child of the person appointing a guardian
- A parent of the person appointing a guardian
- A person nominated by the will

PROBLEMS WITH GUARDIANSHIPS

Reliance on court-ordered guardianships is a cumbersome way to protect your assets and provide for your care in the event of incapacity. State statutes offer you the opportunity to nominate your own guardian. Additionally, planning with the use of a living trust can adequately protect your property in the event of incapacity.

GO TO ▶
Hour 10, "Revocable Living Trusts," discusses the use of a revocable living trust in more detail.

Guardianships also can be very expensive. An attorney is required to handle the preparation and filing of the necessary paperwork seeking a court-appointed guardian. The cost of representation will vary from case to case. As in the case of probate administration, the court usually must approve the fees charged by the attorney. Additionally, the court-appointed guardian is allowed payment for serving as such, along with reimbursement for necessary expenses.

The court will review guardianships periodically. This means that an accounting must be kept of all receipts and expenditures and submitted to the court for approval. This can become a very tedious process for the guardian.

An adult incompetent or a person interested in the welfare of an adult incompetent may petition for an order that the guardianship be terminated.

With regard to a minor, one of the biggest disadvantages from a planning perspective is the mandatory termination provisions found in state law. What this means is that guardianships must terminate at a specific time. This does not allow an opportunity for planning.

State statutes typically provide for the termination of a guardianship no later than when the child attains the age of majority. Because a guardianship proceeding is a protective proceeding instituted on behalf of the minor child, there is no further legal reason to protect the assets of a child once the child attains the age of majority. Unfortunately, this fails to take into account various levels of maturity.

Many parents now provide for their children by establishing trusts that provide for payment over a period of years. There often is a sense that it is not in the child's best interests to turn over relatively large sums of money to a child who is still going to school or who has not demonstrated a sufficient level of financial maturity to handle money.

Unfortunately, by failing to plan for premature death, children who are the subject of guardianships may come into great wealth at age 18. The opportunity to plan for that child is lost since the guardianship statutes do not allow for withholding funds from an adult, unless they continue to suffer from some demonstrable disability.

To prevent a financial windfall from occurring at a relatively early age, proper planning to avoid guardianships is mandatory.

BYPASSING THE GUARDIANSHIP PROCESS

There are at your disposal specific tools that will allow you to completely bypass the guardianship process. The tools you need to do this are as follows:

- Durable Power of Attorney and Health Care Representative Appointment, discussed in Hour 12, "Powers of Attorney, Health Care

Representative Appointments, and Living Wills." In these documents you are allowed in most states to specify who you want to serve as guardian over minor children or yourself, should you become incapacitated in the future.

- Revocable Living Trusts, discussed in Hour 10. The trust is an excellent way to handle the assets of an incapacitated individual. By designating the guardian in your trust, you side step the guardianship procedure entirely. If assets are under the control of the trust through proper re-titling, the designated guardian has the immediate ability to take over control of the assets of an incapacitated individual without seeking court approval.

If these documents are carefully drafted, sufficient power can be given to the representative that eliminates the need to establish a guardianship. If a guardianship is required, the documents will also designate the person desired to serve as guardian.

PROCEED WITH CAUTION

As with all of the material in this book, be certain to consult an estate-planning attorney before implementing any of the techniques discussed in this book. The failure to obtain professional advice could result in additional expenses for administering your estate and could result in additional and unnecessary taxation of your estate. Additionally, the failure to properly prepare documents according to applicable law may render the documents useless.

HOUR'S UP!

Now it's time to see how much you have learned and retained from this lesson. Try to take the following quiz without referring back to the hourly materials.

1. A guardianship over only a person's property sometimes is called:
    a. Craftsmanship
    b. Wardship
    c. Physicianship
    d. Conservatorship

QUIZ

QUIZ

2. A guardianship may be needed when:

    a. A person fails to implement estate planning

    b. A person creates a living will

    c. A person establishes a living trust

    d. A person creates a durable power of attorney

3. Guardianships over a minor child normally terminate when:

    a. The minor demonstrates an ability to manage his finances

    b. The minor files a petition to terminate with the court

    c. The minor reaches the age of majority

    d. The minor graduates from college

4. Guardianships are effective:

    a. In planning your estate

    b. In avoiding the need for a durable power of attorney

    c. In minimizing costs and expenses

    d. To preserve an incompetent's assets for his or her benefit

5. The best tool to reduce the need for a guardianship is:

    a. Durable power of attorney

    b. Health care representative appointment

    c. Revocable living trust

    d. All of the above

Hour 8

Probate

The fact is, there is nothing "good" or "bad" about probate. Probate is simply a process that must be followed whenever there are probate assets in a decedent's estate. This process provides a means for determining heirs, paying creditors, and distributing assets.

HISTORY OF PROBATE

Most of American legal tradition originated in England. The one exception is the state of Louisiana, which has followed French law. This system has developed over time, both in the United States and in England as well as in other countries.

The current law of probate in England is more streamlined than found in the United States. The Probate, Divorce, and Admiralty Division, established in the High Court, has the responsibility to scrutinize instruments that are represented to be testaments as well as wills, which were then considered instruments disposing of real property. Personal representatives receive their power from the will itself. Following appointment by the Probate Division, they are free to act on their own, without court supervision. The court will only become involved in the event of a will contest or other dispute.

Other countries generally have followed the lead of England by simplifying the probate administration process. Unfortunately, the United States still largely

CHAPTER SUMMARY

LESSON PLAN:

In this hour, we'll tackle the topic of probate. Nothing in estate planning has a worse reputation than probate. Yet most people are unaware of what probate is and how it works. Although there are plenty of books and classes created to teach you how to avoid probate, if you're like most people, you're not sure quite what it is you're supposed to avoid. In this hour, you'll learn …

- The history of probate.
- How probate works.
- Who can serve as personal representative.
- What's good and bad about probate.

GO TO ▶
If you need to review what is included in a decedent's probate estate, go to Hour 3, "What Is an Estate?"

operates on a complicated statutory procedure that tends to be expensive and time consuming. In the United States, the probate proceedings are held in what's known as Probate Court, which is called the Surrogate's Court in New York and the Orphan's Court in Pennsylvania. Probate courts in the United States are concerned not just with the estates of decedents, but also with the estates of minors and incompetent individuals.

Probate procedures vary from state to state. Despite some inevitable differences, it is possible to review some general characteristics of the probate process.

PROBATE PROPERTY

GO TO ▶
Review the discussion of tenancy in common and other title issues in Hour 4, "Defining Types of Assets."

To begin with, probate only applies to property in single name or tenancy in common. It also applies to contractual property payable to the estate of the owner, such as life insurance, annuities, and retirement plans.

Second, if there is probate property, the probate process will proceed whether the decedent died with or without a will. Therefore, the first lesson to learn is that you cannot avoid probate with a will.

The corollary to this rule is that you can avoid probate if you own property as a joint tenant with right to survivorship or by designating a beneficiary for your life insurance, retirement accounts, annuities, trusts, and payable on death accounts. As you learned in Hour 4, joint ownership brings along a set of additional problems.

TIME SAVER

 You will still be better off if you use a revocable trust as your primary estate planning tool. It provides far more protection for your assets than does joint tenancy. It also allows you to retain control of your assets.

FUNCTIONS OF PROBATE

The probate process serves several functions, including determining the validity of the will, who has the power to execute the will, and other issues. Let's take a look.

WILL VALIDITY

If you die with a will, the probate court in your county will act to determine the will's validity. Your estate will file the will with the court after your death—probably through an attorney, since many courts will not accept court filings from a non-lawyer.

WHO'S IN CHARGE?

In the United States, we have a system of appointing a person to direct the distribution of a decedent's property. Civil law countries, on the other hand, allow the estate to go directly to the heirs. Civil law is found in continental Europe, and has been adopted in much of Latin America as well as parts of Asia and Africa. In the United States, we call these people "personal representatives," and they are the ones who administrate estates.

Most wills designate, or actually nominate, someone to act as the personal representative on behalf of all of the heirs. This person ensures that the heirs designated in the will receive the decedent's property in the manner he or she intended. Historically, that person was known as an *executor* if that person was male and an *executrix* if female.

WHAT TO DO IF THERE IS NO WILL

If the decedent dies without a will, a personal representative of the decedent files a petition with the probate court to administer an estate without a will. Historically, the person who opened an estate for a decedent who died without a will was called an *administrator* if male and an *administratrix* if female.

The filing of the will or petition with the probate court begins the probate process, and one of the first tasks of the court is to appoint the personal representative. Individuals are actually only "nominated" in a decedent's will to serve as the personal representative. The nominee has no authority over an individual's estate until the court appoints him or her as the personal representative.

You are said to be probating a decedent's will or probating a decedent's estate, depending on whether or not there is a will.

If the decedent had a valid will, the person nominated in the will is usually appointed. If the decedent died without a will, then the court must appoint someone to serve as personal representative of the estate. This appointment usually goes to the nearest available relative, depending on the specifics of state law.

GO TO ▶
Each state has specific requirements that must be followed in the execution of a will for the will to be valid. For a detailed look at the requirements for executing a will, go to Hour 9, "Wills."

In Indiana, for example, those entitled to be appointed personal representative are as follows and in this sequence:

- The executor or executors designated in a will that has been admitted to probate
- A surviving spouse who is a beneficiary of a will that has been admitted to probate
- To a beneficiary of a will that has been admitted to probate
- The surviving spouse, or to the person or persons nominated by the surviving spouse or to the surviving spouse and the person or persons nominated by the surviving spouse
- To an heir, the person or persons nominated by an heir, or an heir and the person or persons nominated by an heir
- If there is not a person listed above, then to any other qualified person

You can't serve as a personal representative if you are …

- Under 18 years of age
- Incapacitated (unless the incapacity is caused only by physical illness, physical impairment, or physical infirmity)
- A convicted felon, either under the laws of the United States or of any state or territory of the United States
- A resident corporation not authorized to act as a *fiduciary* in the state
- A person whom the court otherwise finds unsuitable

STRICTLY DEFINED

A **fiduciary** is a person (or entity) holding a position of trust and confidence with regard to another's assets.

Being a resident of the state where the probate proceedings are pending used to be mandatory, but now many states allow for the appointment of a *resident agent* to serve along with an out-of-state personal representative. This resident agent is often the attorney hired to file the papers.

STRICTLY DEFINED

A **resident agent** is an individual or an entity (such as a financial institution or trust department) that resides (or has a principal place of business) within the state of probate administration and that agrees to accept notices from the probate court and notify the personal representative of all such notices.

LETTERS TESTAMENTARY

Letters testamentary are fancy words for the court papers stating that the personal representative has been duly appointed by the court and is authorized to make decisions on behalf of the estate. These papers must be provided to anyone who intends to deal directly with the personal representative such as financial institutions, the Internal Revenue Service, insurance companies, and the like.

NOTICE TO CREDITORS

Notice of the probate proceedings is published in a newspaper of general circulation in the county of the decedent's residence. This is done to provide notice of the decedent's death to the general public and instruct those with claims against the estate to file such claims within a designated period of time—usually five months.

The notice requirement is one reason why the probate process is often so prolonged. Unfortunately, it is a constitutional requirement that guarantees creditors the right to have their claims presented to the court.

In addition to publication notice, creditors known to the personal representative must be given actual notice of the pending probate proceeding. This requires sending a certified letter to the creditor with information sufficient to inform the creditor of the probate proceeding and the need to file a formal claim.

INVENTORY

Shortly after administration of the decedent's estate begins, the personal representative is usually required to file an inventory with the court listing all of the decedent's assets. The inventory is designed to place the court on notice of the assets being administered. Heirs or any other interested party can review this list, since it is a public record.

 Many states now have simplified administration procedures that eliminate the requirement for the filing of an inventory.

A sample notice of probate administration.

**STATE OF INDIANA
VIGO SUPERIOR COURT
PROBATE DIVISION
2001 TERM**

IN THE MATTER OF THE UNSUPERVISED ADMINIS-TRATION OF THE ESTATE OF WILLIAM Jones DECEASED.

CAUSE NO. 84D02-0101-EU-0000

NOTICE OF ADMINISTRATION

In the Superior Court of Vigo County, Indiana.
Notice is hereby given that Thomas C. Smithwas, on the 28TH day of February, 2001, appointed Personal Representative of the Estate of William Jones, deceased, who died on 21st day of December, 1999
All persons having claims against this estate, whether or not now due, must file the same in said Court within five (5) months from the date of the first publication of this notice, or within one (1) year after the decedent's death, whichever is earlier, or the claims will be forever barred.
Dated at Terre Haute, Indiana, this 28th day of February 2001.

William L. Mansard
Clerk of the Superior Court for Vigo County, Indiana

Keith R. Lyman,
Attorney for Petitioner
6110Ohio Street,

P.O. Box 2222F
Terre Haute, IN 47808
05514142-T/S-March 2nd & 9th, 2001

WILL CONTESTS

If anyone has reason to contest the validity of the will, the probate court is the place to file the contest proceedings. Someone contesting the will can challenge the validity of the will itself for failing to meet the execution requirements of the appropriate state (such as not being properly witnessed), or he or she may challenge the will because it was prepared under undue influence, duress, or fraud. With civil court backlogs, it may be years before there can be a trial.

GO TO ▶
You can find more information on the grounds for challenging a will, including an explanation of what constitutes undue influence, duress, and fraud, in Hour 9, "Wills."

DUTIES OF THE PERSONAL REPRESENTATIVE

The personal representative is responsible for securing the property of the decedent, paying the decedent's bills, collecting any debts due the estate, defending the estate against claims, paying all taxes that might become due because of the decedent's death, and distributing the property of the estate according to the decedent's will or according to law. If the decedent was engaged in business, the personal representative must make sure that the business is operated properly or closed down.

POSTING BOND

The personal representative of the estate usually must post a bond to ensure the faithful performance of his or her duties. Bond usually is determined by statute and set by the probate court. The amount of bond usually is based on the value of the decedent's estate.

FYI Many states now have simplified administration procedures that eliminate the requirement for posting a bond.

SALE OF ASSETS

Sometimes the will of a decedent directs the sale of some or all of the property in the estate. Other times it might be necessary to sell property to liquidate the estate to pay estate expenses, including payment of claims and administrative expenses. If property of the decedent must be sold, the personal representative is responsible for selling such property according to state law, which usually requires the filing of papers with the court for approval. This can be a laborious and time-consuming process.

FYI Many states now have simplified administration procedures that eliminate the requirement for court approval for the sale of estate property.

In a typical supervised probate proceeding, the personal representative first must petition the court for permission to sell property. To do so, he or she usually files court papers and explains the reasons that a sale is in the best interest of the heirs. The court is required to notify all interested parties—primarily the heirs—of the request to sell property. The request is set for a court hearing a few weeks later so the heirs can be notified of the request, and appear and express their approval or disapproval of the request. At the hearing the court will either approve or disapprove the petition. If approved, the personal representative can proceed to sell the property.

As soon as a buyer is found, an agreement to sell can be executed between the personal representative and the buyer, subject to final court approval. At this time, the personal representative again will petition the court to approve the sale of the property and submit the agreement to the court. Again, the court will set a hearing for several weeks later to enable the heirs to appear and then approve or disapprove the sale.

If the court approves the agreement and sale, the personal representative proceeds to close on the sale and collect the proceeds. At this time, the personal representative must file a report of sale with the court and obtain court approval.

State statutes will specify the minimum amount for which estate property can be sold. In Indiana, for example, the personal representative will not be able to sell property for less than fair market value at a private sale, which is one without notice to others. This does not mean that the personal representative should not try to sell the property for more than fair market value. Sometimes a court will direct the personal representative to demonstrate the efforts made to sell property for more than fair market value before it will approve a petition to sell at fair market value.

At a public sale, such as an auction, Indiana permits a personal representative to sell estate property for no less than two thirds its actual fair market value. At a forced sale, as might be required to pay taxes or expenses of administration, this can cause a significant loss in estate value.

PROCEED WITH CAUTION

The law of your state may have provisions that differ from the information contained in this discussion. Be certain to consult with your estate planning attorney.

Getting the Appraisal

The personal representative must determine the value of all estate assets. This is done in different ways, depending on the type of property involved. See Hour 6, "Federal Estate Taxes," for more information.

Estate Property Insurance

All personal representatives have a fiduciary duty to the heirs of an estate. This duty imposes great responsibility on the personal representative, which can create personal liability if estate assets are lost, damaged, or destroyed by fire, theft, and so forth. Always make sure there is adequate insurance on all estate property to protect you from liability to the heirs.

PROCEED WITH CAUTION

If the residence of a decedent is left unoccupied, most homeowners insurance will not cover loss after a specified number of days after the house becomes unoccupied. Additionally, insurance on unoccupied property is quite expensive, but unfortunately necessary. Don't drive the decedent's automobiles either, unless they are insured. If there is an accident, odds are you are not covered as an insured party and the personal representative and/or the estate may become liable to the heirs for damages.

Taxes, Taxes, Taxes

The personal representative also must make sure all taxes—estate, income, inheritance, and fiduciary—are paid before making a final distribution of assets. This task involves paying the taxes and receiving notice of accurate payment from the taxing authority.

JUST A MINUTE

A personal representative should never distribute an estate before all bills are paid, including claims and taxes. Heirs often have a difficult time returning money to the estate for these expenses. The personal representative is also responsible to be certain that these bills are paid before making distribution.

Income Taxes

The personal representative must insure that the decedent's final income tax return is timely filed, which may involve going through tax records, checks, and receipts. It is not unusual for the personal representative to hire an accountant to file these on behalf of the estate. Occasionally the attorney for the estate will prepare these income tax returns.

INHERITANCE TAXES

PROCEED WITH CAUTION

 The law of your state may have provisions that differ from the information contained in this discussion. Be certain to consult with your estate planning attorney.

If the decedent died in a state that imposes inheritance taxes, the personal representative must be certain that the appropriate returns are filed with the state taxing authority. More information on state inheritance taxes is found in Hour 5, "Income Taxes and Inheritance Taxes."

FEDERAL ESTATE TAXES

GO TO ▶
You can find more information on federal estate taxes in Hour 6.

The personal representative also must determine whether the estate value is high enough to require the filing of a federal estate tax return. The appraisals are critical to making this determination.

FIDUCIARY TAXES

Yes, there are even taxes that the estate must pay on *income* received on estate assets. This income is reported on a Federal Form 1041 for estates and trusts.

STRICTLY DEFINED

For fiduciary purposes, **income** is money received from interest, dividends, business income or losses, capital gains and losses, rents, royalties, farm income or loss, ordinary gain or loss, and other types of income.

Form **1041** Department of the Treasury—Internal Revenue Service
U.S. Income Tax Return for Estates and Trusts **2000**

For calendar year 2000 or fiscal year beginning _____, 2000, and ending _____ 20 ____ OMB No. 1545-0092

A Type of entity:
- ☐ Decedent's estate
- ☐ Simple trust
- ☐ Complex trust
- ☐ Grantor type trust
- ☐ Bankruptcy estate–Ch. 7
- ☐ Bankruptcy estate–Ch. 11
- ☐ Pooled income fund

B Number of Schedules K-1 attached (see instructions) ▶

Name of estate or trust (If a grantor type trust, see page 10 of the instructions.)

Name and title of fiduciary

Number, street, and room or suite no. (If a P.O. box, see page 10 of the instructions.)

City or town, state, and ZIP code

C Employer identification number

D Date entity created

E Nonexempt charitable and split-interest trusts, check applicable boxes (see page 10 of the instructions):
- ☐ Described in section 4947(a)(1)
- ☐ Not a private foundation
- ☐ Described in section 4947(a)(2)

F Check applicable boxes: ☐ Initial return ☐ Final return ☐ Amended return ☐ Change in fiduciary's name ☐ Change in fiduciary's address

G Pooled mortgage account (see page 11 of the instructions): ☐ Bought ☐ Sold Date: _____

Income

1	Interest income	1
2	Ordinary dividends	2
3	Business income or (loss) (attach Schedule C or C-EZ (Form 1040))	3
4	Capital gain or (loss) (attach Schedule D (Form 1041))	4
5	Rents, royalties, partnerships, other estates and trusts, etc. (attach Schedule E (Form 1040))	5
6	Farm income or (loss) (attach Schedule F (Form 1040))	6
7	Ordinary gain or (loss) (attach Form 4797)	7
8	Other income. List type and amount _____	8
9	**Total income.** Combine lines 1 through 8 ▶	9

Deductions

10	Interest. Check if Form 4952 is attached ▶ ☐	10
11	Taxes	11
12	Fiduciary fees	12
13	Charitable deduction (from Schedule A, line 7)	13
14	Attorney, accountant, and return preparer fees	14
15a	Other deductions **not** subject to the 2% floor (attach schedule)	15a
b	Allowable miscellaneous itemized deductions subject to the 2% floor	15b
16	**Total.** Add lines 10 through 15b	16
17	Adjusted total income or (loss). Subtract line 16 from line 9. Enter here and on Schedule B, line 1 ▶	17
18	Income distribution deduction (from Schedule B, line 15) (attach Schedules K-1 (Form 1041))	18
19	Estate tax deduction (including certain generation-skipping taxes) (attach computation)	19
20	Exemption	20
21	**Total deductions.** Add lines 18 through 20 ▶	21

Tax and Payments

22	Taxable income. Subtract line 21 from line 17. If a loss, see page 15 of the instructions	22
23	**Total tax** (from Schedule G, line 7)	23
24	**Payments: a** 2000 estimated tax payments and amount applied from 1999 return	24a
b	Estimated tax payments allocated to beneficiaries (from Form 1041-T)	24b
c	Subtract line 24b from line 24a	24c
d	Tax paid with extension of time to file: ☐ Form 2758 ☐ Form 8736 ☐ Form 8800	24d
e	Federal income tax withheld. If any is from Form(s) 1099, check ▶ ☐	24e
	Other payments: **f** Form 2439 _____; **g** Form 4136 _____; Total ▶	24h
25	**Total payments.** Add lines 24c through 24e, and 24h ▶	25
26	Estimated tax penalty (see page 16 of the instructions)	26
27	**Tax due.** If line 25 is smaller than the total of lines 23 and 26, enter amount owed	27
28	**Overpayment.** If line 25 is larger than the total of lines 23 and 26, enter amount overpaid	28
29	Amount of line 28 to be: **a Credited to 2001 estimated tax** ▶ _____ ; **b Refunded** ▶	29

Sign Here

Under penalties of perjury, I declare that I have examined this return, including accompanying schedules and statements, and to the best of my knowledge and belief, it is true, correct, and complete. Declaration of preparer (other than fiduciary) is based on all information of which preparer has any knowledge.

▶ _____ Signature of fiduciary or officer representing fiduciary | Date _____ | ▶ EIN of fiduciary if a financial institution (see page 6 of the instructions)

Paid Preparer's Use Only

Preparer's signature ▶ _____ | Date _____ | Check if self-employed ▶ ☐ | Preparer's SSN or PTIN

Firm's name (or yours if self-employed), address, and ZIP code ▶ _____ | EIN ▶ _____ | Phone no. ( )

For Paperwork Reduction Act Notice, see the separate instructions. Cat. No. 11370H Form **1041** (2000)

Complete this form when reporting income paid to an estate or a trust following the death of the grantor. You can learn more about this form in Hour 5.

ALTERNATE PROBATE PROCEDURES

Nearly every estate has some statutory scheme for the transfer of a decedent's estate without having to go through the formal probate process. The two primary alternate procedures are simplified administration and affidavit.

SIMPLIFIED ADMINISTRATION

Many states have established procedures for the simplified administration of a decedent's estate. These simplified procedures generally allow for the filing of a decedent's will, the preparation (but not necessarily the filing) of an inventory of the decedent's estate, and the administration of the estate without court supervision. A final report usually is filed with the court setting forth all activities of the personal representative, which is distributed to the beneficiaries.

NO ADMINISTRATION

Some states allow for the transfer of estates by affidavit, with some of those permitting only the transfer of personal property by affidavit. Some other states allow for the transfer of real estate title by affidavit. In those states allowing transfer of property by affidavit, there are limits on the value of the estate, ranging from as little as $10,000 to as much as $140,000.

PROCEED WITH CAUTION

 Be certain to consult with an estate planning attorney licensed in your state who can advise you properly on the provisions of your state law.

To administer property subject to these limitations, the beneficiaries to an estate prepare an affidavit, sometimes referred to as a "small estates affidavit," and submit that document to the person in control of the decedent's assets, such as a stock transfer agent, bank account, brokerage firm, and so on.

ADVANTAGES OF PROBATE ADMINISTRATION

Although probate has a bad reputation, there are some good reasons for the probate system. Some of the useful purposes of probate are listed below.

PROTECTING PERSONAL REPRESENTATIVES

One advantage of probate administration is the protection it gives to the personal representative. There is a term for the role the personal representative plays in the probate process. That term is fiduciary.

As a fiduciary, the personal representative is accountable to all of the heirs for the proper administration of the estate. That is why it is so important that all legitimate bills be paid, that all taxes owing be paid, and the estate property be protected pending distribution to the ultimate beneficiaries. The probate process is designed to ensure that all provisions of the law meet compliance. By obtaining appropriate court approval of all actions taken during the supervised administration of the estate, the personal representative is protected from personal liability to others arising out of his or her appointed duty.

PROTECTING CREDITORS

Another advantage to probate administration is the protection of creditors. Whenever there is a formal administration of an estate, the law grants creditors a forum for filing claims against the estate in a timely manner. There is a built-in procedure for handling disputed claims through the trial procedures established by the court. Creditors are guaranteed that they will be afforded due process under the law. There are built-in mechanisms for notifying creditors of the death of a decedent. The personal representative has specific duties and obligations pertaining to notifying creditors of a decedent's death.

PROTECTING HEIRS

Since probate is merely a transition process during which property passes from a decedent to the lawful heirs, it is of paramount importance to the court that all heirs be protected during this process. That is why heirs are entitled to notice of hearing on many proposed actions by the personal representative handling a supervised estate, such as the sale of personal property or real property. Heirs have a forum for any disputes or questions they have during the administration of the estate and, like creditors, they are afforded due process.

RESOLVING DISPUTES

As mentioned above, the court system provides a ready vehicle for the resolution of disputes by creditors or beneficiaries. In addition to will contests mentioned above, there might be questions surrounding the interpretation of a will. For example, the will may be admitted to probate, but may need clarification because of markings or handwriting on the will. The court must decide whether these marks invalidate the entire will or a portion of a will. The court may also ignore the marks under certain circumstances.

DETERMINING HEIRSHIP

Questions are commonly raised about who the decedent's heirs actually are. If the decedent left no will, it may be necessary for the personal representative to determine the identity of the heirs. More information on determining heirship when there is no will is found in Hour 2, "Inheritance and the Laws of Intestate Succession."

DISADVANTAGES OF PROBATE ADMINISTRATION

Although there are some useful aspects to formal probate, there might be reasons an individual wants to avoid probate. Some of these reasons are discussed in the following sections.

ATTORNEYS, PERSONAL REPRESENTATIVES, AND THEIR FEES

Unfortunately, probate is not a do-it-yourself project. When planning your estate, if you utilize a will, you will need to advise your family of the need to hire an attorney to handle your probate estate.

One of the disadvantages of hiring an attorney is that the attorney must be paid for his or her services. Of course, the attorney does not view this as a disadvantage. The amount that an attorney should be paid has been the source of much litigation as well as a concern for many involved in the probate process.

To begin with, attorneys are not allowed to take fees out of a supervised estate without court permission. If the probate is being handled as an unsupervised administration, local court rules must be followed. At the very least, the personal representative and the attorney should come to a written agreement about fees and services.

The American Bar Association has established rules for determining attorney fees in the Rules of Professional Conduct that govern the conduct of attorneys. These rules state simply that a lawyer's fee shall be "reasonable." So exactly what is a reasonable fee? What is reasonable to the attorney might not be reasonable to the personal representative, the heirs, or the court. The ABA issued a formal opinion addressing the question of "reasonableness." Some factors are as follows:

- The time and labor required, the novelty and difficulty of the questions involved, and the skill requisite to perform the legal service properly
- The need for the attorney to decline other employment to concentrate on the probate proceeding
- The fee customarily charged in the locality for similar legal services
- The amount of money involved and the results obtained
- The time limitations imposed by the client or by the circumstances
- The nature and length of the professional relationship with the client
- The experience, reputation, and ability of the lawyer or lawyers performing the services
- Whether the fee is *fixed* or *contingent*

STRICTLY DEFINED

A fee is **contingent** if payment of the fee and the amount of the fee is based upon the outcome of the litigation. A fee is **"fixed"** when payment of the fee and the amount of the fee is predetermined and payable regardless of outcome.

These standards still leave much to the imagination. Accordingly, many local probate courts have established certain fee schedules that the court considers reasonable. If the fee request filed by the attorney falls within the established guidelines, the request will be approved unless an interested party lodges a specific objection.

Sample attorney fee agreement for probate administration.

April 12, 2001

John Client
123 Address Lane
Anytown, ST 00000

Re: Estate of Tom Decedent

Dear Mr. Client

Thank you for retaining our law firm to represent you in the handling of the estate of Tom Decedent.

Our fee for handling this probate and filing any necessary inheritance tax returns and federal estate tax returns is in accordance with the fee schedule for Any County, ST. In addition, the estate will be required to pay any necessary expenses incurred which are necessary for the probate of this estate, including court filing fees, publication expenses, and appraisal fees.

If this estate is supervised, all fees must be approved by the Probate Court. If this estate is unsupervised, no such approval is necessary.

If this is acceptable to you, please indicate your approval by signing in the space provided below.

If you have any questions regarding this matter, please do not hesitate to contact me.

Sincerely,

Your Lawyer

I hereby accept the terms and conditions of employment set forth above based upon the fee established above, and hereby retain LAW OFFICE to represent us in the matter of handling the estate of Tom Decedent.

_____
printed name

Although some courts now authorize only hourly billing on estates, many jurisdictions still utilize the contingent fee as the measure of reasonableness. For example, California attorneys follow a fee schedule that has been codified in the California Probate Code. Section 10800-10810 states:

> "Subject to the provisions of this part, for ordinary services the attorney for the personal representative shall receive compensation based on the value of the estate accounted for by the personal representative, as follows:"

1. 4% on the first $15,000.
2. 3% on the next $85,000.
3. 2% on the next $900,000.
4. 1% on the next $9,000,000.
5. .5% on the next $15,000,000.

For anything more than $25,000,000, the court must determine a reasonable amount. Other states have similar schedules; one Indiana county has the following schedule for probate fees:

Up to $100,000, not to exceed 6%

Next $200,000, not to exceed 4%

Next $700,000, not to exceed 3%

Over $1,000,000, not to exceed 1%

On the other hand, Michigan and Utah require hourly billing. In Nevada, the fee is basically whatever is agreed upon between the personal representative and the attorney. Just about any way you look at it, probate is an expensive proposition. Many people are unhappy to see lawyers make this kind of money. Unfortunately, it doesn't end there. As discussed, not only do the lawyers get paid; the personal representative also gets paid.

PROCEED WITH CAUTION

Be aware that state laws and court rules may have changed by the time you read this book. Be certain to consult with your estate planning attorney licensed in your state to find out about the fees allowed in your jurisdiction.

JUST A MINUTE

Be aware that if a personal representative also is an heir, he or she will inherit something. An inheritance is not taxable. However, if the personal representative charges a fee, this becomes taxable income to the personal representative. The decision on whether to charge a fee, therefore, might not be as easy as it seems.

Also, remember that individuals are not the only ones appointed as personal representatives. Institutional representatives are routinely appointed. All of these institutional representatives will have their own fee structure to follow (as long as it fits within the court's guidelines). Institutional representatives include banks and brokerage firms that have their own trust department that is capable of handling estate administration responsibilities.

PROBATE DELAYS

The typical administration of an estate will last anywhere from 6 months to 18 months, depending on the issues involved. If property needs to be sold, additional delays can result due to market conditions.

MANDATORY CLAIMS PERIOD

The delays that necessarily accompany the probate process can be frustrating. To begin with, every state must provide a reasonable opportunity for creditors to be notified of a pending estate and the right to file a claim against the estate. This often builds in a delay of five to six months.

VALUATION ISSUES

Additional delays are caused by the need to obtain valuations that can take longer than expected, especially if a business is part of a decedent's estate. Appraising a family partnership, family business, or closely held corporation can raise numerous complications in the valuation process because business appraisals can be extremely subjective.

WILL CONTESTS AND CLAIMS

Unexpected will contests or other claims against the estate can result in those matters being placed on the court's trial docket, which can cause delays from one to four years before trial.

ANCILLARY ADMINISTRATION

Never heard of *ancillary administration?* That's what happens when a decedent owns property outside of his home state. Suppose John dies a resident of the state of Indiana. He has a home in Indiana and farmland in Illinois. John also owned land in Louisiana. Because John owned real property in three states, his personal representative must open a probate proceeding in

Indiana, Illinois, and Louisiana! This is called ancillary administration. Filing in more than one state can triple the expenses involved with John's estate, considering costs of administration, appraisal expenses, and attorney and personal representative fees.

STRICTLY DEFINED

Ancillary administration refers to the probate of property the decedent owns in a state other than his resident state.

PUBLIC PROCEEDINGS

For those of you who desire privacy, probate is not the best place for your estate to conclude. All documents filed in the probate court are public records. Any person who wants to see the decedent's will, an inventory of the estate, claims made against the estate, or other matters pending before the court has every right to visit the probate court and look through the official court files. Although this might not be a major concern for most people, some would prefer not to have their estates wind up as a matter of public knowledge.

PROCEED WITH CAUTION

As with all of the material in this book, be certain to consult an estate planning attorney before implementing any of the techniques discussed in this book. The failure to obtain professional advice could result in additional expenses for administering your estate and could result in additional and unnecessary taxation of your estate. Additionally, the failure to properly prepare documents according to applicable law may render the documents useless.

HOUR'S UP!

Now it's time to see how much you have learned and retained from this lesson. Try to take the following quiz without referring back to the hourly materials:

1. The following are examples of probate property:

    a. Life insurance payable to a living spouse

    b. An interest in property held as tenancy in common

    c. Joint tenancy with right of survivorship

    d. Payable on death accounts

2. The best way to avoid probate is …

    a. To execute a will

    b. Own all of your property in single name

    c. Not to own probate property

    d. Have no named beneficiaries on your life insurance

3. Personal representatives have power to act …

    a. Only after the will is probated

    b. Immediately upon the death of the testator

    c. Independently without court appointment

    d. As soon as all of the beneficiaries agree

4. Property can be sold out of an estate …

    a. For whatever the personal representative feels is adequate

    b. At a public sale for no less than full fair market value

    c. At a private sale for no less than two thirds of its value

    d. Only after the court in a supervised estate approves the sale

5. When there is more than one probate required as a result of land in different states, it is referred to as …

    a. Unsupervised administration

    b. Limited administration

    c. Qualified administration

    d. Ancillary administration

QUIZ

PART IV

Using the Primary
Estate Planning Tools

HOUR 9   Wills

HOUR 10   Revocable Living Trusts

HOUR 11   Wills and Trusts: Important
              Provisions

HOUR 12   Powers of Attorney, Health Care
              Representative Appointments,
              and Living Wills

CHAPTER SUMMARY

LESSON PLAN:

In this hour, you'll learn all about wills, from the different types of wills to execution requirements for wills. You also will review the provisions that should be included in every will and some optional provisions for specific situations.

In addition, we'll show you ...

- How a will works.
- How to execute and revoke a will.
- Why a will requires probate.
- What a will can do for you.
- What a will cannot do for you.

A will is nothing more than a document made in which a person sets forth what is to happen to his or her property after death. This is also referred to as a *testamentary disposition* of property. How a person goes about making a will is explained below.

STRICTLY DEFINED

A **testamentary disposition** is a disposition of assets made after death according to the terms of a valid will.

TYPES OF WILLS

Not all wills are the same. Wills can be verbal or written. Each state is allowed to establish its own requirements for the execution of a will. Not all of the wills discussed in the following are valid in every state.

- **Holographic will** The maker of this will prepares it in longhand, as opposed to it being typewritten or printed. In 2000, twenty-eight states approved holographic wills. Pennsylvania recognizes holographic wills by case law, not statutory law. New York recognizes holographic wills only for members of the military serving in armed conflict and some others in the armed services. Maryland also limits its acceptance of these wills to members of the armed forces.

- **Noncupative will**   This type of will is not written at all; it is verbal. Because it is not written it will not comply with the execution requirements of most states. However, sometimes an exception is made if the declarant is facing imminent death; sometimes knows as a *deathbed will*. Some states limit the validity of these wills to personal property only and some impose dollar limits on what is controlled by this type of will.

- **Simple will**   A "simple will" probably is the most misused term pertaining to wills. The simple will is intended to leave all of a decedent's property outright to a select few beneficiaries. A simple will usually contains no provisions for guardianship, trusts, or more complex distributions. This type of will refers to the content of the will, whereas the holographic and noncupative wills refer to the manner of execution.

- **Joint will**   When two individuals create a single will governing the distribution of their separate property, this is referred to as a joint will. This type of will should be avoided because it might limit the ability of the surviving individual to change the terms of the will or dispose of property.

- **Mutual will**   This will is similar to a joint will to the extent that it is prepared pursuant to an agreement between the parties. However, mutual wills are separate wills prepared by each of the parties to the agreement. You should also avoid this type of will because it can create legal problems if the surviving individual does not follow the agreement.

How Do Wills Work?

Understand that a will is *testamentary* in nature, which means it does not have any impact on your life or your property while you are living. In order for a will to have any power over your property after your death, it must be filed with the probate court. Now you know what probate involves, right? If not, review Hour 8, "Probate."

EXECUTION REQUIREMENTS

The requirements for executing a valid will vary from state to state, but do maintain some common themes. Following are the most basic requirements for the execution of a valid will:

- **Sound mind**   The testator must be "of sound mind" at the time the will is executed. Whether a person is of sound mind is sometimes difficult to determine. A generally accepted definition is that the testator:

  - Understands that he or she is executing a will

  - Knows the nature and extent of his or her property

  - Knows the objects of his or her bounty (spouse, descendants, and other relatives)

- **Legal age**   A minor is not able to execute a valid will. Testamentary capacity follows contract law in many respects. Most states have established the legal age at 18. Be certain to check your particular state law.

- **The final say**   A will must be the testator's final expression of intent to dispose of his or her property. Most wills contain a statement to this effect.

- **Self-proving declaration**   A self-proving declaration is a statement by the witnesses and the testator that the document was executed in full conformity with the requirements of state law. With this self-proving declaration, a will can be admitted to probate without additional proof of proper execution. Without this declaration, an affidavit usually is required from at least one of the witnesses that the will was executed in accordance with state law.

- **Voluntary signature**   A valid will must contain the voluntary signature of the testator. Again, state laws usually are quite specific on this issue. Some states will allow for a signature by mark if the individual is unable to sign his or her name. Nearly every state requires that the signature be witnessed or notarized, or both. State law spells out the number of witnesses required. Puerto Rico requires three witnesses and a notary. Usually state law will set forth exact language that should appear in the signature portion of the will, known as the *attestation clause*. The language will indicate that all of the necessary requirements for the execution of a will have been met.

An **attestation clause** is the portion of the will that is signed by the witnesses and which states that the will was executed in his or her presence.

An example of an attestation clause is as follows:

"Signed and declared by [Name of Testator] as his last Will, in the presence of us, who at the request of the testator, and in the presence of the testator and of each other, subscribe our names as witnesses."

SELF-PROVING DECLARATION

A self-proving declaration is a statement by the witnesses and the *testator* or *testatrix* that the document was executed in full conformity with the requirements of state law. With this self-proving declaration, a will can be admitted to probate without additional proof of proper execution Without this declaration, an affidavit is usually required from at least one of the witnesses that the will was executed in accordance with state law. A sample declaration from the Indiana Code appears below.

"UNDER PENALTIES FOR PERJURY, We, the undersigned _____ and the undersigned witnesses, respectively, whose names are signed to the foregoing instrument declare:

(1) That the testatrix executed the instrument and signified to the witnesses that the instrument is her will.

(2) That, in the presence of both witnesses, the testatrix signed or acknowledged her signature already made or directed another to sign for her in her presence.

(3) That she executed the will as her free and voluntary act for the purposes expressed in it.

(4) That each of the witnesses, in the presence of the testatrix and of each other, signed the will as witness.

(5) That the testatrix was of sound mind.

(6) That to the best of her knowledge the testatrix was at the time 18 or more years of age, or was a member of the armed forces or the merchant marine of the United States, or its allies."

Four states have no provisions for self-proving a will: Maryland, Michigan, Ohio, and Vermont. The District of Columbia has no statutory provisions for a self-proved will, but does allow for an abbreviated probate in which the will is presumed to be duly executed.

STRICTLY DEFINED

A **testatrix** is a term applied to a female who executes a will. The term **testator** applies to a male who executes a will.

PROCEED WITH CAUTION

Be aware that state laws may have changed by the time you read this book. Be certain to consult with your estate planning attorney about the requirements for executing a will in your state.

- **Disinterested witnesses** The witnesses to a will must be completely disinterested in the estate of the testator. This means they cannot be relatives of the decedent, nor can they be beneficiaries under the will. The consequences of violating this rule vary. The will might be declared null and void or become open to challenge, or the court might void certain provisions of the will that are in favor of those witnesses.

IMPORTANT WILL PROVISIONS

Every will has certain issues that must be discussed in the document. If a will is going to work properly, the following items must be included. If you already have a will, now is a good time to review it. If you do not yet have a will, read the following to see the issues that will be addressed in your will.

DESIGNATING THE PERSONAL REPRESENTATIVE

One of the most important functions of a will is to allow you the opportunity to select the individual or entity that will be in charge of paying bills, handling claims, and distributing your property in the manner that you have directed. Therefore, take the time to carefully think through your selection.

It is always a good idea to name at least one backup personal representative in case your first choice is unable or unwilling to serve. A good practice is to list two or three backups. This can save you from having to update your will to select a new personal representative.

Each state is allowed to make its own rules about who may serve as a personal representative. Generally, the state sets up the following criteria:

- The personal representative must be an adult.
- The personal representative must not have had any felony convictions.
- The personal representative must be a resident of the state or at least be authorized to do business in the state in the case of an institutional fiduciary.
- The personal representative must not have a disability that would interfere with his or her ability to follow the law and administer the estate.

The court always has some discretion to refuse to appoint a person it finds unsuitable or unable to serve. Some states will allow a non-resident personal representative to serve as long as a *resident agent* is appointed by the probate court and bond is posted.

MAKING SPECIFIC GIFTS

One of the advantages of having a will is the ability to designate who will receive specific gifts at your death.

A specific gift must be clearly set forth in the will and is usually designated as such. Specific gifts normally take priority over general gifts of the remainder of the estate.

A specific gift of property should designate clearly who the intended beneficiary is. Furthermore, any specific gift should make provisions for the disposition of the specific gift if the designated beneficiary predeceases the testator.

STRICTLY DEFINED

The term **lapse** refers to the situation where the intended beneficiary is unable or unwilling to receive a specific gift. This could be caused by the prior death of the beneficiary or it could be caused by the exercise of a disclaimer. The subject of disclaimers is covered later in this hour and in Hour 20.

Whenever a specific gift lapses, absent other instructions, the gift will be invalid and the specific item is distributed along with the remainder of the estate.

Some states have what is called an *anti-lapse statute*. The typical anti-lapse statute provides that whenever there is a specific gift made to a child (or sometimes any lineal descendant) there is a presumption that the gift does not lapse but rather is to be distributed to the heirs of the deceased child (or lineal descendant). Each state's laws must be reviewed carefully to determine whether there is an anti-lapse statute and to whom it applies.

DESIGNATION OF GUARDIANS

Whenever minor children or incapacitated individuals are beneficiaries of your will, it is very important that you designate whom you wish to serve as guardian. Guardianship can be over the person or the estate of an individual. Guardians over the person are responsible for the care and welfare of the individual. Guardians over the estate of an individual are responsible for handling the individual's assets. Most states require that the designation of a guardian be contained in your will. If not set forth in the will, your designation might have no binding effect.

GO TO ▶
Review the discussion of guardianship appointments in Hour 7, "Dealing with Lifetime Issues."

REVOCATION OF WILLS

There are two primary methods to revoke a will. It is very important to understand that each state's laws are different on this issue and must be consulted.

REVOCATION BY WRITTEN DECLARATION OR SUBSEQUENT WILL

The first generally accepted method of revoking a will is to execute a written document that specifically states the intent to revoke a prior will. A standard provision in a will, usually found in the opening paragraph, is that it is the intent of the testator to "hereby revoke any and all prior wills executed by me." With this language any will prepared by the testator will automatically revoke any prior wills.

However, the written document does not have to be another will. Any written instrument usually will suffice so long as the intent to revoke a prior will is made clear.

REVOCATION BY DESTRUCTION

The act of destroying a will, accompanied with the intent to revoke the will, constitutes revocation. The intent element is critical, since a will may be destroyed absent any intent to revoke the will, such as by storm damage, water damage, fire, and so on. There have been many cases of a will being introduced for probate with pencil or ink marks, cross-outs, crossovers, notes, and so on, written on the document. If each page contains a large "X," is that evidence of intent to revoke the will?

 FYI The best way to show intent to revoke a will is to totally destroy the original and all its copies. Anything less than that might be evidence of intent to retain the will as the valid last testament.

THE LAST VALID WILL PREVAILS

Whenever a person prepares a will, it will be presumed that his or her prior will is revoked. A person can have only one valid will disposing of his or her property. However, if there are two valid wills, each dealing with different issues and not contradictory, the court might find the second will to be an amendment to the first will and give both full force and effect.

JUST A MINUTE

 Some attorneys recommend making a new will on a regular basis, even if there is no change in the will. The rationale is that if the last will prepared is successfully contested, the court would then revert back to the next, most recently prepared will. Note that a valid will revokes prior wills, but an invalid will does not revoke anything. Therefore, the last valid will prevails.

AMENDING THE WILL

A will can be amended without revoking the first will. This is done by executing a *codicil* to the original will. The codicil will refer back to the prior will and indicate the provisions being changed. It is important to know that a codicil must be prepared with the same formalities as the original will.

STRICTLY DEFINED

An amendment to a will is known as a **codicil**.

JUST A MINUTE

As a practical and prudent matter, it is best to create a new will rather than amend prior wills. If the codicil is separated from the original will, it might never be probated. Sometimes several codicils can contradict each other, making the will difficult to administer.

Most states have specific statutes regarding the way provisions in a will operate when there has been a divorce. Typically, in the event of divorce, provisions contained in either ex-spouse's will that benefits the other will be declared null and void. However, it is not a good idea to rely on these statutes. Upon your death, the spouse might try to claim that you intended to leave those provisions in your will. Make sure you prepare a new will after a divorce.

UPDATING YOUR WILL

One of the most neglected areas of a person's estate plan is the will. If you are lucky enough to have one, it is entirely likely that it has not been updated for years. Actually, an old, out-of-date will actually could be worse than no will at all. The old will might contain trusts for minor children who are now adults. Guardians might have been appointed who are now deceased. Your personal representatives might no longer be able to serve. You might have children now that you did not have when the prior will was prepared. There might be references to assets that you no longer own. Finally, tax laws probably have changed since your will was prepared, making it obsolete and ineffective from a tax standpoint.

FYI It is always a good idea to review your will annually with your attorney. The cost should be minimal and you actually might learn something that will give you reason to make a change.

WHAT A WILL CAN AND CANNOT DO FOR YOU

Now it is time to put what you have learned about wills in the overall context of estate planning. Let's begin by reviewing some of the basic things that a will can do:

- A will allows you to set forth your wishes regarding how your property should be handled after your demise.

- A will allows you to set forth your wishes regarding how your children should be cared for after your demise.
- A will allows you to say who is going to be responsible for taking care of implementing your wishes.
- A will can give you a chance to save on taxes, depending on how you construct your plan.
- A will can ensure that those who owe you money pay it back.
- A will can provide for the continuation of your business.
- A will can provide for all kinds of contingencies, such as the prior death of a beneficiary, changes in asset ownership, changes in tax laws, and ages of children.

However, there are some things that a will simply is unable to accomplish for you. Some of those things are listed here:

- A will does not avoid the probate administration process.
- A will does not eliminate the need to hire an attorney.
- A will does not get your property to your heirs quickly.
- A will is not a private administration of your estate.
- A will is only effective if it was properly executed.
- A will does not avoid probate in other states where you own land.
- A will does not provide any assistance to you in the event of incapacity.
- A will does not control any non-probate property. Joint assets with right of survivorship, payable upon death accounts, life insurance, retirement accounts, and annuities with beneficiaries all pass by title—regardless of what the will says.

WILLS OF THE FAMOUS

Once you have a good grasp on the fundamentals of wills, it might be helpful—or at least interesting—to see some wills that were prepared by famous people to see how they were written. One will that is astonishingly short came from someone from whom you might expect to see an extensive and intricate will: Former Chief Justice of the United States Supreme Court, Warren Burger. His will is an example of brevity and appears here:

"LAST WILL AND TESTAMENT OF WARREN E. BURGER

I hereby make and declare the following to be my last will and testament.

1. My executors will first pay all claims against my estate.

2. The remainder of my estate will be distributed as follows: one-third to my daughter, Margaret Elizabeth Burger Rose and two-thirds to my son, Wade A. Burger.

3. I designate and appoint as executors of this will Wade A. Burger and J. Michael Luttig.

IN WITNESS WHEREOF, I have hereunto set my hand to this my Last Will and Testament this 9th day of June, 1994.

/s/Warren E. Burger

We hereby certify that in our presence on the date written above WARREN E. BURGER signed the foregoing instrument and declared it to be his Last Will and Testament and that at this request in his presence and in the presence of each other we have signed our names below as witnesses.

/s/Nathaniel E. Brady residing at 120 F St., NW, Washington, DC

/s/Alice M. Khu residing at 3041 Meeting St., Falls Church, VA"

HOUR'S UP!

Now it's time to see how much you have learned and retained from this lesson. Try to take the following quiz without referring back to the hourly materials:

1. A noncupative will is …
   a. Written
   b. Verbal
   c. Revoked
   d. Amended

2. To be valid, a will must always …
   a. Be notarized
   b. Have three witnesses
   c. Be written
   d. Be the final expression of the testator

GO TO ▶
The following wills of the famous are reprinted in the respective appendixes:

• The will of Diana, Princess of Wales, set forth in Appendix B

• The will of former President Richard Nixon, set forth in Appendix C

QUIZ

3. The execution of a valid will always …

    a. Avoids taxes

    b. Disposes of all of your property

    c. Avoids probate

    d. Directs the disposition of your probate property

4. A codicil is …

    a. An amendment to a will

    b. An amendment to a trust

    c. A designation of appointment from the probate court

    d. A document used to revoke a will

5. One good reason to have a will is …

    a. It will dispose of all of your property

    b. It will avoid probate

    c. It will provide for rapid distribution of your property

    d. It can provide for the continuation of your business affairs

HOUR 10
Revocable Living Trusts

CHAPTER SUMMARY

LESSON PLAN:

In this hour, you'll learn about the most popular of all estate planning tools: the revocable living trust. As you read this hour, you will understand how trusts work and how they differ from the use of a will. You'll also discover …

- How to prepare a living trust.
- What a trust does that a will does not do.
- Common misconceptions about living trusts.
- How to integrate your overall estate plan with a trust.
- The importance of funding your trust.

A living trust is a trust created during one's lifetime that owns property during lifetime and directs the disposition of those assets at death. Contrary to what many believe, living trusts are not new. History shows the use of a trust by Plato around 400 B.C.E. to finance a university. The first trust of record in America was drafted in 1765 by Patrick Henry for Robert Morris, governor of the colony of Virginia. This trust, known as the North American Land Company, is still operational.

Wealthy financiers have used trusts through the years. In fact, when people think of trusts, they often think of wealthy individuals setting up trusts run by banks. Fortunately, as individuals utilize the trust for their own family estate planning, some of these preconceptions begin to fade. The truth is, you don't have to be rich to set up a trust.

WHAT IS A TRUST?

The best way to understand a trust is to distinguish between two key issues: ownership and control. Let's start with ownership. Nearly all of us enjoy ownership of property. We all acquire property during our lives, including our home and the land it is built on, our investments, our retirement accounts, and our life insurance. We all love our cars and our clothes. However, if for some reason we were unable to control any of these items, we would be profoundly distraught.

The question is this: Is it the ownership of the assets or the ability to do whatever you want with them that brings you satisfaction? As long as you control all of these items, would it matter to you if you did not technically own them? At first this is difficult to envision. If you think that lack of ownership is the same as loss of control, conceptualizing a trust will be difficult. How can anyone have total control over an item but not own it? Quite simply, this is what a living trust allows. If you can accept that you might be able to control something you do not own, the trust will become a sensible concept.

WHAT IS A LIVING TRUST?

GO TO ▶
Refer back to our discussion of items included in your taxable estate in Hour 3, "What Is an Estate?"

A *living trust* is a legal entity that becomes the title owner to some of your property but allows you to maintain 100% control over that same property. Living trusts are known by various names: *revocable trusts, revocable living trusts,* and *grantor trusts,* to name a few. These names all refer to the same type of trust, which has the following qualities: It is revocable, which means you retain the power to alter, amend, or revoke any of their provisions; and it is "living," which means that it performs during the lifetime of its creator.

In most jurisdictions, the person who creates a trust is referred to as a *grantor* or *settlor.* In particular, the Internal Revenue Code defines these types of trusts as grantor trusts for income tax purposes. The rules that apply to these trusts are referred to as the *grantor trust rules*.

FYI The income tax rules defining a grantor trust are found at I.R.C. Secs. 671–679. There are five categories in which income will be taxed to the grantor based upon ownership. Those categories are reversionary interest, power to control beneficial enjoyment, administrative powers, power to revoke, and income for benefit of the grantor.

THE MECHANICS OF A TRUST

A trust is a legally recognized independent entity, which means that it has the ability to own property the same way as does a corporation, partnership, or other legal entity. Recall our earlier discussion about probate. Remember that certain property owned by an individual will comprise that person's probate estate. Individually owned property, tenancy in common property,

property payable to an estate are all examples of probate property. As you will see, the proper use of a living trust in your estate plan can eliminate the necessity of probate and likewise eliminate probate property from your estate.

How does a separate legal entity own property? It does so by becoming the title owner to that property. If a corporation owns property, the corporate name will appear on the title to the property. Likewise, if a trust owns property, the name of the trust will appear on the title to that property. A trust also can acquire property if it is a beneficiary on life insurance policies, retirement accounts, annuities, or payable on death account.

CONTROL OF A TRUST

The person that controls trust property is called a *trustee*. Normally, you will be the trustee of your own revocable trust. That is how you maintain control over all that is titled in the trust name. If you're married, you might establish a trust in which you and your spouse are co-trustees, which means you'd both maintain control over the trust.

GO TO ▶
Review the discussion of payable on death accounts in Hour 4, "Defining Types of Assets."

AVOIDING PROBATE

What if you own no property on the date of your death? Naturally, there would be no probate because there would be no probate assets in your name. This is exactly the goal when you establish a revocable trust. Property in trust is not subject to probate; instead, it is subject to the terms of the trust.

PROCEED WITH CAUTION

Don't designate your estate as the beneficiary of your trust, since doing so will subject all trust assets to probate administration. There is rarely any reason to name your estate as a beneficiary of your trust. Be certain to seek counsel should you have concerns with long-term care and Medicaid eligibility.

COMPARING WILLS AND TRUSTS

When you create a trust, you, as the grantor or settlor, transfer ownership of your assets to the trust. The trust then becomes the owner of that property. How does the trust transfer ownership to the beneficiaries after your death?

When you create the trust, you'll name the trust's beneficiaries and indicate how the transfer of the property will proceed.

PROCEED WITH CAUTION

The law of your state may have provisions that differ from the information contained in this discussion. Be certain to consult with your estate planning attorney.

As you know, a will also is a written document that contains instructions for the transfer of your property upon your death. However, a will does not contain instructions on the management of your property during lifetime because a will doesn't become effective until after your death.

Thus, a trust usually is more detailed than a will. It must provide instructions for the management of your property in the event of incapacity, something not required in a will. Assets are transferred during lifetime to a revocable living trust. A will does not require retitling assets. Also like a will, a trust contains instructions on who shall be the beneficiaries of the decedent's property and describes the manner in which the transfer should be accomplished. The primary difference here is in the mechanism for accomplishing this goal. A will uses probate administration through a personal representative to transfer property to the heirs of a decedent. A revocable trust uses only private administration through a successor trustee to transfer property to the heirs of a decedent.

EXECUTION REQUIREMENTS

Unlike a will, a trust has fewer technical requirements that must be met. That is one of the big advantages of a living trust: ease of creation. A trust need only be in writing and sufficiently definite enough to identify the following:

- The trust property
- The identity of the trustee
- The nature of the trustee's interest
- The identity of the beneficiary
- The nature of the beneficiary's interest
- The purpose of the trust

Trusts are not executed as testamentary instruments. This means that the laws that pertain to the validity of a last will and testament do not apply to the execution of a trust. Instead, the trust law in the state of residence governs trust execution requirements.

The Uniform Trust Code contains guidelines for creating a valid trust, among that the grantor (or creator) must have the capacity and the intention to create a trust and then designates a beneficiary.

HAVING THE CAPACITY

The grantor must have capacity to create a trust. The test for determining capacity is normally defined in the trust document itself. The following is a sample provision in a trust discussing incapacity.

"Whenever two licensed, practicing medical doctors who are not related by blood or marriage to [the grantor] certify in writing that I cannot discharge the duties of trustee because of mental or physical infirmity, then the office of that person shall be deemed vacated and the alternate trustee provisions shall apply."

EXPRESSING THE INTENTION

The grantor must indicate an intention to create the trust. This intention is made clear by the execution of the trust and the provisions contained in the trust document. The intent to create a trust can also be gleaned from a statement of the purpose of the trust, which should also be clearly stated in the trust document. A sample provision indicating the purpose of a trust follows:

"It is the purpose of this trust, among others, to provide for the management of all trust assets, both presently and during any future period of disability; this being a preferred alternative to guardianship proceedings and a simplified means of accomplishing both lifetime and death transfers of those assets."

DESIGNATING A BENEFICIARY

The trust must have a definite beneficiary. A beneficiary is definite if that beneficiary can be ascertained now or in the future from the language in the document. A clear designation of the name and/or relationship of the bene-ficiary to the grantor is normally sufficient. Interestingly, the Uniform Trust Code contains no requirement for notarization.

PROCEED WITH CAUTION

The law of your state may have provisions that differ from the information contained in this discussion. Be certain to consult with your estate planning attorney.

IMPORTANT TRUST PROVISIONS

There are some basic provisions that should be included in every trust agree-ment. Be certain to include each of the following in your trust agreement. Below is a discussion of some of the most important provisions.

PURPOSE OF THE TRUST

It is very important to establish the purpose of the trust. For example, most states mandate that one spouse cannot disinherit the other spouse. If one attempts in a will to disinherit the other spouse, state law usually gives the surviving spouse the right to choose to inherit according to the will or according to whatever the state law allows a surviving spouse.

Sometimes these statutes, designed to protect a spouse from disinheritance, apply only to probate property controlled by will. However, some courts will apply these statutes to trusts as well if it can be shown that the decedent intended to deprive the surviving spouse of the amount normally allowed by state law. This can be resolved only by examining the intent in establishing the trust. The purpose of the trust should be clearly indicated in the trust document.

When a spouse makes the election to receive what he or she is entitled to receive according to state law, instead of receiving what was given to him or her in the will, this is called "taking against the will."

IDENTIFICATION OF TRUST PROPERTY

Since a trust only controls trust property, it is a good idea to identify the assets that are in the name of the trust. It is very important to remember that your trust will not have any control over assets that are not titled in the name of your trust. Retitling is critical to the effective functioning of your trust.

TRUST FUNDING

Probably the most critical part of using a revocable living trust is the process of *funding your trust.*

STRICTLY DEFINED

Funding a trust refers to the process of transferring title to the name of a trust and designating the trust as beneficiary of certain contractual accounts.

You will recall the discussion in Hour 4 about the different ways we own property and the discussion of contractual assets. With that in mind, review the following:

- Only retitle assets that you want to have in your trust. (We will review assets that you may not want in your trust later in this hour.)
- Don't forget to title new assets in the name of your trust, such as new certificates of deposits, new brokerage accounts, and so on.

PROCEED WITH CAUTION

 Be careful when you identify trust property. Do not assume that assets listed on an attached schedule of property are automatically controlled by the trust. The trust must be the titled owner of those assets, which requires an actual change of ownership.

ASSIGNMENT OF PERSONAL PROPERTY

Remember that some assets—jewelry, clothing, furnishing, and farm implements, for example—do not have a title. With *untitled* assets, the way to transfer title is to make an "assignment" of that property to the trust. The easiest way to do this is to have an assignment provision in your trust. Another way is to use a separate document called a "Bill of Sale" that states your intention to assign all of your property to the trust.

Don't forget to assign untitled personal property to the trust. A failure to do so might require probate administration of those assets.

ASSETS YOU DO NOT WANT IN YOUR TRUST

You may choose not to retitle some assets to the trust. Review the following checklist:

- If you and your spouse have separate trusts (when you are trustee of your trust and your spouse is trustee of a separate trust), keep your personal checking accounts in joint names with right to survivorship. Then add a payable on death beneficiary. This will allow both you and your spouse to write checks on the account. The beneficiary designation will eliminate probate of that account after the death of you and your spouse.

TIME SAVER

Due to tax planning considerations, your attorney may recommend that you be the sole trustee of your trust, and your spouse be the sole trustee of his or her trust. The tip above is useful in this situation and will save you and your spouse many headaches. It is not necessary to keep a checking account out of your trust when you and your spouse have one trust and you are both trustees.

- **Contractual assets** Annuities, retirement accounts, and life insurance share one thing: They all have beneficiary designations. This means that so long as you have a beneficiary designated, the proceeds at death will not go through probate. Furthermore, qualified retirement accounts cannot be owned by a trust, so you would not be able to transfer ownership to your trust, even if you wanted to.

JUST A MINUTE

Be certain to check your beneficiary designations on these contractual assets and list a primary and a contingent beneficiary on all of them. Review these periodically to keep them up to date.

NAME OF TRUST

Unlike a will, every trust must have a name. The name of the trust should appear clearly and conspicuously at the beginning of the document. A trust usually is identified by the name of the trustee, followed by the name of the trust. The title also usually includes some reference to the revocable nature of the document and the date of execution.

JUST A MINUTE

 Using shorthand such as *u/a/d* (*under agreement dated*), *f/b/o* (*for the benefit of*), or *u/t/d* (*under trust dated*) saves space and is appreciated by transfer agents when it comes time to fund the trust.

IDENTIFICATION OF THE TRUSTEE

You must identify the trustee for a trust to be valid. State law will specify the requirements for serving as a trustee. Institutional trustees must have the power to act as trustee. Ordinarily, it is perfectly acceptable to name a beneficiary of the trust as a trustee. You also may serve as your own trustee. You also must designate your *successor trustees*—those people or entities who will serve if you are unable or unwilling to serve as your own trustee.

SELECTING A SUCCESSOR TRUSTEE

Successor trustees—trustees who will take over if the original trustee is unable or unwilling to serve in that capacity—generally will be one of the following:

- Family members
- *Institutional trustees*, such as banks and other corporate trust companies
- Unrelated individuals
- A combination of the above to serve together as joint trustees

STRICTLY DEFINED

The term **institutional trustees** refers to banks, brokerage firms, and other corporate trust companies that are authorized by state law to serve in the capacity of a trustee.

The following are some of the issues to consider when designating successor trustees. Some of these issues pertain to state law; others pertain to considerations that are more practical.

- Is the successor at least 18 years of age? Most state laws require a trustee to be at least 18. Do not attempt to designate a minor as a trustee.

- Where does the successor live? If the successor lives close to you, acting as successor trustee will be easier. This is not, however, a requirement. Many successor trustees live far away and can still efficiently handle the tasks of being a trustee.

- Is the successor a beneficiary? If so, consider whether the gift will be made directly to the beneficiary or held in trust for the benefit of the beneficiary. If the gift is to be held in trust, the beneficiary should not be designated as trustee. Otherwise, it normally doesn't matter whether or not the successor is a beneficiary.

- Is there any advantage to naming two or more successors to serve together? This arrangement is desired in some cases to make sure that not too much power is vested in just one trustee. While in the majority of cases this is not a concern, there may be some consideration given to co-trusteeship, such as ease of administration, joint decision-making, or just sharing of responsibilities.

- Will the appointment of a child as successor create any problems with his or her siblings? Only you can answer this question. If you feel that there may be a problem, consider naming an institutional trustee. The choice of an outside party to serve as trustee can help ease some family tensions.

- Will the successor trustee also be a trustee of a testamentary trust? The administration of a trust can actually extend two levels; the primary trust administration and the subsidiary trust administration. A subsidiary trust is one created in the original trust for beneficiaries, such as minors or disabled beneficiaries. Those subsidiary trusts are sometimes called testamentary trusts. As mentioned above, the trustee of a testamentary trust should not also be a beneficiary of the same trust.

- How many trustees should you designate? From a practical standpoint, consider choosing only one trustee to serve. This makes administration much easier.

Some of the problems found with individual trustees are …

- Lack of knowledge regarding trust administration. Sometimes the individual trustee is not well informed with regard to accounting issues or administration issues. Some individuals are simply not good with money. Those individuals should not be appointed to serve as trustee.

- Lack of knowledge regarding financial investments. This point goes along with the preceding point, which is that some people are not good money handlers. It would be much better for all concerned to use an institutional trustee in this situation.

- Death or incapacity of the individual trustee. If something should happen to your individual trustee, you must provide for the appointment of a successor. With institutional trustees, there is no death or incapacity. There may be buy-outs, but at least there will remain some legal entity in place to serve as trustee.

- Potential non-accountability of individual trustees. Institutional trustees are more accountable than individuals are since institutional trustees must account to appropriate regulatory boards. Professionals are hired to handle trust administration through institutions, whereas an individual trustee may not have the training or ability to properly account to the beneficiaries.

Offsetting these concerns are the following advantages of designating an individual person to act as trustee:

- You may not have to compensate an individual trustee, especially when the individual trustee is a beneficiary of the trust. In any case, the fee will probably be less than the fee an institutional trustee will charge.

- An individual trustee will probably have greater knowledge and familiarity with you, your family, and your intentions and desires.

- Having an individual trustee allows for greater flexibility with investment options, since an individual is not bound by some of the investment regulations that apply to institutional trustees.

When you consider using an individual person as a trustee, you should weigh the following issues carefully. All of these issues have bearing on your selection of trustee.

- **Family dynamics** When you think about naming your children or other family members as successor trustees, be mindful of family relationships. Obviously, if you are in a second-marriage situation, this issue is most apparent. Place yourself fifteen years down the road when your spouse dies and that spouse's child suddenly becomes trustee of a trust for your benefit.

- **Residency** Your trustee does not have to live in your home state. Even institutional trustees may be located out-of-state. Indeed, in today's technological age, residency poses no substantial barrier to qualifying and acting as a successor trustee. Documents can be signed and delivered electronically through fax and e-mail, and overnight mail can be sent most anywhere in the country at relatively minimal expense. Obviously if the choice is between a resident and a non-resident, all things being equal, the resident would be a more efficient choice (a non-resident may have to be bonded, as well).

DISCRETIONARY DISTRIBUTIONS

The trustee may also be a beneficiary of the trust. This fact can influence a trustee's discretionary functions. If appointed because of your incapacity, the successor trustee will usually be empowered to make discretionary distributions of principal and income to you for your health, maintenance, support, and education. If the exercise of this discretion results in diminishing the beneficiary's ultimate share, some undesired influences can exist. If you choose to use an individual beneficiary as a successor trustee, try to minimize the use of discretionary distributions.

ISSUES OF INSTITUTIONAL TRUSTEES

Some people shy away from using an institutional trustee for their trust. Some of the problems perceived with the use of institutional trustees are …

- **Loss of direct control over the trust assets**   An institutional trustee is much less personal and trust departments follow their own investment rules when administering a trust. As a beneficiary, you probably will not be able to direct the investments.

- **Insistence on putting client's investments into the trust institution's common trust funds**   Banks and brokerage firms will normally utilize their own investment sources when handling trust administration. The investments as they existed at death may be sold and/or reinvested in bank securities or brokerage accounts.

- **Lower than desired returns on trust fund investments**   Banks and other institutional investors are bound to follow very strict investment rules when handling trust accounts. They will not invest in risky investments and often will not invest in growth funds. They will not risk principal in their investments.

- **Poor communication with trust officers**   This can occur in large trust departments that may not assign a single individual to the trust account. There may also be varying levels of skill among trust officers as well as delegation of responsibility among various members of the staff, which may result in poor communication and misunderstandings as instructions are related to more than one person.

- **Rotation of trust officers from time to time**   There can be significant turnover in trust departments. This can be frustrating to those who come to associate a trust department with a particular officer, who later leaves the bank, retires, or dies.

- **Expense of institutional trust companies**   Trust companies do not do their work free. They will be paid what they consider a reasonable fee for their services. Some people do not like the idea of paying for these services.

Despite these concerns, institutional trustees are not without their advantages. Some of the benefits of an institutional trustee are as follows:

- Highly trained and professional staff with substantial experience

- Some degree of protection because trust companies are bonded and insured

- Impartiality when it comes to difficult family situations or second marriage situations

- Stability over the long term, especially important when a trust is established for minor children

Institutional trustees can also be of great benefit to an elderly couple or individual that needs assistance with asset management. They can also be of great benefit where an independent, non-family member is desired due to perceived or real family problems.

It is usually best to include a provision in the trust document that will allow a beneficiary to remove an institutional trustee and replace that trustee with either another institutional trustee or an individual trustee.

PROCEED WITH CAUTION

 The power to replace an institutional trustee with an individual trustee may cause serious estate tax problems with larger estates subject to the federal estate tax. If you contemplate using this provision, be certain to discuss this with your estate planning attorney.

DESIGNATION OF CO-TRUSTEES

Clients frequently wish to name two or more children as co-successor trustees. Some of the issues to address with co-trustees are …

- How well do the co-trustees get along?
- Will all co-trustees be required to act together on all issues?
- Will a co-trustee be allowed to act independently from the other co-trustees?
- If one co-trustee is unable or unwilling to serve, will the remaining trustees continue to act or will another successor be appointed to serve with the remaining trustees?

If an individual is serving as co-trustee with an institutional trustee, it is a good idea to speak with a representative of the institutional trustee to gain an understanding as to how that institution handles co-trusteeship with other individuals. Sometimes it may be better to designate one individual trustee and specify an institutional trustee as a "manager" of trust property, accountable to the individual trustee.

A well-drafted document will identify who is authorized to act when there are two or more trustees. Designating two co-successor trustees without providing for the ability of one to act without the other can create some difficult administrative problems.

TRUSTEE PROVISIONS

Trust documents must provide for any number of eventualities, including succession of trustees, who serves as trustee when the one designated is incapacitated, how to compensate trustees, and other details. Let's take a look.

SUCCESSION

By the time a designated trustee is called upon to serve, he or she might be unable or unwilling to serve in that capacity. This could be as a result of death, incapacity, geographic relocation, or a variety of other reasons. Because of this, it is important whenever possible to appoint several successor trustees who will serve if the original successor trustee is unable or unwilling to serve.

In the event all of the named successor trustees are unable or unwilling to serve, then a court will be required to appoint a successor trustee. In order to eliminate judicial involvement in this process, a provision can be inserted in the trust providing a method for the selection of a successor trustee.

RESIGNATION

There is always the possibility that an acting trustee will no longer wish to continue in that capacity. Take care to specify the procedure for resigning as trustee. This not only provides for a definitive method for resigning; it clarifies when a successor trustee becomes responsible for the trust assets.

COMPENSATION

To pay your trustee or not to pay your trustee: That is the question. In many cases, a beneficiary of the trust is named as successor trustee. In these situations, it is customary not to offer the trustee compensation. One reason for this is that the trustee/beneficiary will inherit a share of the trust property and he or she won't have to pay taxes on it, but if you pay him or her, the salary will be taxable income. One exception to the non-compensation idea is if your trustee ends up serving for several years on your behalf because you've become incapacitated. When this occurs, even a trustee who is also a beneficiary may be entitled to compensation.

HOW MUCH IS ENOUGH?

Establishing the amount of compensation is actually quite difficult. Sometimes, an individual will designate a specific dollar amount as compensation. What happens, however, if the successor trustee serves for a short period, is paid the designated dollar amount, and then resigns? Should the next successor trustee be paid the same amount? Will a set dollar amount provide adequate compensation for a successor trustee who serves for several years due to incapacity of the grantor?

You might want to use the phrase "reasonable compensation" in your trust document, but if you do, also establish what "reasonable" is. You might choose to use the fee schedule of an institutional trustee in the community as a guideline, or allow adult beneficiaries to approve any fee paid to the successor trustee.

If you decide to compensate the trustee in an amount based on a percentage of the value of the trust, you have to define that amount with care. Should it be a percentage of the value of the *gross trust property*, the gross taxable estate, the *net trust property*, or net taxable estate? If net, what expenses are subtracted to determine net? Are all reasonable expenses from the trust subtracted first to determine net? If so, arguably compensation to the trustee is a "reasonable expense," resulting in a circular calculation that cannot be solved, since the amount of compensation depends on a determination of the net trust value, which, in turn, requires a determination of the amount of compensation.

STRICTLY DEFINED

The **gross trust property** is the total value of the trust assets, without reduction for debts, taxes, and expenses of administration. **Net trust property** is the value after those deductions. Remember from the discussion in Hour 3 that the gross taxable estate (before reduction) and net taxable estate (after reduction) may include property that is not controlled by the trust, such as life insurance proceeds, retirement accounts, and annuity proceeds.

BOND OF TRUSTEES

A bond is similar to an insurance policy for the personal representative or successor trustee. It provides protection for the beneficiaries in the event the estate or trust property is destroyed, diminished in value, or otherwise affected to the detriment of the beneficiaries.

It is difficult in many cases to obtain a bond for a successor trustee, since there is no court supervision of the trustee. This may also offend the designated successor trustee, who may feel that there was a lack of trust in his or her ability to properly handle the responsibilities of being a trustee. Typically, bond is not required for a successor trustee.

ACCOUNTING REQUIREMENTS

It normally is appropriate for a successor trustee to report his or her estate activities, or *account* to the beneficiaries of a trust. The question is how often the accounting is to take place. One option is to waive all accounting to the beneficiaries. Obviously, this is particularly appropriate if the trustee and the beneficiary are the same person. You also can waive accounting to a court, but require accounting to the beneficiaries on a regular basis, such as every three or six months, or every year. Be certain to specify to whom the accounting is to be made.

TRUSTEE POWERS AND DUTIES

Typically the largest portion of a revocable trust is the designation of trustee powers. You should be careful when listing the powers of the trustee; it is best to be specific. If the power is not specified, some trustees will not risk exercising that power, even if state law indirectly gives that power to the trustee.

Some of the typical powers given to a trustee are ...

- To sell, convey, pledge, mortgage, lease, manage, operate, control, transfer title, divide, convert, or allot the trust property
- To retain nonproductive assets
- To borrow money for any purpose
- To establish lines of credit
- To acquire or dispose of an asset
- To make improvements, alterations, or ordinary or extraordinary repairs of buildings or other trust property
- To vote a security
- To buy, sell and trade in securities of any nature
- To insure the assets of the trust against damage or loss
- To advance money for the protection of the trust and for all expenses, losses, and liabilities sustained in the administration of the trust
- To pay or contest any claim
- To commence or defend litigation with respect to the trust
- To enforce any mortgage
- To pay taxes
- To continue or participate in any business
- To pay the grantor'(s) debts
- To deal with governmental agencies

One of the most significant differences between a will and a trust is the trust's ability to deal with the incapacity of the grantor. It is critical that the trust include instructions and guidelines for the use of trust assets for the grantor and his or her family. The duties of the successor trustee under these circumstances can be divided into four major categories:

- The trustee is required to use the trust assets and income exclusively for the benefit of the grantor. This choice should not be used when trust assets will be needed for the benefit of minor children or other dependents of the grantor.

- The trustee is required to use the trust assets and income for the benefit of the grantor and the children and dependants of the grantor. This choice is appropriate when there are minor children or other dependents.

- The trustee is required to use the trust assets and income for the benefit of the grantor(s) and the spouse of the grantor(s). This choice is appropriate when providing for a spouse.

- The trustee is required to use the trust assets and income for the benefit of the grantor and others who are identified in the document. This will allow for the use of the trust principal and income for individuals other than minor children or dependents such as parents, brothers, sisters, and so forth.

PROVISIONS FOR REVOCATION, AMENDMENT, AND TRANSFER

Unlike a will, a revocable trust is a fully functioning legal entity during the lifetime of the grantor. Thus, it is critical to address lifetime administration issues that are not pertinent in a will. For instance, when creating the trust it is crucial that you include the powers to revoke and amend at any time. When a single trust is used for a married couple be certain to provide that the trust is revocable and amendable by either spouse during their joint lifetime, and that it continues to be revocable and amendable by the surviving spouse until death or incapacity.

Some drafters prefer to make the trust amendable by joint action of the spouses during their joint lifetimes. The idea is to preserve family unity and not allow one spouse to amend the trust without the knowledge of the other spouse. The problem with this approach is the difficulty of planning for the incapacity of one spouse. Is the trust irrevocable if joint action is not possible? Can a guardian of the incapacitated spouse exercise the powers of amendment and revocation along with the other spouse? Allowing either spouse to revoke or amend is cleaner and usually works well.

Furthermore, it's important that you recognize how you own property when you create the trust. Quite often a married couple will own property in a variety of ways. Both might have separate property that they would like to keep separate, plus their jointly owned assets. This is especially true in community property states.

You might want to maintain the basic character of such property in the event of revocation of the trust. If so, you should specify that upon revocation the trust property will be returned to the original owners the same way it was held before the transfer into the trust.

You also could designate that each spouse has a right to withdraw one half of the trust assets at any time without the permission of the other spouse. The inclusion of this power will support an argument that each spouse has an "undivided one-half interest" in the trust. This allows a surviving spouse to disclaim his or her one-half interest if this would facilitate the intentions of the parties, particularly in future estate tax issues.

GO TO ▶
Review the discussion of disclaimers in Hour 20, "Marital Trusts and Disclaimer Planning."

PROCEED WITH CAUTION

The law contains very specific requirements for the proper execution of a disclaimer. Always consult a lawyer before executing a disclaimer.

FURTHER THOUGHTS ON INCAPACITY

One of the most important functions of a living trust (and one most frequently overlooked) is to contain provisions that will provide for continuity of management of assets during a period of time in which you are incapacitated. The failure to address this issue will result in the failure of the document to accomplish one of its most important tasks.

In our previous discussion of the designation of successor trustees, I discussed the various provisions that should be selected which will detail the purposes for which trust property can be utilized during incapacity. These included using the property solely for the grantor; for the grantor and the grantor's spouse; and for the grantor and the grantor's spouse and descendants.

Furthermore, in the event a grantor or, in the case of a married couple, both spouses, become institutionalized in a long term care facility, you must be aware of the impact of such provisions on possible Medicaid eligibility.

When a provision is inserted in the document that requires the trust principal and income to be used *exclusively* for the health, maintenance, and support of the institutionalized spouse, the trustees will be obligated to apply all of the trust property and income generated by the property toward the nursing home expenses of that spouse. This could adversely impact on eligibility for government assistance.

PROCEED WITH CAUTION

Be certain to consult with an estate planning attorney in your state to inquire about the impact of this language on eligibility for government assistance.

When there are separate trusts for a married couple (which is common for estates over $675,000 [in 2001] and also in second marriage situations), a provision that mandates the use of the trust corpus and income exclusively for the individual grantor's health, maintenance and support will deprive the spouse and any dependent children of the use of these assets. This can create problems for all concerned if this is not the intended result.

PROTECTING THE TRUST

Protecting assets is a special consideration when planning your estate. The revocable trust, however, is not designed as an asset-protection tool. Assets within the trust are still subject to claims made by your creditors.

You can, however, protect the assets from certain claims made by creditors of a beneficiary before distribution of the trust.

SPENDTHRIFT PROVISIONS

A spendthrift provision is one that states that the trust assets are unavailable to creditors of a beneficiary and others who may make a claim against the beneficiary's share of the trust. Always include spendthrift provisions in your trust document in order to keep the beneficiary's share free from claims of creditors, marital claims, and bankruptcy claims. Unfortunately, since revocable living trusts are grantor trusts, spendthrift provisions will not protect the trust property from claims made by your creditors.

PROCEED WITH CAUTION

Understand that the assets in your trust remain subject to creditor claims to the same extent as they would had the property not been transferred. It is a good idea, therefore, to purchase an umbrella policy that will cover liability in excess of your existing coverage for homeowners and auto insurance. Consider a two-million-dollar policy.

IN TERROREM PROVISIONS

An in terrorem provision is one that invokes a penalty against anyone contesting the trust. Because of legislative and judicial pronouncements in many states, in terrorem provisions in wills have been declared void as against public policy. This means that those states will not enforce a provision that it does not believe is consistent with other fundamental rights, such as the right to marry and the right to utilize the court system to resolve disputes. The author is unaware of any similar decisions declaring such provisions invalid where they appear in a trust document.

It would be a good idea to include an in terrorem provision in the trust any time there is an unequal distribution of assets or a total disinheritance of one or more heirs.

This provision should address the power of the trustee to elect *arbitration* as a form of dispute resolution in lieu of judicial litigation.

STRICTLY DEFINED

Arbitration is a private determination of the rights of parties to a dispute that, if binding, precludes court involvement.

The inclusion of such provisions would not be void against public policy since arbitration is now a favorite manner of dispute resolution utilized by courts. Furthermore, the inclusion of such a provision may deter potential litigants from challenging the trust. The mere possibility, for example, that a litigant may have to pay all costs and attorney fees if a claim is brought against the trust may stop the filing of a frivolous claim against the trust.

PROCEED WITH CAUTION

If you plan to transfer your home to your trust, be certain to contact your title insurance company and obtain an amendment to your title insurance policy to provide for continued coverage before you make the transfer. A failure to do so might result in a loss of coverage.

COMMON MYTHS CONCERNING LIVING TRUSTS

Following are some of the most common misunderstandings about a revocable living trust.

- **You have to have a bank or other financial institution handle your money and property** *False*. The reason living trusts are gaining such acceptance is because you continue to handle your property just as you would without the trust. It is not necessary for a third party to be a trustee.

- **Living trusts are just for wealthy people** *On the contrary*, a person with a "small" estate has just as much need for a living trust as would someone with an estate in excess of $1,350,000 in 2001 ($675,000 × 2). Unless you have a trust, your estate will likely go through probate, whether you have a will or not. The living trust avoids probate and the costs and time delays so frequently associated with probate.

 FYI The use of separate trusts for a married couple can result in doubling the exemption available to beneficiaries for purposes of calculating state inheritance taxes. Contact an estate planning attorney about this possible benefit.

- **Once your money and property are in trust, you'll never get your property out of the trust** *False*. Unless you create an irrevocable trust for a particular tax reason, you can revoke your trust at any time during your lifetime. This means you can put property into trust, take it out of trust, or just terminate the trust entirely whenever you choose.

- **Once I die, my living trust will continue indefinitely and my heirs might never get my property** *Not true*. You write your own living trust and you decide when your property will be distributed to your named heirs. If you want them to receive your property and to terminate the trust immediately upon your death, your successor trustee will do so. If you want part of your property to remain in trust for some time before distributing such property to your heirs, your trustee must follow your instructions. For example, you might not want your children to receive your property until they reach certain ages; your trust can continue after your death until those children reach those ages.

PROCEED WITH CAUTION

 Whenever you create a trust, be certain to prepare a new will naming your trust as beneficiary. This is referred to as a pour-over will. It does not avoid probate, but will ensure that any assets not covered by the trust or by beneficiary designation will be placed into the trust at death because of the will. It also revokes all prior wills and ensures the consistency of your estate plan.

- **It is very difficult to get your property out of your trust** *False*. It is no more difficult to get your property out of a revocable living trust than it is to put it in the trust. Simply say so in writing and transfer any titles back to your name. You can sell or convey your property held in trust just as you would if you didn't have a trust, except you do so as "trustee" rather than as an individual. You can convey it out of trust back to yourself individually or to a third person. Termination of your trust is as easy as saying so in writing.

- **Placing my property into a living trust will have adverse income tax consequences** *Not so!* Transferring your property into a revocable living trust for which you are your own trustee results in absolutely no adverse income tax consequences because you continue to "own" the property according to the IRS. It is not even necessary to obtain a separate tax identification number for your trust while you are living. Furthermore, you will not lose any income tax deductions by placing your property into a living trust.

- **If I establish a revocable living trust I will have additional tax returns to prepare each year** *Also not true*. A revocable living trust established with you as your own trustee does not create a separate taxable entity during your lifetime; therefore there are no additional tax forms for you to complete. You will continue to complete your tax returns the same way you have in the past.

- **A will is much cheaper than a trust** *Not necessarily*. When weighing your options, remember that a will must be probated if it is to be effective. Therefore, you should add the cost of probate to the cost of the will. Similarly, you should consider the extra cost of a trust along with the potential cost of administering a trust. Your attorney should be able to provide you with some comparisons.

- **When I die, my living trust document will have to be filed with the court before my property can go to my designated heirs** *Not true*. A living trust is a private, legally enforceable document that does not have to be filed with the court when you die. Your successor trustee has the legal obligation to distribute your property in the manner you specify in the trust, much like an executor would have to do in following the terms of your will. A copy of your trust will have to be attached to all tax filings, such as the federal estate tax and state inheritance taxes.

- **I will lose my social security benefits if I establish a living trust**
  Nope. A living trust has absolutely no impact upon your Social Security benefits. Social Security benefits are considered to be income to you, and you do not lose any rights to receive income solely by virtue of establishing a living trust.

- **I will have to assign my mortgage and automobile loans to the trust**
  Not unless you want to. Normally, your debts are not assigned to a trust. The trust holds assets; not liabilities. However, if someone owes you money the promissory note should be assigned to your trust to ensure continuity of payment after your death.

- **Once I prepare a living trust, I will not have to do any follow-up**
  A trust must be reviewed on a regular basis to insure that it meets your needs. Additionally, you must fund your trust for it to work properly.

PROCEED WITH CAUTION

Be certain to notify all lien holders and mortgage holders before making a transfer of your home to your trust. Depending on state law, lien holder rights may be effected by any transfer of property and under certain conditions your mortgage holder may be entitled to accelerate your note under a "due-on-sale" clause. Be certain to discuss this issue with your estate planning attorney.

HOUR'S UP!

Now it's time to see how much you have learned and retained from this lesson. Try to take the following quiz without referring back to the hourly materials:

1. With a living trust, probate will be avoided …
    a. Immediately upon execution of the trust
    b. Never; the trust must be filed with the probate court just like a will
    c. Only if you change beneficiaries
    d. Only if assets are owned by the trust and all assets with beneficiary designations are paid to someone other than your estate.

2. To be valid, a trust must always ...

    a. Be notarized

    b. Have three witnesses

    c. Be written

    d. Be executed one year before death

3. Once a trust is executed ...

    a. You must be sure it is properly funded

    b. There is nothing else to do

    c. You must record it in the recorder's office in the county of your residence

    d. It will guarantee no probate of your estate

4. Properly funding a trust requires ...

    a. That a dollar bill be taped to the document

    b. That you attach a schedule of property to the trust agreement

    c. That you retitle your assets to the name of the trust or designate the trust as a beneficiary

    d. You tell everyone you have a trust

5. One good reason not to have a trust is ...

    a. You have to obtain a separate taxpayer identification number

    b. It will actually increase your taxes on capital gains

    c. A trust is far more expensive to your estate than is a will

    d. None of the above

Hour 11

Wills and Trusts: Important Provisions

Chapter Summary

LESSON PLAN:

In this hour, we'll explore some of the most common provisions found in wills and trusts. You'll find a brief summary of each type of provision, along with tips on when to use them. Understanding some of these basic provisions will help you to understand the document drafted for you by your attorney. You'll also learn ...

- How to provide for the payment of debts and taxes.
- Why you need survivorship provisions.
- Why you need simultaneous death provisions.
- The best way to distribute residue.
- How to provide for the repayment of debt.
- Handling disinheritance.

Every will and trust should contain provisions for the payment of debts and taxes. It is important to use correct wording for the payment of these expenses to insure that you obtain the proper result. For example, a common provision involves *tax apportionment*.

STRICTLY DEFINED

The phrase **tax apportionment** refers to the allocation of taxes to the recipient of property causing the tax.

Many documents simply state that "taxes shall be paid out of the *residuary* estate," which means the debt will be paid after other bequests are made. Here's how it works: Suppose that the decedent left a specific gift of a closely held business to his son, and the entire residue to his daughter. The result would be that the son gets the business without paying any taxes and the daughter only gets what is left over after taxes are paid. In this circumstance, it would be better to have a tax apportionment clause that provides that the beneficiaries pay their portion of taxes based on the value of the property they receive. In this case, the son would pay taxes based on the value of the business.

However, because not all assets are controlled by will or trust, tax and expense apportionment can backfire. As you learned in previous chapters, life insurance, retirement accounts, and annuities all contain beneficiary designations of their own. These assets pass by contract—not by will—and usually are not titled in the name of the trust. Therefore, if your trust's or will's tax apportionment clause states that all expenses are paid out of your probate or trust estate, the beneficiaries of your life insurance, retirement accounts, and annuities will pay none of these taxes or expenses. The burden of paying the taxes falls squarely on those who receive the probate or trust assets.

Herein lies the danger of writing your own document. Although it sounds and looks easy, you can end up with some very unhappy beneficiaries if you don't understand how the tax apportionment clause works. First, take care when you define "debts." If you direct the personal representative or trustee to "pay all debts," you might force him or her to pay an *unenforceable debt*—a debt that actually doesn't need to be repaid under the law. An example of this is a debt for which the statute of limitations has passed.

Second, be careful when you make a bequest that is contingent upon the payment of a debt. An example of this is giving a residence to someone but requiring him or her to pay the existing mortgage. In that case, you'll want to choose an alternate beneficiary in case the beneficiary cannot or will not assume the debt.

Third, make sure you're clear what property, if any, you want to be sold for the payment of expenses of administration, debts, and taxes. Otherwise, the personal representative or trustee will decide, and his or her decision could interfere with your plans to make a specific gift of a particular piece of property. For example, if you don't spell it out in the document, your trustee or personal representative might decide that it is best to sell your residence and some rental properties—even if you specifically left that property to your daughter. This decision could be made due to market conditions, ease of administration, or the need to obtain cash to pay expenses.

SURVIVORSHIP PROVISIONS

You'll also need to specify what should happen to property if a beneficiary dies within a specified period after your death. For instance, suppose you and your spouse, to whom you've left the bulk of your estate, are in a car accident and your spouse dies just after you do. Without a survivorship clause, the beneficiary will inherit from you even if he or she died minutes after your death. If this occurs, your property will pass immediately to the beneficiary's estate, which then distributes it in accordance with his or her will or trust, or in accordance with state law.

You can protect yourself against this by crafting a survivorship provision that allows your estate to be distributed according to your alternate wishes if a beneficiary dies within a specified time—usually 30 days—after your death. On the other hand, if your spouse is your primary beneficiary, you might want to rethink such a survivorship clause. Making gifts to your spouse can result in tax benefits because transfers to surviving spouses are exempt from federal estate tax and most state inheritance taxes (the marital deduction). For example, if you and your spouse should die in a common accident with your spouse dying one minute after you do, it might be better for the property to pass to your spouse so your estate can still benefit from the marital deduction. Obviously, this will depend on the particular circumstances of each estate. This is something you should discuss with your attorney.

SIMULTANEOUS DEATH

But what happens if you and your spouse die at the very same time or there's no real way to know who died first? What happens to distributions to the "surviving spouse"? It's up to you and your attorney to spell out the answer in what's called a simultaneous death provision. You may choose to designate that, in such cases, you will be presumed to predecease your spouse, and the provisions of your will or trust are to be carried out accordingly. This would allow for a marital deduction from your estate to that of your spouse. If you do not want the terms of your spouse's will or trust to control, you may choose to state that the presumption is that you survived (and your spouse predeceased you).

JUST A MINUTE

 Make sure to include a simultaneous death provision—it occurs more often than we care to believe. Consider the deaths of John and Carolyn Kennedy and the couples who died in the crash of Egypt Air Flight 990. Think about how often you and your spouse travel together by automobile.

You and your attorney should review relevant state law when drafting this provision. In fact, most states have some form of simultaneous death statute. There is also a Uniform Simultaneous Death Act that provides that the property of each spouse shall be distributed as if each survived the other, whenever there is no way to determine who actually died first. If both spouses have the same plan of distribution in their wills or trusts, it will not matter who dies first. In second marriages, however, each spouse may be distributing property in their wills or trusts to a different set of beneficiaries. This clause can drastically affect who will benefit from the estates.

Simultaneous death provisions sound contradictory. If the husband is presumed to survive the wife, then the husband's will or trust controls the distribution. But if the wife is also presumed to survive the husband, the wife's will or trust should control the distribution. Which one actually controls the distribution? The answer is that both do. The statute says the "property of each person shall be disposed of ...." The husband's solely owned property, therefore, will be controlled by his will or trust. The wife's solely owned property will be controlled by her will or trust. Jointly owned property will be divided 50/50, with each half controlled by each spouse's respective will or trust. If husband and wife have a single trust with the same dispositive provisions, the issue becomes moot, because either way the distribution plan is the same for both spouses.

PROCEED WITH CAUTION

Don't forget about your beneficiary designations on life insurance, retirement accounts, and annuities. The simultaneous death statute also applies to these assets where the spouse is designated as a primary beneficiary. *Always* designate a contingent beneficiary (or several) who will receive the property in the event the spouse either dies first or is *presumed* to die first.

DISTRIBUTING THE RESIDUE

Ultimately, all the property you own, after debts, taxes, and expenses of administration, must pass to someone. As mentioned earlier, we refer to what's left over as the "residue" of your estate. A common provision is to distribute "all of the rest, residue, and remainder of my estate among my three children, in equal shares." Have you thought about how to accomplish such wishes? Are your assets liquid and ready to be distributed equally? Will property have to be sold to satisfy this directive for equal distribution?

One way to solve this problem is to allow one beneficiary the option of purchasing a particular piece of property at fair market value. The other beneficiaries can receive a portion of that cash as part of their gift. If you're concerned that the beneficiary won't have the cash to pay for the property up front, you can provide that he or she receive it once it is paid for. You then can divide the rest of your property among the remaining beneficiaries.

JUST A MINUTE

Unless the terms of the will or trust provide otherwise, the beneficiaries may agree on the sale of an asset to one of them, with the purchase price deducted from the purchaser's share. This cannot be accomplished, however, if the document stipulates that property must be sold at public sale, or uses similar language.

When a person receives a specific asset it is referred to as a distribution *in kind*. Otherwise, the distribution is said to be *pro-rata*, or in undivided interests.

JUST A MINUTE

Remember, if a beneficiary purchases an asset, this is simply an exchange of cash for the asset itself. The cash is then divided according to the instructions in the residuary clause. On the other hand, when a beneficiary receives specific property as part of their share, the value of that property received must be subtracted from that beneficiary's share of the estate.

PAYING BACK DEBT

Frequently, parents will lend money to their children for such things as buying a home, financing an education, or starting a business. Sometimes these are gifts, and thus the parents don't intend for their children to pay them back. Other times, however, they consider it to be a loan and expect to get the money back. Unfortunately, because the loan exists between parent and child, no promissory note usually exists. Even if there is a note, the due date may be "on demand" or otherwise vague in nature.

When the parents die, must the children repay the debt? That's another question you must answer in your will or trust. Drafting an appropriate debt repayment provision can be tricky, as you can see from the following example.

Suppose you have three children. Child A owes you $50,000, Child B owes you $20,000 and Child C owes you nothing. The net value of your estate is $180,000.

Suppose the will or trust directs an equal distribution among your three children and the debt repayment provision provides that "each child's share shall be reduced by any unpaid debt owed to me at the time of my death."

First, if you calculate "each child's share" this would amount to $60,000 ($180,000 ÷ 3 = $60,000). When you subtract each debt, the children would then receive the following amounts:

Child A: $60,000.00

      –$50,000.00

      $10,000.00

Child B: $60,000.00

      –$20,000.00

      $40,000.00

Child C: $60,000.00

       –$0.00

      $60,000.00

If you add up the total amount distributed to the three children, you get $110,000 ($10,000 + $40,000 + $60,000 = $110,000). However, the total amount available to distribute is $180,000. Who then gets the extra $70,000?

This is an example of how a simple phrase that appears to reflect the intent of the decedent creates an incorrect and problematic result.

Now lets assume you have two children. Child A owes you $20,000; Child B owes you nothing. The value of the net estate available for distribution is $100,000.

Suppose the will or trust directs an equal distribution between the two children and the debt repayment provision provides that *"each child's share shall be reduced by any unpaid debt owing to the decedent at the time of decedent's death."*

If there were *no* debt, each child's share would be $50,000 ($100,000 ÷ 2 = $50,000). If there *was* debt but it was *repaid* before death, the total amount available for distribution would be $120,000 ($100,000 + $20,000 = $120,000), and each child's share would be $60,000 ($120,000 ÷ 2 = $60,000).

Using this language, each child would receive the following amounts:

Child A: $50,000.00

             –$20,000.00

             $30,000.00

Child B: $50,000.00

              –$00.00

             $50,000.00

The total amount distributed to the two children is $80,000 ($30,000 + $50,000 = $80,000), but the total amount available to distribute is $100,000. Who will get the extra $20,000?

If Child B gets the extra $20,000, his share would be $70,000, which is $10,000 more than the $60,000 he would have received had the debt been repaid!

FYI In order for a debt repayment provision to work, make the subtractions for unpaid debt from *the sum of* the total amount available for distribution *plus* the total amount of unpaid debt.

Finally, assume that you have three children. Child A owes you $50,000, Child B owes you $20,000, and Child C owes nothing. The value of the net estate available for distribution is $180,000.

Suppose the will or trust directs an equal distribution among the three children and the debt repayment provision provides as follows:

"The distribution provided for above shall be made by first adding together the total amount of trust assets available for distribution, plus the balance of any remaining unpaid indebtedness owned by any child to me or my spouse at the time of distribution. The amount to be distributed to my children shall be determined from this combined amount. There shall then be deducted from each beneficiary's share the remaining balance of any unpaid indebtedness owned by such beneficiary at the time of distribution."

If there were *no* debt, each child's share would be $60,000 ($180,000 ÷ 3 = $60,000). If there *was* debt, but it was *repaid*, the total amount available for distribution would be $250,000 ($180,000 + $70,000 = $250,000), and each child's share would be $83,333.33 ($250,000 ÷ 3 = $83,333.33). Using this calculation, each child would then receive the following amounts:

Child A:	$83,333.33
	−$50,000.00
	$33,333.33
Child B:	$83,333.33
	−$20,000.00
	$63,333.33
Child C:	$83,333.34
	−$00.00
	$83,333.34

The total amount distributed to all three children is $180,000 ($33,333.33 + $63,333.33 + $83,333.34 = $180,000), and the total amount available to distribute is $180,000. Now everything comes out even!

PROCEED WITH CAUTION

In some cases it is the desire of the drafter of the will or trust to forgive a debt owing from a beneficiary at death. If this is your wish, you would not want to use a debt-reduction clause.

DISINHERITANCE

Sometimes families are not a cohesive unit and a child does not have any meaningful communication with his or her parents for years. Other times there may be the wrong kind of communication, including threats of lawsuits by beneficiaries who thought they should get more and other trouble for the other legitimate beneficiaries. If your family is in such a state, you'll want to pay close attention to this section.

WHO YOU CAN DISINHERIT

To begin with, you must be clear on whom you can disinherit. If it is your intent to disinherit a spouse, for example, you must be mindful of the ramifications. Spousal rights, also known as the *spousal allowance*, are protected by statute. This protection consists of a statutory guarantee that the spouse will inherit from her deceased spouse's estate, despite any contrary provisions contained in the will of the deceased spouse.

STRICTLY DEFINED

The **spousal allowance** is a right provided by state law allowing a surviving spouse a minimum guaranteed percentage of probate property at the death of the first spouse to die.

These guarantees usually consist of specific dollar amounts that are guaranteed to the surviving spouse. The law of each state varies, but a general rule of thumb is that the surviving spouse will be allowed at least $1/3$ of the probate estate of the deceased spouse. It is difficult to generalize since each state differs considerably.

Some states base the percentage share on the length of the marriage, which percentage can go as high as 50%. Some states authorize $1/3$–$1/2$ of the estate regardless of the length of marriage.

FYI There are variations in the spousal share, depending on factors such as whether or not there are surviving children and whether or not the marriage is a first marriage or a subsequent marriage.

The spousal share is usually only guaranteed out of the probate property. This means that the only assets available to satisfy a spousal share are probate assets. If there are no probate assets or if there are insufficient probate assets to satisfy an allowance, the entire spousal allowance will not be satisfied. The spousal share does not typically extend to non-probate property, such as accounts with beneficiary designations or jointly owned property with rights to survivorship. Some states limit the allowance out of the probate estate.

If probate property becomes non-probate property, such as where a single name account becomes joint with right to survivorship, the issue then becomes whether or not there was an intent to defeat the spousal allowance by making the change in ownership. If it is judicially determined that there was a wrongful intent to prevent property from being subject to a spousal allowance, the courts will likely hold that the property must be counted in determining the spousal allowance.

The general conclusion that can be drawn from this is that a spouse is a "protected person" and cannot be arbitrarily disinherited without consequences.

 FYI This does not mean that a person cannot make single name property joint with someone other than a spouse, or transfer individually owned property to a trust for the benefit of someone other than a surviving spouse. The issue is not whether or not it can be done, but whether or not the primary motivation in doing so was to deny the spouse his or her elective rights. Intent, therefore, becomes the critical issue.

How to Disinherit

Any time there is a desire to disinherit someone, you must be very careful to document your intentions. It is this author's opinion that the best way to "disinherit" someone is to identify the individual and include a statement, without explanation, that it is your desire not to provide for that individual. When explanations are included in a will or trust for disinheriting someone, there is fertile soil to challenge the logic and factual basis for the explanation.

Likewise, contrary to popular opinion, when a client chooses to disinherit someone, there is no legal requirement to leave him or her "one dollar." If this language is used, the successor trustee or personal representative will be required to search for the individual and obtain an address for that person, then send the check for $1.00 to the individual. This can create headaches when the individual cannot be located or refuses the payment.

 FYI Contrary to popular belief, children are not "protected" from disinheritance. While many believe that you must leave something to a child, the author is unaware of any state that prohibits disinheriting a child.

PROCEED WITH CAUTION

 Another effective method to disinherit someone is to state that you have "intentionally and with full knowledge omitted to provide for all heirs not specifically mentioned in the terms of this document." This is sometimes referred to as a "general disinheritance."

IDENTIFICATION OF BENEFICIARIES

As is true for most aspects of drafting wills and trusts, the more specific, the better when it comes to identifying your beneficiaries. If you aren't specific, your intentions might be difficult to discern. For instance, if you designate your "children" as beneficiaries, does that mean only the children alive when you draft the will, or would you want to include any children born after you've done so? The same problem crops up if you designate "nieces and nephews" or other groups of family members. You may choose to specify the names of the children. If you might have more children after you draft the document, define what you mean as well as you can.

SPECIFIC GIFTS

Many people like to leave a beneficiary a specific item of property. Typically, these items are family heirlooms, such as wedding rings, jewelry, or pictures. They may also be collectibles, such as antiques, coins, or gun and sport collections. Occasionally, a parcel of real estate, such as a farm, may be given to one person to live on and/or farm, especially when that person has expressed an interest in the farm and also when the other siblings, for example, live elsewhere and are not interested in farming.

The document should be clear with regard to when the gift is to take place. If a spouse survives the decedent, typically the gift provisions will not be accomplished until after the death of the surviving spouse. If this is not specified, certain gifts of valuable property could be gifted to beneficiaries when the first spouse dies, even though the other spouse survives. This can create problems when the property gifted is expected to belong to the surviving spouse, such as household goods and furnishings and jewelry.

Similarly, it is a good practice to identify what happens to the specific gift if the designated recipient dies first or disclaims the gift. Will the property pass to the heirs of the designated recipient; to the spouse of the designated recipient; or along with the residue of the will or trust to the remainder beneficiaries? Clarifying this when you have your document drafted can save time and litigation expenses.

HOW TO MAKE SPECIFIC GIFTS

You may wish to designate that certain items of personal property, such as family heirlooms, tools, or jewelry, be designated to pass to a particular beneficiary. Either these specific designations can be placed within the will or trust document itself or can be made in a separate writing.

Most states require that a separate writing be executed prior to the execution of the will referencing that writing. The will can reference this pre-existing document, but cannot reference a document that is not yet in existence. This is an area where trusts have more flexibility than a will. Trusts are usually able to reference a document not yet in existence at the time the trust was prepared. When using a separate writing, be certain to include a provision in the document that refers to the separate writing and provides that those provisions are to be incorporated "by reference" into the document itself.

A specific gift form is a list of assets along with the intended beneficiary of each, which is attached to a trust. The use of a specific gift form rather than designating the specific gifts in the trust document can prove beneficial for the reason that it will not be necessary to amend the trust document to change specific gifts. All that would need to be amended would be the specific gift form. This saves you the expense of a trust amendment and is much more convenient.

There is, however, a downside to the use of a separate writing for specific gifts. Although extremely convenient, a separate writing can easily be the subject of litigation or claims. Some of the problems that can arise include:

- Claims that you did not have sufficient mental capacity to execute the separate document
- Claims that you were operating under undue influence at the time your executed the separate writing
- The potential that your intent may be unclear where there are several amendments
- The potential for the separate writing somehow to mysteriously "disappear"
- The potential for the language to be ambiguous, making your intent uncertain

In order to avoid these serious problems, it is recommended that you sign the separate writing in front of at least two independent, disinterested witnesses whose names appear on the separate writing. Notarization would also help in the event of future litigation.

Another important issue to make clear in both the trust agreement itself and the separate writing is when the gift shall become effective. Should it be effective upon the first death or upon the death of both spouses? Remember that the surviving spouse may be able to amend the trust after the death of the first spouse and alter the specific gift instructions. In fact, the surviving spouse may make his or her own gift of that item during the lifetime of that surviving spouse, making the specific gift a nullity.

DISTRIBUTION PROVISIONS

The next step is to outline how the will or trust property is to be administered following your death. All wills and trusts must choose among a few options for distribution. These options are as follows:

- Distribute the entire trust or probate property among the beneficiaries outright.
- Distribute a portion of the trust or probate property among the beneficiaries (or selected beneficiaries) outright and retain the remainder in trust for specified purposes, for a specified period of time.
- Retain the entire trust or probate property in trust for specified purposes, for a specified period of time.

Under the first option, the personal representative or trustee must make a distribution of all property within a reasonable time following your death. You should decide whether you want the property to be distributed as is, or sold and the proceeds distributed. You might leave instructions for specified property to be sold.

When distribution instructions are drafted, be certain to do the following:

- Identify the specific beneficiaries by name and relationship (spouse, each child [and possible future children], and so forth).
- Specify the share of each such beneficiary.
- Provide for alternate distributions if the named beneficiary dies first, becomes incapacitated, or disclaims the gift.
- Utilize percentages whenever possible. Rather than specify a dollar amount for a gift, it is better to leave a percentage of your residuary estate to the beneficiaries. In this manner you are assured that a proportionate amount of what you have to give at death is divided among the beneficiaries. Your estate may not have the amount specified if you mentioned a dollar amount.

Identifying the beneficiaries by name and relationship will help the personal representative or trustee accurately distribute the estate to the appropriate beneficiaries. For example, if in the will or trust you request a distribution "among all of my nieces and nephews," the personal representative or trustee has the burden of identifying those nieces and nephews. This task can expose the personal representative or trustee to liability for failure to use due diligence in determining heirship and might even require a court determination of heirship. This creates additional expense and delay.

If you want an equal distribution among the named beneficiaries, be certain to include language such as "in substantially equal shares among." Including the word "substantially" eliminates liability of the trustee or personal representative for the minor variations in value that can occur when distributing property *in kind*.

STRICTLY DEFINED

In kind refers to the distribution of specific assets to a beneficiary, as opposed to an equivalent cash value.

Of great importance is the question of what happens if the intended beneficiary predeceases the decedent. The complexity of this issue cannot be overstated. A few examples might be helpful to show you what can happen.

Imagine you're a widow and have three children, A, B and C. Each child is married and has three children. You want the property to pass equally among the three children. Suppose Child A predeceases you. Do you want the property to pass to the surviving spouse or the surviving grandchildren or both? Suppose you want the property to pass among the surviving grandchildren. Will the distribution be *per stirpes*, whereby the one-third share of Child A will pass to the grandchildren, one-ninth each; or will the distribution be *per capita*, whereby the two surviving children and the three grandchildren share equally one fifth each? (Per capita is extremely rare, as it tends to create very angry children!)

STRICTLY DEFINED

As you may remember from Hour 2, "Inheritance and the Laws of Intestate Succession," the phrase **per capita** means to take (acquire) by head count. **Per stirpes** means to take (acquire) by representation. The phrase **by representation** refers to a manner of distribution whereby the beneficiaries receive the same share that would have been received by a deceased ancestor.

If you decide to include the spouse of a deceased child, be aware that the share passing to the surviving spouse might end up in a subsequent marriage and might result in a disinheritance of the surviving grandchildren. You might wish to establish an irrevocable trust with an independent trustee distributing the gift for the benefit of the surviving spouse and the grandchildren. This will ensure that the grandchildren will inherit as you intend.

Now carry this scenario one step further: Suppose the children of Child A receive a one-sixth share each. Suppose further that these are minor children and the property is to be held in a trust for their health, maintenance, education, and support until they reach 30 years of age. Assume one of the grandchildren dies unexpectedly at the age of 21. What provisions have been included in the will or trust document for the distribution of that deceased grandchild's remaining share? Do you want that share to pass to the siblings of the deceased grandchild or divided in equal shares between your surviving two children?

What if the grandchild is married at the age of 18 and dies at the age of 21? Should the spouse of the deceased child inherit the share of the deceased grandchild? What if the grandchild has a child? Do you want the share of the deceased grandchild to go to the great-grandchild? These are issues you must consider and clarify in your will or trust.

JUST A MINUTE

I recommend that you designate percentage distributions rather than specific dollar amounts because you won't know now what the size of your estate will be at the time of your death. Specific dollar gifts in small amounts might be relatively safe, but larger sums might not be available in liquid form for distribution, which might require that property be sold to satisfy the specific gift even if that wasn't your intent. Percentages will work with any size estate and can allow for pro-rata distributions of probate or trust property.

I also recommended that a "catch-all" phrase be included covering the unlikely situation in which all of your named beneficiaries predecease you. A typical phrase would simply provide that the will or trust would be distributed to your heirs. Some people select a charity for the beneficiary if all other beneficiaries are deceased or to a friend or relative.

PROCEED WITH CAUTION

As with all of the material in this book, be certain to consult an estate planning attorney before implementing any of the techniques discussed in this book. The failure to obtain professional advice could result in additional expenses for administering your estate and could result in additional and unnecessary taxation of your estate. Additionally, the failure to properly prepare documents according to applicable law may render the documents useless.

HOUR'S UP!

Now it's time to see how much you have learned and retained from this lesson. Try to take the following quiz without referring back to the hourly materials:

1. The importance of a tax apportionment clause is …

    a. It ensures that the taxes are paid out of the residuary estate.

    b It allocates the tax burden to those receiving the taxable property.

    c. Only probate property is affected by this clause.

    d. Trust property is never affected by this clause.

2. The problem with distributing a specific dollar amount is …

    a. The beneficiary might not think it is enough.

    b. Percentage distributions are too hard to calculate.

    c. The tax burden is disproportionately allocated.

    d. Your estate might not have that much in liquid assets.

3. A distribution of property in kind means …

    a. A specific asset is given to the beneficiary.

    b. The gift to the beneficiary is thought to be very considerate.

    c. All property is divided proportionately among the beneficiaries.

    d. Only one beneficiary can receive the residue of the estate.

4. A debt repayment provision should provide ...

    a. That all unpaid debt is forgiven

    b. That all unpaid debt is to be paid by the estate

    c. That all unpaid debt should be paid by the other beneficiaries

    d. That the combined assets available for distribution plus the unpaid debt is divided up, followed by a subtraction of debt owed by each particular beneficiary from that beneficiary's share

5. When considering the disinheritance of a beneficiary ...

    a. One dollar is the least amount that can be given to a beneficiary.

    b. You cannot disinherit your children.

    c. It is not necessary to leave them one dollar.

    d. You should give very specific reasons for choosing to leave them nothing.

QUIZ

HOUR 12

Powers of Attorney, Health Care Representative Appointments, and Living Wills

Most people have seen or might even have signed some type of power of attorney. Powers of attorney are commonly used to allow someone to sign your name on tax returns or to sign checks when you are unable to do so yourself.

STRICTLY DEFINED

The person executing a power of attorney is called the **principal**. The person who is appointed to act on behalf of the principal is called the **attorney-in-fact**.

The use of a power of attorney in the context of estate planning is vital. The power of attorney will help to cover gaps left as a result of the use of some other estate planning tools.

Most individuals are not aware of the various types of powers of attorney that are available and do not understand clearly the uses for each type. The following discussion will clarify the numerous types of powers of attorney that can be used for estate planning.

GENERAL POWER OF ATTORNEY

Powers of attorney can be categorized by whether they are *general* or *special*. A general power of attorney is a document that gives someone broad powers to act on your behalf. The validity and effectiveness of a power of

CHAPTER SUMMARY

LESSON PLAN:

In this hour, you'll learn the value of having these three documents in your estate planning toolbox. You will understand how these documents work together to avoid guardianship. In many respects these three documents may prove more valuable to you than either your will or your trust, at least in regard to lifetime issues involving illness or incapacity. You will also learn ...

- The different types of powers of attorney.
- All about health care representative appointments.
- The relationship between a living will and a health care appointment.

attorney is not affected by its status as general or specific. Instead, the term "general" refers only to the extent of the power being conveyed.

It is important to note that the principal does *not* have to be disabled or incapacitated for the power of attorney to be effective.

The following is a sample of the introductory paragraph of a general power of attorney:

> I, [name of principal], do hereby appoint [name of attorney-in-fact] as my true and lawful attorney-in-fact, for me, in my name, and on my behalf, to do any and all acts which I could do if I were personally present. My attorney-in-fact may perform for me and in my name and on my behalf any act pertaining to the care, supervision, and management of my affairs that I personally have authority to perform. My attorney-in-fact may exercise for me and in my name and on my behalf all, but not limited to, those powers set forth below. This power of attorney shall apply to all property owned by me.

SPECIAL OR LIMITED POWER OF ATTORNEY

A special power of attorney conveys very specific, limited powers to the attorney-in-fact. This type of power of attorney conveys no powers other than those designated. You'll often see a special power of attorney used in real estate transactions in which the owners have moved to another state and they appoint an attorney-in-fact to represent them at the closing of the sale of their former home. Sample language from a special power of attorney for real estate closings follows:

> I give to my attorney-in-fact the powers prescribed by section (2) of Ind. Code §30-5-5, _Real Property Transactions_, which powers are incorporated herein by reference. The powers given herein shall specifically authorize my attorney-in-fact to act on my behalf with regard to the sale of certain real estate located at [address], [city], [state], and all associated property involved in the sale thereof (including personal property which might be sold along with said real estate) and to execute any and all necessary documents required at the closing of said property transaction on my behalf.

DURABLE POWER OF ATTORNEY

Powers of attorney also can be categorized in terms of whether or not they are *durable*. When a power of attorney is durable, it will continue to be effective even if the principal later becomes incapacitated. Most special or limited powers of attorney are not durable. They are executed for a particular purpose and are not intended to be effective after that particular purpose has been fulfilled.

General powers of attorney may or may not be durable. It is very easy to visit a local office supply company and find legal forms, including powers of attorney. The most common powers of attorney are written to convey powers, special or general, to an attorney-in-fact during the lifetime and competency of the principal. Most of these documents specifically state that if the principal becomes incompetent the power of attorney terminates and the authority granted to the attorney-in-fact ceases.

Although valuable in some circumstances, this type of power of attorney serves no useful purpose when it comes to estate planning. The value of a power of attorney in estate planning is to make sure someone has the power to act on your behalf if you are unable to so act. To accomplish this, you must be certain to have a durable power of attorney. By including the term "durable," this power of attorney will authorize an individual to act on behalf of the principal. The attorney-in-fact can act as such while the principal is competent and continue through the principal's incapacity until his or her death.

The following is a sample of the type of language used to indicate that a power of attorney is *not* durable:

> *"This power of attorney shall continue to be effective until such time as I am determined to no longer be capable of handling my affairs. Such determination shall be made by at least two licensed physicians."*

Following is a sample of language making the power of attorney durable:

> *"My disability or incompetence shall not affect or terminate this Power of Attorney."*

Springing Durable Power of Attorney

One type of power of attorney that is quite valuable in estate planning is called the *springing* durable power of attorney. A springing durable power of attorney gives authority to an attorney-in-fact to act on behalf of the principal only if at some later time the principal becomes incompetent. It will not convey authority to the attorney-in-fact until a physician determines that the principal is incapacitated. This document is useful for people who do not wish to give authority to any other person so long as they are competent and able to handle their own affairs.

The following language designates a springing durable power of attorney:

> *"This power of attorney shall be effective upon the determination that I am disabled or incapacitated, or no longer capable of managing my affairs. My disability or incapacity may be established by the certificate of a licensed physician stating that I am unable to manage my affairs."*

JUST A MINUTE

Most powers of attorney are immediate, meaning they convey powers to the attorney in fact upon execution of the document. Special language is normally required to make a power of attorney "springing."

PROCEED WITH CAUTION

One of the goals of estate planning is to have documents in place so that they are ready when needed. The springing power of attorney requires an additional step before it is effective: the physician's statement of incapacity. Problems may also arise when the principal becomes *physically* ill and unable to handle his or her affairs, but does not become *mentally* incapable of handling his or her affairs.

TERMINATION AT DEATH

It is most important to know that there is no power of attorney that conveys any power to act on behalf of a deceased principal. Powers of attorney are not testamentary. The only value of a power of attorney is to act on behalf of the principal during lifetime. Upon death, the power of attorney terminates as a matter of law. Any further acts taken on behalf of the principal must be made by the duly appointed personal representative.

As effective as they are, powers of attorney are not a panacea for estate planning purposes because they do not lend any assistance to the testamentary distribution of the principal's estate.

PROCEED WITH CAUTION

The law of your state may have provisions that differ from the information contained in this discussion. Be certain to consult with your estate planning attorney.

REQUIREMENTS FOR EXECUTION

The requirements for execution of a power of attorney actually are quite simple. A power of attorney must be signed by the principal in writing and either witnessed or signed in the presence of a notary public, depending on state law. These documents are state law–specific and must be created to conform to state law requirements.

COMPENSATION AND REIMBURSEMENT

Attorneys-in-fact can be authorized to receive reimbursement for expenses in addition to a reasonable fee for serving as such. The power of attorney document must be very specific on these issues. Courts construe powers of attorney *strictly*, meaning that if the document does not specify a particular power or a particular fee, the court will not infer such power or fee from the document.

RECORDATION REQUIREMENTS

Again, state law will control whether a power of attorney must be recorded to be effective. Most statutes require only that the document be recorded when used as part of a real estate transaction. State law will also specify where the document is to be recorded.

REVOCATION

You can revoke a power of attorney at any time, as long as you do so in writing and notify all relevant parties of the revocation. Consider the following language, which is common in powers of attorneys:

> "I hereby ratify and confirm all that my attorney-in-fact shall do by virtue hereof. Further, I agree to indemnify and hold harmless any person who, in good faith, acts under this power of attorney or transacts business with my attorney-in-fact in reliance upon this power, without actual knowledge of its revocation."

This indemnification language is needed to allow others to rely upon representations made within the power of attorney. Otherwise, financial institutions and others would not risk liability by acting in accordance with a power of attorney. The mere fact that the principal has revoked the power of attorney does not mean the institution relying upon it is aware of the revocation.

Care must be taken in the use of a power of attorney because third parties (those relying upon the authority granted in a power of attorney document) do not need to inquire into the authority granted by the document and may rely on the document until such time as the third party is notified of the death of the principal or the revocation of the power of attorney document.

Therefore, you must give notice of revocation to all who may be operating on the assumption that it is still valid. Additionally, if the power of attorney document has been recorded, you must also record the revocation.

ADVANTAGES

There are numerous advantages to having a valid power of attorney. Some of those advantages are as follows:

- A power of attorney is relatively inexpensive.
- Using a power of attorney can eliminate the need for guardianships over the assets of an incompetent person.
- Use of a power of attorney can authorize steps for the preservation of assets for long-term care purposes as well as tax reduction purposes.

PROCEED WITH CAUTION

Granting someone an immediate general power of attorney will empower that individual to exercise full control over your assets, even if you are still competent. Be extremely careful when using these documents and do not give them out to the attorney-in-fact until necessary.

HEALTH CARE REPRESENTATIVE APPOINTMENT

PROCEED WITH CAUTION

The law of your state may have provisions that differ from the information contained in this discussion. Be certain to consult with your estate planning attorney.

The health care representative appointment is much like a special durable power of attorney. The special power granted in this power of attorney is to make health care decisions on behalf of the principal.

Like other powers of attorney, you must comply with state law to ensure that your document will be useful when needed. Most of the ordinary provisions discussed above are included in the health care power of attorney.

Some lawyers incorporate the health care powers into the durable power of attorney. Although there is nothing wrong with this approach, the following are reasons for making the document separate:

- You might want to have someone other than your attorney-in-fact serve as your health care representative. For example, a son happens to be a nurse and would be excellent for making health care decisions, but a daughter might be a banker and be an excellent choice for attorney-in-fact. You must evaluate your own situation to make this determination.

- You may prefer to make only the health care document available to the medical provider, without giving the medical provider the rest of the power of attorney document. This keeps those provisions separate from the provisions in the power of attorney that pertain only to property.

- It's often better to create the health care appointment along with the living will (which we will discuss next) and to keep those documents separate from the durable power of attorney.

JUST A MINUTE

The health care appointment does more than a living will. This appointment provides for the making of any medical decision, regardless of whether it involves artificial life support. This might be more valuable than the living will and undoubtedly would be used more often.

Following is a sample of some of some of the powers that might be included in your health care appointment.

"Consent, refuse consent, or withdraw consent to any care, treatment, service or procedure to maintain, diagnose or treat a physical or mental condition and to make decisions about organ donation, autopsy and disposition of the body;

Make all necessary arrangements at any hospital, psychiatric hospital or psychiatric treatment facility, hospice, nursing home or similar institution; to employ or discharge health care personnel to include physicians, psychiatrists, psychologists, dentists, nurses, therapists or any other person who is licensed, certified, or otherwise authorized or permitted by the laws of this state to administer health care as the agent shall deem necessary for my physical, mental and emotional well being; and

Request, receive, and review any information, verbal or written, regarding my personal affairs or physical or mental health including medical and hospital records and to execute any releases of other documents that might be required in order to obtain such information."

LIVING WILLS

The living will is a fundamentally important document to include in your estate plan. Frequently mistaken for a "living trust," this document will convey your wishes regarding artificial life support and artificially supplied nutrition and hydration. As is true for most estate documents, living wills are creatures of state law and you must comply with the execution requirements of state law to make the document valid. Most living wills include instructions for whether life-prolonging measures should be rendered and usually contain some request that you receive pain medicine or other care necessary for your comfort. Needless to say, it's important to have a living will to clarify your wishes.

PROCEED WITH CAUTION

The law of your state may have provisions that differ from the information contained in this discussion. Be certain to consult with your estate planning attorney.

EXECUTION REQUIREMENTS

Most living wills require the signatures of two to three witnesses. You also should give a copy of the document to your health care provider and, if he or she will not comply with your wishes, you might want to find another doctor who will. Most hospitals now offer, and in some cases, require, that a patient execute a living will upon being admitted to the facility.

PROCEED WITH CAUTION

As with all of the material in this book, be certain to consult an estate planning attorney before implementing any of the techniques discussed in this book. The failure to obtain professional advice could result in additional expenses for administering your estate and could result in additional and unnecessary taxation of your estate. Additionally, the failure to properly prepare documents according to applicable law may render the documents useless.

HOUR'S UP!

Now it's time to see how much you have learned and retained from this lesson. Try to take the following quiz without referring back to the hourly materials:

1. If you want to have a power of attorney that continues to be effective after a determination of incapacity, you want one that is …

    a. Springing

    b. Powerful

    c. Durable

    d. Special

2. The difference between a general and a special power of attorney is …

    a. A general power of attorney applies only to specific events.

    b. A special power of attorney is one that you worked hard to get.

    c. A special power of attorney covers only specified transactions.

    d. A general power of attorney does not include health care powers

3. The person appointed in a power of attorney is called …

    a. Special

    b. Attorney-at-law

    c. Health care representative

    d. Attorney-in-fact

4. A living will is …

    a. Binding on the physician

    b. Not binding on the physician

    c. The same as a living trust

    d. The same as a health care representative appointment

5. If you need someone to make medical decisions for you in situations that do not require life support, you will need …

    a. A living will

    b. A living trust

    c. A health care representative appointment

    d. A will

Part V
Special Assets

Hour 13   Life Insurance

Hour 14   Retirement Plans

Hour 15   Business Entities

HOUR 13

Life Insurance

LESSON PLAN:

Life insurance is one of the most versatile and common products. However, there is good news and bad news: Although life insurance creates unexpected solutions to many estate planning problems, it also might require paying some unexpected taxes when not titled correctly. In this hour you will learn …

- The different types of life insurance.
- How life insurance is taxed.
- Advantages of life insurance.

Recall our discussion of life insurance as a part of your taxable estate in Hour 3, "What Is an Estate?" Usually overlooked when examining your estate, *life insurance* can increase an estate to the point where federal estate taxes become a planning issue.

The fact that insurance is not paid until the insured's death is probably the very reason why most people do not consider this part of their taxable estate. Most people have a tendency to include only the *cash value* of a life insurance policy as an item of value in their taxable estate. This happens because the cash value is the only part of the insurance that the owner has access to during lifetime.

Life insurance is an important estate planning tool to provide cash for the payment of estate and inheritance taxes, debts, administrative costs, and other estate expenses. We have already discussed how life insurance death benefits add to the value of the taxable estate. In this chapter, we will review the various types of life insurance available. With this understanding, you will be in a better position to appreciate some of the estate planning techniques available to reduce estate taxes.

Life insurance is a contract under which the insurer agrees to pay to the insured, in return for a premium, a defined amount upon the death of the insured.

LIFE INSURANCE POLICIES—A CLOSER LOOK

GO TO ▶
One of the most valuable tools available is the irrevocable life insurance trust. This trust is discussed in detail in Hour 17, "Irrevocable Life Insurance Trusts."

There are many different types of available life insurance. Each of these types of policies has a specific purpose. Understanding these purposes will help you find the right product for your needs. Below is a short description of the most basic types of life policies.

Life insurance **cash value** is the portion of a life insurance policy that represents accumulated premiums plus earnings on those premiums remaining after policy expenses have been deducted.

TERM INSURANCE

Term insurance is "pure protection." There is no cash value built into this type of policy. The amount of the premium is based upon the amount of coverage. In early years, the premium is relatively inexpensive. The owner receives the maximum short-term protection for a minimum cash outlay. In later years, however, the cost increases dramatically due to the age of the insured in relation to mortality tables.

Following is a sample illustration of a term life policy with a coverage amount of $500,000 for a male non-smoker who was born on September 11, 1953, and lives in Indiana. This is a 30-year policy, guaranteed level premium for 10 years (The premium will not increase during the first 10 years of this policy. After that, the premiums will increase.)

Policy Year	Age	Annual Premium
1	47	$1,195
2	48	$1,195
3	49	$1,195
4	50	$1,195
5	51	$1,195
6	52	$1,195
7	53	$1,195

Policy Year	Age	Annual Premium
8	54	$1,195
9	55	$1,195
10	56	$1,195
11	57	$9,565
12	58	$10,495
13	59	$11,545
14	60	$12,715
15	61	$14,015
16	62	$15,595
17	63	$17,185
18	64	$19,095
19	65	$21,205
20	66	$23,475
21	67	$25,935
22	68	$28,575
23	69	$31,455
24	70	$34,705
25	71	$38,985
26	72	$42,635
27	73	$47,515
28	74	$52,995
29	75	$58,875
30	76	$65,135
30-Year Total		$593,650

FYI As you probably know, all life insurance companies have different premiums for the same amount of coverage. This is true even when comparing policies of the same type, such as whole life, universal life, and so on. This is simply an illustration. You must consult with your insurance agent to get a real quote for you.

The question you must ask yourself is whether the term insurance payment schedule makes sense for you. As you can see, the first 10 years have a relatively inexpensive annual premium for the amount of death benefit, which can make it appear attractive. However, if your goals are to use this policy to pass along the death benefit to your heirs, you must continue to look at the increased premiums after year 10. For example, the difference between years 10 and 11 is a shocking $8,370!

You must ask yourself if it is economically feasible to continue making these enormous payments until the age of 76, which will cost you a total of $593,650 over the entire term of the policy, with a death benefit $93,650 less than the premium paid into the policy. Remember, term insurance has no cash value. All of the money you pay in is used to purchase insurance. Nothing is left over after the premiums are paid except the value of the death benefit.

Term insurance is best used for short-term needs. During the initial years of a term policy, the rate is low enough to allow the policy owner to save extra money in a separate investment. As that separate investment grows in value, the need for insurance might diminish, allowing the policy owner to reduce the death benefit; thus reducing the premium.

JUST A MINUTE

The efficiency of "buy term and invest the difference" is a hotly debated topic and is beyond the scope of this book. Because cash value builds up within a policy tax free, it may be difficult to find a comparable investment outside the policy. A financial planner will be happy to compare investment programs with you.

Another type of life insurance is called decreasing term insurance. It has a death benefit that gradually decreases over time, which this allows the premium to remain relatively constant but the same dollars will buy less insurance each year of the policy. This type of policy can be an effective substitute for credit life policies, which tend to be more expensive than traditional term policies. Credit life insurance will pay off a particular debt in the event of death if there is still a balance owing at that time. Before taking out this type of policy, compare the premium expense with a decreasing term policy. You will likely find that the decreasing term policy is cheaper than the credit life policy.

WHOLE LIFE INSURANCE

The oldest form of insurance with a cash reserve is what is known as whole life insurance. Although still available, whole life has largely been replaced with some of the other types of insurance described in the following sections. The major characteristics of whole life insurance are as follows:

- The premium for a whole life insurance contract remains level throughout the life of the contract.
- Cash value builds up within the contract to maintain a reserve, which the insurance company needs to maintain a level premium as the insured ages. (This cash value increases annually and the policyholder can borrow against it or take it as surrender proceeds, which are close in amount to the cash value but tend to be a little less than the cash value due to some insurance expenses incurred upon surrender of the policy.

The most traditional form of whole life insurance is *ordinary* life (sometimes called *straight* life). With this policy, your annual premiums remain constant throughout the life of the policy. The premiums will be higher initially than the rates charged by term life insurance, but will be less than term life insurance as you age.

There are two major components to whole life insurance: the insurance component and the cash value component. This policy uses up a portion of your premium for insurance costs (the insurance component) and deposits the remainder of the premium into a cash reserve (the cash value component). This cash reserve earns a moderate rate of interest. If premium payments are missed, the insurance carrier will use the cash value to satisfy the premium costs.

An online request for a whole life policy paying a $500,000 death benefit and issued to a 47-year-old male non-smoker, born on September 11, 1953 and residing in Indiana, revealed the following quote:

Annual Rate
$1,115
$1,185
$1,195
$1,205
$1,215
$1,225
$1,230
$1,235
$1,250
$1,260
$1,300
$1,310
$1,325

These rates are not guaranteed, which means that the company actually might increase any given annual premium at any time during the life of the policy.

Whole life insurance does accumulate cash value in addition to providing permanent protection. You can borrow against the cash value for emergencies or for retirement, and the cash value grows on a tax-deferred basis. However, traditional whole life policies pay a comparatively low return on the cash value, making it a less attractive investment. Other policies discussed in the following offer a better growth rate for your cash value.

UNIVERSAL LIFE INSURANCE

A *universal* life policy has three separate components: investment, expense, and mortality. It works this way: The owner selects a death benefit level. The death benefit can be one that increases over time or remains level. From the premium paid by the owner, the insurer deducts a load (expense) for policy expenses and mortality charges. The remaining premium is credited toward the owner's cash value. The cash value earns interest at rates based on current investment earnings.

The terms of universal life policies vary from company to company. They are unique in that the policy owner selects the level of premium and death benefit desired and the length of time he or she will pay a premium. Significant flexibility in premium payments is possible. Although the contract owner usually has to pay a certain minimum premium during the first policy year, after that he or she can vary the amount, the payment date, or frequency of subsequent premiums.

The insurance company invests the cash value component of universal life in interest-sensitive investments, such as money market funds, whereas a whole life policy earns interest at a predetermined rate. The cash value in a universal life policy earns interest at a variable rate. There usually is a minimum interest rate earned by the cash value.

VARIABLE LIFE INSURANCE

With a *variable* life insurance policy, unlike the interest-sensitive investment of universal life, the policy owner can invest the cash value in equities (stock) and manage the investment decisions personally. For this reason, neither the death benefit nor the *surrender value* available during life are guaranteed, which makes this policy unique. Both can increase or decrease depending upon the investment performance of the assets in the policy. Usually the death benefit will not decrease below the initial face amount of the policy, as long as the policy owner pays all premiums. The tradeoff is that the policy owner will lose the cash value guarantee in exchange for the potential investment growth of his or her investment decisions.

The policy owner can allocate the premium, after the insurance company makes certain deductions, to a particular sub-account held by the insurance company, with investment options similar to those found with mutual funds. Some of the investments available are money market accounts, growth stock accounts, bond accounts, balanced fund accounts, and real estate accounts. The death benefit normally will be adjusted once a year. The cash value will be adjusted on a daily basis. Premiums are fixed and always remain the same.

Variable life enjoys the same favorable income tax treatment as other insurance policies. Earnings from the investments are income tax deferred. Death benefits, regardless of growth, pass free of income tax.

VARIABLE UNIVERSAL LIFE INSURANCE

Variable universal life is a combination of universal life insurance and variable life insurance. It's like universal life in that it has flexible premiums, adjustable death benefits, and policy loan and partial withdrawal privileges. However, like variable life, the owner of the life contract decides where to invest the premiums within categories similar to those available to variable life insurance premiums. The typical variable universal life policy carries a guaranteed minimum death benefit in the event that the underlying investments are not profitable. This policy actually is a combination insurance policy and securities investment.

SURVIVORSHIP LIFE INSURANCE

Survivorship life insurance, sometimes called joint and survivor life or second-to-die, typically insures two people. The underlying policy can be a whole life, term, universal, or variable type of policy. However, the death benefit under a survivorship policy is not paid until the last of the insured individuals die. Quite frequently the cash value will be sufficient to cover future premiums after about 10 years.

This policy typically is used by husband and wife, parent and child, or two related business people such as business owners or key employees. This type of policy can be an extremely effective tool for the payment of taxes, including federal estate, inheritance, and income taxes. This is especially useful for couples relying on the unlimited marital deduction at the first death, creating a bigger tax burden at the second death.

JUST A MINUTE

Ownership of a second-to-die policy is crucial when planning your estate. Recall that ownership of a policy can cause the death benefit to be included in the owner's taxable estate. When the policy pays off at the second death, the owner who is last to die will include the death benefit in his or her taxable estate. Go to Hour 17 on irrevocable life insurance trusts for more on available insurance strategies.

FIRST TO DIE LIFE INSURANCE

First to die life insurance is a life insurance policy that insures two or more people. The policy can be a whole life, term, universal, or variable life type of policy. The death benefit is realized when the first insured dies. Some policies, through a rider, allow the survivor to continue coverage after the first insured dies. The policy can be used in business or personal planning—wherever there is a need for coverage only until the death of one of the two insured parties. Using a single first to die policy to insure multiple parties usually costs less in premiums than the purchase of two separate policies.

TAXATION OF DEATH BENEFITS

As the old expression goes, nothing is certain except death and taxes. In the case of life insurance, taxes of all kinds follow right after death. They are discussed in the following list:

- **Income tax** Generally speaking, insurance proceeds payable upon the insured's death are exempt from income tax; therefore they are excludable from the gross income of the beneficiary. When the beneficiary chooses to receive death proceeds under a life income settlement option in which payments are made in installments to the beneficiary, the annual interest produced by the death proceeds is taxable to the beneficiary. The balance is recoverable income tax free.
- **Estate tax** The proceeds of a life insurance policy usually are subject to the federal estate tax. Life insurance proceeds are included in the

decedent's gross estate if 1) the proceeds are payable to or for the benefit of his or her estate, 2) at the time of death the insured possessed any incidents of ownership in the policy (such as the right to change the beneficiary, the right to surrender the policy, or the right to obtain a policy loan), and 3) the policy is transferred to someone else by the decedent within three years prior to his or her death. Also, the fair market value of a policy (generally the sum of the cash value plus unearned premiums) owned on another person's life is includable in the owner's gross estate.

- **Gift tax**   Gifts of life insurance policies might be subject to the federal gift tax. The value of the gift is based on the fair market value of the insurance policy at the time of the gift. The gift tax value of a policy generally can be obtained from the insurance company.

 In general terms, the gift tax value of a policy is roughly equal to the cash value.

- **State inheritance taxes**   Most inheritance tax laws exempt death benefits paid from life insurance policies from taxation if the proceeds are payable to a named beneficiary. However, if the beneficiary is the owner's estate or if there is no beneficiary, the death benefit normally will be included in the taxable estate for state inheritance tax purposes.

PROCEED WITH CAUTION

 Since inheritance tax laws vary from state to state, seek the advice of an estate-planning attorney licensed to practice in your state of residence to learn about your own state inheritance tax laws.

THE VALUE OF LIFE INSURANCE

Life insurance has acquired a bad name through the years. Visions of the life insurance salesman knocking on your door and sitting across the kitchen table trying to convince you to buy life insurance still appears in the minds of many people. However, from an estate planning perspective life insurance is one of the most valuable of all estate planning strategies.

The primary reason for this is the effects of *leveraging*. Leveraging occurs whenever a certain amount of money is used to acquire a much greater amount of money. In this case, the insurance is acquired as a result of the payment of premiums. Premiums can be either inexpensive or costly; but either way they are far less than the death benefit paid to the beneficiaries, unless it is term life insurance, which can cost more than the death benefit.

GO TO ▶
This technique is discussed in Hour 17.

Depending on who the owner is, you can have as much insurance on your life as you can afford and have none of it included in your estate for federal estate tax purposes. The strategies for doing this will be discussed in subsequent hours.

Don't shy away from life insurance simply because you "don't need any more insurance." In the context of estate planning, insurance is not usually purchased for the sole purpose of insuring your life; rather, it is purchased to finance death taxation on the state and federal level.

ADVANTAGES OF LIFE INSURANCE

Life insurance is extremely valuable. It can provide cash in the event of premature death. When you did not have the opportunity to build funds for your retirement or funds to pay for the cost of raising children or providing for a spouse, life insurance will provide the necessary money for all of these purposes. Some of the other advantages of having life insurance include the following:

- You can use life insurance for special needs such as college expenses, mortgage balances, or other large expenses.
- You can use life insurance as a tool to help build credit, or as security on a loan.
- Life insurance can be used to compensate a company if one of the company's key employees dies.
- Life insurance can be used to finance charitable gifts.

PROCEED WITH CAUTION

Be certain to obtain proper financial and legal advice when purchasing life insurance as a part of an estate plan. Financial professionals and legal professionals should work together in formulating the right plan for you.

Hour's Up!

Now it's time to see how much you have learned and retained from this lesson. Try to take the following quiz without referring back to the hourly materials:

1. Insurance that has no cash value is called …

    a. First-to-die insurance

    b. Universal life insurance

    c. Term insurance

    d. Variable life insurance

2. Insurance that has a separate fund for extra cash that earns a contractual rate of return is called …

    a. First-to-die insurance

    b. Universal life insurance

    c. Term insurance

    d. Variable life insurance

3. Insurance that is frequently used by married couples to pay estate taxes is …

    a. First-to-die insurance

    b. Universal life insurance

    c. Term insurance

    d. Survivorship life insurance

4. Insurance that provides flexibility in both the amount of premium paid and the type of investment for the cash value is called …

    a. Second-to-die insurance

    b. Universal life insurance

    c. Term insurance

    d. Variable life insurance

5. Insurance that has a fixed premium and a fixed return on the cash value is called …

    a. Whole life insurance

    b. Universal life insurance

    c. Term insurance

    d. Variable life insurance

HOUR 14
Retirement Plans

CHAPTER SUMMARY

LESSON PLAN:

Retirement plans have become one of the most valuable parts of an estate. In this hour, you will learn about both qualified and non-qualified retirement accounts. You will develop an understanding of the importance of these various plans in connection with the planning of your estate. You will also learn ...

- The different retirement accounts that are available.
- How qualified and non-qualified accounts are taxed.
- The rules for making distributions from both qualified and non-qualified accounts.
- The rights of a spouse to qualified and non-qualified accounts upon the death of the owner.
- Estate planning strategies for retirement accounts.

A discussion of retirement accounts will necessarily encompass many different types of plans. Initially, it's helpful to compare *non-qualified accounts*, which receive no special tax treatment, with *qualified accounts*, which offer such tax breaks as deductibility for income tax purposes. Let's first define some of the more technical terms that you will soon become familiar with.

STRICTLY DEFINED

A **non-qualified retirement account** is one in which the contribution receives no special tax treatment such as deductibility for income tax purposes. A **qualified retirement account** is an account that allows for special tax treatment of contributions, deferral of taxes on income and capital gains, and which is subject to minimum distribution rules.

When we speak of non-qualified retirement accounts, we're referring to accounts used as vehicles for the investment of funds for retirement. Those investments tend to be in tax-deferred accounts, such as annuities and variable life insurance.

PROCEED WITH CAUTION

Don't confuse tax-free, tax-deferred, and tax-deductible investments. Tax-free investments are not subject to income taxation when the funds are withdrawn. Interest and dividends earned on tax-deferred investments are not subject to taxation until they're withdrawn from the account. If you have a tax-deductible investment, the investment itself can be deducted on your individual income tax return.

TAXABILITY OF RETIREMENT ACCOUNTS

Retirement accounts present very special and sometimes complicated tax issues. Due to the nature of these accounts as tax-deferred and sometimes tax-deductible, it is easy to become confused about the tax ramifications of these accounts. Read on to learn more about how the various taxes impact on these investments.

INCOME TAXATION

Contributions to non-qualified accounts are not tax-deductible. Earnings within non-qualified accounts grow tax-deferred but are taxable during the year in which the earnings are withdrawn.

Contributions to a qualified account are tax-deductible for income tax purposes. Earnings within qualified accounts are tax-deferred until the time that distributions are made.

FEDERAL ESTATE TAX

Both qualified and non-qualified accounts are included in the taxable estate of the owner for purposes of calculating the federal estate tax. The value used is measured as of the date of death, which will include both principal (the money deposited into the account) and accumulated income (earnings on the principal contributions).

If a surviving spouse is the primary beneficiary of the retirement account, the estate of the deceased owner will be allowed to deduct the full *value* of the account as part of the unlimited marital deduction.

STRICTLY DEFINED

The **value** of the retirement account will be a combination of both the principal deposited into the account and the interest and growth of the investment.

PROCEED WITH CAUTION

Although most of a decedent's assets are entitled to a step up in basis, assets contained within an annuity do not qualify for the stepped-up basis. You must anticipate and plan for potentially significant income tax issues to occur upon the death of the owner.

The phrase **stepped-up basis** refers to a provision in the tax code that substitutes the date of death value of an appreciated asset as the basis for that asset instead of the decedent's original cost basis.

STATE INHERITANCE TAXES

Both qualified and non-qualified accounts typically are included in the taxable estate of the owner when calculating state inheritance taxes. The value, which will include both principal and accumulated income, is measured as of the date of death.

You'll also have to check state law to make sure your estate complies with any inheritance tax requirements. As is the case with the federal estate tax, if a surviving spouse is the primary beneficiary of the retirement account, state laws usually allow the estate of the deceased owner to deduct the full value of the account as part of the unlimited marital deduction for inheritance tax purposes.

PROCEED WITH CAUTION

By definition, state inheritance taxes vary from state to state. Be certain to consult with an estate planning attorney licensed in your state who can advise you properly on the provisions of your state inheritance tax laws.

NON-QUALIFIED PLANS

We begin our discussion with a review of the rules of non-qualified plans. Because these plans are not qualified to receive special tax treatment, generally there are no *minimum required distributions*. Again, because any plan that is not a qualified plan is by definition non-qualified, this category includes accounts that are not intended for retirement such as checking accounts, savings accounts, money market accounts, certificates of deposit, and so forth. Some investments are better suited as retirement accounts because of the tax-deferred nature of the investment earnings. Annuities often are used for retirement funds, as is variable life insurance.

STRICTLY DEFINED

Minimum required distributions are rules issued by the Internal Revenue Service governing the amount and timing of mandatory distributions from qualified retirement accounts.

ANNUITIES

Annuities are investments issued by insurance companies. Contributions to annuities are not tax-deductible. All annuities are governed by contract. The contract contains all of the terms of the agreement between the investor and the insurance company.

STRICTLY DEFINED

An **annuity** is an investment contract in which the owner deposits a sum of money, either as a lump sum or in periodic installments, which accumulate tax-deferred, and in which the owner agrees to certain restrictions on the right of withdrawal.

The terms of a typical annuity will allow the owner to withdraw no more than 10% of the investment annually without penalty.

Additional withdrawal privileges exist but will be subject to early withdrawal penalties for a specific number of years. Penalties will be imposed for a period of time anywhere from 7 to 15 years. The following is an illustration of what the penalty might be on a typical annuity contract imposed on amounts in excess of the annual 10% amount:

Year 1   7%

Year 2   6%

Year 3   5%

Year 4   4%

Year 5   3%

Year 6   2%

Year 7   1%

Under this penalty scenario, the contract owner would be allowed to remove all of the investment from the annuity in year 8 or thereafter without penalty.

JUST

gh there might be no
come withdrawn from the

PROCE

a particular annuity con-
e certain to read your pol-
isor or to the company

VARIABL

Va ... ndous opportunity to
de ... ng-term needs. Because
th ... iction available for
co ... igs within the policy
gr ... nagic takes over.
Th ... , the investment and
th ... ne costs for exercising
th ... nal, especially com-
pa

So ... etirement funds are as
fol

GO TO ▶
A more detailed
discussion of vari-
able life insurance
is found in Hour
13, "Life Insur-
ance."

- There is no minimum required distribution.
- There is no required beginning date for making withdrawals.
- Funds can be withdrawn at any time, as long as the policy provisions are complied with. This allows the funds to be used for college education and other expenses aside from retirement.

FYI As with all loans, they must be paid back. Usually, the payback occurs at the time the policy pays the death benefit by reducing the death benefit in accordance with the balance due on the policy loan.

QUALIFIED PLANS FOR INDIVIDUALS

Now let's take a closer look at the many qualified retirement plans that are available for individuals who do not own their own business. These plans can be very attractive to non-business owners.

THE TRADITIONAL IRA

Individual Retirement Accounts are qualified retirement accounts for individuals and their spouses, with limits on deductible contributions of $2,000 per year.

PROCEED WITH CAUTION

 Be certain to consult with an estate planning attorney licensed in your state or your financial planner who can advise you properly on the details pertaining to your IRA account.

Any person under the age of $70^1/_2$ who has received *compensation* during the taxable year can make a deductible contribution to a traditional IRA. All contributions are fully vested, which means that your investment cannot be taken away from you.

 Actually, anybody can make a non-deductible contribution to an IRA account, but must meet the preceding requirements in order to deduct the contribution.

A married spouse who has received compensation can make contribution to the other non-working spouse's IRA account if filing a joint return and if the income of the other spouse is less than the income of the contributing spouse. The total amount of tax-deductible contributions for each working spouse is 100% of compensation or $2,000 per year, whichever is less. Deductible contributions to an IRA must be made by April 15 to deduct on the prior year's return.

ROTH IRA

The relatively new Roth IRA presents some exciting possibilities for the individual or couple planning for retirement. Whereas the primary benefit of a traditional IRA is tax deferral, the primary benefit of a Roth IRA is tax-free earnings growth. Amounts contributed to a Roth IRA are fully vested.

Be certain to consult with an estate planning attorney licensed in your state or your financial planner who can advise you properly on investing in a Roth IRA.

Because this is a qualified plan, there are some restrictions on the amount that can be contributed and the timing of the withdrawals. For example, individuals with adjusted gross income less than $95,000 ($150,000 for joint filers) are eligible to contribute $2,000 each per year to a Roth IRA (2001). If income exceeds these limits, the allowable contribution is reduced. Spouses without earned income can contribute if they file jointly with a working spouse.

Unlike the traditional IRA, individuals older than $70^1/_2$ can continue to contribute to a Roth IRA as long as they continue to have earned income or are married to a person with earned income.

FYI Roth IRAs also benefit from an unusual IRS rule that considers withdrawals to be from principal contributed to the account first, then from earnings. This means that the initial withdrawals will be tax-free since the contributions were not deductible going into the account.

QUALIFIED PLANS FOR BUSINESSES

Now we will review some of the qualified retirement plans that are available for business owners. There are a wide variety of available plans to choose from. Read on to gain an understanding of some of the most popular plans.

SIMPLIFIED EMPLOYEE PENSION (SEP)

Simplified employee pension, or SEP, is designed for the self-employed person or the owner of a small business who is interested in setting up a retirement plan that is easy to maintain. This plan allows for a much larger tax-deductible contribution than either the traditional IRA or the Roth IRA. An eligible employer can contribute the lesser of $30,000 or 15% of compensation (with some restrictions). Amounts deposited into a SEP account are fully vested.

As an employer, there is a requirement that all employees who are at least age 21 and who have earned at least $450 in three of the past five years be included in all contributions made by the employer. However, the employer can elect not to make any contribution in a given year. There are no matching contributions by employees.

SAVINGS INCENTIVE MATCH PLAN FOR EMPLOYEES (SIMPLE)

The savings incentive match plan for employees, or SIMPLE IRA, also is designed with ease of administration in mind; it is for businesses with less than 100 employees. This plan is a bonus for employees in that the employee contribution is pre-tax, thus reducing the employee's taxable income. The SIMPLE IRA must include all employees who earn at least $5,000 during the preceding two years and who are expected to earn at least as much in the current year. The maximum contribution eligible for tax deferral is $6,000 per employee, indexed for inflation. All contributions to the account are fully vested.

Employees can choose the percent of their income to *defer* into a SIMPLE IRA subject to a percentage cap.

STRICTLY DEFINED

The term **defer** refers to the ability to have monies withheld from income and deposited into a qualified retirement account pre-tax, meaning withholding taxes are not taken from the amount withheld.

The employer elects to contribute in one of two ways:

- The employer can elect to make a dollar-for-dollar match of the amount the employee elects to defer, with a maximum match of 3% of compensation.
- The employer can elect to make a contribution equal to 2% of compensation for each eligible employee.
- Employees need not match the employer's contribution.

403(B)(7) PLAN

These qualified plans are designed specifically for employees of a public school or qualified tax-exempt organization including museums, colleges, and non-profit hospitals. As with the SIMPLE IRA, employee contributions are made pre-tax, thus reducing taxable compensation. The yearly contribution limits on this plan generally are $10,500 or 25% of gross compensation;

whichever is less. If an employee has been with the same employer for at least 15 years, a greater contribution limit of $15,000 is allowed. All contributions are 100% vested.

401(K) PLAN

One of the most common corporate plans is the 401(k) plan. This is available to all companies—large and small—and offers employees a variety of investment options. All employees at least 21 years old with one year of service with the company must be included (with some exceptions); tax-deferred contributions are limited to $10,500. Yearly contributions may not exceed 25% of gross compensation or $30,000 per individual.

Employers can match employee contributions; however, they are limited to 15% of total eligible payroll. These plans tend to be funded mostly by employees, with pre-tax contributions allowed. There is a window of opportunity beginning with a time when withdrawals can be and the time when distributions become mandatory. At age 59$^1/_2$ distributions may begin without penalty. There is no minimum amount that can be withdrawn at this time. After reaching the age of 70$^1/_2$ distributions must be made. There is also a requirement that a certain amount be withdrawn annually. This is called the minimum required distribution.

PENALTY-FREE DISTRIBUTIONS

Generally speaking, all of the preceding qualified plans allow the owner to begin making withdrawals without penalty once the owner reaches the age of 59$^1/_2$. Prior to that, the IRS will assess a penalty for any distributions from these plans, except for specified purposes. Early distributions from these plans can be made for specified reasons, which generally include the following:

- Financial hardship
- Permanent disability
- Death
- Separation from service (in the case of 403[b][7] and 401[k] plans).

With respect to Traditional IRAs, Roth IRAs, SEP IRAs, and SIMPLE IRAs, early withdrawal is allowed without penalty for the purchase of a first home, with a cap of $10,000.

MINIMUM REQUIRED DISTRIBUTIONS

The IRS requires that all owners of qualified retirement plans begin making distributions at a specified age. Minimum distributions must begin by April 15 of the year following the year the account owner reaches the age of $70^1/_2$. On January 11, 2001 the IRS issued new proposed regulations for calculating the amount that must be withdrawn after age $70^1/_2$. These are called *minimum required distributions*.

FYI The old minimum distribution rules are called "proposed regulations," even though they have been used since 1987. These new rules also are proposed, but can be used by taxpayers.

The rules and regulations for distributing funds from a qualified retirement account are among the most complex of all areas of the law. Entire books have been written on the topic of retirement plan distributions. It is important that you understand that the information that follows is intended only as a general overview of some of the rules that govern distributions from both qualified and non-qualified accounts.

The goal here is to make some of the most basic rules understandable. Decisions regarding minimum distributions must be made only after careful consultation with a retirement planning specialist. The information that follows will allow you to understand that specialist better and help you to make a more informed decision.

The amount of the minimum distribution is based on the life expectancy of the owner and the beneficiary. Under the old rules, complicated calculations were required under several different options, using the actual age and life expectancy of the named beneficiary. If the actual named beneficiary was more than ten years younger than the owner, there was an assumption that the beneficiary was really only ten years younger than the owner. If there was no named beneficiary, special rules applied. There were options to calculate life expectancy based upon the age of the owner, the joint life expectancy of the owner and the beneficiary, and in some cases the calculation was redone every year.

Under the new rules the minimum distribution is calculated on the assumption that the beneficiary is ten years younger than the owner. This assumption applies regardless of the beneficiary's actual age or identity, or whether there even is a beneficiary. To make this an easy calculation, the IRS uses a uniform life expectancy table. This table makes it easy to figure the life expectancy to use when calculating the minimum distribution.

The New Uniform Life Expectancy Table

Age of IRA Owner	Life Expectancy (in Years)
70	26.2
71	25.3
72	24.4
73	23.5
74	22.7
75	21.8
76	20.9
77	20.1
78	19.2
79	18.4
80	17.6
81	16.8
82	16.0
83	15.3
84	14.5
85	13.8
86	13.1
87	12.4
88	11.8
89	11.1
90	10.5
91	9.9
92	9.4
93	8.8
94	8.3
95	7.8
96	7.3
97	6.9
98	6.5
99	6.1
100	5.7
101	5.3

continues

The New Uniform Life Expectancy Table (continued)

Age of IRA Owner	Life Expectancy (in Years)
102	5.0
103	4.7
104	4.4
105	4.1
106	3.8
107	3.6
108	3.3
109	3.1
110	2.8
111	2.6
112	2.4
113	2.2
114	2.0
115	1.8

The only time this table is not used is when the spouse of the account owner actually is more than 10 years younger than the account owner. In this situation the joint life expectancy of both spouses is used based upon joint life expectancy tables and actual ages. For example, Suppose Bill is 71½ and is ready to make his minimum distribution calculation. Bill has an IRA valued at $500,000. Bill is married to Susan, who is 67. Bill will use the new uniform life expectancy table for his age, and will divide the account balance by 25.3. The result, $19,762.85, is his minimum distribution.

Here's another example: Suppose the same facts as previously discussed, but assume Susan is 60. Because Susan is more than 10 years younger than Bill, the joint life expectancy tables will be used. The life expectancy result is 26.0. The result, $19,230.77, is his minimum distribution.

Following are the old joint life expectancy tables:

IRS Joint Life and Last Survivor Expectancy Table

Ages	70	71
35	47.5	47.5
36	46.6	46.6

Ages	70	71
37	45.7	45.6
38	44.7	44.7
39	43.8	43.8
40	42.9	42.8
41	41.9	41.9
42	41.0	41.0
43	40.1	40.1
44	39.2	39.1
45	38.3	38.2
46	37.4	37.3
47	36.5	36.5
48	35.7	35.6
49	34.8	34.7
50	34.0	33.9
51	33.1	33.0
52	32.3	32.2
53	31.5	31.4
54	30.7	30.5
55	29.9	29.7
56	29.1	29.0
57	28.4	28.2
58	27.6	27.5
59	26.9	26.7
60	26.2	26.0
61	25.6	25.3
62	24.9	24.7
63	24.3	24.0
64	23.7	23.4
65	23.1	22.8
66	22.5	22.2
67	22.0	21.7
68	21.5	21.2

continues

IRS Joint Life and Last Survivor Expectancy Table   (continued)

Ages	70	71
69	21.1	20.7
70	20.6	20.2
71	20.2	19.8
72	19.8	19.4
73	19.4	19.0
74	19.1	18.6

SPOUSAL ROLLOVERS

As the rule was before, a surviving spouse is allowed under the new rules to rollover the IRA inherited from a deceased spouse. The surviving spouse then can designate a new beneficiary and therefore stretch out the distribution period.

The advantage of a spousal rollover is that the spouse is allowed to withdraw the funds from the account of the deceased spouse and deposit those funds into a new individual retirement account with a different custodian. Utilizing the rollover prevents taxation on any part of the rollover amount until it is later withdrawn.

The spouse can establish a brand new individual retirement account and deposit these funds into it, or the spouse can deposit those funds into an existing individual retirement account. The spousal rollover is a very powerful technique allowing for continued deferral of the income within the retirement plan.

PROCEED WITH CAUTION

As with all of the material in this book, be certain to consult an estate planning attorney before implementing any of the techniques discussed in this book. The failure to obtain professional advice could result in additional expenses for administering your estate and could result in additional and unnecessary taxation of your estate. Additionally, the failure to properly prepare documents according to applicable law may render the documents useless.

Hour's Up!

Now it's time to see how much you have learned and retained from this lesson. Try to take the following quiz without referring back to the hourly materials:

1. Earnings on a qualified retirement account grow …
    a. Tax-free
    b. Tax-deferred
    c. Subject to tax
    d. Subject to double taxation

2. Contributions to a non-qualified retirement annuity …
    a. Are fully deductible, but subject to 50% of the owner's adjusted gross income
    b. Are pre-tax contributions
    c. Are not deductible
    d. Are fully deductible in the year of contribution

3. The difference between a traditional IRA and a Roth IRA is …
    a. Distributions from a Roth IRA are tax-deductible.
    b. Earnings in a Roth IRA are taxable.
    c. Contributions to a Roth IRA are not tax-deductible.
    d. Contributions to a Roth IRA are pre-tax.

4. The minimum age for making penalty-free distributions from an IRA generally is set at age …
    a. $70^1/_2$
    b. $59^1/_2$
    c. $57^1/_2$
    d. $62^3/_4$

5. Under the new minimum distribution rules, with the exception of spouses, the age of the beneficiary is assumed to be how many years younger than the account owner …
    a. 15
    b. 11
    c. 5
    d. 10

HOUR 15
Business Entities

CHAPTER SUMMARY

LESSON PLAN:

In this hour, you'll learn about the various types of business entities. Choosing the correct entity for your business is extremely important from an estate planning perspective. In this hour you will learn ...

- The major types of entities.
- The advantages of each type of entity.
- The disadvantages of each type of entity.

Estate planning extends beyond just personal assets. For those of you who are business owners, or who may be contemplating some type of business in the future, you should spend time carefully considering the type of form the business should take. The selection of entity should never be taken lightly. Liability issues pervade the decision on how to operate your business. Tax issues also play a significant role in the entity choice.

The following are the basic types of business entities. You will learn about the characteristics of each, followed by a discussion of the advantages and the disadvantages of each business form.

SOLE PROPRIETORSHIP

If you are looking for the easiest way to do business, the sole proprietorship is the way to go. There are no special filings or paperwork that have to be completed before you can do business this way.

The way to use this business format is to start doing business. That's about it. You may choose a name for your business, like Bob's Computer Repair, or any other name you wish. When you identify your business on legal documents or tax returns, you simply use the selected name for your business.

LEGAL DOCUMENTS NEEDED

GO TO ▶
To review the application for taxpayer identification number, see Hour 5, "Income Taxes and Inheritance Taxes."

No special legal documents are needed to operate this type of business. As a business, if you have employees, you will need to apply for a taxpayer identification number from the IRS.

LIABILITY ISSUES

Unfortunately, this is one of the worst forms of business from a liability perspective. Second only to the general partnership, covered later in this chapter, this form of business will expose you personally to any liability arising out of the operation of this business.

When you do business as a sole proprietorship, there is no separate legal entity doing the business. Instead, you alone, along with any employees, are running the business. Therefore, you and all of your personal assets are subject to any claims made by creditors.

TAXATION

Income and expenses for your business are reported on your personal income tax return on Schedule C. The net income or net loss is then carried over to your 1040 return. You must also pay self-employment tax on your business. This will be reported and calculated on Schedule SE, also attached to your personal tax return. The rate of taxation is the same as your personal income tax rate.

ADVANTAGES

Doing business as a sole proprietorship is easy. That alone is the reason many people choose this form of doing business. To do business as a sole proprietor, you simply "open up shop" and start doing business.

DISADVANTAGES

As mentioned earlier, the single biggest disadvantage is the exposure to unlimited liability from any business activity performed by you or your employees. The only assets that are exempt from liability claims from judgment creditors are assets protected by your state statutes. These commonly include your personal residence, some household goods and furnishings, and a car. Some cash may be exempt as well.

If you're looking for the easiest way to do business, the sole proprietorship is the way to go. You won't have to complete any special paperwork before you begin doing business. You simply choose a name for your business and identify it this way on legal documents and tax returns. This form of business sometimes is referred to as a *d/b/a*, or *doing business as*. Any time you see a d/b/a you are looking at a sole proprietorship.

THE GENERAL PARTNERSHIP

Operating as a general partnership requires something that is not present when operating as a sole proprietorship: more than one individual engaged in the business as an owner. A general partnership exists when all partners participate in the management of the business and share the profits and losses from the business.

Although not mandatory from a legal standpoint, the terms of any general partnership should be in writing. It is not necessary, however, that the writing be filed with the recorder's office.

LEGAL DOCUMENTS NEEDED

To run your partnership properly, you should have a written partnership agreement containing all of the operating conditions pertinent to the business. Some of the points to include are …

- Names and addresses of partners
- The amount of the initial and subsequent contributions by each partner
- The allocation of profits and losses among the partners
- Terms pertaining to dissolution of the partnership
- Terms pertaining to amending the partnership agreement
- Terms pertaining to the management of the partnership

The general partnership agreement usually does not have to be recorded. Sometimes, however, it is a good idea to record the agreement or at least some certificate of partnership that discloses the name of the partnership and the identity of the partners. This can be helpful when the partnership buys or sells real estate.

LIABILITY

The only form of business that is worse than a sole proprietorship from a liability perspective is a general partnership. The reason? With a sole proprietorship you are liable for anything you do in the scope of your business. With a general partnership, you are liable, not only for your own actions, but you are also personally liable for the actions of each general partner—you and your partners are *jointly and severally liable* for each other's actions.

STRICTLY DEFINED

Joint and several liability means that all general partners are equally liable for partnership activities and each of them is liable individually for all of the liabilities.

A general partnership is a separate legal entity. Nevertheless, all general partners are jointly and severally liable for the partnership activities.

Suppose that Tom Partner and Bill Smith are general partners with XYZ general partnership. Tom thinks that the partnership needs capital and signs for the partnership on a bank loan for $100,000. The partnership is not able to make the payments on the loan, so bank sues the partnership, Tom, and Bill. The bank easily obtains a court judgment against all of the above. The partnership does not have many assets, so the bank looks to Tom and Bill for payment. Tom, unfortunately, has no assets except a home and a car, which are all exempt from creditors. The bank therefore seeks to collect the entire judgment from Bill. Bill is actually quite wealthy and has significant personal assets. Bill would be forced to pay the judgment in full if he has enough non-exempt assets.

Note in the above example that Bill never signed the note with the bank. Even if Bill was unaware that Tom signed on behalf of the partnership, Bill is liable for the entire debt. The fact is that Tom is also liable for the entire debt, but he has nothing the creditors can take to satisfy the judgment.

Now suppose that Bill and Tom both have enough non-exempt assets to satisfy this judgment. The bank may choose to collect all of the debt from just

Bill and ignore Tom altogether. Why? Bill is jointly and severally liable for the debt. Severally means individually, regardless of whether Tom is also liable and regardless of Tom's ability to pay.

The partner who has to pay the debt may be able to obtain "contribution" from the other liable parties. This allows all liable partners and the partnership to equalize the obligation to pay the debt. This right of contribution, however, has no bearing on the right of the judgment creditor to collect from any and all liable parties.

TAXATION

A general partnership is a separate legal entity and is required to file its own tax return. This does not mean, however, that it pays taxes separately. A partnership is a "flow-through" entity, meaning that all net income is taxed to the general partners on the individual returns of the general partners.

The applicable tax rate may vary, depending on the individual tax brackets of the general partners. The amount distributed to each general partner is determined by reference to the partnership agreement.

For example, assuming the partnership agreement provides for equal distribution of profits and losses, if the general partnership had a net profit of $60,000, Partner A will report $30,000 of income on his or her 1040, and Partner B will do likewise.

ADVANTAGES

One advantage to operating your business as a general partnership is that there is minimal paperwork involved in the creation of the entity. The general partnership agreement may be retained in your office without any filing requirements. It has many of the same advantages as a sole proprietorship, but is designed to accommodate more than one owner.

It is also quite easy to allocate profits and losses in a manner that is agreeable to all general partners. Furthermore, all general partners have an active role in the management of the partnership.

Tax reporting is quite easy, with the partnership filing the information return, and the net profits and losses passing over to the individual partners for inclusion on their personal returns.

File this return to report income for U.S. partnerships.

Form **1065** Department of the Treasury Internal Revenue Service	**U.S. Return of Partnership Income**	OMB No. 1545-0099
	For calendar year 2000, or tax year beginning .... , 2000, and ending .... , 20...... . ► **See separate instructions.**	**2000**

A Principal business activity	Use the IRS label. Other- wise, print or type.	Name of partnership	D Employer identification number
B Principal product or service		Number, street, and room or suite no. If a P.O. box, see page 13 of the instructions.	E Date business started
C Business code number		City or town, state, and ZIP code	F Total assets (see page 13 of the instructions) $

G   Check applicable boxes: **(1)** ☐ Initial return   **(2)** ☐ Final return   **(3)** ☐ Change in address   **(4)** ☐ Amended return
H   Check accounting method: **(1)** ☐ Cash   **(2)** ☐ Accrual   **(3)** ☐ Other (specify) ► ....
I   Number of Schedules K-1. Attach one for each person who was a partner at any time during the tax year ► ....

Caution: *Include **only** trade or business income and expenses on lines 1a through 22 below. See the instructions for more information.*

Income	**1a** Gross receipts or sales	**1a**	
	b Less returns and allowances.	**1b**	**1c**
	2 Cost of goods sold (Schedule A, line 8)		**2**
	3 Gross profit. Subtract line 2 from line 1c.		**3**
	4 Ordinary income (loss) from other partnerships, estates, and trusts *(attach schedule)*. . .		**4**
	5 Net farm profit (loss) *(attach Schedule F (Form 1040))*		**5**
	6 Net gain (loss) from Form 4797, Part II, line 18.		**6**
	7 Other income (loss) *(attach schedule)*.		**7**
	8 **Total income (loss).** Combine lines 3 through 7		**8**

Deductions (see page 14 of the instructions for limitations)	**9** Salaries and wages (other than to partners) (less employment credits)		**9**
	10 Guaranteed payments to partners		**10**
	11 Repairs and maintenance		**11**
	12 Bad debts		**12**
	13 Rent		**13**
	14 Taxes and licenses		**14**
	15 Interest		**15**
	16a Depreciation (if required, attach Form 4562)	**16a**	
	b Less depreciation reported on Schedule A and elsewhere on return	**16b**	**16c**
	17 Depletion **(Do not deduct oil and gas depletion.)**		**17**
	18 Retirement plans, etc..		**18**
	19 Employee benefit programs		**19**
	20 Other deductions *(attach schedule)*		**20**
	21 **Total deductions.** Add the amounts shown in the far right column for lines 9 through 20 .		**21**
	22 **Ordinary income (loss)** from trade or business activities. Subtract line 21 from line 8 . .		**22**

Sign Here	Under penalties of perjury, I declare that I have examined this return, including accompanying schedules and statements, and to the best of my knowledge and belief, it is true, correct, and complete. Declaration of preparer (other than general partner or limited liability company member) is based on all information of which preparer has any knowledge.	
	► Signature of general partner or limited liability company member	► Date

Paid Preparer's Use Only	Preparer's signature ►	Date	Check if self-employed ► ☐	Preparer's SSN or PTIN
	Firm's name (or yours if self-employed), address, and ZIP code ►		EIN ►	
			Phone no. ( )	

For Paperwork Reduction Act Notice, see separate instructions.   Cat. No. 11390Z   Form **1065** (2000)

The name of the partnership business is whatever you want it to be. To properly identify it as a partnership, it is best to add the words "a partnership" after the name.

DISADVANTAGES

Liability is the single biggest disadvantage to operating this type of business. Another disadvantage is that there are multiple managers of the business, which can lead to conflict in management style as well as in meeting management objectives.

THE LIMITED PARTNERSHIP

Limited partnerships share most of the same attributes as a general partnership. The primary difference between a general and a limited partnership is the fact that some partners in a limited partnership do not participate in management of the partnership business.

STRICTLY DEFINED

A **limited partner** is one who invests in the partnership but does not participate in management. The liability of the limited partner is limited to his or her investment in the partnership.

LEGAL DOCUMENTS NEEDED

The same advice for general partnerships also applies here. The partnership agreement must be written in order to clarify the objectives of all partners. Also, with a limited partnership, some partners will not be participating in management, but have made an investment in the partnership. The investment should be well documented and the limited partner fully advised on partnership activities.

TAX REQUIREMENTS

The tax reporting requirements for a limited partnership are the same as for a general partnership. Always be certain to obtain a taxpayer identification number.

ADVANTAGES

To the general partners, the advantages of operating a limited partnership are the same as for a general partnership, plus there is the extra benefit of working with the investment made by the limited partners. This investment may help make the business a success.

To the limited partner, the biggest advantage is limited liability. As mentioned, liability extends only to the investment made. Personal assets of the limited partner are not subject to partnership debts.

It is imperative that the limited partner not participate in the management of the partnership. Even though he or she is referred to as a limited partner, a judgment creditor of the partnership may try to prove that the limited partner really did participate in management of the partnership, thereby making the limited partner a general partner. If this argument is successful, the limited partner will be subject to partnership liabilities just as if he or she was a general partner. In other words, the title alone is not enough to protect the limited partner from liability.

DISADVANTAGES

From the perspective of the general partners, the biggest disadvantage is that liability is not shared equally among all partners. Of course, all of the disadvantages associated with doing business as a general partnership apply here as well.

From the perspective of the limited partner, the biggest disadvantage is that there is no voice in management. The investment by the limited partner must be based upon the belief in the abilities of the general partners to operate the business properly and profitably.

THE CORPORATION

The corporation is probably the most common form of ownership of a business. The corporation is a separate legal entity from the owners. There are different types of corporations created for different purposes.

LEGAL DOCUMENTS NEEDED

The corporation, unlike the sole proprietorship, requires that it be created into a separate legal entity. To do this, there are certain documents that must be prepared.

ARTICLES OF INCORPORATION

The articles of incorporation are the documents that must be prepared to organize the corporation.

JUST A MINUTE

The authority for a corporation to act is derived from the appropriate state agency, usually the Secretary of State. This authority is evidenced by a "Certificate of Incorporation."

A corporation may not conduct business without first obtaining the permission of the state. The articles of incorporation will usually specify the identity of the individuals who are creating the entity, as well as the name of the corporation and its stated purpose.

These articles are filed, with an appropriate fee, with the state agency in charge of corporate filings. The state will first conduct a search to insure that the proposed corporate name is available. If so, the certificate of incorporation will be returned to the incorporators as evidence of authority to conduct business.

BY-LAWS

The by-laws of a corporation contain the detailed rules that will govern the conduct of the corporation. Typical provisions will include:

- The number of shares to be issued
- The various classes of stock with appropriate descriptions (Classes of Stock refers to certain privileges that a shareholder has that a shareholder of a different class would not, such as voting rights)
- The manner in which directors will be elected
- The manner in which officers will be elected
- The manner in which notice shall be given for meetings of both the directors and the shareholders

- How a meeting will be conducted and who will preside over the meetings
- How often meetings will be held
- Quorum requirements (the number of directors/shareholders that must be in attendance for business to be conducted)

MINUTES OF MEETINGS

All corporations conduct business by holding meetings. Meetings will be held of directors as well as shareholders. In order to document that meetings actually took place, the secretary of the corporation will prepare the minutes of the meetings and keep those minutes in the corporate record book.

The corporation will always begin its business operations by holding an initial meeting of shareholders and an initial meeting of directors. At these initial meetings, directors will be appointed and the corporate by-laws will be ratified.

STOCK

The stockholders own a corporation. Certificates of stock will be issued to the stockholders as evidence of the number of shares owned by the shareholder and the class of stock held.

TAXATION OF CORPORATIONS

Since corporations are separate legal entities, they are taxed separately from its owners. There are, however, two primary types of corporations that impact on this method of taxation.

"C" CORPORATIONS

A "C" corporation is one that operates completely separate from its shareholders and is taxed separately. A "C" corporation will be required to file a corporate tax return.

Use this form to report "C" corporation profits and losses.

Form **1120-A**	**U.S. Corporation Short-Form Income Tax Return**	OMB No. 1545-0890
Department of the Treasury Internal Revenue Service	For calendar year 2000 or tax year beginning................ , 2000, ending .... , 20..... See separate instructions to make sure the corporation qualifies to file Form 1120-A.	**2000**

A Check this box if the corp. is a personal service corp. (as defined in Temporary Regs. section 1.441-4T—see instructions) ☐	Use IRS label. Other-wise, print or type.	Name	**B** Employer identification number
		Number, street, and room or suite no. (If a P.O. box, see page 7 of instructions.)	**C** Date incorporated
		City or town, state, and ZIP code	**D** Total assets (see page 8 of instructions) $

E Check applicable boxes: **(1)** ☐ Initial return **(2)** ☐ Change of address

F Check method of accounting: **(1)** ☐ Cash **(2)** ☐ Accrual **(3)** ☐ Other (specify) ▶

Income

1a	Gross receipts or sales	**b** Less returns and allowances	**c** Balance ▶	1c	
2	Cost of goods sold (see page 14 of instructions)	2	
3	Gross profit. Subtract line 2 from line 1c	3	
4	Domestic corporation dividends subject to the 70% deduction	4	
5	Interest	5	
6	Gross rents	6	
7	Gross royalties	7	
8	Capital gain net income (attach Schedule D (Form 1120))	8	
9	Net gain or (loss) from Form 4797, Part II, line 18 (attach Form 4797) . .	9	
10	Other income (see page 8 of instructions)	10	
11	**Total income.** Add lines 3 through 10 . . . . ▶	11	

Deductions (See instructions for limitations on deductions.)

12	Compensation of officers (see page 10 of instructions)	12	
13	Salaries and wages (less employment credits)	13	
14	Repairs and maintenance	14	
15	Bad debts	15	
16	Rents	16	
17	Taxes and licenses	17	
18	Interest	18	
19	Charitable contributions (see page 11 of instructions for 10% limitation) .	19	
20	Depreciation (attach Form 4562)	20		
21	Less depreciation claimed elsewhere on return	21a		21b	
22	Other deductions (attach schedule)	22	
23	**Total deductions.** Add lines 12 through 22 . . . . ▶	23	
24	Taxable income before net operating loss deduction and special deductions. Subtract line 23 from line 11	24	
25	**Less: a** Net operating loss deduction (see page 13 of instructions)	25a			
	b Special deductions (see page 13 of instructions)	25b		25c	
26	**Taxable income.** Subtract line 25c from line 24	26	
27	**Total tax** (from page 2, Part I, line 8)	27	

Tax and Payments

28	**Payments:**		
a	1999 overpayment credited to 2000	28a		
b	2000 estimated tax payments	28b		
c	Less 2000 refund applied for on Form 4466	28c ( )	Bal ▶	28d	
e	Tax deposited with Form 7004	28e	
f	Credit for tax paid on undistributed capital gains (attach Form 2439)	28f	
g	Credit for Federal tax on fuels (attach Form 4136). See instructions	28g	
h	Total payments. Add lines 28d through 28g	28h	
29	Estimated tax penalty (see page 14 of instructions). Check if Form 2220 is attached . . ▶ ☐	29	
30	**Tax due.** If line 28h is smaller than the total of lines 27 and 29, enter amount owed	30	
31	**Overpayment.** If line 28h is larger than the total of lines 27 and 29, enter amount overpaid . .	31	
32	Enter amount of line 31 you want: **Credited to 2001 estimated tax** ▶		**Refunded** ▶	32	

Sign Here

Under penalties of perjury, I declare that I have examined this return, including accompanying schedules and statements, and to the best of my knowledge and belief, it is true, correct, and complete. Declaration of preparer (other than taxpayer) is based on all information of which preparer has any knowledge.

▶ Signature of officer _____ Date _____ ▶ Title _____

Paid Preparer's Use Only

Preparer's signature ▶	Date	Check if self-employed ☐	Preparer's SSN or PTIN
Firm's name (or yours if self-employed), address, and ZIP code ▶		EIN	
		Phone no. ( )	

For Paperwork Reduction Act Notice, see page 1 of the instructions. Cat. No. 11456E Form **1120-A** (2000)

Since a corporation is a separate taxpayer, it has its own tax rate table.

Corporations (for Tax Years Beginning in 2001)

Taxable Income Over	Not Great Than	Taxes on Col. 1	Rate on Excess
$0	$50,000	$0	15%
$50,000	$75,000	$7,500	25%
$75,000	$100,000	$13,750	34%
$100,000	$335,000	$22,250	39%
$335,000	$10,000,000	$113,900	34%

The corporation, not the shareholders, pays the appropriate tax. Dividends from the corporation paid to the shareholders are also taxable to the shareholder.

 FYI This creates the concept of "double-taxation," a drawback to a "C" corporation. There are ways to reduce or eliminate this double-taxation with proper planning. Be certain to consult with an estate planning attorney.

"S" CORPORATIONS

In order to escape from these corporate tax rates, many individuals opt under subchapter S of the Internal Revenue Code to be taxed as a partnership. This taxation is a pass-through tax explained above under partnerships.

 FYI Some confuse the "C" and "S" corporations as being different types of legal entities. In fact, these two types of corporations are only different in the manner in which they are taxed.

In order to elect to operate as an "S" corporation, the corporation must meet certain requirements. Some of those requirements are …

- The corporation cannot have more than 75 shareholders
- The election must be made by filing Form 2553, Election by a Small Business Corporation
- The corporation must be a domestic corporation organized under the laws of any state or U.S. territory
- The only authorized shareholders can be individuals, estates, and certain exempt organizations or trusts

- All shareholders must be U.S. citizens or residents (no non-resident aliens)

- There may only be one class of stock

- All shareholders must consent to the election

Form **2553** (Rev. January 2001) Department of the Treasury Internal Revenue Service	**Election by a Small Business Corporation** (Under section 1362 of the Internal Revenue Code) ► See Parts II and III on back and the separate instructions. ► The corporation may either send or fax this form to the IRS. See page 1 of the instructions.	OMB No. 1545-0146

Notes:
1. This election to be an S corporation can be accepted only if all the tests are met under **Who May Elect** on page 1 of the instructions; all signatures in Parts I and III are originals (no photocopies); and the exact name and address of the corporation and other required form information are provided.
2. Do not file **Form 1120S**, U.S. Income Tax Return for an S Corporation, for any tax year before the year the election takes effect.
3. If the corporation was in existence before the effective date of this election, see Taxes an S Corporation May Owe on page 1 of the instructions.

Part I   Election Information

Please Type or Print	Name of corporation (see instructions)	A Employer identification number
	Number, street, and room or suite no. (If a P.O. box, see instructions.)	B Date incorporated
	City or town, state, and ZIP code	C State of incorporation

D Election is to be effective for tax year beginning (month, day, year) . . . . ►   /   /

E Name and title of officer or legal representative who the IRS may call for more information | F Telephone number of officer or legal representative ( )

G If the corporation changed its name or address after applying for the EIN shown in A above, check this box . . . . ► ☐

H If this election takes effect for the first tax year the corporation exists, enter month, day, and year of the **earliest** of the following: (1) date the corporation first had shareholders, (2) date the corporation first had assets, or (3) date the corporation began doing business . . . . ►   /   /

I Selected tax year: Annual return will be filed for tax year ending (month and day) ►
If the tax year ends on any date other than December 31, except for an automatic 52-53-week tax year ending with reference to the month of December, you **must** complete Part II on the back. If the date you enter is the ending date of an automatic 52-53-week tax year, write "52-53-week year" to the right of the date. See Temporary Regulations section 1.441-2T(e)(3).

J Name and address of each shareholder; shareholder's spouse having a community property interest in the corporation's stock; and each tenant in common, joint tenant, and tenant by the entirety. (A husband and wife (and their estates) are counted as one shareholder in determining the number of shareholders without regard to the manner in which the stock is owned.)	K Shareholders' Consent Statement. Under penalties of perjury, we declare that we consent to the election of the above-named corporation to be an S corporation under section 1362(a) and that we have examined this consent statement, including accompanying schedules and statements, and to the best of our knowledge and belief, it is true, correct, and complete. We understand our consent is binding and may not be withdrawn after the corporation has made a valid election. (Shareholders sign and date below.)		L Stock owned		M Social security number or employer identification number (see instructions)	N Share-holder's tax year ends (month and day)
	Signature	Date	Number of shares	Dates acquired		

Under penalties of perjury, I declare that I have examined this election, including accompanying schedules and statements, and to the best of my knowledge and belief, it is true, correct, and complete.

Signature of officer ►   Title ►   Date ►

For Paperwork Reduction Act Notice, see page 4 of the instructions.   Cat. No. 18629R   Form **2553** (Rev. 1-2001)

Use this form to elect subchapter "S" status for your corporation.

ADVANTAGES

The single biggest advantage of operating a business as a corporation is the limited liability afforded to shareholders. A corporation is liable for its debts to the extent of corporate assets. The shareholders of a corporation are not personally liable for corporate debts beyond their investment in the corporation.

As with limited partners, shareholders must go to great lengths to ensure that a corporation is actually operated as a corporation. This means that the shareholders must follow certain guidelines:

- All corporate transactions must be carried out in the name of the corporation. All corporations must identify in the name that they are corporations. Designations such as "Inc." or "Corporation" are the most common. The importance of this is that all who deal with the corporation must be put "on notice" that they are dealing with a corporation and not a sole proprietorship (d/b/a).

- All letterhead, business cards, advertising, and so on must clearly set forth the corporation name.

- All bank accounts used by the corporation must be set up only in the name of the corporation. All checks must likewise have the corporate name clearly printed on them.

- No individual officer, director, or shareholder should ever sign his or name individually to a corporate obligation, and must always identify the capacity in which he or she is signing. For example, Paula Petunia, secretary of the XYZ Corporation, should never sign her name like this:

_____

Paula Petunia

The proper way for her to sign would be as follows:

_____

Paula Petunia, Secretary for

XYZ Corporation

- Shareholders, officers, and directors should never commingle personal money with corporate money. The quickest way to become liable for a corporate obligation is to treat the corporation as a sole proprietorship. Reliance on the name of the corporation is not enough to prevent liability from attaching.

"If it walks like a duck, talks like a duck, and sounds like a duck, it is probably a duck." This phrase has never been more appropriate than when used in connection with corporations. Even though a corporation has been properly formed, if money is exchanged freely between the corporation and the personal accounts of individual shareholders, officers, directors; if corporate advertising fails to use the term "Inc." or "Corporation"; or if corporate records are not maintained regularly, the individuals will be liable for corporate debt. This is called "piercing the corporate veil."

- Always keep corporate records current. Always keep minutes of initial and annual meetings of both the shareholders and the directors in the corporate record book.

- Be certain to pay and file all necessary information with the state office in charge of corporations. Reports must typically be filed on an annual basis.

Due to variations in state law, be certain to consult with an attorney in your state who can advise you on the requirements contained in your state law.

DISADVANTAGES

The biggest disadvantage of operating a business as a corporation is the paperwork required to organize and operate it properly. Separate tax returns are required. Consistent and periodic bookkeeping must be maintained for the corporate record book and other accounts. Commingling of personal funds with the corporate funds must be avoided at all costs.

SOME OTHER BUSINESS ENTITIES

Many individuals are now running their businesses as limited liability companies (LLCs). This is a relatively new business entity, created by statute. Members, who are much like general partners, manage the limited liability company. The difference is that the members are not personally liable for liabilities of the LLC. In this sense, they are like limited partners. Members, therefore, are basically limited partners who manage the business.

The LLC is taxed the same as a partnership. Net income and losses are passed through to the individual members in proportion to their respective interests in the LLC.

Unlike an "S" corporation, the LLC is not restricted with regard to classes of stock or number of "shareholders" (members) as is the "S" corporation. There is more flexibility with the operation and management of an LLC than with an "S" corporation.

One of the hottest business entities has been the family limited partnership (FLP). The family limited partnership is basically a limited partnership organized under applicable statutes that are used to provide tax and non-tax benefits for family-owned and operated businesses. FLPs typically contain restrictions on transferability of interests in the partnership. State law also limits creditor claims against the FLP by compelling the filing of a *charging order*, which allows the creditor a right to its pro rata share of distributions from the FLP.

An FLP is run the same as a limited partnership. There must be a general partner to operate and manage the partnership. Limited partner interests can be given to members of the family. The general partner might, for example, own only 1% interest in the FLP, with the remaining 99% owned by other family members as limited partners.

Gifting of partnership interests can be made to family members while the general partner continues to maintain control over all partnership assets. As a result of the restrictions on transferability, the valuation of partnership interests generally will be discounted below fair market value, which can provide for some significant savings in estate and inheritance taxes. There are significant costs associated with maintaining a FLP, including periodic appraisals and tax reporting requirements.

PROCEED WITH CAUTION

 The Internal Revenue Service does not like family limited partnerships. As a result, they are regularly and routinely audited. Careful valuations and record keeping are essential.

Hour's Up!

Now it's time to see how much you have learned and retained from this lesson. Try to take the following quiz without referring back to the hourly materials:

1. The business organization form with the greatest personal liability exposure is …

   a. Corporation

   b. Limited liability company

   c. General partnership

   d. Sole proprietorship

2. All of the following are pass-through tax entities, which pass income and losses on to the owners, except …

   a. Partnership

   b. "C" corporation

   c. Sole proprietorship

   d. "S" corporation

3. Which corporate document must be filed with a state agency?

   a. Articles of incorporation

   b. By-laws

   c. Minutes

   d. Stock certificates

4. A sole proprietorship must file which of the following with a state agency?

   a. Certificate of business registration

   b. Certificate of incorporation

   c. By-laws

   d. None of the above

5. An "S" corporation is …

   a. Taxed at the corporate level and again at the shareholder level.

   b. Taxed only at the corporate level

   c. A partnership that is taxed like a corporation

   d. A corporation that is taxed like a partnership

PART VI

Tax Saving Techniques

HOUR 16   Credit Shelter Trusts

HOUR 17   Irrevocable Life Insurance Trusts

HOUR 18   Minor's Trusts and Education Planning

HOUR 19   Charitable Trusts

HOUR 20   Marital Trusts and Disclaimer Planning

HOUR 21   Gifting of Assets

HOUR 22   Planning for Non-Residents

Hour 16
Credit Shelter Trusts

Chapter Summary

LESSON PLAN:

In this chapter you will learn ...

- All about the credit shelter trust.
- How to set up a credit shelter trust.
- How to use formula marital deduction clauses.
- How to provide for the surviving spouse.
- Who should be the trustee of the credit shelter trust.
- What happens when the surviving spouse dies.

Hour 6, "Federal Estate Taxes," detailed the nature of the federal estate tax. With any luck, you remember that people who have a taxable estate in excess of $675,000 (for year 2001) require special tax planning to reduce the impact of the federal estate tax. This exemption is available to each individual, which means husband and wife each have an exemption equivalent of $675,000 (in 2001). Therefore it would seem logical that a married couple would be able to own a combined $1.35 million and pay no federal estate tax at the time of each of their deaths. Unfortunately, the use of these two exemptions is thwarted by the ineffective use of joint ownership.

As you know, joint ownership of property with right of survivorship means that when one spouse dies, the other spouse inherits the decedent's entire share and owns the property outright. For example, if husband and wife jointly own property worth $1,375,000 (in 2001) the first spouse to die would have a value of $675,000 (half the total) in his or her taxable estate. However, because of the unlimited marital deduction, there would be no federal estate tax owing at the death of the first spouse because the entire one-half interest of the deceased spouse is transferred to the surviving spouse.

When the second spouse dies there is no spouse surviving (except in the event of remarriage) and the unlimited marital deduction is no longer available. At this time the entire $1,375,000 is part of the taxable estate of the surviving spouse. The surviving spouse is allowed only his or her individual exemption of $675,000 (in 2001). The result is a tax beginning at the rate of 37% imposed on the excess $675,000.

This "marital deduction-joint property" trap is the most common problem facing married couples. It has been said that the estate tax is a voluntary tax, paid by those people who have neglected to plan. If the husband and wife properly utilize marital deduction tax planning, the result can be completely reversed.

For example, suppose husband and wife own $1.35 million in property, but assume the husband owns $675,000 in his name alone and his wife owns the other $675,000 in her name alone. In this situation, there is no joint tenancy property with right of survivorship. Although husband's taxable estate is $675,000, his estate will be allowed to utilize the $675,000 individual unified credit resulting in no federal estate tax (in 2001).

As long as that property does not pass to his wife, her taxable estate also will be valued at $675,000 (assuming for this illustration that there is no appreciation or additions). Her estate also will use the $675,000 individual unified credit and will owe no federal estate tax. (You're probably wondering what happens if you *want* to leave money to your spouse. Don't worry: We'll get to that in just a minute!)

By simply eliminating the use of joint tenancy with right of survivorship, the estates of this couple would pay no federal estate tax on the entire $1.35 million in assets. From a tax standpoint, the savings amounts to $220,550! Not too bad for simply eliminating joint tenancy!

JUST A MINUTE

When two trusts are established for husband and wife, this will also result in doubling the applicable exemptions available under state inheritance tax laws. For example, if the first $100,000 is exempt under state law on assets passing to a child, husband can leave $100,000 to the child, and wife can do the same. Since the inheritance is received from different people, the exemption applies each time. If, however, all of husband's assets passed directly to wife, child would only benefit from the single $100,000 exemption.

Marital deduction planning is designed to avoid the problem created by joint ownership of assets with right of survivorship. By limiting the amount of property passing from the first spouse to die to the surviving spouse, the survivor has a better chance of keeping his or her estate under $675,000.

Because individual ownership creates a probate estate, utilize a revocable living trust for each spouse. This attains the advantage of reducing and in some cases eliminating a federal estate tax on the first 1.35 million in the couple's taxable estate, and eliminating probate.

In Indiana, a home owned jointly between husband and wife is exempt from general creditors. If husband and wife transfer their home into a trust, this property is no longer owned by them as individuals, but instead is owned by them as trustees. The result is a loss of the unlimited exemption afforded to the residence. This result can be minimized through the use of umbrella liability coverage.

SETTING UP A CREDIT SHELTER TRUST

You've now learned how to earn incredible tax savings by choosing not to transfer property to your surviving spouse. However, taxes are not everything. Most spouses wish to provide for the other regardless of tax issues. However, transferring property directly to the surviving spouse creates an additional tax burden when that surviving spouse dies. There must be some way to provide for the surviving spouse and still not transfer property to the surviving spouse. The solution is to provide for the surviving spouse without transferring any assets *directly* to him or her. This is the function of the credit shelter trust.

The credit shelter trust is simply a vehicle for retaining sufficient assets to apply against the unified credit; then use for the benefit of the surviving spouse. As long as the surviving spouse does not have too much control over the credit shelter trust, the mere presence of these trust assets will not cause those assets to be taxed as part of the surviving spouse's taxable estate.

A credit shelter trust can be established in a will or in a living trust; either will accomplish the same tax objectives. If you use the will, the credit shelter trust will be written into your will. You will maintain individual ownership of your assets until death. Your will then will be probated and your assets used to "fund" the credit shelter trust.

If you use a living trust, the credit shelter trust will be written into your trust. Rather than maintain individual ownership of your assets, you will retitle your assets into the name of the revocable trust. You will maintain your trust until death, at which time the credit shelter trust automatically becomes operative. No probate would be required and your trust is already funded.

PROCEED WITH CAUTION

The failure to properly retitle all assets that are to be placed in the trust will result in those assets not being controlled by the trust provisions and will likely result in probate over those assets.

JUST A MINUTE

It is important to consider non-trust assets when dividing assets between spouses, because a credit shelter-funding clause takes into account all assets in the decedent's taxable estate; not just trust assets.

FORMULA MARITAL DEDUCTION

What happens when a married individual has more than the unified credit amount? Suppose Bob owns $800,000 in property and investments. He sets up a credit shelter trust with a goal of sheltering from taxation $675,000 (in 2001). How does he shield the remaining $125,000 from federal estate taxes?

Assuming Bob does not want to make charitable gifts, which are deductible, he has little choice but to defer taxes on the $125,000. How does he do that? He transfers that $125,000 to his wife. By using the unlimited marital deduction, he will avoid all federal estate taxes at his death, partially by exempting $675,000; partially by deferring $125,000.

PROCEED WITH CAUTION

The IRS has some very strict rules to follow when it comes down to writing the document that will reach the above goal. You should never even attempt to "do it yourself" or it is quite likely that your heirs will be paying federal estate taxes.

These formula marital deduction clauses are quite complex, but there are several methods you can use to achieve the best result. For the sake of illustration, here is a description of how these formulas work:

- One formula will first fund the credit shelter trust with up to $675,000 (in 2001), and transfer the remainder directly to the surviving spouse.

- Another formula leaves everything to the surviving spouse that qualifies for the marital deduction, except the amount that is exempt ($675,000 in 2001). This sounds the same as the first choice, but it actually can have different results.

These formulas are written to apply even if the law changes. Rather than referring to a specific dollar amount, such as $675,000, it will refer to the amount that is exempt from taxation as a result of the applicable unified credit. It is beyond the scope of this book to go into more detail on these various formulas. Suffice it to say that a professional accountant or estate planner can help you use these formulas so that you achieve significant tax savings.

Another issue concerns the valuation of the decedent's assets. Different valuation dates can produce different results. One of the valuation dates that can be used is date of death value; another is date of distribution. Your document must specify the valuation date.

PROVIDING FOR YOUR SURVIVING SPOUSE

Even if the first spouse to die does not give the first $675,000 (in 2001) directly to the surviving spouse, there are assets providing for the surviving spouse as needed. Making the credit shelter trust available to the surviving spouse attains this goal. This can be accomplished using one of several "open doors" that are authorized by the IRS. These are described in the following.

PROCEED WITH CAUTION

 Don't give your surviving spouse too much control or access to the credit shelter trust. Too much control results in the credit shelter assets being taxed in the estate of the surviving spouse, thus negating all of the planning.

PROVIDING INCOME

The first open door is to make any income generated by the trust assets payable to the surviving spouse. Full access to this income does not jeopardize the shelter provided over the trust principal. There are both practical and tax reasons for allowing income to be distributed to the surviving spouse. Providing a means of support usually is of paramount importance to the couple. Depending on the type of investment, the credit shelter trust assets might produce significant returns.

A fully funded credit shelter trust ($675,000 in 2001) invested in insured money market funds earning 7% would net $47,250 annually. Many couples would consider this sufficient for the support needs of the surviving spouse without that spouse having to touch the principal. Usually, the spouse could supplement this income with retirement and social security benefits, as well as from income generated from the separate assets belonging to the surviving spouse.

You can make the income payable to your spouse either mandatory, which means it happens automatically, or discretionary, which leaves the decision to pay the income to the spouse to the trustee. If you know your spouse will expect and rely on this income for as his or her primary support, you'll want to make the distribution mandatory. If you want to make the income available just in case your surviving spouse needs the income at a later date, leaving the distribution decision to the trustee makes good sense.

GO TO ▶
Review the discussion of income taxation of estates and trusts in Hour 5.

From a tax standpoint, the payment of income to the surviving spouse most likely is the best plan. As pointed out in Hour 5, "Income Taxes and Inheritance Taxes," income taxation of trusts can be more severe than individual tax rates. For example, the tax on income over $$8,900 from a trust is taxed at the rate of 39.6%.

THE FIVE AND FIVE POWER

Recall in our discussion of the general power of appointment in Hour 3, "What Is an Estate?" that a person who has a general power of appointment must include the value of the property he or she controls in his or her taxable estate. If Bill has an estate valued at $400,000 and also a general power of appointment over a trust with a value of $500,000, Bill's taxable estate will be $900,000. If the power of appointment was limited, Bill's taxable estate would only be $400,000. With the general power, Bill would have total use and enjoyment of the $500,000 held in trust. With the limited power Bill would have no ability to use the $500,000 for himself, his creditors, or his estate or the creditors of his estate.

Fortunately, there is another option that can allow Bill use of a small portion of the trust assets. If Bill has a general power over no more than $5,000 or 5%—which is why they call it the *five and five power*—of the value of the trust on an annual basis, only that value will be included in Bill's taxable estate. If Bill had a power to use up to $8,000 or 8% of the value of the trust annually, Bill's taxable estate at death would include the full value of the trust.

Remember that even if the power is not used during the year of the power holder's death, the value that could have been used will be included in the taxable estate of the power holder.

LIMITED POWER OF APPOINTMENT

We described the limited power of appointment in detail in Hour 3. A limited power is one that allows the individual with the power to have control over the entire asset, but is restricted from using the property for his or her self, his or her creditors, or the estate of either. Granting the surviving spouse a limited power of appointment over the credit shelter trust assets can allow for early termination of the credit shelter trust before the death of the surviving spouse. This is particularly useful when the surviving spouse has sufficient assets to maintain a comfortable standard of living. This type of power usually limits distributions to children or lineal descendants, but need not be limited in that manner so long as it does not become a general power.

THE ASCERTAINABLE STANDARD

The *ascertainable standard* is well established as a safe method of allowing a surviving spouse access to the trust's assets if needed. The reasons for the spouse to receive assets from the trust include his or her "health, education, maintenance, and support (HEMS)."

Unlike the five and five power and the limited power of appointment, both of which are exercisable by the spouse alone, the ascertainable standard is a power exercisable by the trustee of the trust. So long as a surviving spouse has the right to use trust assets in accordance with this standard, there is little risk of tax inclusion in the surviving spouse's estate. This meets the goal of providing for the surviving spouse with assets sheltered in the trust.

This standard is quite broad. As long as the trustee documents that the spouse requires the funds for health, education, maintenance, and support, the spouse in need actually can use none of it or all of it as needed. Unlike the five and five power, the mere ability to distribute the trust for health, maintenance, support and education does not cause any assets not distributed to be included in the taxable estate of the surviving spouse.

CHOOSING THE TRUSTEE

There is some disagreement in the estate planning community over whether or not the surviving spouse should serve as trustee of a credit shelter trust. The debate centers primarily on the tax ramifications of the choice. Most couples would prefer that the surviving spouse serve as trustee of the credit shelter trust because it gives the surviving spouse a certain degree of power over the assets. It also keeps "outsiders" out of the loop, at least while the surviving spouse is alive. Another reason is that surviving spouses usually will not be paid for being trustee, whereas another individual might and a financial institution will charge a fee for serving as trustee.

All of these are good reasons to name a spouse as trustee. A few planners believe, however, that the IRS will view this control by the surviving spouse over the trust assets as sufficient to include those assets in the surviving spouse's taxable estate. If the surviving spouse serves as trustee, the existence of the power to distribute income to him- or herself will not cause inclusion of any trust assets in the taxable estate of the surviving spouse except, of course, the income. Nor will the existence of the limited power of appointment or five and five power have any adverse income tax consequences.

Some planners reason that without any method of judicial review (the right to go to court to review actions of the trustee) by the ultimate beneficiaries of the trust (children, for example), this standard, exercised by the spouse in his or her own favor, is too broad and is tantamount to a general power of appointment. Others assert that as long as the standard is properly applied, anybody, including the surviving spouse, can exercise it.

The safest approach is to name someone other than the surviving spouse as trustee. Another option is to name co-trustees, with the surviving spouse having power over investment of trust assets and the distribution of income, exercise of the limited power of appointment, and exercise of the five and five power. The co-trustee could have exclusive authority over the discretionary distributions pursuant to the ascertainable standard (health, maintenance, support, and education).

A third approach would be to allow the surviving spouse to serve as trustee, but eliminate the ascertainable standard from the powers of the trustee. The drawback would be the inability to reach trust principal except to the extent of the annual five and five power.

PROCEED WITH CAUTION

As with all of the material in this book, be certain to consult an estate planning attorney before implementing any of the techniques discussed in this book. The failure to obtain professional advice could result in additional expenses for administering your estate and could result in additional and unnecessary taxation of your estate. Additionally, the failure to properly prepare documents according to applicable law may render the documents useless.

Hour's Up!

Now it's time to see how much you have learned and retained from this lesson. Try to take the following quiz without referring back to the hourly materials:

1. A credit shelter trust can be established ...

    a. In a trust

    b. In a will

    c. Both of the above

    d. None of the above

2. The value of assets in a credit shelter trust can be as much as ...

    a. $10,000; $20,000 if a married couple

    b. $1.35 million in the year 2001

    c. One half of $675,000 in the year 2001

    d. The applicable unified credit exemption amount

3. With the use of a credit shelter trust by the deceased spouse, the surviving spouse ...

    a. May have access to trust principal and income

    b. May have no access to trust principal

    c. May have access only to trust income

    d. May get only $5,000 annually

4. Which of the following might be a trustee of a credit shelter trust ...

    a. Children

    b. Financial institution

    c. Spouse

    d. Any of the above

5. The exercise of the limited power of appointment will result in ...

   a. All of the trust passing directly to the surviving spouse

   b. All of the trust passing directly to the children

   c. Any portion of the trust passing to any member of a class that does not include the surviving spouse, the estate of the surviving spouse, or the creditors of the surviving spouse or the creditors of the estate of the surviving spouse

   d. All of the trust passing directly to a charity

HOUR 17

Irrevocable Life Insurance Trusts

CHAPTER SUMMARY

LESSON PLAN:

In this chapter you will learn about the most powerful of all estate planning tools: the irrevocable life insurance trust. Unparalleled in its simplicity and results, this irrevocable trust can provide the solutions to most tax problems. You will learn about the power of leveraging. You will also learn …

- All about the irrevocable life insurance trust (ILIT).
- How it operates and why it works so well.
- What to consider when you're drafting a life insurance trust.
- Who can be the trustee.
- What tax ramifications to consider.
- Some alternatives to the ILIT.

Whoever said life insurance is boring didn't know about the irrevocable life insurance trust (ILIT). The capability of an irrevocable life insurance trust to pay taxes, pass on a legacy, provide liquidity for the operation of a business, and to do it all on a leveraged basis really is quite phenomenal.

Recall in Hour 3, "What Is an Estate?" the discussion of items included in your taxable estate. The one asset that most people do not consider to be a part of their taxable estate is life insurance. Even without cash value, life insurance death benefits are included in the taxable estate of the owner for federal estate tax considerations. That a death benefit, paid only after the death of the insured, can be taxed in the estate of the owner is quite a shock to some people. But as discussed in Hour 6, "Federal Estate Taxes," the key to taxation of life insurance is the existence of "incidences of ownership." The most common of these are as follows:

- Power to change the beneficiary
- Power to surrender or cancel the policy
- Power to assign the policy or revoke an assignment
- Power to pledge the policy for a loan
- Power to obtain from the insurer a loan against the surrender value of the policy
- Power to change beneficial ownership

PROCEED WITH CAUTION

You need to be aware that if you transfer ownership of an existing policy of life insurance to a new owner, you'll be activating a *three-year inclusionary rule*. This rule provides that any policy transferred within three years of the death of the original owner will be included in the taxable estate of the original owner for federal estate tax purposes.

Basically, if you own the policy, your estate will be taxed on it. So what can you do to escape taxation? The answer is simply to avoid "owning" the life insurance policy. Again, because ownership includes more than being the technical owner, all incidents of ownership must be carefully avoided.

UNDERSTANDING THE PLAN

An irrevocable life insurance trust is a vehicle that owns life insurance policies insuring your life. The primary goal of this trust is to shift ownership of life insurance policies away from you to remove the policy proceeds from taxation at your death. By transferring ownership of that policy to an irrevocable trust, or by having an irrevocable trust purchase a new policy, the death benefit will not be included in the estate of the insured.

CHOOSING THE RIGHT POLICY

Because of the three-year inclusionary rule, you have to plan in advance for this tax planning to work. If you already have a life insurance policy, it's time to evaluate the benefits of this policy. If you bought the policy to provide liquidity in the event of your premature death, for example, then this policy should be retained.

Most likely, you have a single policy insuring your life—and if so, you're probably the husband. One reason the husband usually is the one insured is that mortality tables indicate the male will predecease the female. Additionally, although not necessarily true today, the male historically was the wage earner and it was his income that was needed by the surviving spouse and children to survive. Maintaining this type of policy is important from a retirement planning perspective. Should the husband die prematurely, the wife will need the death benefit to maintain her care and comfort and to provide an education for the children. You don't want to transfer this kind of policy to an irrevocable trust since it would be unavailable for this purpose.

On the other hand, if you don't need your life insurance for retirement, or childcare and education, consider transferring it to a trust. You might be single or may be a retired couple who have amassed sufficient funds to care for yourselves. You might be reluctant to transfer these funds to a trust if you've owned insurance most of your life or have invested considerable sums in the policy. Although you might no longer need the funds, you might not want to cancel the policy and give up the death benefit. Another consideration is the type of insurance held. For example, term insurance has no cash value but can have premiums in later years that are prohibitive.

GO TO ▶

For a discussion of the various types of insurance, review Hour 13, "Life Insurance."

This type of policy will tend to terminate in later years due to the high premiums involved. If the premiums are too high to afford, the policy will not be able to provide much of a death benefit anyway. Transferring this policy will normally not be worth doing.

The policy that most likely will be a candidate for an irrevocable life insurance trust is one that builds cash value. These include universal life, variable life, whole life, and variable-universal life. If enough money is deposited in early years, the cash value may be sufficient to pay the premiums without any additional deposits being necessary. Even if you have another life insurance policy, you should get someone else to purchase a new policy—it can't be in your name—and put it into an irrevocable trust. If you never own the title to the new policy, the benefits will not be included in your estate. Being the insured is not an incident of ownership.

THE IRREVOCABLE LIFE INSURANCE TRUST

As the name implies, an irrevocable life insurance trust is nothing more than an irrevocable trust that owns life insurance. This is not the same as a living trust, which by definition is a revocable trust. The life insurance trust must be irrevocable because if you have the power to revoke the trust it means that the assets will become part of your taxable estate—exactly what you hoped to avoid by establishing the trust in the first place.

The good news is that this irrevocable trust can actually own any asset; not just life insurance. The name "irrevocable life insurance trust" actually is a misnomer because not only can the trust own life insurance, it can own real estate or other types of investments. The reason the descriptive term "life insurance" is used is to distinguish this trust from many other irrevocable trusts such as irrevocable children's trusts and irrevocable charitable trusts.

Who's in Charge?

Basically anybody except the insured can be the trustee of this trust. If the insured were the trustee, IRS rules would require that the insurance be included in the estate of the insured, based upon the degree of control exercised by the insured/trustee. To avoid inclusion in the insured's estate, neither the insured nor the insured's spouse should ever serve as trustee of an irrevocable life insurance trust.

A financial institution probably is best to serve as trustee. There are certain record keeping requirements that are best handled by an institutional trustee. This is especially true since this trust is irrevocable. Whereas an institutional trustee likely will be around when the policy pays off, an individual might not. Individuals might decide not to serve, requiring that the trusteeship pass to someone else designated in the document.

For these reasons it is a good idea to have a financial institution as trustee. This corporate trustee would know its legal duties and obligations for providing notices to the beneficiaries upon receiving contributions to the trust. It also would have knowledge of investment obligations for any amount received in excess of the premium amount.

On the other hand, many people prefer to have their children serve as trustees. This approach has merit, because the children will be the ultimate beneficiaries anyway. Another factor in favor of children as trustees is saving the expense of an institutional trustee. For liability purposes, many financial institutions charge fairly high annual fees to serve as trustees. Children usually will be happy to serve without pay, because the trust actually benefits them in the end.

What Happens After the Trust Is Created?

GO TO ▶
To review the discussion of the grantor trust rules, see Hour 10, "Revocable Living Trusts."

The first step you must take after executing the trust is applying for a taxpayer identification number. Because this trust does not fit within the grantor trust rules, and is a legal entity separate from the insured, it must operate with a separate taxpayer identification number. This number must be used to report taxable income attributable to the trust.

As a practical matter, there rarely will be any taxable income on an irrevocable life insurance trust until the policy pays the death benefit, because income earned on investments within the policy (the cash value) is tax-deferred.

Once the insured and the trustee execute the document and a taxpayer identification number is obtained, the next step is to prepare an application for new insurance on the life of the insured. This step can be skipped when no new insurance is applied for and only existing insurance is transferred to the trust.

The IRS reviews these trusts quite closely to be certain the insured has no incidents of ownership in the policy. Thus, it is imperative that the trustee make application for the insurance and not the insured. If the IRS finds that the insured made application for the policy it is likely that the policy will be included in the insured's taxable estate for federal estate tax purposes.

PAYING THE PREMIUMS

Once an existing policy has been transferred, or a new policy issued to the trust, the trustee of that trust becomes the owner of the policy. As such, all premium notices will come to that trustee. The trustee will need funds to pay the premium on any such policy of insurance. For the trustee to obtain the funds necessary to pay the premium costs, the individual grantor will need to contribute sufficient assets to that trust to accomplish that purpose.

The insured can contribute any dollar amount to the trust at any time. The insured therefore must contribute enough to the trust to allow the trustee to finance the life policy. The transfer of money from the insured to the trustee is a gift, because the insured never gets this money back. The amount that can be gifted tax-free depends on the number of beneficiaries of the trust. If you want those contributions to qualify for the $10,000 per person, per year annual gift exclusion, the insured shouldn't contribute more than $10,000 per year, per beneficiary. Obviously sufficient assets must be contributed to insure that the trustee has sufficient funds with which to pay the insurance premium.

For a gift of cash from the insured to the trustee of the irrevocable trust to qualify for the $10,000 per person, annual gift tax exclusion, the beneficiaries of that trust must have an immediate right to possess the funds contributed to the trust. Without this present interest, the gift to the trust is taxable to the insured. This requires that the trustee of the trust give the beneficiaries written notice that they have an unrestricted right to demand and receive their proportionate share of the money contributed to the trust within a specified period of time. This time usually is between 15 and 60 days. If the beneficiaries elect to receive those funds, the trustee will be obligated to deliver those funds to the individual beneficiaries.

JUST A MINUTE

This written notification of the right of withdrawal is referred to as a *crummey power*, stemming from the Federal 9th Circuit Court of Appeals case entitled *Crummey* v *Comm.*

Naturally, if the beneficiaries demand their share of the contribution to the trust, there will be nothing left to pay the insurance premiums and eventually the policy will lapse. This would work to the disadvantage of the beneficiaries and destroy the purpose for creating the trust. If the individual beneficiaries elect not to receive their proportionate share of the contribution, once the designated period of time passes those funds are no longer available to the beneficiary. They then can be used by the trustee according to the terms of the trust to pay the premium on any policy of life insurance.

PROCEED WITH CAUTION

There can be no agreement, formal or informal, in which the beneficiaries agree not to exercise this right of withdrawal. Even an informal family discussion about this has led to the disqualification of the annual gift exclusion.

TRUST FUNDAMENTALS

As a general rule, you can contribute any amount of money to this trust at any time. The issue really is whether you'll have to pay taxes as a result of the gift. The answer, is that any gift in excess of the annual exclusion amount will result in a taxable gift to the one making the gift. Without a valid crummey notice, any gift to the trust would be taxable to the one making the gift.

Exploring Beneficiary Tax Implications

Whenever a beneficiary has an unrestricted right to take possession and enjoyment of assets contributed to a trust, a failure to exercise that right is treated by the Internal Revenue Code as a gift from the beneficiary back to the trust. The reason for this is that this unrestricted right of withdrawal for the benefit of the beneficiary is a general power of appointment. Assets over which an individual has a general power of appointment are considered to be part of that individual's taxable estate.

GO TO ▶
To review the discussion of general and limited powers of appointment, see Hour 3.

This gift from the beneficiary back to the trust is a taxable gift if the amount the beneficiary chooses not to receive is more than $5,000 or 5% of the total value of the assets that could have been used to satisfy the withdrawal right.

JUST A MINUTE

A carefully drafted trust will provide special language that will prevent a potential gift from being taxable to the beneficiary. Be certain to consult with your legal advisor about this issue.

One such provision would allow the beneficiary a continuing right to withdraw up to the $5,000/5% limit in any given year and carry over the excess of that amount from year to year until there is no gift tax consequence. Another approach would be to give to the beneficiary a general testamentary power to appoint the excess over the $5,000/5% limit in any year to anyone that he or she chooses. This appointment would be designated in his or her last will and testament.

Whenever an insured transfers ownership of an insurance policy to an irrevocable trust or to any other new owner, a taxable gift has occurred. Valuation of these gifts varies depending on the type of policy.

- The value of a new policy generally is the amount of the gross premium paid for the policy.

- If a person owns a single premium or a paid-up policy, the gift value is the single premium the company would charge for a comparable contract with the same face value on the life of a person the insured's age at the time of the gift.

- If further premium payment must still be made on the policy, the value is a result of a calculation to determine the *interpolated terminal reserve* and the value of the unearned portion of the last premium paid. This calculation comes somewhat close to the cash value of the policy.

Some Alternatives to an Irrevocable Life Insurance Trust

Instead of creating an irrevocable life insurance trust, you can simply transfer ownership of an existing policy to another person such as one of your children. As an alternative, your child could take out a policy of insurance on your life, as a child has an insurable interest in a parent's life. If you opt for this plan your children will own the policy, thereby removing the value of the life insurance from the estate of the insured and making the policy a part of the child's/owner's estate. Of course, if you decide to go this route, you'd better have confidence that your children will cooperate and retain the policies so the proceeds can be available for payment of taxes.

However, keep in mind that the inclusion of this policy in the estate of the child could cause a tax problem should the child predecease the insured. This alternative also exposes the policy value to the creditors of the child/owner and makes it subject to divorce and bankruptcy proceedings involving the child/owner. Furthermore, the child/owner would have the power as owner to change beneficiaries, which could upset the plan desired by the insured.

Applying the Death Benefit

The terms of the trust will determine the disposition of the death benefit. Ordinarily, those provisions are similar to those that might be contained in the insured's will or trust. The trustee might be required to distribute the death benefits immediately to the heirs, or invest those sums and make distributions over a period of time or for specific purposes. Using this technique, a family can create a cash fund from the death proceeds and use it to loan money to or purchase assets from a decedent's estate. Doing so will provide cash to pay estate taxes and inheritance taxes but not trigger additional estate and inheritance taxes.

PROCEED WITH CAUTION

Remember: This type of trust is irrevocable. You won't be able to make any changes to the document after it is prepared. Be certain to obtain proper financial and legal advice when contemplating the use of an irrevocable life insurance trust in your estate plan.

OTHER TWISTS AND TURNS

When insuring yourself using an irrevocable life insurance trust, you can't use any of its parts for your benefit. This means you'll have no access to the cash value building within the policy. For some people, especially younger couples who might need access to the growing cash value, the inability to access the cash value is unacceptable. Although not perfect, the following plan might help to accomplish the goal of being able to use the cash value. A second to die (survivorship) policy is required to use this plan.

GO TO ▶
If you need to brush up on this type of policy, review Hour 13.

THE STANDBY TRUST

The first part of this plan is to make an educated guess at which spouse is expected to outlive the other. In addition to mortality tables, actual ancestral longevity and current health issues should be accounted for in this decision making process. The individual with the shortest anticipated life expectancy will be designated as owner of the survivorship policy. The designated owner then will create an irrevocable life insurance trust. This irrevocable trust will be named as the contingent owner and also will be named as the primary beneficiary of the policy.

If the owner dies first as anticipated, the irrevocable trust becomes the owner of the policy. As a survivorship policy, the death benefit is not paid until both spouses are deceased. Upon the death of the surviving spouse, the death benefit should not be included in the taxable estate of the surviving spouse because the surviving spouse never had any incident of ownership in the life insurance policy or its cash value.

The advantage of this plan is that the cash value remains accessible to the couple until the first spouse dies. However, the cash value portion will remain as an includable item in the estate of the owner, and will be subject to federal estate tax.

JUST A MINUTE

If the cash value is paid at the death of the owner to the surviving spouse, the surviving spouse will have the proceeds included in his or her estate at the subsequent death of the surviving spouse.

One problem with this plan is that the order of deaths might not occur as anticipated. Suppose the husband is the owner of the policy and the wife is the first to die. The husband, as owner of the life insurance policy, must transfer ownership of the policy to the irrevocable life insurance trust if he wants to keep the death benefit out of his taxable estate—but he'll have to do that at least three years before he dies. Otherwise, the entire death benefit will be included in his estate. This also will result in a taxable gift of the cash value of the policy to the trust, and gift taxes will have to be paid.

The result is not a perfect scenario but one that does minimize some of the estate tax issues that would be present if no life insurance trust was involved and both spouses were owners of the policy.

PROCEED WITH CAUTION

Don't create a plan like this without the advice of counsel. The purpose of this illustration is merely to show an alternate use of the irrevocable life insurance trust.

ADVANTAGES OF AN IRREVOCABLE LIFE INSURANCE TRUST

The primary benefits of this trust are that …

- The death proceeds will escape taxation for income, estate and inheritance tax purposes (subject to the three-year inclusion period) and that
- The proceeds can be used to reimburse the heirs for the expenses of administration of an estate, including death taxes and income taxes.

PROCEED WITH CAUTION

As with all of the material in this book, be certain to consult an estate planning attorney before implementing any of the techniques discussed in this book. The failure to obtain professional advice could result in additional expenses for administering your estate and could result in additional and unnecessary taxation of your estate. Additionally, the failure to properly prepare documents according to applicable law may render the documents useless.

Hour's Up!

Now it's time to see how much you have learned and retained from this lesson. Try to take the following quiz without referring back to the hourly materials:

1. How many years prior to death must a life insurance policy be transferred to keep the policy out of the taxable estate of the original owner?

    a. Seven years

    b. Five years

    c. Three years

    d. One year

2. What type of insurance is not favored for inclusion in a life insurance trust?

    a. Term

    b. Whole

    c. Universal

    d. Variable

3. All of the following might be a trustee of an irrevocable life insurance trust except …

    a. A child of the insured

    b. A corporate fiduciary

    c. The insured

    d. A competent non-resident adult

4. The transfer of money from the insured to the trustee of a properly drafted irrevocable trust is …

    a. Never a taxable gift, regardless of the amount of the gift

    b. Not a taxable gift up to the annual gift exclusion amount

    c. Always a taxable gift to the beneficiary

    d. Always a taxable gift

5. A crummey power is …

    a. The power vested with the insured to withdraw $5,000 or 5% of the amount in the trust on an annual basis.

    b. The right to transfer money to an irrevocable trust to fund a life insurance policy

    c. A very poorly worded power

    d. The power of a beneficiary to withdraw funds contributed to a trust

Hour 18

Minor's Trusts and Education Planning

M any people are interested in making lifetime gifts to minors but would like to maintain control over the investment. Tax considerations are important, although sometimes not as important as making the funds available to the *minor*. In this hour we'll review some of the trusts and other methods that exist and illustrate how these trusts and other methods can benefit you and your beneficiary.

STRICTLY DEFINED

> For purposes of the trusts discussed in this chapter, 2503(b) and trusts, a **minor** is defined as any individual under the age of majority.

Sometimes you won't want to make a direct gift to a minor because he or she will have unfettered control over all assets. This also will be true of assets gifted into an account created under the Uniform Transfers to Minors Act. Fortunately, the IRS approves certain types of trusts for purposes of making gifts to minors, including the Section 2503(c) and 2503(d) trusts. Let's take a look.

SECTION 2503(C) TRUST

A Section 2503(c) trust is an irrevocable trust for the benefit of a minor that allows gifts to the trust to qualify for the annual gift tax exclusion. The key requirement of this trust is that both income and principal must be available to the minor when he or she reaches age 21.

CHAPTER SUMMARY

LESSON PLAN:

You will learn a variety of methods for providing funds for minor children as well as individuals over the age of 18. We also will discuss new state programs that help finance educational expenses. You will also learn …

- How to use the 2503(b) and 2503(c) trusts.
- How to use Education IRAs.
- How to use a qualified state tuition program.

GO TO ▶
For a more detailed discussion of gifting, go to Hour 21, "Gifting of Assets." There you will find a detailed discussion of how to make non-taxable gifts.

The interesting part about these trusts is that the annual gift exclusion can be used even though the minor does not have immediate possession of the property.

The 2503(c) trust should be considered when …

- The person making the gift is in a high income tax bracket and the minor's income tax bracket is low.
- The person making the gift owns an asset likely to appreciate over time and would like to remove the appreciated asset from his or her gross estate.
- The use of the gift tax annual exclusion is desirable.

The interesting part about these trusts is that the annual gift exclusion may be used even though the minor does not have immediate possession of the property.

Note that neither income nor principal must be paid out to the minor prior to the time the minor attains the age of 21.

JUST A MINUTE

There is a variation in the minimum age a minor must attain to gain access to funds held in a 2503(c) trust (21) compared to a gift to minors account (18), transfers to minors account (21), and a 2503(b) account (whatever the document states).

Any portion of the trust that remains when the minor reaches age 21 must be available to the minor, free from the trust.

If the minor dies before he or she reaches 21, the remaining assets in the trust must go either to the minor's estate or to someone designated in the minor's will.

TAX IMPLICATIONS

Any income that is distributed to the minor is taxable to the minor at the minor's tax rate. If any trust income is not distributed in a taxable year, it will be taxed to the trust at the trust tax rates. Even though the gift to the trust is not immediately in the possession of the minor, the IRS allows for gifts to the trust to constitute a present interest gift and qualify for the annual gift tax exclusion. Not only do transfers to this trust qualify for the annual gift tax exclusion, all of the appreciation on the property from the date it is placed in the trust will not be included in the grantor's gross estate.

GO TO ▶
To view the tax rates for trusts and estates, see Hour 6, "Federal Estate Taxes." Because these rates are high, usually it is advisable to distribute the income annually so the income will be taxed at the minor's rate.

PROCEED WITH CAUTION

Note that the entire value of a 2503(c) trust will be included in the grantor's estate if the grantor is the trustee at the time of his or her death. (Typically, the gross estate of a decedent does not include the value of transfers made by a decedent within three years of death except for transfers of life insurance.) Therefore, if estate reduction is the desired goal, the grantor should select a different trustee for the trust.

ADDITIONAL STRATEGIES

One of the disadvantages of this trust is the requirement that all trust property be turned over to the minor when the minor reaches age 21. To allow for the continuation of this trust beyond age 21, the minor can be given a right to compel distribution for a limited time. If the minor does not exercise his or her withdrawal privilege, the trust can again become irrevocable; thus provide for continuing maintenance for future years.

FYI The right of withdrawal is very similar to the right of withdrawal provided in irrevocable life insurance trusts. For a closer look at these crummey powers, review Hour 17, "Irrevocable Life Insurance Trusts."

DISADVANTAGES

As a general rule, if the intent is to make relatively small gifts to a minor, the complexities and expenses of creating this trust outweigh the advantages. As mentioned above, if the donor acts as the trustee and dies in that capacity before the minor has reached age 21, the assets in the trust may be includable in his or her taxable estate anyway.

The primary disadvantages of a 2503(c) trust include the following:

- Expenses of drafting the trust
- Expenses of filing tax returns and estimated quarterly payments
- The requirement that this trust can have only one beneficiary
- The requirement that this trust be irrevocable resulting in a loss of control by the grantor

Section 2503(b) Trust

A 2503(b) trust differs from the 2503(c) trust in that it requires a *mandatory* distribution of income to the trust beneficiary on at least an annual basis. Assets placed into this trust need not be distributed when the minor attains the age of 21. Therefore, there is more flexibility with the timing of distributions. This trust can extend for the lifetime of the minor, if desired.

Additionally, the principal can be preserved in the trust indefinitely and can even be paid to someone other than the income beneficiary. The trust can even give power to the beneficiary to designate someone who will receive the principal of the trust.

Tax Implications

GO TO ▶
Go to Hour 21 for more discussion of gifting and future interest gifts.

The problem with this trust lies with the unfavorable tax treatment of the trust. Gifts to this type of trust are divided into two portions: an income portion and a principal portion. Only the income portion qualifies for the $10,000 annual exclusion. The principal portion is considered by the IRS as a gift of a future interest and as such does not qualify for the gift tax annual exclusion.

Despite the tax drawbacks of all trusts for minors, this one probably is the most flexible of all. Whereas other trusts have restrictions on when distributions of principal must be made, this one does not. However, it does have the restriction on mandatory distribution of income that the other trusts do not.

Strategy

One strategy for utilizing this trust and still protecting the distribution of income from going directly to the minor is to use this trust in conjunction with a gift to minors account. When income is distributed, the trustee may make distribution directly into a custodial account and use it for the benefit of the minor. In the alternative, it can be left to accumulate in the custodial account until the minor reaches the age of majority under the state statute.

When the beneficiary reaches the applicable age for distribution of the custodial account, the income will then have to be made available to the minor.

TAXATION

If the minor is under the age of 14, income will be taxed according to special rules, known as the "kiddie tax." If the minor is at least 14, all income is taxed at the minor's bracket. There is, therefore, an opportunity to save taxes by transferring assets to a minor child.

GO TO ▶
To learn more about how the "kiddie tax" operates, see Hour 21.

The following is a chart comparing these two children's trusts.

Comparison of 2503(c) and 2503(c) Trusts

	2503(b)	2503
Payment of Income	Mandatory Age 21	Discretionary
Payment of Principal	Discretionary Age 21	Mandatory
Annual Gift Exclusion Allowed	Partial (income only)	Yes

EDUCATIONAL TRUSTS

Considering the cost of tuition, planning for your child's education might seem daunting; all the more reason to do so as soon as possible. Some of the opportunities for educational planning are discussed below. Let's explore these in more detail.

EDUCATION IRAS

An Education IRA (Education Individual Retirement Account) is a trust that is created to help pay for educational expenses. Only expenses that fit within the definition of *qualified educational expenses* will be allowed. Any expenses must be reduced by any payment received from other sources, such as scholarships and other educational assistance. Gifts and inheritances, however, are excluded from this requirement.

Qualified educational expenses include tuition, fees, books, supplies, and equipment. Some provision is made for room and board for students attending college at least half time. Any accredited post-secondary educational institution in the United States, both graduate and undergraduate, qualifies.

Any expenses must be reduced by any payment received from other sources, such as scholarships and other educational assistance. Gifts and inheritances are excluded from this requirement.

For example, suppose that both parents and grandparents would all like to contribute $500 each to a child. Unfortunately, the rules will only permit a *total* of $500 to be contributed to that child's education IRA in any one year.

There are significant tax benefits to an Education IRA. Income earned by an Education IRA is exempt from taxation. Distributions from Education IRAs for qualified expenses are not includable as taxable income to the beneficiary.

Other disadvantages to the Education IRA are that contributions are not deductible, all must be made in cash, and all must be made prior to the beneficiary's 18th birthday.

Perhaps the biggest problem with Education IRAs is that they have annual limit of $500. Depending on when the IRA contributions begin relative to the age of the beneficiary, and also depending upon the school selected by the beneficiary, it will be difficult to fund a four-year college education with only the Education IRA.

The Education IRA's limit can be reduced based upon the donor's adjusted gross income. For example, adjusted gross income over $95,000 will trigger a calculation that reduces the allowable contribution. This annual limit also is reduced if any contribution is made to a qualified state tuition program during the year unless, of course, the contribution to the state tuition program was made from an Education IRA.

An **eligible educational institution** includes any vocational school, college, university, and some post-secondary educational institutions.

There are penalties if contributions are made in excess of the allowable amount. If excess contributions are not returned before the date for filing the donor's tax return, any excess contributions are subject to a 6% excise tax. Be careful, therefore, that your contributions are within the allowable limits.

To grant tax benefits, the IRS imposes some restrictions on the use of an Education IRA. Some of those restrictions are as follows:

- No part of the assets of an Education IRA can be used to purchase life insurance.

- No part of the assets of an Education IRA can be commingled with other property except in a common trust fund or common investment fund.

- If the beneficiary encumbers the account as security for a loan, the amount encumbered will be treated as a distribution from the account.

- Rollovers from one Education IRA to another Education IRA are allowed so long as the beneficiaries are the same (or are members of the beneficiary's family). Only one rollover per 12-month period is allowed.

- If a beneficiary dies before the complete distribution of the balance remaining in an Education IRA, the remaining balance must be paid to the estate of the beneficiary within 30 days of death.

ESTATE AND GIFT TAX CONSEQUENCES

Fortunately, contributions to an Education IRA are eligible for the annual gift tax exclusion. Even if a contribution to an Education IRA exceeds the annual exclusion amount of $10,000, the donor can prorate the gift over a five-year period.

FYI Although contributions qualify for the annual gift tax exclusion, they do not qualify for the exclusion for qualified transfers for educational purposes. Therefore, the $10,000 limitation applies.

QUALIFIED STATE TUITION PROGRAMS

One of the most important developments in education planning is the advent of qualified state tuition programs. All state programs were created in accordance with Internal Revenue Code 529, but vary from state to state. Most states have enacted a qualified state tuition program.

PROCEED WITH CAUTION

These programs vary from state to state. Some of the information that follows may be out of date by the time you read this. Be certain to consult with an estate planning attorney licensed in your state or your financial planner who can advise you properly on investing in these programs.

From a planning standpoint, these programs have outstanding features, ranging from tax deferral to estate reduction, and have many advantages over the Education IRA. For example, contributions to an Education IRA are limited to $500 per year, but those to a qualified state tuition program are unlimited as far as federal law is concerned. However, both are considered to be gifts, which means that from a tax standpoint, contributions to a qualified state tuition program are limited to $10,000 per person, per year. A married couple can each contribute $10,000, making the total annual gift $20,000.

JUST A MINUTE

Because each state can design its own statute, some have imposed limits on contributions to qualified state tuition programs. For example, no additional contributions can be made to a Massachusetts tuition savings plan once the account value has reached $158,750. Iowa has an annual contribution limit of $2,000. (These numbers may have changed. Be certain to check these figures with your financial planner or estate planning attorney.)

PROCEED WITH CAUTION

Because a contribution to a qualified state tuition program constitutes a taxable gift, the amount of the contribution must be combined with any other gifts made to the same beneficiary during the calendar year in meeting the annual $10,000 gift exclusion. Also, if the lump sum method described in the preceding is used, the donors will not be able to make any additional contributions to that qualified state tuition program for an additional four years. This method also prohibits any other tax-free gifts during this time to the same beneficiary.

The qualified state tuition programs operate like a mutual fund investment. The contributor to the program does not control the investment; instead it is handled by large financial services companies such as Fidelity Investments and TIAA-CREF. This is handled much like a mutual fund insofar as an investment manager makes investment decisions.

Although you do not control the investments, the growth of the original investment is tax deferred until you withdraw it. At the time you withdraw the investment for qualified educational expenses, the earnings are taxed at the child's rate for federal purposes. Earnings are potentially taxable for state purposes, although some states exempt this income when it is used for qualified educational expenses.

Another advantage to investing in a qualified state tuition program is that the contributor controls who gets the investment. For example, if any portion of the investment is not used for qualified educational expenses, it can be cashed in. If the remaining investment is cashed in, earnings will be taxed to the contributor at the contributor's tax rate. There also will be a penalty imposed by the state, which must be "more than de minimis." Proposed regulations indicate that a 10% penalty is sufficient.

To avoid this penalty, the contributor can simply select a new beneficiary, as long as that person is a *member of the family* of the original beneficiary. Until someone withdraws them, the invested funds will continue to grow tax deferred. Unfortunately, you can't invest in a qualified state tuition program in the same taxable year as you contribute to an Education IRA if it is for the same beneficiary. Therefore, choose your vehicle for educational investing and stick to it, at least during that calendar year.

STRICTLY DEFINED

Member of the family means a person's child or grandchild, stepchild, sibling or step-sibling, parents and their ancestors, stepparents, nieces or nephews, aunts and uncles, or in-laws, and the spouses of any of the preceding.

An interesting aspect of these programs is that most plans allow one individual to be both account owner and designated beneficiary. Future regulations might clarify this point.

You might want to do a little comparison shopping because rates and other terms of investment differ from state to state. No matter what state program you invest in, you can use your investment at any qualified educational institution in the country.

Some states offer incentives to encourage education at a state school. Mississippi and Virginia offer state tax deductions for contributions made to their qualified tuition plans. Earnings from the plan investment are exempt from state taxes if used for state college expenses. Louisiana and New Jersey offer grants to those who attend in-state schools. Some states protect assets invested in a state tuition program from creditor claims and disregard the account value in determining eligibility for state level financial aid programs. (This information may have changed. Be certain to check these figures with your financial planner or estate planning attorney.)

ROTH IRA ACCOUNTS

Another technique for saving for educational expenses is the Roth IRA. The advantage of the Roth IRA is that earnings are tax free. However, Annual contributions are limited to $2,000 per year. All other conditions for owning a Roth IRA must be met, including the requirements of earned income and the phase-out for higher income taxpayers.

PROCEED WITH CAUTION

Be certain to consult with an estate planning attorney licensed in your state or your financial planner who can advise you properly on investing in a Roth IRA.

PREPAID TUITION PROGRAMS

Another option is the prepaid tuition program offered in many states. In essence, you would prepay tuition at the current rate and the institution would guarantee your child's enrollment for that sum. The "growth rate" on this type of investment simply is the rate of tuition inflation, which has been historically anywhere from two to three times that of the Consumer Price Index.

PROCEED WITH CAUTION

As with all of the material in this book, be certain to consult an estate planning attorney before implementing any of the techniques discussed in this book. The failure to obtain professional advice could result in additional expenses for administering your estate and could result in additional and unnecessary taxation of your estate. Additionally, the failure to properly prepare documents according to applicable law may render the documents useless.

HOUR'S UP!

Now it's time to see how much you have learned and retained from this lesson. Try to take the following quiz without referring back to the hourly materials:

1. A 2503(b) trust requires:

   a. Mandatory principal payout at age 21

   b. Mandatory income payout annually

   c. Mandatory principal payout at age 18

   d. Discretionary income payout at age 21

2. A 2503(c) trust requires:

   a. That contributions to the trust qualify for the annual gift exclusion.

   b. Mandatory principal payout at age 18

   c. Mandatory income payout annually

   d. Mandatory principal payout at age 21

3. The most that can be contributed to an Education IRA annually is …

   a. $500

   b. $10,000

   c. $5,000

   d. $100

4. Earnings on contributions to a qualified state tuition program …

   a. Tax-free

   b. Taxable annually to the beneficiary

   c. Tax-deferred

   d. Taxable annually to the contributor

5. Contributions to a qualified state tuition program are …

   a. Tax-deductible

   b. Limited in amount by federal law

   c. Limited by state law to $10,000

   d. Taxable gifts

HOUR 19
Charitable Trusts

Charitable giving has become a major source of tax savings for the affluent and is increasingly being used by others in various tax brackets as part of their estate planning. There are basically two types of charitable giving: outright gifts and gifts in trust. In this hour we will review gifts in trust and compare the many types of trusts that provide charitable benefits to the donor as well as the charity. The type of trust examined in this chapter is referred to as a *split-interest* trust.

STRICTLY DEFINED

A **split-interest** trust is one that has both charitable and non-charitable beneficiaries.

The primary functions of charitable split interest trusts are: to provide income to the donor, other members of the family, or both; provide for a future gift to charity; and benefit from income, estate, or gift tax charitable deductions. All of these benefits are attainable with proper planning. Read on to see which tax benefits you can enjoy with each type of charitable trust described below.

CHARITABLE REMAINDER TRUSTS

A *charitable remainder trust* is a common split-interest trust that pays income to a non-charitable beneficiary for a period of time. At the end of the term of the trust, the remaining principal is paid to a qualified charity. There

CHAPTER SUMMARY

LESSON PLAN:

In this hour, you'll explore the world of charitable trusts and compare several different types of trusts. You will discover that you and others can still benefit from the charitable gift during lifetime and get a charitable deduction at the same time. You will learn how gifting to a charitable trust compares to outright gifts. You will learn how insurance works together with charitable planning. You'll also discover ...

- The difference between an annuity trust and a unitrust.
- The varieties of charitable trusts .
- The benefits of non-charities.
- The connection between life insurance and charitable gifting.

are two types of charitable remainder trusts: the charitable remainder unitrust and the charitable remainder annuity trust; they will be discussed in the following.

 FYI Only three types of split-interest trusts allow the donor a charitable deduction. Those three are the annuity trust, unitrust, and the pooled income trust. If a trust does not meet the requirements of these trusts, no charitable deduction will be allowed.

CHARITABLE REMAINDER UNITRUST

A *charitable remainder unitrust* pays income to one or more non-charitable income beneficiaries for a period of time specified in the trust document. The balance remaining at the end of the term is paid to a qualified charity. The amount of income paid from a unitrust is a fixed percentage of the net fair market value of the trust. The trustee determines the value of the trust on an annual basis.

The donor irrevocably transfers money or securities to a trustee of a charitable remainder unitrust. In return, the trustee pays the donor (or other beneficiary) a unitrust amount from the property for a specified term or for life. The donor also can provide for his or her spouse to receive a unitrust amount from the donated property for life if the donor dies first. The income beneficiary would receive payments based on a fixed percentage of the fair market value of the assets placed in trust; the assets would be revalued each year.

One primary motivation for this trust is to transfer appreciated property to the trust. A charitable remainder trust is exempt from federal income tax because the beneficiary of the trust is a qualified charity. This means you can transfer a highly appreciated asset to the trustee, the trustee will sell it and incur no capital gain! The trustee then reinvests the proceeds to generate a high-income yield.

 JUST A MINUTE

The minimum payout from a charitable remainder trust is 5%. The greater the payout, the less the charitable deduction will be.

For example, Bob Thompson, aged 65, donates $1,000,000 to a charitable remainder trust on August 1, 2001. He decides to receive a minimum payout of 5%, with income paid monthly. He names himself and his wife Susan as income beneficiaries. The trust is set up to terminate upon the death of both Bob and Susan, at which time the trustee will pay the remaining trust property to a *qualified charity* of his choosing.

STRICTLY DEFINED

A **qualified charity** is one that allows the donor of the trust to gain either an income, gift, or estate tax deduction. The Internal Revenue Service publishes a book (Publication 78) known as *The Cumulative List* that lists all organizations qualified to receive gifts for which an income tax charitable deduction is allowed.

Based upon some technical assumptions, the following illustrates the benefits of this gift to the Thompsons.

The Thompsons will realize a charitable deduction of $335.010 as a result of the transfer of the $1,000,000 investment. Additionally, they will receive an income stream as illustrated in Figure 19.2.

Figure 19.1 is based on an assumed 10% growth rate for the investment in the charitable remainder trust. Over a 24-year period, the investment grows from $1,000,000 to $3,063,103, after annual payouts ranging from $50,000 to $146,176 in year 24. The charity receives the ending principal of $3,063,103 and the Thompsons benefit from the charitable deduction of $335,010.

You can take the deduction in the year that you irrevocably place the funds in trust. The deduction is measured by the present value at the date of the gift of the charity's right to eventually receive the unitrust's assets. The charity does not get what you put in, because you and/or someone else gets an income stream for either a set period of time or for your lifetime (or the lifetime of others). Therefore, since you are allowed to take a charitable deduction in the year the gift is made, there must be some way to calculate how much of that gift will actually be left at the end of the term of the trust to go to charity. This calculation is referred to as a "present value" calculation. It's simply a way to "guess" how much will really be going to the charity.

PROCEED WITH CAUTION

The type of charity will determine the amount that can be deducted for income tax purposes in any given taxable year. See the discussion of types of charities later in this hour. Carry-forward rules will apply for excess deductions.

Figure 19.1:
Illustration of
charitable remainder
unitrust.

(Provided with
permission of
zcalc software,
on the Web at
www.zcalc.com)

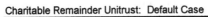
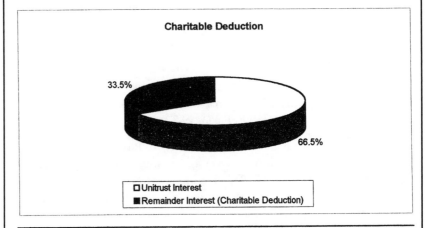

Charitable Remainder Unitrust: Default Case

Charitable Deduction

Bob Thompson

Charitable Deduction

Total Interest	1,000,000
Unitrust Interest	664,990
Remainder Interest (Charitable Deduction)	335,010

Charitable Deduction

33.5%

66.5%

☐ Unitrust Interest
■ Remainder Interest (Charitable Deduction)

General

Type of Trust	Life
Date of Transfer	13-Apr-01
Section 7520 Rate	8.0%
Beginning Principal	1,000,000
Nearest Age of Life 1	65
Nearest Age of Life 2	62
Life Status	Last to Die
Unitrust Payout Rate	5.000%
Unitrust Payout Period	Monthly
Months by which Valuation Precedes Payout	1

Charitable Remainder Unitrust: Default Case

Annual Cash Flow and Payments
Bob Thompson

General

Type of Trust	Life
Unitrust Payout Rate	5.000%
Unitrust Payout Period	Monthly
Months by which Valuation Precedes Payout	1
Years of Trust Duration	24
Cumulative Unitrust Payouts	2,160,420

Year	Beginning Principal	Annual Growth	Annual Payout	Ending Principal
1	1,000,000	97,748	50,000	1,047,748
2	1,047,748	102,415	52,387	1,097,775
3	1,097,775	107,305	54,889	1,150,192
4	1,150,192	112,429	57,510	1,205,111
5	1,205,111	117,797	60,256	1,262,652
6	1,262,652	123,421	63,133	1,322,941
7	1,322,941	129,314	66,147	1,386,108
8	1,386,108	135,489	69,305	1,452,292
9	1,452,292	141,958	72,615	1,521,635
10	1,521,635	148,736	76,082	1,594,290
11	1,594,290	155,838	79,715	1,670,414
12	1,670,414	163,279	83,521	1,750,172
13	1,750,172	171,075	87,509	1,833,739
14	1,833,739	179,244	91,687	1,921,296
15	1,921,296	187,802	96,065	2,013,034
16	2,013,034	196,769	100,652	2,109,151
17	2,109,151	206,165	105,458	2,209,859
18	2,209,859	216,009	110,493	2,315,374
19	2,315,374	226,323	115,769	2,425,928
20	2,425,928	237,129	121,296	2,541,761
21	2,541,761	248,451	127,088	2,663,124
22	2,663,124	260,314	133,156	2,790,282
23	2,790,282	272,744	139,514	2,923,512
24	2,923,512	285,767	146,176	3,063,103

Figure 19.2: Illustration of estimated cash flow from charitable remainder unitrust.

(Provided with permission of zcalc software, on the Web at www.zcalc.com)

Figure 19.3 shows a comparison of various payout rates. For example, had the Thompson's chosen a 9% payout rate, instead of a 5% rate, the charitable deduction would be reduced to $150,390.

Figure 19.3:
Comparison of
payout rates from
charitable remainder
unitrust.

(Provided with per-
mission of zcalc
software, on the
Web at www.
zcalc.com)

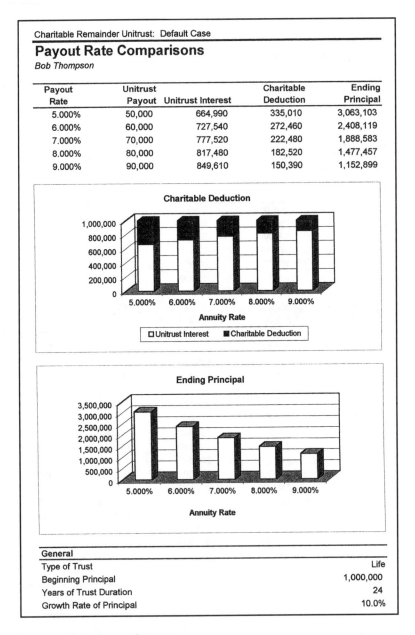

Charitable Remainder Unitrust: Default Case

Payout Rate Comparisons

Bob Thompson

Payout Rate	Unitrust Payout	Unitrust Interest	Charitable Deduction	Ending Principal
5.000%	50,000	664,990	335,010	3,063,103
6.000%	60,000	727,540	272,460	2,408,119
7.000%	70,000	777,520	222,480	1,888,583
8.000%	80,000	817,480	182,520	1,477,457
9.000%	90,000	849,610	150,390	1,152,899

Charitable Deduction

1,000,000
800,000
600,000
400,000
200,000
0

5.000% 6.000% 7.000% 8.000% 9.000%

Annuity Rate

☐ Unitrust Interest ■ Charitable Deduction

Ending Principal

3,500,000
3,000,000
2,500,000
2,000,000
1,500,000
1,000,000
500,000
0

5.000% 6.000% 7.000% 8.000% 9.000%

Annuity Rate

General	
Type of Trust	Life
Beginning Principal	1,000,000
Years of Trust Duration	24
Growth Rate of Principal	10.0%

CHARITABLE REMAINDER ANNUITY TRUSTS

A *charitable remainder annuity trust* is designed to permit fixed payment annually to a non-charitable beneficiary with the remainder going to charity. This trust works basically the same as the charitable remainder unitrust. The donor transfers money or securities to a trust, which pays him or her a fixed dollar amount each year for a specified term or for life.

If the income of the trust is insufficient to meet the required annual payment, the difference is paid from *capital gains* or principal. (But see "makeup" provisions below) If the income is greater than the amount required in any given year, the excess is reinvested in trust.

STRICTLY DEFINED

Capital gain refers to an income tax on appreciation of an asset that has been sold for more than its cost basis.

The income tax deduction is computed in the year funds are irrevocably placed in trust and is measured by the present value of the charity's right to receive the trust assets at the death of the income beneficiary. If all the necessary tests are met, the donor of a charitable remainder annuity trust will be entitled to an income tax deduction limited to the value of the remainder interest.

Assume the same facts as outlined in the preceding for Bill and Susan Thompson, only now assume that Bill selected a charitable remainder annuity trust instead of the unitrust. Figure 19.4 illustrates the charitable deduction allowed to the Thompsons.

The Thompsons will realize a charitable deduction in the amount of $477,211 because of the transfer of the $1,000,000 investment. Additionally, they will receive a fixed income stream as illustrated in Figure 19.5.

The preceding is based upon an assumed 10% growth rate for the investment in the charitable remainder trust. Over a 24-year period, the investment grows from $1,000,000 to $5,225,549, after equal annual payouts of $50,000 annually. The charity receives the ending principal of $5,225,549 and the Thompson's benefit from the charitable deduction of $477,211.

Figure 19.6 shows a comparison of various annuity rates. For example, had the Thompson's chosen a 9% annuity rate, instead of a 5% rate, the charitable deduction would be reduced to $81,164.

Figure 19.4:
Illustration of
charitable remainder
annuity trust.

(Provided with
permission of
zcalc software,
on the Web at
www.zcalc.com)

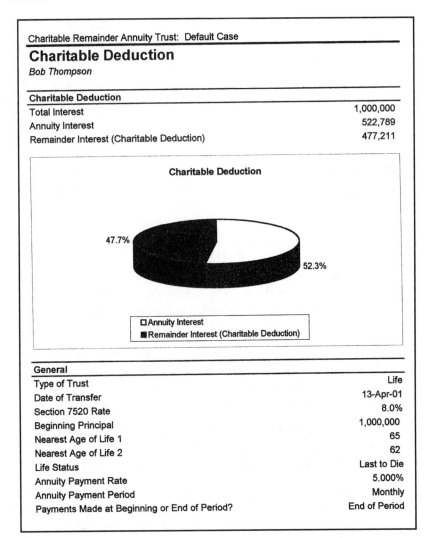

Charitable Remainder Annuity Trust: Default Case

Charitable Deduction
Bob Thompson

Charitable Deduction

Total Interest	1,000,000
Annuity Interest	522,789
Remainder Interest (Charitable Deduction)	477,211

Charitable Deduction

47.7%   52.3%

☐ Annuity Interest
■ Remainder Interest (Charitable Deduction)

General

Type of Trust	Life
Date of Transfer	13-Apr-01
Section 7520 Rate	8.0%
Beginning Principal	1,000,000
Nearest Age of Life 1	65
Nearest Age of Life 2	62
Life Status	Last to Die
Annuity Payment Rate	5.000%
Annuity Payment Period	Monthly
Payments Made at Beginning or End of Period?	End of Period

Charitable Remainder Annuity Trust: Default Case

Annual Cash Flow and Payments

Bob Thompson

General

Type of Trust	Life
Annuity Payment Rate	5.000%
Annuity Payment Period	Monthly
Payments Made at Beginning or End of Period?	End of Period
Annuity Payment Per Period	4,167
Years of Trust Duration	24
Cumulative Annuity Payments	1,200,000

Year	Beginning Principal	Annual Growth	Annual Payment	Ending Principal
1	1,000,000	97,748	50,000	1,047,748
2	1,047,748	102,523	50,000	1,100,270
3	1,100,270	107,775	50,000	1,158,045
4	1,158,045	113,552	50,000	1,221,597
5	1,221,597	119,908	50,000	1,291,505
6	1,291,505	126,898	50,000	1,368,403
7	1,368,403	134,588	50,000	1,452,991
8	1,452,991	143,047	50,000	1,546,038
9	1,546,038	152,352	50,000	1,648,390
10	1,648,390	162,587	50,000	1,760,976
11	1,760,976	173,845	50,000	1,884,822
12	1,884,822	186,230	50,000	2,021,052
13	2,021,052	199,853	50,000	2,170,905
14	2,170,905	214,838	50,000	2,335,743
15	2,335,743	231,322	50,000	2,517,065
16	2,517,065	249,454	50,000	2,716,519
17	2,716,519	269,400	50,000	2,935,919
18	2,935,919	291,340	50,000	3,177,259
19	3,177,259	315,474	50,000	3,442,732
20	3,442,732	342,021	50,000	3,734,753
21	3,734,753	371,223	50,000	4,055,976
22	4,055,976	403,345	50,000	4,409,322
23	4,409,322	438,680	50,000	4,798,002
24	4,798,002	477,548	50,000	5,225,549

Figure 19.5: Illustration of estimated cash flow from charitable remainder annuity trust.

(Provided with permission of zcalc software, on the Web at www. zcalc.com)

Figure 19.6:
Comparison of
payout rates from
charitable remainder
annuity trust.

(Provided with
permission of
zcalc software,
on the Web at
www.zcalc.com)

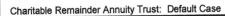

Charitable Remainder Annuity Trust: Default Case

Annuity Rate Comparisons

Bob Thompson

Annuity Rate	Annuity Payment	Annuity Interest	Charitable Deduction	Ending Principal
5.000%	50,000	522,789	477,211	5,225,549
6.000%	60,000	627,347	372,653	4,300,713
7.000%	70,000	731,904	268,096	3,375,876
8.000%	80,000	836,459	163,541	2,451,040
9.000%	90,000	918,836	81,164	1,526,203

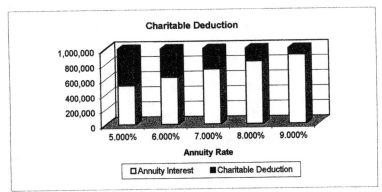

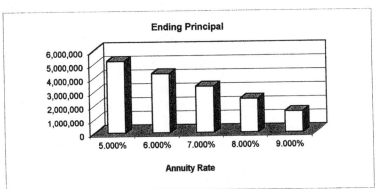

General	
Type of Trust	Life
Beginning Principal	1,000,000
Years of Trust Duration	24
Growth Rate of Principal	10.0%

MAKEUP PROVISIONS

A charitable remainder trust pays either a set amount annually (annuity trust) or a percentage of the net value of the trust on an annual basis (unitrust). What happens if the income generated by the trust is insufficient to cover the required payment? The trust agreement must specify whether or not the trustee is obligated to invade the principal annually to make the required payment. If the trust agreement allows for invasion of principal, it is entirely possible that the amount available to charity will be reduced.

Therefore, some trusts do not permit the trustee to invade principal to make an annuity or unitrust payment. In this event, a lesser amount is paid to the income beneficiary. The question then is whether the trustee has the power to make up for this shortfall in later years when there is sufficient income.

If a trust has a makeup provision, the trustee, in future years, actually might pay an amount greater than the annuity or unitrust amount (in order to "make up" for the amount not paid in earlier years).

If the trust does not contain the makeup provision, the shortfall is permanent and the income beneficiaries simply will receive less than the annuity or unitrust amount in those years.

CHARITABLE LEAD TRUST

A *charitable lead annuity* or *unitrust* is basically the reverse of the charitable remainder trust. The income beneficiary of a charitable lead trust is the charity. The trust will provide for either a unitrust or annuity payment to one or more qualified charities during the term of the trust. At the end of that term, the property typically is transferred either to the donor or members of the donor's family.

The donor transfers income-producing property to a trust. The trust in turn provides the charity with a guaranteed annuity or annual payments equal to a fixed percentage of the fair market value of the trust property, which will be recomputed annually. At the end of the specified period, the property is returned to the donor (or go to a non-charitable beneficiary of the donor's choice).

The primary advantage of a charitable lead trust is to provide a high-income taxpayer with a charitable income tax deduction. If certain requirements are met, the donor will be allowed a current deduction for the value of the annuity or unitrust interest given annually to a charity.

FYI For a charitable lead trust to give the donor a charitable deduction, the donor must be considered the owner of the trust for tax purposes. If the donor is the owner of the trust, it falls within the grantor trust rules contained in the Internal Revenue Code. As a grantor trust, the donor is taxed on all income generated by the trust.

The donor does not take an annual charitable deduction. As the owner of the income and principal of the trust, the donor takes an immediate deduction when the trust is funded under the grantor trust rules. The deduction is based on the present value of the charity's future rights to annuity or unitrust payments.

JUST A MINUTE

The charity gets an income stream for either a set period of time or for your lifetime (or the lifetime of others). Therefore, since you are allowed to take a charitable deduction for this stream of future payments to the charity, there must be some way to calculate how much that future stream of payments will actually be during the anticipated term of the trust. This calculation is referred to as a "present value" calculation. It's simply a way to "guess" how much will really be going to the charity.

Let's again go back to the example of Bill and Susan Thompson. Suppose Bill uses a charitable lead unitrust for his planning needs. Based on the same assumptions, Figure 19.7 illustrates the extent of the charitable deduction.

The Thompson's will realize a charitable deduction in the amount of $667,200 as a result of the transfer of the $1,000,000 investment. Additionally, the charity will receive an income stream as illustrated in the following chart.

Figure 19.8 is based upon an assumed 10% growth rate for the investment in the charitable lead trust. Over a 24-year period, the investment grows from $1,000,000 to $3,034,081, after annual payouts to the charity ranging from $50,000 to $144,848. A non-charitable beneficiary will receive the ending principal of $3,034,081 and the Thompson's benefit from the charitable deduction of $667,200.

Figure 19.9 shows a comparison of various payout rates. For example, had the Thompson's chosen a 9% payout rate, instead of a 5% rate, the charitable deduction would be increased to $851,240.

Charitable Lead Unitrust: Default Case

Charitable Deduction
Bob Thompson

Charitable Deduction

Total Interest	1,000,000
Remainder Interest	332,800
Unitrust Interest (Charitable Deduction)	667,200

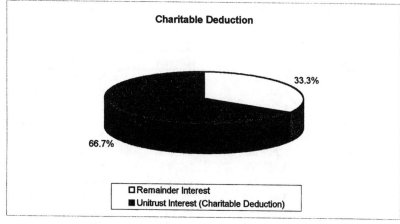

Charitable Deduction

- □ Remainder Interest
- ■ Unitrust Interest (Charitable Deduction)

33.3%

66.7%

General

Type of Trust	Life
Date of Transfer	13-Apr-01
Section 7520 Rate	8.0%
Beginning Principal	1,000,000
Nearest Age of Life 1	65
Nearest Age of Life 2	62
Life Status	Last to Die
Unitrust Payout Rate	5.000%
Unitrust Payout Period	Quarterly
Months by which Valuation Precedes Payout	1

*Figure 19.7:
Illustration of
charitable lead
unitrust.*

*(Provided with
permission of zcalc
software, on the
Web at www.
zcalc.com)*

Figure 19.8:
Illustration of esti-
mated cash flow
from charitable lead
unitrust.

(Provided with per-
mission of zcalc
software, on the
Web at www.
zcalc.com)

Charitable Lead Unitrust: Default Case

Annual Cash Flow and Payments
Bob Thompson

General

Type of Trust	Life
Unitrust Payout Rate	5.000%
Unitrust Payout Period	Quarterly
Months by which Valuation Precedes Payout	1
Years of Trust Duration	24
Cumulative Unitrust Payouts	2,148,727

Year	Beginning Principal	Annual Growth	Annual Payout	Ending Principal
1	1,000,000	97,332	50,000	1,047,332
2	1,047,332	101,939	52,367	1,096,905
3	1,096,905	106,764	54,845	1,148,824
4	1,148,824	111,818	57,441	1,203,200
5	1,203,200	117,110	60,160	1,260,150
6	1,260,150	122,653	63,008	1,319,796
7	1,319,796	128,459	65,990	1,382,265
8	1,382,265	134,539	69,113	1,447,690
9	1,447,690	140,907	72,385	1,516,213
10	1,516,213	147,576	75,811	1,587,979
11	1,587,979	154,561	79,399	1,663,141
12	1,663,141	161,877	83,157	1,741,861
13	1,741,861	169,539	87,093	1,824,307
14	1,824,307	177,564	91,215	1,910,656
15	1,910,656	185,968	95,533	2,001,092
16	2,001,092	194,771	100,055	2,095,808
17	2,095,808	203,990	104,790	2,195,007
18	2,195,007	213,645	109,750	2,298,901
19	2,298,901	223,757	114,945	2,407,714
20	2,407,714	234,348	120,386	2,521,676
21	2,521,676	245,440	126,084	2,641,033
22	2,641,033	257,058	132,052	2,766,038
23	2,766,038	269,225	138,302	2,896,961
24	2,896,961	281,968	144,848	3,034,081

Charitable Lead Unitrust: Default Case

Payout Rate Comparisons
Bob Thompson

Payout Rate	Unitrust Payout	Remainder Interest	Charitable Deduction	Ending Principal
5.000%	50,000	332,800	667,200	3,034,081
6.000%	60,000	270,280	729,720	2,380,490
7.000%	70,000	220,480	779,520	1,863,072
8.000%	80,000	180,670	819,330	1,454,436
9.000%	90,000	148,760	851,240	1,132,501

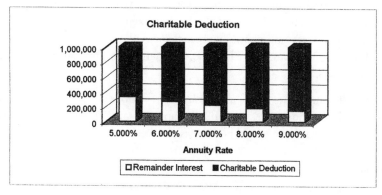

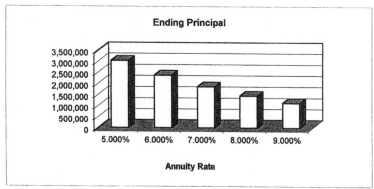

General	
Type of Trust	Life
Beginning Principal	1,000,000
Years of Trust Duration	24
Growth Rate of Principal	10.0%

Figure 19.9: Comparison of payout rates from charitable lead unitrust.

(Provided with permission of zcalc software, on the Web at www.zcalc.com)

CHARITABLE LEAD ANNUITY TRUST

The following charts and tables illustrate a charitable lead annuity trust for Bill and Sharon Thompson.

The Thompson's will realize a charitable deduction in the amount of $519,408 as a result of the transfer of the $1,000,000 investment. Additionally, the charity will receive an income stream as illustrated in the following chart.

Figure 19.11 is based upon an assumed 10% growth rate for the investment in the charitable lead annuity trust. Over a 24-year period, the investment grows from $1,000,000 to $5,262,228, after fixed annual payouts to the charity of $50,000. A non-charitable beneficiary will receive the ending principal of $5,262,228 and the Thompson's benefit from the charitable deduction of $519,408.

The following figure shows a comparison of various annuity rates. For example, had the Thompson's chosen a 9% annuity rate, instead of a 5% rate, the charitable deduction would be increased to $915,678.

JUST A MINUTE

Remember that there are three different deductions available with a charitable split-interest trust; income, gift, and estate. The deduction available to you will depend on when you make the gift. The amount of your deduction depends upon the type of charity you have selected.

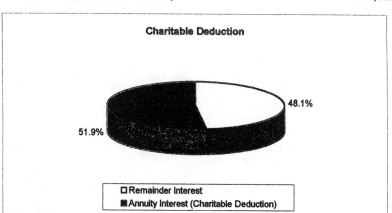

Charitable Lead Annuity Trust: Default Case

Charitable Deduction

Bob Thompson

Charitable Deduction

Charitable Deduction	
Total Interest	1,000,000
Remainder Interest	480,592
Annuity Interest (Charitable Deduction)	519,408

Charitable Deduction

48.1%

51.9%

☐ Remainder Interest
■ Annuity Interest (Charitable Deduction)

General	
Type of Trust	Life
Date of Transfer	13-Apr-01
Section 7520 Rate	8.0%
Beginning Principal	1,000,000
Nearest Age of Life 1	65
Nearest Age of Life 2	62
Life Status	Last to Die
Annuity Payment Rate	5.000%
Annuity Payment Period	Quarterly
Payments Made at Beginning or End of Period?	End of Period

Figure 19.10: Illustration of charitable lead annuity trust.

(Provided with permission of zcalc software, on the Web at www.zcalc. com)

Figure 19.11:
Illustration of esti-
mated cash flow
from charitable lead
annuity trust.

(Provided with per-
mission of zcalc
software, on the
Web at www.zcalc.
com)

Charitable Lead Annuity Trust: Default Case

Annual Cash Flow and Payments

Bob Thompson

General	
Type of Trust	Life
Annuity Payment Rate	5.000%
Annuity Payment Period	Quarterly
Payments Made at Beginning or End of Period?	End of Period
Annuity Payment Per Period	12,500
Years of Trust Duration	24
Cumulative Annuity Payments	1,200,000

Year	Beginning Principal	Annual Growth	Annual Payment	Ending Principal
1	1,000,000	98,162	50,000	1,048,162
2	1,048,162	102,978	50,000	1,101,141
3	1,101,141	108,276	50,000	1,159,417
4	1,159,417	114,104	50,000	1,223,521
5	1,223,521	120,514	50,000	1,294,035
6	1,294,035	127,566	50,000	1,371,601
7	1,371,601	135,322	50,000	1,456,923
8	1,456,923	143,855	50,000	1,550,778
9	1,550,778	153,240	50,000	1,654,018
10	1,654,018	163,564	50,000	1,767,582
11	1,767,582	174,920	50,000	1,892,502
12	1,892,502	187,412	50,000	2,029,915
13	2,029,915	201,154	50,000	2,181,068
14	2,181,068	216,269	50,000	2,347,337
15	2,347,337	232,896	50,000	2,530,233
16	2,530,233	251,186	50,000	2,731,419
17	2,731,419	271,304	50,000	2,952,723
18	2,952,723	293,435	50,000	3,196,158
19	3,196,158	317,778	50,000	3,463,936
20	3,463,936	344,556	50,000	3,758,491
21	3,758,491	374,011	50,000	4,082,503
22	4,082,503	406,412	50,000	4,438,915
23	4,438,915	442,054	50,000	4,830,969
24	4,830,969	481,259	50,000	5,262,228

Charitable Lead Annuity Trust: Default Case

Annuity Rate Comparisons
Bob Thompson

Annuity Rate	Annuity Payment	Remainder Interest	Charitable Deduction	Ending Principal
5.000%	50,000	480,592	519,408	5,262,228
6.000%	60,000	376,710	623,290	4,344,727
7.000%	70,000	272,828	727,172	3,427,226
8.000%	80,000	168,945	831,055	2,509,725
9.000%	90,000	84,322	915,678	1,592,224

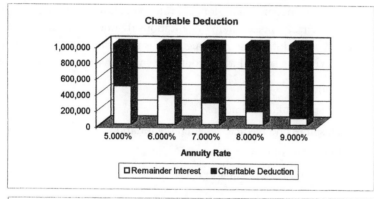

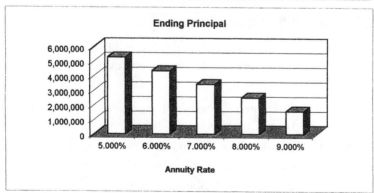

General	
Type of Trust	Life
Beginning Principal	1,000,000
Years of Trust Duration	24
Growth Rate of Principal	10.0%

Figure 19.12: Comparison of payout rates from charitable lead annuity trust.

(Provided with permission of zcalc software, on the Web at www.zcalc.com)

TYPES OF CHARITIES

The Internal Revenue Code is full of citations and references to various charitable organizations. The first one we will look at is called a Section 170(b)(1)(A) Organization.

I.R.C. SECTION 170(B)(1)(A) ORGANIZATIONS

These organizations will qualify the donor to receive an income tax charitable deduction. Additionally, these organizations are referred to as *50% charities*, meaning they allow the donor to deduct up to 50% of his or her adjusted gross income. Carry-forward rules will allow additional deductions in future years. Some common organizations that qualify as 50% charities are listed in the following. Although this is not a comprehensive list, it should give you a general idea about the type of charity that is eligible:

- Churches
- Educational organizations
- Hospitals and medical research organizations
- Governmental units
- Certain private foundations

I.R.C. SECTION 2055(A) ORGANIZATIONS

Organizations that are described in this Internal Revenue Code section will allow the donor's estate an estate tax deduction when he or she donates to them.

- The United States, any state and any political subdivision thereof, and the District of Columbia, when used exclusively for public purposes
- Any corporation organized and operated exclusively for religious, charitable, scientific, literary, or educational purposes
- A trustee or a fraternal society, order, or association operating under the lodge system when used exclusively for religious, charitable, scientific, literary, or educational purposes, or for the prevention of cruelty to children or animals
- A veterans' organization

There is considerable overlap of the charities that qualify for an income tax deduction and those that qualify for an estate tax deduction. However, there are some differences that you must be careful to note. For example, the organizations listed as qualifying for the income tax deduction must be domestic organizations, but you can take estate tax deductions for foreign organizations.

I.R.C. SECTION 2522(A) ORGANIZATIONS

To qualify the donor for the gift tax charitable deduction, the charity must qualify as one described in this code section. Generally speaking, the types of organizations listed as qualifying for the estate tax deduction also qualify for the gift tax deduction. The gift tax law does recognize a community chest, fund, or foundation as a qualified donee, without any requirement that it be in the form of a corporation.

I.R.C. SECTION 509(A) PRIVATE FOUNDATIONS

A final category of qualified charities is the private foundation. The specific requirements for qualification are somewhat extensive and will not be covered in this hour.

POOLED INCOME FUND

The donor of a pooled income fund gives property to the fund and retains a lifetime income interest in the property. The property is for the benefit of more than one individual. The remainder interest then goes to a qualified charity.

The primary characteristic of this type of fund is that property in the fund is commingled with property transferred to the fund by other donors. The trustee must be independent and cannot be a donor to the fund or a beneficiary of the fund. The amount of income from the fund is determined by the rate of return earned by the trust for such year.

ADVANTAGES AND DISADVANTAGES

There are many advantages to using a charitable-split interest trust. Some of these advantages are tax-related, some are non-tax related. Let's look at some of the more important benefits:

- Charitable trusts can provide significant savings on the sale of appreciated assets by avoiding taxation on the capital appreciation.
- Charitable trusts can provide significant income, gift, and estate tax deductions.
- Contributions to a charitable trust can significantly reduce federal estate taxes and the taxable value of the decedent's estate.
- Charitable trusts can help achieve charitable goals and benefit charities of your choice while providing a benefit to non-charitable beneficiaries.

The primary drawback to the use of charitable split-interest trusts is the loss of the value of the trust assets to the donor and his or her family. This in turn leads to the concept of the wealth replacement trust, generally an irrevocable life insurance trust. The idea is that the additional income stream to the donor that results from the use of this device can be used to pay premiums on life insurance on the donor held in the a trust, which ultimately is distributed to the family to replace the "wealth," i.e., the value of the assets in the charitable remainder trust.

Figure 19.13 illustrates this wealth replacement strategy. This figure shows that although $1,000,000 was transferred to a charitable remainder annuity trust, thus depriving the family of the asset, an irrevocable life insurance trust was created and funded with a second-to-die life insurance policy for $530,000. During the lifetime of both husband and wife, they will receive $50,000 annually in annuity payments for 24 years (estimated). Although not shown on this diagram, the premiums on the $530,000 life insurance can be paid out of the $50,000 annual annuity payment. Additionally, the $530,000 death benefit, payable upon the second death to the irrevocable life insurance trust, is then paid out to the beneficiaries, income, estate and inheritance tax free! The charity gets $477,211! In the meantime, husband and wife both get the income tax charitable deductions based upon the charitable value of the donation to the charitable remainder trust, which is $477,211! Also, husband and wife do not have to pay income tax on the sale of the appreciated asset that was transferred to the charitable remainder trust! The beneficiaries receive, in addition to the $530,000 death proceeds from the irrevocable life insurance trust, whatever is left of the annual annuity payments made during Bob's and Susan's lifetime.

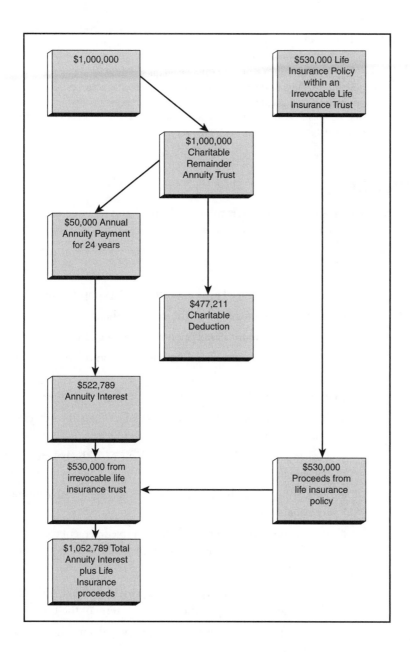

Figure 19.13:
Illustration of chari-
table remainder
annuity trust with
irrevocable life
insurance trust.

PROCEED WITH CAUTION

 As with all of the material in this book, be certain to consult an estate planning attorney before implementing any of the techniques discussed in this book. The failure to obtain professional advice could result in additional expenses for administering your estate and could result in additional and unnecessary taxation of your estate. Additionally, the failure to properly prepare documents according to applicable law may render the documents useless.

Hour's Up!

Now it's time to see how much you have learned and retained from this lesson. Try to take the following quiz without referring back to the hourly materials:

1. A unitrust pays out …

    a. A fixed percentage based upon the initial contribution

    b. A fixed amount that stays the same for the term of the trust

    c. A variable amount based upon the type of charity

    d. A fixed percentage recalculated annually on the net trust asset value

2. A charitable remainder trust …

    a. Pays no income, but pays the principal to a qualified charity at the end of the term of the trust

    b. Pays income to one or more individuals with the balance payable to a qualified charity

    c. Pays principal to the donor only, with income payable annually to a qualified charity

    d. Pays income to only one individual a fixed percentage payable to the charity each year during the term of the trust

3. A charitable lead trust …

    a. Pays income to a charity, with the principal payable to a non-charitable beneficiary at the end of the term of the trust

    b. Pays income to a charity, with the principal annually to a non-charitable beneficiary

QUIZ

   c. Pays principal annually at the rate of 5% of net asset values to a charity, with the balance payable to a non-charitable beneficiary at the end of the term of the trust

   d. Pays principal annually at the rate of 5% of net asset values to a non-charitable beneficiary, with the balance payable to a charitable beneficiary at the end of the term of the trust

4. Wealth-replacement involves the use of which product along with a charitable split-interest trust …

   a. Mutual funds

   b. Variable annuity

   c. Life insurance

   d. Stock options

5. A contribution to a 50% charity means …

   a. The donor is denied the income tax deduction.

   b. The donor is denied the charitable deduction.

   c. The donor is allowed to deduct the entire gift in the year of the transfer.

   d. The donor is allowed to deduct up to 50% of the donor's adjusted gross income.

Hour 20

Marital Trusts and Disclaimer Planning

When planning your estate, providing for your surviving spouse is more than just making sure that he or she has proper maintenance and support; you also want to reduce taxes as much as possible. Additionally, you'll want to consider the issue of who will have control over the estate, especially if you're in a second marriage.

As a spouse, you have a choice to make when planning your estate: Should the property pass directly to your surviving spouse or should it be held in trust, designed to support him or her? What are the tax ramifications of this decision? What are the practical ramifications? We will discuss these issues and more in this hour.

THE UNLIMITED MARITAL DEDUCTION

As discussed in Hour 6, "Federal Estate Taxes," there is now an unlimited marital deduction for transfers from a deceased spouse to a surviving spouse. Unlimited means just that: no limit on how much is tax-deferred. One of the requirements for the marital deduction is that you must give the property to your surviving spouse, either directly or through a trust set up for his or her benefit. The two most common marital trusts are the power of appointment trust and the QTIP trust. Let's take a look.

POWER OF APPOINTMENT TRUST

This is a trust established for the benefit of the surviving spouse. The property transferred to this trust by the first

CHAPTER SUMMARY

LESSON PLAN:

In this hour, you'll learn about the types of marital trusts that are commonly used in estate planning. You can use these trusts to save on estate taxes and help with problems associated with second marriages. We'll also cover the process of disclaiming a gift made by will or trust and the effect of a disclaimer on the property involved. You'll also learn …

- The definition of the marital deduction.
- All about a power of appointment trust.
- All about a QTIP trust.
- How you can disclaim a gift.
- What happens to the disclaimed gift.
- The definition of a disclaimer trust.

spouse to die qualifies for the marital deduction, which keeps the estate tax free.

GO TO ▶
Go back to Hour 6 to review the marital deduction and see Hour 16, "Credit Shelter Trusts," to review credit shelter trusts.

For example, Bob sets up a power of appointment trust and a credit shelter trust. Remember, the credit shelter trust can hold assets valued up to $675,000 (in 2001) free from federal estate tax. When Bob dies in 2001, his taxable estate is valued at $1,300,000. Because Bob's credit shelter trust can hold only approximately $675,000 in value, the remaining $625,000 will incur a federal estate tax unless he either donates that sum to a charity or gives it to his surviving spouse.

The transfer to the surviving spouse uses the unlimited marital deduction and defers taxation on the $625,000 until the death of the surviving spouse. However, using this trust retains the property for the use and benefit of the surviving spouse.

Suppose that Bob has established a trust during his lifetime but his wife Susan did not. Bob knows the value of avoiding probate and knows that Susan is not interested in managing money. Likewise, Susan knows the importance of financial management and would prefer not to handle money.

Bob creates the power of appointment trust. Upon his death, the assets that would have gone directly to Susan instead go to the power of appointment trust. XYZ Trust Company is appointed as trustee. Susan is to receive all income generated by the trust assets on a quarterly basis. Additionally, Susan is granted the power to take any portion of the principal that she desires at any time.

The power of appointment trust accomplishes all of their objectives. All of the $625,000 is tax-deferred, resulting in no tax at Bob's death. Bob has a trust to use as she sees fit, created by Bob in Bob's trust. Susan has the power to change trustees, even making herself a trustee if she chooses. She can take all of the money out of the trust if she wants or leave it in the trust and designate its recipient in her will. These trusts are not used much in estate planning.

JUST A MINUTE

One requirement for this trust to qualify for the unlimited marital deduction is that all income must be payable to the spouse, and only the spouse can be the recipient of income from the trust. Furthermore, the spouse then has the power to designate who will receive the property at his or her death.

The reason this trust is called a power of appointment trust is because the surviving spouse has a "general power of appointment" over the trust. As you will recall, this means whatever is left over in the trust will be taxed to the estate of the surviving spouse. The trust provides a means of managing the assets for the surviving spouse as a trust, rather than making an outright gift to the spouse.

QTIP Trust

QTIP stands for qualified terminable interest trust. A QTIP trust is specially designed to provide for a surviving spouse but, at the same time, prevent the surviving spouse from changing beneficiaries. Here are the primary objectives accomplished when using this trust:

- Qualify all of the property passing into the QTIP trust for the unlimited marital deduction
- Provide an income stream to the surviving spouse
- Prevent the surviving spouse from changing beneficiaries of the QTIP trust
- Protect the principal in the QTIP trust for other beneficiaries

STRICTLY DEFINED

QTIP is an abbreviation for qualified terminable interest trust. It is recognized by the Internal Revenue Service as qualifying for the marital deduction.

The trust is called a qualified terminable interest trust because the interest the surviving spouse has in the trust terminates at his or her death. Normally, a terminable interest does not qualify for the unlimited marital deduction. Because this trust is an exception to this rule, it is referred to as a terminable interest trust that is qualified for the marital deduction.

The requirements for qualification of this trust for the marital deduction are as follows:

- The income must be payable at least annually only to the surviving spouse.
- The surviving spouse cannot be a beneficiary of any part of the principal when the trust terminates.
- The surviving spouse has no power to appoint any portion of the trust to anyone during lifetime or at death.

- The surviving spouse may be given the power to withdraw no more than $5,000 or 5% of the value of the trust assets on an annual basis. This power lapses each year if not used.

One of the most important uses of the QTIP trust is in a second marriage in which each spouse has children from a prior marriage. This trust allows each spouse to provide for the surviving spouse during lifetime and to protect the principal for the benefit of the children of the grantor of the trust. For example, Bob and Susan each are on their second marriage, each with children from the first marriage. Both wish to ensure that their respective children are provided for, but they also wish to provide for each other as long as one of them is living.

If either Bob or Susan simply leaves what he has to the other, there is a possibility that the surviving spouse will not make adequate provisions for the children of the first spouse to die. If Bob and Susan each separate some or all of their assets, they could direct that their respective property be placed into a QTIP trust for the benefit of the other spouse. While living, that surviving spouse would receive all of the income from the trust. At the death of the surviving spouse, the children of the first spouse to die inherit the principal from the trust.

USING DISCLAIMERS

There actually are times when a beneficiary of a will or trust (or even an heir to an intestate estate) does not want to receive the inheritance. In other words, just because someone is given something, it doesn't mean that he or she necessarily wants it. Some of the reasons for disclaiming an inheritance are as follows:

- The gift will increase the taxable estate of the beneficiary, creating additional taxation.
- The gift is of an undesirable item (such as land in another state and carries with it administrative and maintenance responsibilities).
- The beneficiary prefers that a different heir or beneficiary receive the property.

There's another reason to execute a disclaimer: to correct an erroneous designation of a beneficiary.

THE QUALIFIED DISCLAIMER

Not all disclaimers are the same. Our attention first turns to the subject of *qualified disclaimers*. A qualified disclaimer is one that will keep the disclaimed asset out of the taxable estate of the beneficiary. We will explain a non-qualified disclaimer in the following paragraphs.

STRICTLY DEFINED

By definition, a **qualified disclaimer** is an irrevocable and unqualified refusal by the potential recipient of property to accept that gift.

For a disclaimer to be qualified it must meet certain requirements; they are as follows:

- The disclaimer must be irrevocable and without qualification.
- The disclaimer must be in writing.
- The writing must be delivered to the one who transferred the interest, such as the legal title owner, person in possession of the property, or the legal representative of the owner. This usually is the personal representative of the estate.
- The execution and delivery of the disclaimer must be completed within nine months from the date of the transfer, which usually is the date of death in the case of testamentary gifts.
- The person disclaiming must not have accepted the interest being disclaimed or accepted any of its benefits.
- The disclaimed interest must pass either to the spouse of the decedent or someone other than the disclaimant without any direction by the disclaimant.

EFFECT OF A DISCLAIMER

Whenever property is effectively disclaimed, the IRS treats it as if it never passed to the person who disclaims it. Instead, it is treated as if it passed directly to the party who is entitled to receive it. In other words, the person who disclaims with a qualified disclaimer is not considered to have made a gift to the person who ultimately receives the item, which eliminates any gift tax liability as a result of the execution of a disclaimer.

If you want to disclaim any property, you have nine months from date of death to execute a valid disclaimer. However, don't receive any benefit from the property in the interim, or you won't be allowed to make the qualified disclaimer.

For example, suppose Tom inherits a brokerage account investment. Tom waits five months to execute a valid qualified disclaimer. During this five-month period, Tom receives interest and dividends on this account and deposits the interest and dividends in his personal bank account. The IRS will disallow the disclaimer on the basis that Tom enjoyed the benefits of the investment account before executing the disclaimer.

FORM OF QUALIFIED DISCLAIMER

So long as all of the requirements are met, there is no mandatory form for the disclaimer; however, it's very important that you get legal advice before executing a disclaimer. If you don't word the document correctly or cover all the possible contingencies, you might end up getting stuck with a undesired result.

WHY DISCLAIM AT ALL?

As mentioned earlier, there are many reasons to disclaim an inheritance or gift. In addition to those listed, one reason to execute a disclaimer is to correct an erroneous designation of a beneficiary.

For example, suppose that Carl dies owning a $1,000,000 individual retirement account. Carl named his daughter as primary beneficiary and his wife as contingent beneficiary. If the property passes as directed to his daughter, Carl's estate would be forced to pay an estate tax on the amount over $675,000 that does not pass directly to his spouse. The tax, figured just on this one item, could amount to over $96,300!

To avoid this result, daughter could execute a qualified disclaimer of the amount over the exemption of $675,000, which would be $325,000. Without any direction on her part, the plan administrator would then pay the $325,000 directly to the contingent beneficiary, Carl's spouse. This gift would qualify for the marital deduction and eliminate the estate tax on this item.

FYI In addition to the savings on estate taxes, in this example the spouse will get all of the rollover benefits available to a spousal beneficiary of a qualified retirement account, thus allowing for continuing tax deferral over an extended period of time on the disclaimed amount.

THE NON-QUALIFIED DISCLAIMER

The requirements for the execution of a non-qualified disclaimer are found in state law. If the disclaimer does not comply with the requirements for a qualified disclaimer according to the Internal Revenue Code, then no tax benefits will be achieved by virtue of the disclaimer. Therefore, a person making a non-qualified disclaimer will be deemed by the IRS to have received the property and then gifted that property to the person who receives it as a result of the disclaimer. This means the gift would be subject to the gift tax laws.

THE DISCLAIMER TRUST

The disclaimer trust specifies exactly what will happen to the disclaimed property if the original recipient exercises a disclaimer. This trust allows a beneficiary to receive the property which he or she is entitled to receive under the terms of the trust. In the alternative, if the beneficiary exercises a disclaimer, the property subject to that disclaimer will pass to what's called a *subsidiary trust*. The subsidiary trust will be governed by its own terms. Frequently, one of the terms of the subsidiary trust is to provide for the health, maintenance, support, and education of the disclaimant.

For example, a husband and wife have separate trusts. The husband's trust names his wife as primary beneficiary. The husband's trust provides that if his wife disclaims her interest in the trust, the property shall instead pass to a credit shelter trust. At the husband's death, his wife chooses to exercise her right of disclaimer. The assets held in the husband's trust would then pass to the credit shelter trust. This credit shelter trust will provide for the health, maintenance, support, and education of his spouse for so long as she lives, with the remaining assets to pass to the children at the wife's death.

GO TO ▶
For more information of credit shelter trusts and how they work, see Hour 16.

The advantage of this type of trust is that the wife may postpone the decision whether or not to fund a credit shelter trust until the time of her husband's death. This adds to the flexibility of the couple's estate plan.

PROCEED WITH CAUTION

As with all of the material in this book, be certain to consult an estate planning attorney before implementing any of the techniques discussed in this book. The failure to obtain professional advice could result in additional expenses for administering your estate and could result in additional and unnecessary taxation of your estate. Additionally, the failure to properly prepare documents according to applicable law may render the documents useless.

HOUR'S UP!

Now it's time to see how much you have learned and retained from this lesson. Try to take the following quiz without referring back to the hourly materials:

1. A person disclaiming a gift …

   a. Can select the ultimate beneficiary

   b. Is going to receive it anyway

   c. Is unable to direct who gets it

   d. Forces the property to go to the state

2. A qualified disclaimer must be executed …

   a. Within nine months of the probate of decedent's estate

   b. Within nine months of the decedent's death

   c. Within six months of the decedent's death

   d. Before the decedent's death

3. One of the requirements for the execution of a qualified disclaimer is that …

   a. The disclaimer be made either verbally or in writing

   b. The disclaimant receive no interest in the disclaimed property

   c. The disclaimant state specifically who will get the disclaimed property

   d. One may not disclaim real estate

4. A power of appointment marital trust requires which of the following:

    a. Discretionary income to the spouse; distribution of principal subject to ascertainable standard; health, maintenance, support and education

    b. Mandatory income to the spouse; general power to appoint principal to spouse for any reason

    c. Spouse cannot designate new beneficiaries

    d. Income to spouse only; no principal is available to spouse

5. A qualified terminable interest trust (QTIP) ...

    a. Requires that mandatory income is payable only to spouse

    b. Requires that spouse has general power of appointment over principal

    c. Provides that spouse can designate new beneficiaries

    d. Does not qualify for the marital deduction

QUIZ

HOUR 21
Gifting of Assets

It certainly seems like common sense: A *gift* is when you give away something, right? Almost. Technically speaking, a gift occurs whenever someone gives up possession and control of property for less than what the property is worth. Although this sounds like common sense, there are some everyday situations in which you might not think you are making a gift—when in fact you are.

STRICTLY DEFINED

A **gift** is any transfer of money or property for less than full value, in which the donor loses use, possession, and control over the property.

Consider some of these examples:

- You sign the title of your house, worth $100,000, over to your children in return for them paying you $50,000. The gift is the value of the portion you did not get back; in this case $50,000.

- You sell your car to your brother for one dollar. The car is worth $2,000. You've made a gift of $1,999.

- You set up a savings account with your money; then put your son's name on the account as a joint owner. Whenever the son makes a withdrawal from the account, you have made a gift equal to the amount withdrawn.

Gifts must be voluntary. If you make a payment that discharges a legal obligation, such as a judgment, creditor, or child support, you can't consider that a gift. Additionally,

CHAPTER SUMMARY

LESSON PLAN:

In this hour, you'll learn about most of the issues that you must consider when contemplating a gift. Specifically, you will learn about the many advantages of gifting such as how to avoid probate and how to reduce income taxes through gifting. You also will become familiar with the annual gift tax exclusion, the relationship between the estate and gift taxes, gifts to non-citizen spouses, the marital deduction as it relates to gifting, and certain qualified gifts. You'll also learn …

- How to reduce your estate for tax purposes.

- How to make charitable gifts work for you.

- How to utilize the gift tax laws.

- How to use the laws regarding charitable and educational gifting.

a gift must be made by an individual; however, you can make a gift to any entity capable of owning property including an individual, a trust, or a business. Also, a gift must be complete; for example, if Bob gives Tom the right to use his car but Bob retains the title, Bob hasn't made a gift to Tom. Although Bob has given up use and enjoyment of the car, he still has some control over it.

Other types of transactions also cannot be considered gifts, including money used to …

- Fund a joint bank account
- Purchase U.S. savings bonds
- Fund a joint brokerage account in which the joint owner is not the spouse

These transactions are not gifts as long as the person who transfers the money retains the right to regain the entire fund without the consent of the other joint owner. However, if consent is required to withdraw funds, a gift has been made.

PROCEED WITH CAUTION

If you add another name to your account, you'll increase your liability. If your joint owner files bankruptcy, becomes the subject of a lawsuit, or is later entangled in a divorce proceeding, your account is at risk of loss to those creditors. The risk increases with each additional joint owner.

VALUATION OF GIFTS

A gift is valued as of the date of the gift. The general rule is to use the fair market value of the item transferred. This is basically the price agreed upon by a reasonable willing buyer and a reasonable willing seller. Some assets are capable of accurate valuation, such as cash, securities, bonds, and certificates of deposit.

Other assets are not quite as easy to value. For example, you can obtain a value on an automobile from someone who regularly deals with automobile sales. Values also can be obtained on the Internet or from valuation sources such as the National Automobile Dealers Association, available in most libraries and online.

Harder still is figuring out the value of income-producing property, such as farmland. With farmland, you must compare similar land in the area; usually you'll need to hire a certified appraiser to do so.

Even non-income-producing property, such as a residence, sometimes is difficult to value, as the true value can vary significantly with the economy and the community. Changes in the neighborhood can make significant changes in valuation in a short time, such as a commercial development that might serve to increase values in neighboring areas, or an environmental hazard that will serve to sharply decrease values.

JUST A MINUTE

The Federal Estate Tax allows the use of *alternate valuation* to reduce the value of an estate and minimize taxes. Alternate valuation is the value of all of a decedent's assets determined six months following death. This can be beneficial if the value of estate property declines sharply following death.

NON-TAX ADVANTAGES OF GIFTING

Apart from providing tax breaks, which we discuss in the next section, there are many other practical reasons for making lifetime gifts. Some gifts provide funds for children, grandchildren, or others who lack the resources to attend college, purchase a home, or start a business. In many cases, receiving gifts from others is the only way some people will be able to get the college education they need.

Gifting can provide an opportunity for a child to gain valuable experience with managing money and provide the foundation of a savings plan. The earlier you give the gift, the longer the interest on the investment will compound. Gifting also avoids probate of the gifted asset.

GO TO ▶
For a more detailed discussion of probate, go to Hour 8, "Probate." There you will find a detailed discussion of what probate is and how it works.

INCOME TAX BENEFITS

Significant income tax benefits—sometimes called *kiddie taxes*—result from giving a gift to a child. To understand how this tax works, let's first look at the type of person who might qualify for the kiddie tax and then examine the amount of income the beneficiary can earn from this tax.

The recipient must be both a dependent child and under the age of 14. Any recipient who does not meet both of these tests will not benefit from the kiddie tax. A dependent child is defined as one who is dependent on at least one living parent for support at the end of any given taxable year. The amount of the income that can benefit from the kiddie tax is $1,400 or less.

The benefit of qualifying for the kiddie tax is that the first $750 of a dependent child's unearned income (in 2001) is exempt from taxation due to the child's standard deduction. The next $750 of unearned income is taxed at the child's (usually) lower tax bracket compared to the parent. For example, if an adult taxpayer in the 37% tax bracket has unearned income from dividend-paying stock of $1,500, and assuming that other earned income uses up the adult's standard deduction, this income would be taxed as follows:

Total unearned income	$1,500.00
Taxation at adult's rate	×.37
Total tax	$555.00

Now let's assume this same adult taxpayer gifts the stock to a qualified dependent child. This gift will cause future dividends to be taxed according to the kiddie tax rules. The tax would be calculated as illustrated in the following:

Total unearned income	$1,500.00
Standard deduction	−$750.00
Net unearned income	$750.00
Taxation at child's rate	×.15
Total tax	$112.50
Total tax savings	$442.50

Before making this gift, it helps to identify what is considered *earned income* and what is considered *unearned income*. Federal tax regulations specify that Social Security and pension payments received by a child are unearned income. Income generated by an investment in a *Uniform Transfers to Minors Act* is unearned income. In contrast, earned income generally refers to compensation for personal services rendered by the child. What happens if the total unearned income of a dependent child exceeds $1,500? Children under the age of 14 must pay tax on this excess unearned income at their parents' marginal rate.

STRICTLY DEFINED

A **Uniform Transfers to Minors Account** is an account created under state law for the benefit of a minor child, where the child is entitled to the account at age 21.

JUST A MINUTE

In addition to the benefits of taxing income at a lower tax rate, there is another big advantage to gifting assets that appreciate in value. Although not taxable until an asset is sold, appreciation will be attributed to the estate of the child rather than the estate of the parent making the gift. This reduces the value of the parent's estate by removing future appreciation.

ESTATE TAX BENEFITS

As you learned in Hour 6, "Federal Estate Taxes," the estate tax is imposed on the value of assets owned by a decedent on the date of death. Obviously, if the decedent gives away assets before death, it would seem logical that the decedent's estate will be reduced by the value of the gift.

Many people have heard that you must give away an asset at some designated period of time before death to reduce the value of your estate. The truth is that only gifts of life insurance are subject to this *look-back rule*. A transfer of an ownership interest in a life insurance policy will take the value of that policy out of the decedent's estate only if the transfer occurred at least three years prior to the decedent's death. However, this three-year rule does not apply to gifts of other types of assets.

STRICTLY DEFINED

A **look-back period** applies to a period of time where assets given away will nevertheless be included in an individual's taxable estate. There is a three-year look-back period pertaining to transfers of ownership of a life insurance contract.

These deathbed transfers are perfectly effective for reducing the size of a decedent's estate, as long as the decedent was competent to make the gift.

COMMUNITY PROPERTY CONSIDERATIONS

In *community property* states—Arizona, California, Idaho, Louisiana, Nevada, New Mexico, Texas, Washington, and Wisconsin—a gift of community property will be treated as if the gift is divided equally between spouses. It is similar in application to the gift-splitting technique described earlier.

STRICTLY DEFINED

> **Community property** is a form of ownership between husband and wife in which each spouse has a separate, undivided interest in property acquired during marriage. This applies only in community property states. such as Arizona, California, Idaho, Louisiana, Nevada, New Mexico, Texas, Washington, and Wisconsin.

ANNUAL GIFT EXCLUSION

A person can give as much as $10,000 each to any number of recipients every calendar year without any tax. To qualify for the annual gift exclusion, gifts must be outright gifts or gifts of a *present interest*. Basically, the recipient of the gift must be able to use, possess, and enjoy the gift upon receipt, without restriction.

For example, a parent can give each of his or her four children $10,000 each calendar year for 10 years (a total of $100,000) with no tax on any of these gifts. The gift exclusion is a "use it or lose it" exemption. A gift not made in one year cannot be made in a subsequent year and qualify for the prior year's exclusion.

The giver does not have to file a tax return for any of the outright gifts that qualify for the annual exclusion. However, amounts in excess of $10,000 given to any one person in any calendar year must be reported on a gift tax return, with the exclusion applied against the total gift made.

 Taxable gifts are reported on Federal Form 709, United States Gift Tax Return, or on Federal Form 709A, United States Short Form Gift Tax Return.

FUTURE INTEREST GIFTS

A future interest gift is one made now but where the beneficial enjoyment of the gift is delayed until a future time. Normally, for a gift to be exempt as a tax-free annual gift, it must be unqualified. This means that the beneficiary of the gift must be able to use it immediately, without restriction. This is called a present-interest gift. The following are, nevertheless, gifts of a future interest that still qualify for the annual gift tax exemption.

UNIFORM TRANSFERS TO MINORS ACCOUNTS

One exception to the present interest requirement is to establish a Uniform Transfers to Minors Account (UTMA). This is simply an account created under state law that provides for the management of the deposits by a custodian until the child reaches age 21. The predecessor to the Uniform Transfers to Minors Act was the Uniform Gifts to Minors Act (UGMA). The primary difference between UTMA and UGMA is that the minor child is entitled to the account at age 18 under UGMA and at age 21 under UTMA. Another difference is that UGMAs will permit only transfers of bank deposits, securities, and insurance policies while UTMAs permit the transfer of any kind of property.

Anyone can be the custodian, including the parent of the minor child, which brings us to a very unusual provision in estate and gift tax law. If you are the custodian for your own child, the value of the account will still be included in your taxable estate even though you are allowed to count your contribution as a gift. Therefore, if gifting to such an account is motivated by estate tax considerations, you will not want to be the custodian of the account.

PROCEED WITH CAUTION

Transferring funds into a minor's account might interfere with the child's ability to receive financial aid. Financial aid programs often require money in a student's name to be used for college expenses before they will qualify for financial aid. Consider making payment of college expenses directly to the institution instead.

Under the Uniform Transfers to Minors Act, the minor acquires both legal and equitable title to the subject matter of the gift. Custodial gifts avoid many of the problems and expenses of other methods of transferring property to a minor such as outright gifts, trusts, or guardianship arrangements. This type of account is valuable when a parent would like to gift money or property for a minor's benefit without giving it to him or her outright and without having to set up a trust.

Here are a few more things to note about gifting:

- Property must be transferred to a custodian who holds it for the minor under the relevant state's Gifts or Transfers to Minors Act.

- A separate custodial account must be established for each beneficiary. Only one custodian can be appointed for each account. However, any number of separate gifts may be made.

- Custodial property is for the "use and benefit" of the minor.
- Custodial property passes to the administrator or executor of the minor's estate.
- If a custodian dies before the minor is legally an adult and the custodian has not chosen a successor, the minor can pick the successor if the minor is at least 14. If the minor does not pick a successor or is less than 14, the minor's guardian will be appointed. If there is no guardian, the court (upon petition) will select a successor.
- If the minor is under age 14, all unearned income in excess of $1,500, although it will be taxed to the minor, will be taxed at the parents' tax bracket. The first $750 of a minor's unearned income will bear no tax because of the minor's standard deduction. The next $750 will be taxed to the minor at the minor's tax bracket and any excess will be taxed to the minor at the parents' bracket. All unearned income will be taxed to minors 14 and over at their appropriate bracket.

Use of this type of account is beneficial when …

- The gift is one of a present interest and qualifies for the $10,000 annual gift tax exclusion.
- A parent would like to shift some of the income tax burden from his or her high tax bracket to a minor's lower bracket.
- The $10,000 annual gift tax exclusion is desired.
- A parent would like to reduce his or her potential estate tax burden by shifting future appreciation in the value of an asset to a minor.
- The donor does not object to the donee receiving the property outright upon reaching the age of twenty-one (21).

The following points should be kept in mind when contemplating a gift to a minor's account:

- If there are two or more minors to whom a parent wishes to make gifts, a custodian must be appointed for each minor.
- Once made, a custodial gift is irrevocable.
- The property must be distributed to the minor when he or she reaches the age of 21.
- Income from any custodial property will be taxed to the minor whether distributed or not, except to the extent it is used to discharge a legal obligation of some other person (for example, a parent's

obligation to support a minor). Where income produced by a custodial gift relieves an individual such as a parent of a legal obligation, the income is taxed to that parent.

- The value of property transferred generally will be included in the estate of a deceased minor-donee. So if the donee dies, assets in the custodial account will be includable in the minor's estate.

- Custodial property will be included in the estate of the donor if the donor appoints himself or herself as custodian and dies while serving in that capacity.

- Gifts of insurance are still included in the decedent's gross estate at their date of death value, regardless of the value of the policy, if the policy is transferred by the insured within three years of his death.

GIFT SPLITTING

Married couples have a bonus when it comes to gifting. Each spouse may exclude $10,000 per person per year, making the effective exclusion for the couple $20,000 per recipient per year. However, with a married couple, one spouse actually can give $20,000 to a single recipient in any one calendar year, as long as the other spouse signs a consent to split the gift on the Federal Gift Tax Return, Form 709.

An example is helpful to see how gift splitting actually works: Suppose Bob wishes to give $10,000 in a calendar year to each of his four children. Under gift tax laws, he could do this out of his own funds without any tax consequences. Bob's wife also could choose to make identical gifts from her own funds, again without any tax consequences.

However, if Bob wanted to gift $20,000 to each child out of his own funds, he could do this with the consent of his wife. She would merely sign the U.S. gift tax return and consent to split the gift. This is significant because one spouse can gift twice the annual exemption to a single recipient out of his or her own funds.

Once a gift is split with the consent of the other spouse, all gifts made by either spouse during the calendar year must be split. In other words, the election to split gifts applies not only to a single gift but applies to all gifts made by either spouse during the calendar year.

Use this form to report annual gifts in excess of $10,000 per beneficiary.

Form **709-A** (Rev. November 2000) Department of the Treasury Internal Revenue Service	**United States Short Form Gift Tax Return** Calendar year 20.........	OMB No. 1545-0021

1 Donor's first name and middle initial	2 Donor's last name	3 Donor's social security number

4 Address (number, street, and apartment number)	5 Legal residence (domicile)

6 City, state, and ZIP code	7 Citizenship

8 Did you file any gift tax returns for prior periods? . . . . ☐ Yes ☐ No

If "Yes," state when and where earlier returns were filed ►

9 Name of consenting spouse	10 Consenting spouse's social security number

Note: *Do not use this form to report gifts of closely held stock, partnership interests, fractional interests in real estate, or gifts for which the value has been reduced to reflect a valuation discount. Instead, use Form 709.*

List of Gifts

(a) Donee's name and address and description of gift	(b) Donor's adjusted basis of gift	(c) Date of gift	(d) Value at date of gift

Consent

I consent to have the gifts made by my spouse to third parties during the calendar year considered as made one-half by each of us.

Consenting spouse's signature ►   Date ►

Sign Here

Under penalties of perjury, I declare that I have examined this return, and to the best of my knowledge and belief, it is true, correct, and complete. Declaration of preparer (other than donor) is based on all information of which preparer has any knowledge.

► Signature of donor   Date

Paid Preparer's Use Only

Preparer's signature ►	Date	Check if self-employed ► ☐

Firm's name (or yours if self-employed), address, and ZIP code ►   Phone no. ► (   )

For Disclosure, Privacy Act, and Paperwork Reduction Act Notice, see the instructions.   Cat. No. 10171G   Form **709-A** (Rev. 11-2000)

UNLIMITED MARITAL DEDUCTION

The Internal Revenue Code allows for the transfer of assets having unlimited value between spouses without taxation. This is the same rule that applies to transfers to a surviving spouse after death, which was discussed in Hour 6 on federal estate taxes. There is, therefore, no tax imposed on a transfer of money or property between spouses, regardless of the value of the transfer and regardless of how often the transfers occur. Special rules apply to transfers to a non-citizen spouse, discussed below.

GO TO ▶
If planning for a non-citizen spouse, go to Hour 22, "Planning for Non-Residents." There you will find more information on how the absence of the marital deduction for non-citizens impacts your planning.

COMPARING GIFT AND ESTATE TAXES

One of the little known facts about the gift tax is that it actually is the same tax as the federal estate tax. These taxes are collectively referred to as the "United States Gift and Estate Tax." Although most people think this tax is imposed only following death, it also applies to gifts made during one's lifetime that exceed the annual exclusion. Anytime a gift is made that does not qualify for either the marital deduction or the annual gift exclusion, the gift must be reported to the Internal Revenue Service on a gift tax return.

Another common misconception is that a tax must be paid when a gift tax return is filed. In actuality, payment does not routinely accompany a gift tax return. As you might recall from the discussion of estate taxes, each individual has an amount excluded from the imposition of an estate tax, commonly referred to as the unified credit. In 2001, the amount was $675,000. Because the gift and estate taxes are one and the same tax, this exemption also applies to these lifetime taxable gifts. Therefore, when a gift tax return is filed, the individual typically uses a portion of his or her unified credit.

When you stop to think about it, you will discover that an individual can actually gift up to $685,000 (in 2001) to one individual in one year and suffer no adverse tax consequences. For example, Bob has an estate valued at $450,000. Bob would like to gift as much as possible to his only son without any adverse gift tax consequences. If Bob gives his son all of the $450,000, would there be any tax owing? No. Bob's gift would be treated as follows:

Total Gift	$450,000.00
Amount of annual exclusion	–$10,000.00
Amount of Taxable Gift	$440,000.00
Total Tax	–$135,400.00
Less Unified Credit	–$220,550.00
Balance Due	$0.00

The only requirement is that Bob will have to file a gift tax return by April 15 of the year after he made the gift. Bob will still have an unused credit of $85,150, which will be applied at Bob's death against any tax that might be owed at that time. Because Bob gave everything away, any tax would be imposed only on what Bob owned on the date of his death.

JUST A MINUTE

The actual calculation for both gift and estate taxes is to calculate the tax owing and then deduct any applicable credit. People are easily confused by references to the unified credit and the exemption equivalent amount. In 2001 the actual credit is $220,550. Taxable assets having a value of $675,000 will produce a tax of $220,550. Therefore, the "exemption equivalent amount" is $675,000.

More on Gifts and Taxes

Whenever there is a taxable gift, a Federal gift tax return must be filed. This is true even if no tax will be payable along with the return. Gift tax returns must be filed no later than April 15 following the year in which the gift was made. The obligation to file and pay any taxes is the responsibility of the person who made the gift. A gift tax return is not required if the amount gifted qualifies for the annual exclusion.

Timing of Gifts

With a few exceptions, gifts are immediately effective for tax reduction purposes. Therefore, a gift made two days before death is effective to remove the gifted property from the estate of the donor for federal estate taxes. One exception concerns the transfer of ownership in a life insurance policy, which requires that the donor live for three years following the date of the gift. If death occurs within that time, the value of the life insurance will be included in the taxable estate of the donor. The other exception concerns transfers in which the donor still retains some rights to the property, such as the reservation of a life estate in real estate. If those requirements are met, the entire value of the gifted item is included in the estate of the donor for tax purposes.

GO TO ▶
For a discussion of ways to avoid the problems with the three-year look-back period on life insurance, go to Hour 17, "Irrevocable Life Insurance Trusts."

TAX IMPACT ON RECIPIENT

One of the most frequently asked questions is whether the recipient of a gift must pay tax on the gift itself. The answer is no. The recipient of a gift pays no gift tax on the gifts and the gift is not treated as income to the recipient. However, any income realized from the investment of the gift will become taxable income to the recipient.

STEPPED-UP BASIS

A more serious problem with lifetime gifting occurs when the gift involves an appreciated asset such as real estate or equities. To understand the concept of the stepped-up basis, we will start with a definition of the word *basis*. Basis is what someone pays for something. If you paid $200,000 for your home, your "basis" is $200,000.

PROCEED WITH CAUTION

 Be certain to contact your accountant or other financial advisor when making decisions concerning the tax treatment of the sale of an appreciated asset.

You need to know your basis because when you sell that same property, you will be taxed on the difference between the selling price and the basis. This is commonly known as *capital gain*. The same is true of any appreciated asset, such as stock. This is important in gifting because the donor's basis in appreciated property is passed on to the recipient. Therefore, the recipient assumes the tax liability upon the realization of that gain through sale of the donated asset.

A better approach from a tax standpoint would be for the original owner to retain the asset and allow the recipient to inherit it. This way, the recipient will get the benefit of a stepped-up basis on the appreciated property determined by its fair market value on the donor's date of death. For example, Bob owns stock in XYZ Corporation. He paid $5 per share for the stock and bought 200 shares. The stock is now valued at $50 per share. Bob does not want to pay capital gains tax on this stock, so he wants to give it away to his daughter.

If Bob chooses to give away the stock, he will be transferring to his daughter his basis, which is $1,000. If his daughter decides to sell the stock at $50 per share, the sale price will net her $10,000. She will have to pay capital gains tax on the gain of $9,000.

If Bob retains the stock until he dies, he could make a specific gift of the stock in his will or trust to his daughter. If the stock is valued at $75 per share on Bob's date of death, the basis to his daughter will be $15,000. If she then decides to sell the stock at $75 per share, the sale price will net her $15,000. She will not have to pay any capital gains tax.

JUST A MINUTE

In addition to the exclusion of gains on the sale of a principal residence, you can also exclude gains on the sale of another house if you have lived in the house for at least two out of five years ending with the sale of the house.

PROCEED WITH CAUTION

Not all assets are allowed a stepped-up basis at the owner's death. For example, U.S. Government E bonds accumulate interest until the bonds are cashed in. When the owner of E bonds dies, the estate or the heirs will eventually cash them in. The new owner will pay income tax on all untaxed income.

QUALIFIED TRANSFERS

Sometimes when an asset is given away, it is not considered a gift. This type of gift is called a *qualified transfer*. There are two primary gifts considered to be qualified. The first is tuition paid directly to an educational organization for education or training. The second is any amount paid to any medical provider on behalf of another. Because these gifts are qualified, they are non-taxable and are not limited by the annual exclusion amount.

JUST A MINUTE

Don't ever give away an asset you might need for your own care and comfort. Tax reduction is important, as is providing for a child's education. However, neither is as important as providing for yourself first.

As you have now learned, the simple gift might be the most effective of all of the estate planning techniques discussed in this book. A gift can have significant impact on estate and income taxes. You also have discovered that gifting can have a serious adverse effect on the recipient of the gift when the asset has appreciated significantly in value. Be aware also that gifting can result in a disqualification for public assistance programs such as Medicaid.

PROCEED WITH CAUTION

As with all of the material in this book, be certain to consult an estate planning attorney before implementing any of the techniques discussed in this book. The failure to obtain professional advice could result in additional expenses for administering your estate and could result in additional and unnecessary taxation of your estate. Additionally, the failure to properly prepare documents according to applicable law may render the documents useless.

HOUR'S UP!

Now it's time to see how much you have learned and retained from this lesson. Try to take the following quiz without referring back to the hourly materials:

1. A married spouse can give the following amount to a single recipient in a single year without tax:
   a. $15,000
   b. $40,000
   c. $20,000
   d. $10,000

2. The amount of income that can benefit from the kiddie tax is ...
   a. $1,000
   b. $1,500
   c. $750
   d. $10,000

3. A gift of which of the following assets must be made at least three years prior to death to exclude the asset value from the decedent's taxable estate?
   a. Life insurance
   b. Stock
   c. Home
   d. Cash

4. The tax imposed on a taxable gift made during lifetime can be offset by which of the following:

   a. Unlimited marital deduction

   b. Income tax paid during year of gift

   c. Annual exclusion

   d. Charitable deduction

5. A gift of an appreciated asset during lifetime is not a good idea for which of the following reasons:

   a. It is not a qualified gift

   b. The annual exclusion is unavailable

   c. Loss of stepped-up basis

   d. The marital deduction is unavailable

HOUR 22

Planning for Non-Residents

An alien is a person who cannot hold or is not eligible for a U.S. passport. It is important to understand that an alien may become a United States resident. One test for determining whether an individual is a resident alien essentially says that an alien is a resident during a calendar year if the alien is a lawful permanent resident of the United States at any time during that calendar year.

Another test finds that an alien is considered a United States resident if he or she is present in the Unites States for at least 31 days during the current calendar year and for a total of 183 days during the current year and the 2 preceding calendar years.

THE TAXABLE ESTATE OF THE ALIEN

The issue of estate planning for a non-resident alien comes up only if he or she owns property in the United States.

As a general rule, whenever a non-resident owns property in the United States, the property will be subject to federal estate taxation. That's true whether the non-resident alien owns property individually or in the form of a partnership, corporation, or other entity.

The following is a short summary of how various types of property owned by aliens are treated for federal estate tax purposes. Note that there are always exceptions to the general nature of this table.

LESSON PLAN:

In this hour, we'll discuss the special planning required for *aliens*—residents of the United States who are not citizens, which means they can't vote or hold a U.S. passport. Many of these people need special attention for their planning needs, and many of the assumptions used in traditional planning do not apply in this context. However, there are some special techniques available to effectively plan the estate of the resident and the non-resident alien. You'll also learn ...

- How the unified credit applies to aliens.
- How the unlimited marital deduction applies to aliens.
- Whether aliens get to use the gift tax annual exclusion.
- Whether assets outside of the United States are subject to the federal estate tax.

Taxation of Aliens with U.S. Assets

Real estate	Subject to estate tax
Tangible personal property	Physically located in the United States; subject to estate tax
U.S. bank deposits	Issued by a U.S. bank; not subject to estate tax
Corporate stock	If issued by a U.S. corporation, subject to estate tax
Partnership interests	The IRS will not rule concerning the status of a partnership interest for estate tax purposes
Limited liability company	Treated either as corporation or partnership, depending on specific facts
Revocable trust	If created with a U.S. fiduciary, subject to estate tax
Business assets	If associated with a U.S. trade or business, subject to estate tax

MARITAL DEDUCTION FOR ALIENS

As you will see in a moment, the question of whether or not there will be a marital deduction depends on the citizenship status of the surviving spouse. A transfer at death to a non-citizen surviving spouse is not eligible for the marital deduction, even if the surviving spouse is a resident.

If the surviving spouse is a U.S. citizen, the estate of the non-resident alien will be entitled to use the unlimited marital deduction. If the surviving spouse is not a U.S. citizen, the estate of the non-resident alien will not be able to use the unlimited marital deduction.

UNITED STATES TREATIES

The United States has entered into certain treaties with other countries that offer at least a partial marital deduction for transfers to aliens. There are some treaties that provide a marital deduction of up to one half of the decedent's gross taxable estate. Two such treaties are the U.S.–Germany Estate Tax Treaty and the U.S.–Sweden Estate Tax Treaty. The U.S.–France Estate Tax Treaty offers a marital deduction equal to one half of the decedent's gross taxable estate or $250,000, whichever is greater. The U.S.–U.K. Estate Tax Treaty and the U.S.–Denmark Estate Tax Treaty authorize the unlimited marital deduction.

FYI Treaties are in effect with the following countries that pertain to the imposition and amount of federal estate tax due from the estate of a non-resident alien: Australia, Austria, Canada, Denmark, Finland, France, Germany, Greece, Ireland, Italy, Japan, Netherlands, Norway, Republic of South Africa, Sweden, Switzerland, and the United Kingdom.

UNIFIED CREDIT FOR ALIENS

Aside from the issue of the marital deduction is the issue of whether the unified credit is available to the estate of deceased resident aliens. Estates of U.S. citizens and U.S. residents are allowed to receive the full unified credit against federal estate taxes.

The estates of non-resident aliens, however, are allowed a unified credit of only $13,000, the equivalent to the exclusion of only $60,000 from the gross taxable estate of the alien's estate. This has a significant impact on the estate tax paid by an alien.

JUST A MINUTE

 Consult an international advisor if you're a married non-resident alien with property in this country. There are tax treaties that are in place with some countries that might allow at least some relief with the unified credit.

AVAILABILITY OF THE GIFT TAX ANNUAL EXCLUSION

Gifts made by non-resident aliens are subject to the U.S. Gift Tax if the property is situated within the United States. However, the gift tax does not apply to transfers of *intangible property* by a non-resident alien.

STRICTLY DEFINED

Intangible property includes items of personal property that have no intrinsic (built-in) value but represent something of value. Examples include money on deposit, such as bank accounts.

Gift-splitting, which is afforded to married U.S. citizens so that a gift made by one spouse can be treated as if made one half by each spouse, is not available to a non-resident alien. Review Hour 21, "Gifting of Assets," to refresh your memory on gift-splitting by married couples.

The non-resident alien is granted some relief, however. He or she is allowed to make gifts up to $103,000 per year per donee, even if the donee is also a non-resident alien. This opens up a significant planning opportunity for non-resident aliens if there is advance planning.

QUALIFIED DOMESTIC TRUST (QDOT)

One method of obtaining the benefits of citizenship for federal estate tax purposes is if the transfer is from the estate of a non-resident alien to a qualified domestic trust. This trust offers some immediate benefits to the estate of the non-resident alien. As you will see, however, the benefits can be lost over time.

GO TO ▶
To review those requirements, see Hour 20, "Marital Trusts and Disclaimer Planning."

The following are the basic requirements for the establishment of a valid qualified domestic trust:

- The trust must meet all of the same requirements for a trust to qualify for the marital deduction. This includes the requirements for a power of appointment trust or a QTIP trust.

- One trustee must be a U.S. citizen or a domestic corporation.

- The trustee must have the power to withhold taxes on any distributions made from the trust.

- The property of the non-resident alien must be transferred to the QDOT or to another trust that has been modified to meet the requirements of a QDOT, or the surviving spouse must make the transfer.

- The marital deduction will be allowed if the surviving spouse becomes a U.S. citizen.

- The marital deduction will be allowed if there is an applicable treaty involved.

A QDOT actually is a means of deferring estate taxes. Upon the occurrence of any of the following, an estate tax will be imposed ...

- If there is any distribution other than income to the surviving spouse or distribution to the surviving spouse based upon hardship.

- Upon the death of the surviving spouse, in which case the entire balance remaining in the QDOT is subject to estate tax.

- If the QDOT fails at any time to meet the necessary requirements, in which case the amount in the trust will be subject to estate tax.

PROCEED WITH CAUTION

It also is important to note that if a tax is imposed and paid by way of distribution from the trust, the distribution itself triggers an additional estate tax!

Of all the strategies available to a non-resident alien, the annual gift of $103,000 (in 2001, indexed annually) is the best planning strategy available. Although this does not require any special trusts, it does require advance planning. If you are an alien, you must be certain to advise your estate planning attorney of your non-citizenship status since this will dramatically impact the advice given to you.

PROCEED WITH CAUTION

As with all of the material in this book, be certain to consult an estate planning attorney before implementing any of the techniques discussed in this book. The failure to obtain professional advice could result in additional expenses for administering your estate and could result in additional and unnecessary taxation of your estate. Additionally, the failure to properly prepare documents according to applicable law may render the documents useless.

HOUR'S UP!

Now it's time to see how much you have learned and retained from this lesson. Try to take the following quiz without referring back to the hourly materials:

1. With regard to a non-resident alien:
   a. Property situated in the United States is not subject to estate tax.
   b. Property situated in the United States is subject to estate tax.
   c. Property situated outside the United States is subject to estate tax.
   d. Property situated in the United States is subject to a $13,000 estate tax.

2. With regard to transfers from a non-resident alien to a United States citizen spouse:
   a. There is no marital deduction allowed.
   b. There is only a $103,000 marital deduction allowed.
   c. The unlimited marital deduction is allowed.
   d. These transfers are illegal.

3. A non-resident alien is allowed the following unified credit at death:

   a. $10,000

   b. $1,000,000

   c. $675,000

   d. $13,000

4. A non-taxable gift from a non-resident alien to another non-resident alien …

   a. Cannot exceed $103,000

   b. Cannot be done

   c. Can be done with only a QDOT

   d. Is limited to $13,000

5. A QDOT …

   a. Is the only way to make lifetime gifts to a non-resident spouse

   b. Is the only way to use the $13,000 uniform credit

   c. Allows for the use of the marital deduction upon the death of the non-resident alien

   d. Prevents the trust assets from ever being taxed for federal estate tax purposes

QUIZ

PART VII
Putting It All Together

HOUR 23   Case Study 1: Single Individuals

HOUR 24   Case Study 2: Married Couples

HOUR 23

Case Study 1: Single Individuals

CHAPTER SUMMARY

LESSON PLAN:

Now that you've reached this point in the book, it is time to pull together some of the concepts discussed and apply them to real-life situations. Because planning for single individuals is sometimes substantially different than planning for married couples, this chapter will focus on how to implement planning strategies for the single individual. In this hour, you'll learn …

- How to gather our assets effectively.
- How to prioritize your goals.
- How to choose the right estate planning tools to achieve your goals.
- How to implement your plan.

 Let's consider the case of Karl Jennings, age 45, single. His net worth statement appears in the following, showing all asset values in present value. For purposes of this illustration, assume that all of Karl's assets are in single ownership.

PROCEED WITH CAUTION

As pointed out in Hour 1, "The Estate Planning Process," it is important to consider future values when planning an estate. This will be illustrated later in this hour.

Notice that Karl's asset tabulation includes the types of assets—which we shall assume are all in single name—the current fair market value, and liabilities. Karl's goals are to reduce the expense of probate administration and to reduce taxation as much as possible. As you'll see, it will be important for Karl to know how his assets might grow in the future. You'll be amazed at how much his assets will grow, even using conservative estimates, and this will make you aware of why future growth calculations are so very important.

Net Worth Statement (in Present Value)

Category	Description	Asset Value
Personal property	CD	$5,000
Personal property	Money market	$3,000
Personal property Intangible	Checking	$2,000
Personal property Intangible	Savings	$3,000
Personal property Intangible	Bonds	$5,000
Personal property Intangible	Brokerage account	$100,000
Personal property Intangible	Life insurance	$200,000
Personal property Intangible	IRA	$300,000
Real estate Tangible	Primary residence	$180,000
Liability	Mortgage	$90,000
TOTAL		$708,000

Karl's estate consists of the following:

- Investments $208,000
- Retirement $300,000
- Life insurance $200,000

Let's assume that Karl dies with a will in 2001, at age 45. We'll also assume Karl has his estate listed as beneficiary on his IRA and life insurance. Funeral expenses and administrative expenses are subtracted automatically.

The graph in Figure 23.1 shows estimated taxes and expenses of $119,400. The net to Karl's heirs would be $588,600. You can see the inefficiency of this plan caused by Karl's failure to plan properly.

The next illustration shows a detailed breakdown of the tax analysis for Karl's estate.

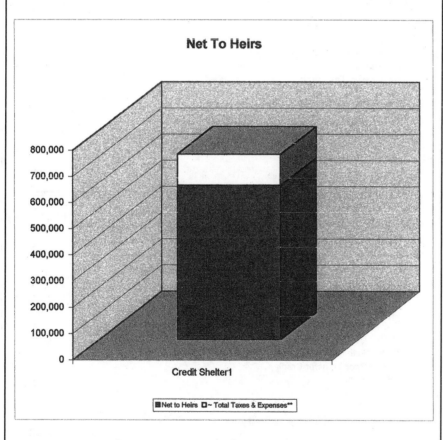

Estate Plan Scenarios: Default Case

Net to Heirs - Comparison
Karl Jennings

Future Values in 2001*	Credit Shelter1
Future Value of Current Estate	708,000
~ Total Taxes & Expenses**	119,400
Net to Heirs	588,600

Net To Heirs

800,000
700,000
600,000
500,000
400,000
300,000
200,000
100,000
0

Credit Shelter1

■ Net to Heirs □ ~ Total Taxes & Expenses**

*Assumes a 0.0% Growth Rate.

**The future value of taxes & expenses paid on first death plus those paid on last death.

Figure 23.1: Graph showing effects of insufficient planning in present value.

(Provided with permission of zcalc software, on the Web at www.zcalc. com www.zcalc. com)

Figure 23.2:
Table showing tax
calculations—
present value.

(Provided with per-
mission of zcalc
software, on
the Web at
www.zcalc.com)

Estate Plan Scenarios: Default Case

Tax Details - All To Heirs

Karl Jennings

First to Die (Spouse) in 0

Net Estate	0
~ Admin Expenses	0
~ FOBI Deduction	0
~ Marital Deduction	0
Taxable Estate	0
Adjusted Taxable Gifts	0
Tentative Tax Base	0
Tentative Tax	0
~ Gift Tax Paid Credit	0
~ Unified Credit	220,550
~ State Death Tax Credit	0
~ Other Credits	0
Federal Estate Tax	0
State Death Tax	0
Total Death Taxes (0% Marginal Bracket)	0
Income Tax on IRD	0
Administrative Expenses	0
Total Taxes and Expenses	0

Last to Die (Karl) in 2001

Net Estate	508,000
~ Admin Expenses	25,400
~ FOBI Deduction	0
Taxable Estate	482,600
Adjusted Taxable Gifts	0
Tentative Tax Base	482,600
Tentative Tax	149,884
~ Gift Tax Paid Credit	0
~ Unified Credit	220,550
~ State Death Tax Credit	0
~ Tax on Prior Transfer Credit	0
~ Other Credits	0
Federal Estate Tax	0
State Death Tax	0
Total Death Taxes (0% Marginal Bracket)	0
Income Tax on IRD	84,000
Administrative Expenses	25,400
Total Taxes and Expenses	109,400

The tax calculation in Figure 23.2 discloses that even though Karl's estate is not going to incur a federal estate tax, it will incur income taxes on the retirement account as a result of payment to the estate. These taxes are shown near the bottom of the chart as "income tax on IRD," which stands for "income in respect of a decedent." This tax is not cheap; the calculation estimates $84,000.

ANALYSIS

Karl has done no significant planning, although he has accumulated significant assets. Because Karl died with a will and without a trust, his estate, being in single name, will pass through probate. The total value of his estate, minus liabilities, is $708,000. Like many people, he has a mortgage on his primary residence.

Karl has made some significant mistakes due to his failure to plan his estate. To begin with, all of Karl's assets are in single name. This means that all of his assets will pass directly through the probate process. This example does not illustrate who Karl's heirs might be, but assuming Karl has some beneficiaries in mind, he could have designated those individuals as beneficiaries payable on death accounts. All of Karl's bank accounts, bonds, and brokerage account could have been made into a payable upon death (or transfer on death) designation. The result of this simple change would eliminate $118,000 from passing through probate. At an estimated probate expense of 5%, this would amount to a savings of $5,900.

The second big mistake made by Karl was his failure to designate a beneficiary on his retirement IRA and his life insurance. Because of his failure to make this important designation, these two accounts will be payable to the personal representative of his estate. This subjects $500,000 to unnecessary probate fees and state inheritance taxation, if the state of his residence on date of death imposes an inheritance tax. Because life insurance and retirement accounts are paid into the probate estate both become subject to creditor claims against the estate. Most states would exempt these assets from creditor claims if they were paid directly to a named beneficiary. There will most likely be a delay of over a year before Karl's heirs will receive their inheritance.

ALTERNATIVE 1: PROJECTING FUTURE GROWTH

Using all of the assumptions and asset information provided in he preceding, a good plan will attempt to project future growth of assets. Assume an estimated growth rate of 7% on Karl's property until his death in 10 years, in 2011. (Note that no growth is calculated on the life insurance, because that death benefit remains the same.)

The graph in Figure 23.3 demonstrates the effects of future growth on an estate and the tax impact of that growth. This chart estimates total taxes and administrative expenses of $313,783.

JUST A MINUTE

If 7% seems like too much growth, consider the rule of 72s. This rule provides that if you divide 72 by the rate of return on the investment, the result is the number of years required to double your investment. For example, $100,000 at 7% growth will take approximately 10 years to double. 72 ÷ 7 = 10.28. Using this formula, you can see how the estate nearly doubled in the 10-year time frame with assumed growth of 7%.

ANALYSIS AND SUGGESTIONS

Karl's estate has grown to $1,269,265, which will now increase his anticipated administrative expenses to approximately $63,463.

In Figure 23.4, notice the federal estate tax estimate of $84,379! Coupled with the administrative expenses, the total loss to his estate will be approximately 147,842!

Karl should consider the following:

- Prepare a revocable living trust.
- Name a beneficiary (other than his estate) to receive his life insurance and his retirement accounts.
- Transfer his CD, money market, checking account, savings account, bonds, brokerage account, and residence to the name of his trust.
- Transfer his life insurance policy to an irrevocable life insurance trust.

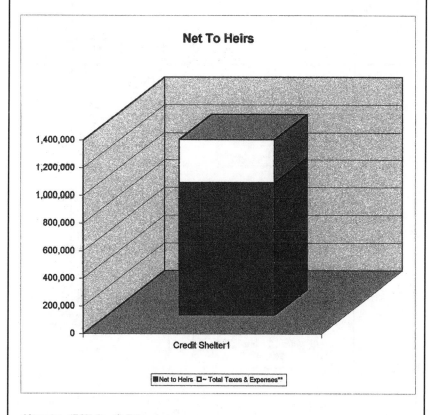

Estate Plan Scenarios: jennings estate plan

Net to Heirs - Comparison
Karl Jennings

Future Values in 2011*	Credit Shelter1
Future Value of Current Estate	1,269,265
~ Total Taxes & Expenses**	313,783
Net to Heirs	955,481

Net To Heirs

Credit Shelter1

■ Net to Heirs □ ~ Total Taxes & Expenses**

*Assumes a 7.0% Growth Rate.

**The future value of taxes & expenses paid on first death plus those paid on last death.

*Figure 23.3:
Graph showing
effects of insufficient
planning in future
value.*

*(Provided with per-
mission of zcalc
software, on the
Web at www.
zcalc.com)*

Figure 23.4:
Chart showing
expenses and net to
heirs—future value.

(Provided with
permission of zcalc
software, on the
Web at www.
zcalc.com)

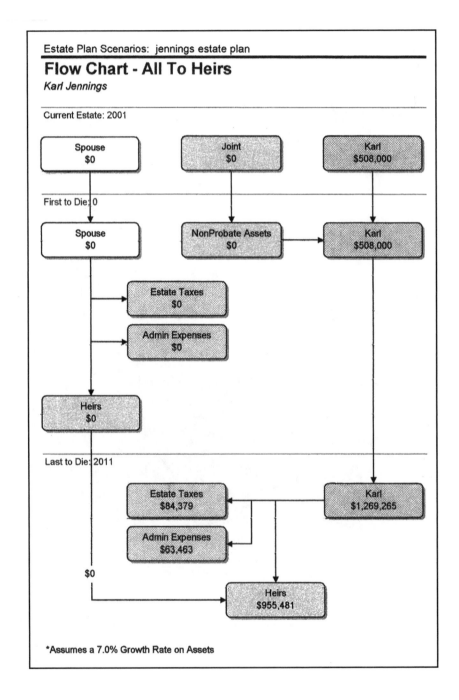

Estate Plan Scenarios: jennings estate plan

Flow Chart - All To Heirs
Karl Jennings

Current Estate: 2001

| Spouse $0 | Joint $0 | Karl $508,000 |

First to Die: 0

| Spouse $0 | NonProbate Assets $0 | Karl $508,000 |

Estate Taxes $0

Admin Expenses $0

Heirs $0

Last to Die: 2011

Estate Taxes $84,379

Admin Expenses $63,463

Karl $1,269,265

$0

Heirs $955,481

*Assumes a 7.0% Growth Rate on Assets

ALTERNATIVE 2

If Karl does the preceding, here is what his plan will look like, assuming his death occurs in 10 years, in 2011.

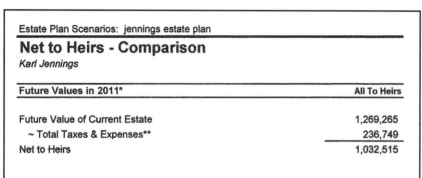

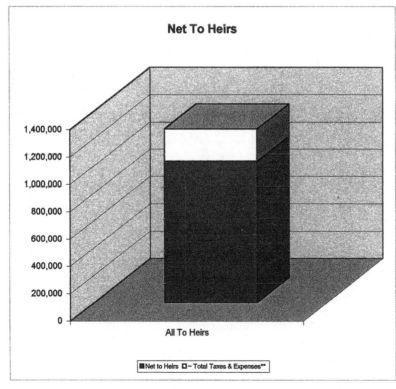

Estate Plan Scenarios: jennings estate plan

Net to Heirs - Comparison
Karl Jennings

Future Values in 2011*	All To Heirs
Future Value of Current Estate	1,269,265
~ Total Taxes & Expenses**	236,749
Net to Heirs	1,032,515

Net To Heirs

■ Net to Heirs □ ~ Total Taxes & Expenses**

All To Heirs

*Assumes a 7.0% Growth Rate.
**The future value of taxes & expenses paid on first death plus those paid on last death.

Figure 23.5: Graph showing effects of planning in future value.

(Provided with permission of zcalc software, on the Web at www.zcalc. com)

ANALYSIS OF PLAN IMPLEMENTATION

These simple changes have reduced the tax from an estimated $84,379 to $6,479—a savings of $77,900! The other major change was the removal of the $200,000 life insurance policy from the taxable estate more than three years before Karl's death.

Now let's see the effects of the irrevocable life insurance trust.

Figure 23.6:
Chart showing effects of utilizing irrevocable life insurance trust.

(Provided with permission of zcalc software, on the Web at www.zcalc. com)

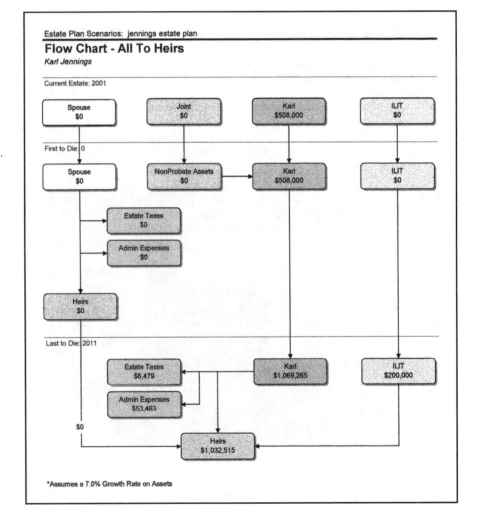

Note that the insurance contained in the life insurance trust passes to the beneficiaries free from federal estate tax, state inheritance tax, and income tax. The insurance in the life insurance trust consists of the $200,000 policy transferred to the trust. Premiums on both policies are paid by lifetime gifts to the trustee from Karl that qualify for the annual gift tax exclusion.

As a result of this planning, Karl has gone from giving his heirs $955,481 to giving them $1,032,515.

PROCEED WITH CAUTION

 As with all of the material in this book, be certain to consult an estate planning attorney before implementing any of the techniques discussed in this book. The failure to obtain professional advice could result in additional expenses for administering your estate and could result in additional and unnecessary taxation of your estate. Additionally, the failure to properly prepare documents according to applicable law may render the documents useless.

HOUR'S UP!

Now it's time to see how much you have learned and retained from this lesson. Try to take the following quiz without referring back to the hourly materials:

1. The biggest problem with Karl's original estate plan is …
    a. There is no probate.
    b. Taxes are minimized as well as can be expected.
    c. All his assets are in single name and payable to his estate.
    d. Karl has too much wealth.
2. The problem with naming the estate as beneficiary of his retirement plans and life insurance is …
    a. His beneficiaries inherit everything faster.
    b. It slows down the distribution of his retirement account.
    c. It causes life insurance to be subject to income tax.
    d. It subjects all to probate expenses and creditor claims.

3. To keep the existing policy out of his taxable estate at death, he must transfer the policy to the irrevocable trust how many years before his death:

   a. Three years

   b. One year

   c. Five years

   d. It is out of his taxable estate immediately upon transfer to the trust.

4. The proceeds from the irrevocable life insurance trust are ...

   a. Taxable for state inheritance tax, tax free for federal estate and income taxes

   b. Tax-free for federal estate, state inheritance, and income taxes

   c. Tax-free for federal estate, but taxable for state inheritance and income taxes

   d. Tax-free for income tax, but taxable for federal estate and state inheritance taxes

5. The revocable trust helps Karl:

   a. Avoid taxes

   b. Avoid all attorney fees

   c. Avoid creditors

   d. Avoid probate

QUIZ

HOUR 24

Case Study 2: Married Couples

CHAPTER SUMMARY

LESSON PLAN:

In this final hour we will review some of the problems encountered by married couples when planning their estates. Like the previous hour, we will review the assets of the couple, followed by a look at administrative expenses and tax liabilities. We then will review some future value calculations. In this hour you will learn …

- How joint ownership can cause increased taxation.
- How credit shelter planning actually works.
- How to benefit from a life insurance trust.

In the last hour you saw how the single individual can significantly reduce the administrative expenses of his or her estate and dramatically reduce taxes. Additionally, he or she can significantly increase the amount passing to the beneficiaries. Now we will examine how a married couple can achieve similar savings as they plan their estate.

EXAMPLE 1—ALL TO SPOUSE

John Smith, 50, and Linda Smith, 46, are married. For future value comparisons, assume that John dies in the year 2026 at age 77. Further assume that Linda dies at age 77 in the year 2030. Further assume they own the following assets:

- Investments—jointly owned with survivorship—$400,000
- Retirement—owned by John payable to Linda—$300,000
- Life Insurance—owned by John payable to Linda—$200,000

The following illustrations assume future values, calculated at 7% growth.

From a tax standpoint, the failure to plan is devastating. To begin with, the amount at the first death passes to the surviving spouse tax free due to the unlimited marital deduction. However, at the second death two things happen: First, the entire estate goes through probate. Second, estate taxes are due within nine months of the second death. As the chart in Figure 24.1 illustrates, no estate taxes are due at John's death. This is due to the use of the unlimited marital deduction. John's retirement account, life insurance and all joint property passes to Jane.

*Figure 24.1:
Chart showing
effects of joint
ownership in future
value.*

*(Provided with permission of zcalc
software, on the
Web at www.
zcalc.com)*

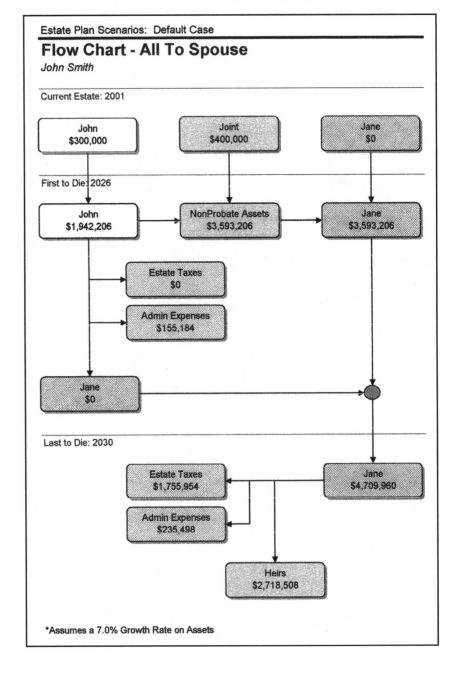

Estate Plan Scenarios: Default Case

Flow Chart - All To Spouse

John Smith

Current Estate: 2001

| John $300,000 | Joint $400,000 | Jane $0 |

First to Die: 2026

| John $1,942,206 | NonProbate Assets $3,593,206 | Jane $3,593,206 |

Estate Taxes $0

Admin Expenses $155,184

Jane $0

Last to Die: 2030

Estate Taxes $1,755,954

Admin Expenses $235,498

Jane $4,709,960

Heirs $2,718,508

*Assumes a 7.0% Growth Rate on Assets

All of those assets continue to grow until Jane's death. The estimated value of the estate at Jane's death is $4,709,960. Federal estate taxes are estimated to be $1,755,954, and administrative expenses estimated to be $235,498. The net to the heirs is $2,718,508.

EXAMPLE 2—USE OF CREDIT SHELTER TRUSTS

Now we are going to assume that, rather than pass everything to the surviving spouse, each spouse will have a credit shelter trust in place. The only assets that John can place into his trust during lifetime is $1/2$ of the joint assets. So he and Jane decide to split the joint assets between them.

- Each places $200,000 into their own trust.

- John, as owner of life insurance, names his trust as beneficiary of his $200,000 life insurance policy. This will shelter those proceeds at his death.

- John leaves the retirement account alone, with Jane as beneficiary, for income tax reasons, allowing Jane to roll-over the retirement account into her IRA account.

- Since John dies first, he will be able to shelter up to $1,000,000 at his death by transferring this amount to his credit shelter trust.

In this situation, not everything passes to Jane at John's death. You will see that $1,000,000 passes without any estate tax at John's death to his credit shelter trust. This amount continues to grow until Jane's death to $1,310,769. Here it is important to see that this amount is not subject to federal estate tax at Jane's death; it all passes directly to the heirs.

Jane has her own trust assets, plus John's retirement proceeds. At her death, her estate has grown to $3,166,698. Federal estate taxes will be approximately $1,090,884, and administrative expenses will be approximately $171,855.

Compared to using joint ownership of assets, the results are quite impressive!

- Federal Estate taxes have been reduced from $1,755,954 to $1,090,884, a savings of $665,070!

- Administrative expenses have been reduced from $235,498 to $171,855, a savings of $63,643!

- Total savings using these techniques: $728,713!

Figure 24.2:
Chart showing
effects of using
credit shelter trust
planning.

(Provided with per-
mission of zcalc
software, on the
Web at www.
zcalc.com)

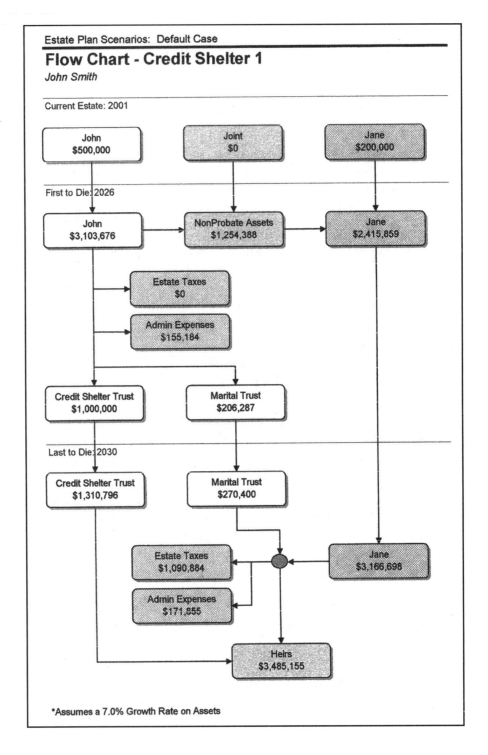

EXAMPLE 3—USE OF IRREVOCABLE LIFE INSURANCE TRUST

As good as all of this planning is, there is still more that can be done. John and Jane have done their very best by sheltering $2,000,000 combined using separate credit shelter trusts. But there is still a federal tax owing because their estate is larger than $2,000,000. They have the following choices to make about how to arrange for the payment of the federal estate taxes and administrative expenses totaling $1,262,739:

- Let the heirs pay it out of their inheritance other than retirement funds.

- Let the heirs borrow money to pay it.

- Let the heirs pay it out of the retirement funds, thus incurring additional income tax on those distributions.

- Make annual gifts during their lifetimes to the trustee of an irrevocable life insurance trust, who will in turn purchase a second-to-die life insurance policy with a death benefit of $1,000,000.

Let's see the results of the irrevocable life insurance trust in Figure 24.3.

Notice in the following figure that the $1,000,000 proceeds from the second-to-die insurance pays at Jane's death to the heirs free from any taxes. Although the taxes are the same at Jane's death, the heirs now have $1,000,000 in tax-free money to pay the taxes. The net to heirs is now $4,485,155!

PROCEED WITH CAUTION

As with all of the material in this book, be certain to consult an estate planning attorney before implementing any of the techniques discussed in this book. The failure to obtain professional advice could result in additional expenses for administering your estate and could result in additional and unnecessary taxation of your estate. Additionally, the failure to properly prepare documents according to applicable law may render the documents useless.

Figure 24.3:
Chart showing
effects of using
irrevocable life
insurance trust.

(Provided with per-
mission of zcalc
software, on the
Web at www.
zcalc.com)

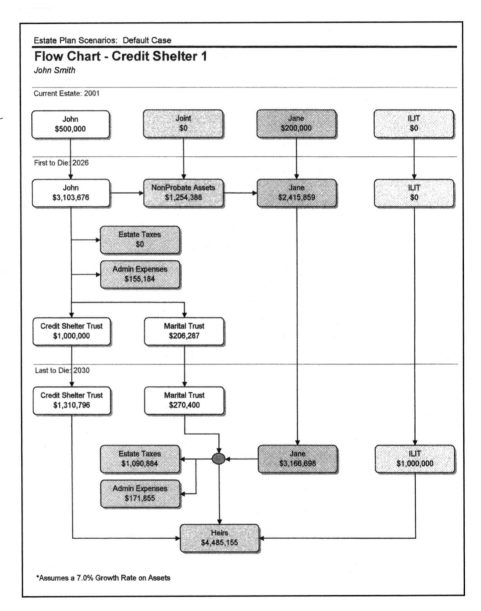

Estate Plan Scenarios: Default Case

Flow Chart - Credit Shelter 1
John Smith

Current Estate: 2001

John	Joint	Jane	ILIT
$500,000	$0	$200,000	$0

First to Die: 2026

John	NonProbate Assets	Jane	ILIT
$3,103,676	$1,254,388	$2,415,859	$0

Estate Taxes
$0

Admin Expenses
$155,184

Credit Shelter Trust	Marital Trust
$1,000,000	$206,287

Last to Die: 2030

Credit Shelter Trust	Marital Trust
$1,310,796	$270,400

Estate Taxes
$1,090,884

Admin Expenses
$171,855

Jane	ILIT
$3,166,698	$1,000,000

Heirs
$4,485,155

*Assumes a 7.0% Growth Rate on Assets

Hour's Up!

Now it's time to see how much you have learned and retained from this lesson. Try to take the following quiz without referring back to the hourly materials:

1. One very important aspect of planning your estate is …
   a. To project future values
   b. To ignore future values
   c. To disregard anticipated probate expenses
   d. To sell all of your assets

2. Proceeds from the life insurance trust …
   a. Must be paid to the attorney for the estate
   b. Are not subject to probate or estate taxes
   c. Are subject to estate taxes but not probate
   d. Are subject to probate but not estate taxes

3. When planning your estate, you should consider …
   a. Federal estate taxes only
   b. State inheritance taxes only
   c. Income taxes only
   d. Federal estate taxes, inheritance taxes, and income taxes

4. Once assets have been placed into a credit shelter trust …
   a. They continue to grow, subject only to state inheritance taxes.
   b. They continue to grow, subject to estate taxes at the second death.
   c. They continue to grow estate tax free.
   d. They do not appreciate in value.

5. Estate planning is …
   a. Not worth the time it takes
   b. Not worth the expense
   c. Does not benefit the heirs
   d. None of the above

Part VIII
Appendixes

A   Answers to Quiz Questions

B   Lady Di's Will

C   Last Will and Testament of
Richard M. Nixon

D   References and Further Readings

E   Glossary

APPENDIX A

Answers to Quiz Questions

Hour 1

1. d
2. c
3. a
4. d
5. b

Hour 2

1. d
2. b
3. c
4. b
5. a

Hour 3

1. c
2. d
3. a
4. a
5. d

Hour 4

1. c
2. b
3. d
4. d
5. b

Hour 5

1. a
2. d
3. a
4. b
5. c

Hour 6

1. a
2. d
3. c
4. c
5. d

Hour 7

1. d
2. a
3. c
4. d
5. d

Hour 8

1. b
2. c
3. a
4. d
5. d

Hour 9

1. b
2. d
3. d
4. a
5. d

Hour 10

1. d
2. c
3. a
4. c
5. d

Hour 11

1. b
2. d
3. a
4. d
5. c

Hour 12

1. c
2. c
3. d
4. b
5. c

Hour 13

1. c
2. b
3. d
4. d
5. a

Hour 14

1. b
2. c
3. c
4. b
5. d

Hour 15

1. c
2. b
3. a
4. d
5. d

Hour 16

1. c
2. d
3. a
4. d
5. c

Hour 17

1. c
2. a
3. c
4. b
5. d

Hour 18

1. b
2. d
3. a
4. c
5. d

Hour 19

1. d
2. b
3. a
4. c
5. d

Hour 20

1. c
2. b
3. b
4. b
5. d

Hour 21

1. c
2. b
3. a
4. b
5. c

Hour 22

1. b
2. c
3. d
4. a
5. c

Hour 23

1. a
2. b
3. d
4. c
5. d

Hour 24

1. b
2. c
3. d
4. a
5. d

Lady Di's Will

This is the Last Will and Testament of Princess Diana, Princess of Wales. Consider as you read this that it was written in England in accordance with English law, which is somewhat different than the law in the United States.

Nevertheless, note the inclusion of important provisions, some of which were discussed in Hour 9, "Wills," including provisions in the event of the death of a primary beneficiary; appointment of guardians; appointment of personal representatives; valuation of the estate; fees; signature and witnessing; and the execution of a codicil.

The Will of Diana, Princess of Wales

I, DIANA PRINCESS OF WALES of Kensington Palace London W8, **HEREBY REVOKE** all former Wills and testamentary dispositions made by me **AND DECLARE** this to be my last Will which I make this First day of June One thousand nine hundred and ninety three.

1. I **APPOINT** my mother **THE HONOURABLE MRS FRANCES RUTH SHAND KYDD** of Callinesh Isle of Seil Oban Scotland and **COMMANDER PATRICK DESMOND CHRISTIAN JERMY JEPHSON** of St James's Palace London SW 1 to be the Executors and Trustees of this my Will.

2. I WISH to be buried.

3. SHOULD any child of mine be under age at the date of the death of the survivor of myself and my husband I APPOINT my mother and my brother **EARL SPENCER** to be the guardians of that child and I express the wish that should I predecease my husband he will consult with my mother with regard to the upbringing, education, and welfare of our children.

4. (a) I GIVE free of inheritance tax all my chattels to my Executors jointly (or if only one of them shall prove my Will to her or him).

(b) I DESIRE them (or if only one shall prove her or him).

(i) To give effect as soon as possible but not later than two years following my death to any written memorandum or notes of wishes of mine with regard to any of my chattels (ii) Subject to any such wishes to hold my chattels (or the balance thereof) in accordance with Clause 5 of this my Will.

(c) FOR the purposes of this Clause "chattels" shall have the same meaning as is assigned to the expression "personal chattels" in the Administration of Estates Act 1925 (including any car or cars that I may own at the time of my death).

(d) I DECLARE that all expenses for the safe custody of and insurance incurred prior to giving effect to my wishes and for packing, transporting, and insurance for the purposes of the delivery to the respective recipients of their particular chattels shall be borne by my residuary estate.

5. SUBJECT to the payment or discharge of my funeral testamentary and administration expenses and debts and other liabilities I GIVE all my property and assets of every kind and wherever situate to my Executors and Trustees Upon trust either to retain (if they think fit without being liable for loss) all or any part in the same state as they are at the time of my death or to sell whatever and wherever they decide with power when they consider it proper to invest trust monies and to vary investments in accordance with the powers contained in the Schedule to this my Will and to hold the same UPON TRUST for such of them my children **PRINCE WILLIAM** and **PRINCE HENRY** as are living three months after my death and attain the age of twenty five years if more than one in equal shares PROVIDED THAT if either child of mine dies before me or within three months after my death and issue of that child are living three months after my death and attain the age of twenty one years such issue shall take by substitution if more than one in equal shares per stirpes the share that the deceased child of mine would

have taken had he been living three months after my death but so that no issue shall take whose parent is then living and so capable of taking.

6. MY EXECUTORS AND TRUSTEES shall have the following powers in addition to all other powers over any share of the Trust Fund.

(a) POWER under the Trustee Act 1925 Section 31 to apply income for maintenance and to accumulate surplus income during a minority but as if the words "my Trustees think fit" were substituted in sub-section (1)(i) thereof for the words "may in all the circumstances be reasonable" and as if the proviso at the end of sub-section (1) thereof was ommitted.

(b) POWER under the Trustee Act 1925 Section 32 to pay or apply capital for advancement or benefit but as if proviso (a) to sub-section (1) thereof stated that "no payment or application shall be made to or for any person which exceeds altogether in amount the whole of the presumptive or vested share or interest of that person in the trust property or other than for the personal benefit of that person or in such manner as to prevent limit or postpone his or her interest in possession in that share or interest."

7. THE statutory and equitable rules of apportionment shall not apply to my Will and all dividends and other payments in the nature of income received by the Trustees shall be treated as income at the date of receipt irrespective of the period for which the dividend or other income is payable.

8. IT is my wish (but without placing them under any binding obligation) that my executors employ the firm of Mishcon de Reya of 21 Southampton Row London WC IB 5HS in obtaining a Grant of Probate to and administering my estate.

9. ANY person who does not survive me by at least three months shall be deemed to have predeceased me for the purpose of ascertaining the devolution of my estate and the income thereof.

10. IF at any time an Executor or Trustee is a professional or business person charges can be made in the ordinary way for all work done by that person or his firm or company or any partner or employee.

THE SCHEDULE

MY Executors and Trustees (hereinafter referred to as "my Trustees") in addition to all other powers conferred on them by law or as the result of the terms of this my Will shall have the following powers.

1. a) FOR the purposes of any distribution under Clause 5 to appropriate all or any part of my said property and assets in or toward satisfaction of any share in my residuary estate without needing the consent of anyone.

(b) FOR the purposes of placing a value on any of my personal chattels (as defined by the Administration of Estates Act 1925) so appropriated to use if they so decide such value as may have been placed on the same by any Valuers they instruct for inheritance tax purposes on my death or such other value as they may in their absolute discretion consider fair and my Trustees in respect of any of my personal chattels which being articles of national scientific historic or artistic interest are treated on such death as the subject of a conditionally exempt transfer for the purposes of the Inheritance Tax Act 1984 Section 30 (or any statutory modification or re-enactment thereof) shall in respect of any such appropriation place such lesser value as they in their absolute discretion consider fair after taking into account such facts and surrounding circumstances as they consider appropriate including the fact that inheritance tax for which conditional exemption was obtained might be payable by the beneficiary on there being a subsequent chargeable event.

(c) TO insure under comprehensive or any other cover against any risks and for any amounts (including allowing as they deem appropriate for any possible future effects of inflation and increasing building costs and expenses) any asset held at any time by my Executors and Trustees And the premiums in respect of any such insurance may be discharged by my Executors and Trustees either out of income or out of capital (or partly out of one and partly out of the other) as my Executors and Trustees shall in their absolute discretion determine and any monies received by my Executors and Trustees as the result of any insurance insofar as not used in rebuilding reinstating replacing or repairing the asset lost or damaged shall be treated as if they were the proceeds of sale of the asset insured PROVIDED ALWAYS that my Executors and Trustees shall not be under any responsibility to insure or be liable for any loss that may result from any failure so to do.

2. (a) POWER to invest trust monies in both income producing and nonincome producing assets of every kind and wherever situated and to vary investments in the same full and unrestricted manner in all respects as if they were absolutely entitled thereto beneficially.

(b) POWER to retain or purchase as an authorised investment any freehold or leasehold property or any interest or share therein of whatever nature proportion or amount (which shall be held upon trust to retain or sell the same) as a residence for one or more beneficiaries under this my Will and in the event of any such retention or purchase my Trustees shall have power to apply trust monies in the erection alteration improvement or repair of any building on such freehold or leasehold property including one where there is any such interest or share And my Trustees shall have power to decide (according to the circumstances generally) the terms and conditions in every respect upon which any such person or persons may occupy and reside at any such property (or have the benefit of the said interest or share therein).

(c) POWER to delegate the exercise of their power to invest trust monies (including for the purpose of holding or placing them on deposit pending investment) and to vary investments to any company or other persons or person whether or not being or including one or more of my Trustees and to allow any investment or other asset to be held in the names or name of such person or persons as nominees or nominee of my Trustees and to decide the terms and conditions in every respect including the period thereof and the commission fees or other remuneration payable therefor which commission fees or other remuneration shall be paid out of the capital and income of that part of the Trust Fund in respect of which they are incurred or of any property held on the same trusts AND I DECLARE that my Trustees shall not be liable for any loss arising from any act or omission by any person in whose favour they shall have exercised either or both their powers under this Clause.

(d) POWER to retain and purchase chattels of every description under whatever terms they hold the same by virtue of the provisions of this my Will And in respect thereof they shall have the following powers

(i) To retain the chattels in question under their joint control and custody or the control and custody of any of them or to store the same (whether in a depository or warehouse or else-where)

(ii) To lend all or any of the chattels to any person or persons or body or bodies (including a museum or gallery) upon such terms and conditions as my Trustees shall determine

(iii) To cause inventories to be made

(iv) Generally to make such arrangements for their safe custody repair and use as having regard to the circumstances my Trustees may from time to time think expedient

(v) To sell the chattels or any of them and

(vi) To treat any money received as the result of any insurance in so far as not used in reinstating replacing or repairing any chattel lost or damaged as if it were the proceeds of sale of the chattel insured

(e) POWER in the case of any of the chattels of which a person of full age and capacity is entitled to the use but when such person's interest is less than an absolute one

(i) To cause an inventory of such chattels to be made in duplicate with a view to one part being signed by the beneficiary for retention by my Trustees and the other part to be kept by the beneficiary and to cause any such inventory to be revised as occasion shall require and the parts thereof altered accordingly

(ii) To require the beneficiary to arrange at his or her expense for the safe custody repair and insurance of such chattels in such manner as my Trustees think expedient and (where it is not practicable so to require the beneficiary) to make such arrangements as are referred to under paragraph (iv) of sub-clause (d) of this Clause

PROVIDED THAT my Trustees shall also have power to meet any expenses which they may incur in the exercise of any of their powers in respect of chattels out of the capital and income of my estate or such one or more of any different parts and the income thereof as they shall in their absolute discretion determine AND I FURTHER DECLARE that my Trustees shall not be obliged to make or cause to be made any inventories of any such chattels that may be held and shall not be liable for any loss injury or damage that may happen to any such chattels from any cause whatsoever or any failure on the part of anyone to effect or maintain any insurance.

IN WITNESS whereof I have hereunto set my hand the day and year first above written

SIGNED by HER ROYAL HIGHNESS

in our joint presence and

then by us in her presence

I, DIANA PRINCESS OF WALES of Kensington Palace London W8, DECLARE this to be a First Codicil to my Will which is dated the first day of June One thousand nine hundred and ninety three.

1. My Will shall be construed and take effect as if in clause 1 the name and address of Commander Patrick Desmond Christian Jermy Jephson were omitted and replaced by the following:

my sister Elizabeth Sarah Lavinia McCorquodale (known as The Lady Sarah McCorquodale) of Stoke Rochford Grantham Lincolnshire NG33 5EB

2. In all other respects I confirm my said Will.

IN WITNESS whereof I have hereunto set my hand this First day of February One thousand nine hundred and ninety six.

SIGNED by HER ROYAL HIGHNESS

in our joint presence and then

by us in her presence

APPENDIX C

Last Will and Testament of Richard M. Nixon

This is the Last Will and Testament of former President Richard M. Nixon. Notice how the introductory paragraph revokes all prior wills and codicils (amendments) to prior wills. You will also note references to the Internal Revenue Code sections pertaining to charitable gifts, which was discussed in Hour 19, "Charitable Trusts."

You should also notice the careful description of personal property as well as the provisions covering the death of a primary beneficiary. You will also note the specific gifts (Article III) and the residue clause (Article IV), simultaneous death (Article VII), and the use of the attestation clause.

I, RICHARD M. NIXON, residing in the Borough of Park Ridge, County of Bergen and State of New Jersey, being of sound and disposing mind and memory, do hereby make, publish and declare this to be my Last Will and Testament, revoking all prior Wills and codicils.

ARTICLE ONE

I give and bequeath to THE RICHARD NIXON LIBRARY AND BIRTHPLACE (hereinafter sometimes referred to as the "Library") for its uses, an amount equal to the "adjusted proceeds amount" (as hereinafter defined); provided, however, that if there are any outstanding and unpaid amounts on pledges I have made to the Library, including, specifically, any amounts unpaid on the One Million Two Hundred Thousand Dollar pledge made in 1993, then the adjusted proceeds amount under this bequest shall be paid first directly to the Library to the extent necessary to satisfy such charitable pledge or pledges, and provided further, that if at the time of my death or distribution the Library is not an organization described in Sections 170(c) and 2055(a) of the Internal Revenue Code of 1986, as amended (the "Code"), which would entitle the estate to a charitable deduction for Federal Estate Tax purposes, I give and bequeath such property to THE NIXON BIRTHPLACE FOUNDATION, provided further, if THE NIXON BIRTHPLACE FOUNDATION is not then an organization described in Sections 170(c) and 2055(a) of the Code, I give and bequeath such property to such organization or organizations described in said Sections of the Code in such shares as my executors shall designate by written and acknowledged instrument filed within six months from the date of my death with the clerk of the court in which this Will shall have been admitted to probate.

In the event such property is distributed to an organization other than the RICHARD NIXON LIBRARY & BIRTHPLACE, I request such organization to bear in mind my wish that such property ultimately repose in such Library, if and when it qualifies as a charitable organization under Sections 170(c) and 2055(a) of the Code.

The term "adjusted proceeds amount" shall be defined as the excess of

(i) the amount due or paid to me and/or my estate under the judgment entered following the decision of the United States Court of Appeals for the District of Columbia Circuit in the case of Richard Nixon v United States of America, decided on November 17, 1992, and/or any concurrent or subsequent proceedings relating

pertaining thereto, and any related or subsequent case, provided that any such amounts paid during my life shall only be included as adjusted proceeds to the extent such amounts as of the date of my death are held or invested in a segregated and traceable account or accounts over

(ii) the sum of (a) the amount of all attorneys' fees and other costs or expenses, whether previously paid or unpaid, associated with or incurred in connection with such proceedings or any case similar to or relating thereto and all other attorneys' fees from 1974 on, which my estate or I have paid or which are outstanding, excluding, however, any attorneys' fees paid to the firm of which William E. Griffin has been a member, and (b) One Million Four Hundred Fifty Thousand Dollars, the amount equal to my contribution to the Library made in 1992. The amounts under (a) and (b) of this subparagraph (ii) shall be part of my residuary estate.

It is my intention, by this bequest, to make a charitable gift of any "windfall" received under the lawsuits referred to above, and to first make my family whole by recovering all of the legal expenses I have incurred or my estate is to incur because of these and other lawsuits.

ARTICLE TWO

A. Subject to the restrictions contained in this paragraph and any other restrictions contained in this Will, I give and bequeath all items of tangible personal property that I shall own at my death which relate to events of my official or personal life or the official or personal life of my deceased wife, PATRICIA R. NIXON, which have had historical or commemorative significance, except for my "personal diaries", which are defined and disposed of in Paragraph B of this Article, to THE RICHARD NIXON LIBRARY & BIRTHPLACE; provided, however, that if at the time of my death or distribution such Library is not an organization described in

Sections 170(c) and 2055(a) of the Code, which would entitle the estate to a charitable deduction for Federal Estate Tax purposes, I give and bequeath such property to THE NIXON BIRTHPLACE FOUNDATION, provided further that if THE NIXON BIRTHPLACE FOUNDATION is not then an organization described in Sections 170(c) and 2055(a) of the Code, I give and bequeath such property to such organization or organizations described in said Sections of the Code in such shares as my executors shall designate by written and acknowledged instrument filed within six months from the date of my death with the clerk of the court in which this Will shall have been admitted to probate.

In the event such property is distributed to an organization other than the RICHARD NIXON LIBRARY & BIRTHPLACE, I request such organization to bear in mind my wish that such property ultimately repose in such Library, if and when it qualifies as a charitable organization tinder Sections 170(c) and 2055(a) of the Code. Such tangible personal property shall include, without limitation, awards, plaques, works of art of all kinds, medals, membership or achievement certificates, commemorative stamps and coins, religious items, commemorative and personalphotographs and all correspondence, documents, notes, memoranda, letters and all other writings that I own at my death, of whatever kind and nature, personal or public, whether inscribed by me or not inscribed by me and whether written by me or to me. I direct that the determination as to which items of my tangible personal property are included in this bequest, and which items are items of tangible personal property disposed of under Paragraph C of this Article, shall be based on the decision of my executors; however, it is my wish that my executors consult with my surviving daughters in making this determination. The determination of my executors shall be conclusive and binding upon all parties interested in my estate.

Notwithstanding the above provisions, my daughters, PATRICIA NIXON COX and JULIE NIXON EISENHOWER, or the survivor, or if neither daughter is surviving, my executors, shall have the right, within six months of my date of death, to go through all of such tangible personal property, to take any such property appraised at no value, or any other items of such tangible personal property, provided that under no circumstances shall the amount of such property taken by my daughters exceed in value three percent (3%) of the total value of all such property included in this Paragraph A.

B. I give and bequeath me "personal diaries" (as hereinafter defined) in equal shares to my daughters, JULIE NIXON EISENHOWER and PATRICIA NIXON COX, or all to the survivor. If either or both of my daughters shall, disclaim some or all or parts of my "personal diaries", such disclaimed items shall be distributed to THE RICHARD NIXON LIBRARY AND BIRTHPLACE (the "Library") for its uses; provided, however, that if at the time of my death or distribution the Library is not an organization described in Sections 170(c) and 2055(a) of the Internal Revenue Code of 1986, as amended (the "Code"), which would entitle the estate to a charitable deduction for Federal Estate Tax purposes, I give and bequeath such property to THE NIXON BIRTHPLACE FOUNDATION, provided further that if THE NIXON BIRTHPLACE FOUNDATION is not then an organization described in Sections 170(c) and 2055(a) of the Code, I give and bequeath such property to such organization or organizations described in said Sections of the Code in such shares as my executors shall designate by written and acknowledged instrument filed within six months from the date of my death with the clerk of the court in which this Will shall have been admitted to probate.

In the event such property is distributed to an organization other than the RICHARD NIXON LIBRARY & BIRTHPLACE, I request such organization to bear in mind my wish that such property ultimately repose in such

Library, if and when it qualifies as a charitable organization under Sections 170(c) and 2055(a) of the Code.

If neither of my daughters survives me, I direct my executors to collect and destroy my "personal diaries. "Notwithstanding any other provisions of this Will, if neither of my daughters survives me, the property constituting my "personal diaries" shall be subject to the following restrictions: At no time shall my executors be allowed to make public, publish, sell, or make available to any individual other than my executor (or except as required for federal tax purposes) the contents or any part or all of my "personal diaries" and, provided further, that my executors shall, within one year from the date of my death or, if reasonably necessary, upon the later receipt of a closing estate tax letter from the Internal Revenue Service, destroy all of my "personal diaries".

My "personal diaries" shall be defined as any notes, tapes, transcribed notes, folders, binders, or books that are owned by me or to which I may be entitled under a judgment of law including, but not limited to, folders, binders, or books labeled as Richard Nixon's Diaries, Diary Notes, or labeled just by dates, that may contain my daily, weekly, or monthly activities, thoughts or plans. The determination of my executors as to what property is included in this bequest shall be conclusive and binding upon all parties interested in my estate; however, it is my wish that my executors consult with my surviving daughters and/or my office staff in making this determination.

C. If at the time of my death any lawsuit or lawsuits are pending regarding the ownership of any of my tangible personal property including, but not limited to, all of the tangible personal property listed in Paragraph A above, I specifically direct my executors to continue such lawsuits for as long as they, in their discretion, deem it appropriate to do so, knowing my wishes in this matter.

D. I give and bequeath the balance of the tangible personal property I shall own at my death, not otherwise effectively disposed of in this Will, to my issue, per stirpes. If both of my daughters, PATRICIA NIXON COX and JULIE NIXON EISENHOWER, shall survive me, such tangible personal property shall be divided between my daughters in such manner as they shall agree, or in the absence of agreement, or if any child is a minor, as my executors determine, which determination shall be conclusive upon all persons interested in my estate.

E. I authorize and empower my executors to pay, and to charge as administration expenses of my estate, the expenses of storing, packing, insuring and mailing or delivering any article of tangible personal property hereinabove disposed of.

ARTICLE THREE

A. If my granddaughter, MELANIE EISENHOWER, survives me, I give and bequeath to her the sum of Seventy Thousand ($70,000.00) Dollars.

B. If my grandson, ALEXANDER RICHARD EISENHOWER, survives me, I give and bequeath to him the sum of Thirty Thousand Dollars ($30,000.00).

C. If my grandson, CHRISTOPHER COX, survives me, I give and bequeath to him the sum of Ten Thousand Dollars ($10,000.00) .

The specific bequests to my grandchildren named above are made to equalize the gifts made to all of my grandchildren during my life. The disparity in amounts, or lack of a bequest, is not intended and should not be interpreted as a sign of favoritism for one grandchild over another.

ARTICLE FOUR

All of the rest, residue and remainder of my estate, real and personal, wherever situated, including any lapsed or ineffective legacies or devises (but excluding any property over which I may have a power of appointment, it being my intention not to exercise any such power), herein sometimes referred to as my "residuary estate," I dispose of as follows:

A. I give and bequeath the sum of Fifty Thousand Dollars ($50,000.00) to each grandchild of mine who survives me.

B. I give, devise, and bequeath the balance of my residuary estate to my issue, per stirpes.

C. Notwithstanding any other provisions of this will, if any bequest or share of my estate under this Article FOUR would be payable to a grandchild of mine for whose benefit a separate trust created under the Will of my deceased wife, PATRICIA R. NIXON, is then in existence, I direct that such bequest or share of my estate shall be distributed to the trustee(s) of such trust, to be added to, administered and disposed of as part of the principal of such trust in accordance with the terms Of such trust; and, provided further, that if the addition of any portion or all of this residuary bequest or share of my estate to a trust for a grandchild under the Will of PATRICIA R. NIXON shall cause such trust to have an inclusion ratio greater than zero for purposes of the Generation Skipping Transfer Tax provisions of Article 13 of the Code (the "GST tax"), then any portion, up to the whole, of such bequest or share of my estate, that is not exempt from the GST tax shall not be added to the trust, but shall be given to such trustee(s) to be held in a separate trust under the same terms and conditions, my intention being to create two separate trusts, one of which has, for GST tax purposes, an inclusion ratio of zero, and one of which has an inclusion ratio greater than zero.

ARTICLE FIVE

If upon my death no issue of mine shall then be living, I give, devise and bequeath my residuary estate, or the then remaining principal and, except as hereinabove otherwise provided, any undistributed or accrued income of such trust, as the case may be, to THE RICHARD NIXON LIBRARY & BIRTHPLACE, and if such organization is not then in existence, to the persons who would have been my heirs under the laws of intestate distribution of New Jersey then in effect had I died on the data, of the event requiring a distribution.

ARTICLE SIX

I direct that all estate, inheritance and other death taxes (including any interest and penalties thereon) imposed by any jurisdiction whatsoever by reason of my death upon or with respect to any property includable in my estate for the purposes of any such taxes, or upon or with respect to any person receiving any such property, whether such property shall pass under or outside, or shall have passed outside, the provisions of this Will, except for additional estate taxes imposed by Section 4980 (A)(d) of the Code and generation-skipping transfer taxes imposed under Section 13 of the Code ("GST taxes") which may be payable by reason of my death, shall be paid, without apportionment, from the principal of my residuary estate. Any GSTtax payable by reason of my death shall be charged and the liability for the payment of such GST taxes shall be determined according to the law of the jurisdiction imposing such GST tax.

ARTICLE SEVEN

If any beneficiary under this Will and I shall die simultaneously or in such circumstances as to render it difficult or impossible to determine who predeceased the other, it shall conclusively be presumed for the purposes of this Will that I survived.

ARTICLE EIGHT

I hereby nominate, constitute, and appoint my friends, WILLIAM E. GRIF-FIN, and JOHN R. TAYLOR, to be the co-executors of this Will.

The appointment of my attorney, WILLIAM E. GRIFFIN, as a co-executor is made with my knowledge and approval of his receipt of commissions as provided by law, and his law firms receipt of compensation for legal services rendered to my estate.

The individuals named in the foregoing paragraph are granted the continuing discretionary power, exercisable while in office, and exercisable only unanimously if more than one of them is then in office, to designate one or more successors or co-fiduciaries or a succession of successors or co-fiduciaries in such office to act one at a time or together with co-fiduciaries, to fill any vacancy occurring in such office after any successor designated herein shall have failed to qualify or ceased to act, by written instrument, duly acknowledged, and to revoke any such designation prior to the happening of the event upon which it is to become effective, by a written instrument, duly acknowledged, and a new designation may be made as above provided. If there shall be more than one such designation of successor fiduciary or co-fiduciary in effect and unrevoked, they shall be effective in the reverse of the order in which they were made.

Any fiduciary may resign at any time by delivering or mailing a notice in writing of such resignation to his or her co-fiduciaries, or, if none, to his or her designated successor, if such designee has indicated his or her willingness to act, and thirty days thereafter such resignation shall take effect. If any fiduciary becomes disabled, that determination of disability shall also constitute that individual's immediate resignation as a fiduciary without any further act. For the purposes of this paragraph, a person shall be considered disabled if either (i) a committee, guardian, conservator, or similar fiduciary shall have been appointed for such person or (ii) a court shall have determined, or two physicians shall have certified, that the person is incompetent or otherwise unable to act prudently and effectively in financial affairs.

Each successor fiduciary and co-fiduciary shall have all rights and discretions which are granted to the executors named herein, except those which may be specifically denied in this will.

At any time that there are two or more fiduciaries then in office, all decisions regarding my estate shall be made by both or the majority of my fiduciaries in much office. However, my fiduciaries may from time to time authorize one of their number, or each of them acting singly, to execute instruments of any kind on their behalf (including, but not by way of limitation, any check, order, demand, assignment, transfer, contract, authorization, proxy, consent, notice or waiver). Insofar as third parties dealing with my fiduciaries are concerned instruments executed and acts performed by one fiduciary pursuant to such authorization shall be fully binding as if executed or performed by all of them. An authorization shall be valid until those acting in reliance on it receive actual notice of its revocation.

No fiduciary shall be required to give any bond or other security for the faithful performance of such fiduciary's duties in any jurisdiction whatsoever; or if any such bond shall be required, no such fiduciary shall be required to furnish any surety thereon. No executor shall be required to file a bond to secure the return of any payment or payments on account of commissions of such executor.

My individual executors may receive the commissions allowable under New Jersey Law from time to time during the period of the administration of my estate and any trusts hereunder.

Any corporate executor serving hereunder shall receive compensation in accordance with its Schedule of Fees in effect from time to time during the period over which its services are performed.

ARTICLE NINE

I give to my fiduciaries, with respect to any and all property, whether real or personal, which I may own at the time of my death, or which shall at any time constitute part of my estate, including funds held hereunder for persons under the age of 21 years, and whether constituting principal or income therefrom, in addition to the authority and power conferred upon them by law, express authority and power to be exercised by them as such fiduciaries, in their discretion, for any purpose, without application to, authorization from, or confirmation by any court:

a) To retain and to purchase or otherwise acquire stocks, whether common or preferred, bonds, obligations, shares or interests in investment companies or investment trusts, securities issued by or any common trust fund maintained by any corporate fiduciary, partnership interests, or any other property, real or personal, of whatsoever nature, wheresoever situated, without duty to diversify, whether or not productive of income and whether or not the same may be authorized by law for investment of estate funds, it being my intention to give my fiduciaries the same power of investment which I myself possess with respect to my own funds.

b) To deposit funds in the savings or commercial department of any corporate fiduciary or of any other bank without limit as to duration or amount.

c) To sell, without prior authorization or confirmation of the court, at public or private sale, exchange, mortgage, lease without statutory or other limitation as to duration, partition, grant options in excess of six months on, alter, improve, demolish buildings, or otherwise deal with any property, real or personal, upon any terms and whether for cash or upon credit, and to execute and deliver deeds, leases, mortgages or other instruments relating hereto.

d) To exercise in person or by proxy all voting, conversion, subscription, or other rights incident to the ownership of any property, including the right to participate in any corporate reorganization, merger, or other transaction and to retain any property received thereunder and the right to delegate discretionary power.

e) To borrow from any person, including any corporate fiduciary, and to lend money to any person, including any person beneficially interested hereunder, with or without security.

f) To compromise or arbitrate claims, to prepay or accept prepayment of any debt, to enforce or abstain from enforcing, extend, modify or release any right or claim, or to hold any claim after maturity without extension, with or without consideration.

g) To hold separate shares or trusts in solido, and to hold property in bearer form or in the name of a nominee or nominees.

h) To execute and deliver deeds or other instruments, with or without covenants, warranties, and representations and with or without consideration, including releases which shall discharge the recipient from responsibility for property receipted for thereby.

i) To abstain from rendering or filing any inventory or periodic account in any court.

j) Without the consent of any beneficiary, to make division or distribution in cash or in kind or partly in each. Any such distribution in kind shall be made at the fair market value on the date or dates of distribution and may be made without regard to the tax basis of such property and without any duty to distribute such assets pro rata among beneficiaries or to equalize the tax basis recovered by such beneficiaries, any provision of this will or rule of law to the contrary notwithstanding.

k) To employ legal and investment counsel, custodians, accountants and agents for the transaction of any business of my estate or any trust hereunder or for services or advice, to pay reasonable compensation therefor out of my estate or such trust, as may be applicable, and to rely and act or decline to rely or act upon any information or opinion furnished by them.

l) To retain or acquire the stock of any corporation in which any individual fiduciary hereunder or any officer or director of any corporate fiduciary hereunder may have an interest, whether as officer, director, employee, or otherwise.

m) To make or join in elections and joint returns under any tax law; to agree in the apportionment of any joint tax liability; to exercise or forbear to exercise any income, gift or estate tax options; to determine the allocation of exemptions or exercise other elections available to my executors for generation-skipping transfer tax purposes; and to make or refrain from making adjustments between principal and income or between shares of my estate by reason of any deduction taken for income tax instead of estate tax purposes or any election as to the date of valuation of my estate for estate tax purposes, all in such manner as my executor may deem advisable, and any such determination made by my executor shall be conclusive and binding upon all persons affected thereby.

n) To pay out of my general estate in respect of any real or tangible personal property situated outside the state of the principal administration of my estate at the time of my death any administration expense payable under the laws of the state or country where such property is situated.

o) To pay themselves, individually, at such time or times and without prior approval of any court or person interested in my estate or, any trust hereunder or payment of interest or the securing of any bond or rendering of any annual statement, account or computation thereof, such sum or sums on account of commissions to which they may eventually be entitled hereunder as they, in their discretion, may determine to be just and reasonable, to charge the same wholly against principal or wholly against income, or partially against principal and partially against income, as they may, in their discretion, determine advisable, and in the case of any trustee, to retain commissions which they may determine shall be payable out of income from income derived from any year preceding or succeeding the year with respect to which such commissions shall have been earned.

p) Generally, to exercise in good faith and with reasonable care all investment and administrative powers and discretions of an absolute owner which may lawfully be conferred upon a fiduciary.

ARTICLE TEN

A. Whenever income or Principal is to be distributed or applied for the benefit of a person under the age of 21 years (referred to as a "minor" in this Article) or a person who in the sole judgment of my fiduciaries is incapable of managing his or her own affairs, my fiduciaries may make payment of such property in any or all of the following ways:

1. By paying such property to the parent, guardian or other person having the care and control of such minor for such minor's benefit or to any authorized person as custodian for such minor under any applicable Gifts to Minors Act, with authority to authorize any such custodian to hold such property until the minor attains the age of 21 years where permitted under applicable law.

2. By paying such property to the guardian, committee, conservator, or other person having the care and control of such incapable person.

3. By paying directly to such minor or incapable person such sums as my fiduciaries may deem advisable as an allowance.

4. By expending such property in such other manner as my fiduciaries in their discretion shall determine will benefit such minor or incapable person.

B. If principal becomes vested in and payable to a minor, my fiduciaries may make payment thereof in any of the ways set forth in the preceding paragraph of this Article, or may, defer payment of any part or all thereof meanwhile paying or applying to or for the use of such minor so much or all of such principal and of the income therefrom, as my fiduciaries in their discretion may deem advisable. Any income not so expended by my fiduciaries shall be added to principal. My fiduciaries shall pay any remaining principal to such minor upon such minor's attaining the age of 21 years or to such minor's estate upon death prior to such payment in full.

C. Any payment or distribution authorized in this Article shall be a full discharge to my fiduciaries with respect thereto.

ARTICLE ELEVEN

All interests hereunder, whether in principal or income, while undistributed and in the possession of my executors, and even though vested or distributable, shall not be subject to attachment, execution or sequestration for any debt, contract, obligation, or liability of any beneficiary, and, furthermore, shall not be subject to pledge, assignment conveyance or anticipation by any beneficiary.

ARTICLE TWELVE

The account (intermediate or final) of any executor may be settled by agreement with the adult beneficiaries interested in the account and a parent or guardian of those beneficiaries who are minors, who shall have the full power on the basis of such settlement to release such fiduciary from all liability for such fiduciary's acts or omissions as executor for the period covered thereby. Such settlement and release shall be binding upon all interested parties hereunder including those who may be under legal disability or not yet in being and shall have the force and effect of a final decree, judgment, or order of a court of competent jurisdiction rendered in an action or proceeding for an accounting in which jurisdiction was duly obtained over all necessary and proper parties. The foregoing provisions, however, shall not preclude any fiduciary from having such fiduciary's accounts judicially settled if such fiduciary shall so desire. In any probate, accounting or other persons interested in my estate are required by law to be served with process, if a party to the proceeding has the same interest as or a similar interest to a person under a legal disability (including, without limitation, an infant or an incompetent) it shall not be necessary to serve process upon the person under a disability or otherwise make such person a party to the proceeding, it being my intention to avoid the appointment of a guardian ad litem wherever possible.

ARTICLE THIRTEEN

The validity, construction, effect, and administration of the testamentary dispositions and the other provisions contained in this will shall, in any and all events, be administered in accordance with, and construed and regulated by, the laws of the State of New Jersey from time to time existing.

ARTICLE FOURTEEN

A. Wherever "child," "children," or "issue" appears in this Will, it shall be deemed to include only lawful natural issue and persons deriving their relationship to or through their parent or ancestor by legal adoption prior to such adopted person's attainment of the age of 18 years.

B. A disposition in this Will to the descendants of a person per stirpes shall be deemed to require a division into a sufficient number of equal shares to make one share for each child of such person living at the time such disposition becomes effective and one share for each then deceased child of such person having one or more descendants then living, regardless of whether any child of such person is then living, with the same principle to be applied in any required further division of a share at a more remote generation.

ARTICLE FIFTEEN

A. All references herein to this Will shall be construed as referring to this Will and any codicil or codicils hereto that I may hereafter execute.

B. Wherever necessary or appropriate, the use herein of any gender shall be deemed to include the other genders and the use herein of either the singular or the plural shall be deemed to include the other.

C. Except as otherwise specifically, provided in this will:

1. Each reference to my "fiduciaries" shall be deemed to mean and refer to my executor and, where applicable, to a custodian hereunder;

2. Each reference to my "executors" shall be deemed to mean and refer to the fiduciary or fiduciaries, natural or corporate, who shall be acting hereunder in such capacity from time to time; and

3. Any and all power, authority and discretion conferred upon my executor or my fiduciaries may be exercised by the fiduciary or fiduciaries who shall qualify and be acting hereunder from time to time in the capacity in which such power, authority and discretion are exercised.

IN WITNESS WHEREOF, I have hereunto set my hand and seal this (24th) day of February, 1994.

/s/ Richard M Nixon

ATTESTATION CLAUSE

WE the undersigned, do hereby certify that on the 24th of February, 1994, RICHARD M. NIXON, the Testator above named did, in the presence of the undersigned and of each of us, subscribe, publish and declare the foregoing instrument to be his last Will and Testament and then and there requested us and each of us to sign our names thereto as witnesses to the execution thereof, which we hereby do in the presence of the said Testator and of each other on this 24th day of February, 1994.

(signed by three witnesses) each being duly sworn, depose and say:

That they witnessed the execution of the Will of RICHARD M. NIXON, dated February 24 1994, consisting of eighteen pages. That the Will was executed at Woodcliff Lake, New Jersey, under the supervision of Karen J. Walsh an attorney at law with offices at 51 Pondfield Road, Bronxville, New York. That this affidavit is made at the request of the Testator.

That the Testator, in our presence, subscribed his name to the Will at the end thereof, and at the time of making such subscription, published and declared the same to be his Last Will and Testament; thereupon we, at his request and in his presence and in the presence of each other, signed our names thereto as subscribing witnesses.

That the said Testator, at the time of such execution, was more than 18 years of age and, in our opinion, of sound mind, memory and understanding, not under any restraint or in any respect incompetent to make a Will.

That the Testator indicated to us that he had read the Will, knew the contents thereof, and that the provisions therein contained expressed the manner in which his Estate is to be administered and distributed.

That the Testator could read, write and converse in the English language and was suffering from no defect of sight, hearing or speech, or from any physical or mental impairment which would affect his capacity to make a valid Will.

That the Testator signed only of the said Will on said occasion.

Sworn to before me this 25th day of February, 1994.

PAUL G. AMICUCCI

Notary Public, State of New York

No. 5001747

Qualified in Westchester County

APPENDIX D
References and Further Readings

BOOKS

2000 Multistate Guide to Estate Planning, Jeffrey A. Schoenblum, A Panel Publication.

Financial Planner's Guide to Estate Planning, 3rd Ed. Paul J Lochray College for Financial Planning, Denver, Co.

Life and Death Planning for Retirement Benefits—The Essential Handbook for Estate Planners, 3rd Ed. Natalie B. Choate

Macmillan Teach Yourself Personal Finance in 24 Hours, Janet Bigham Bernstel and Lea Saslav

Tax Economics of Charitable Giving, 11th Ed, Arthur Andersen & Co., S.C.

Tax Facts 1—2001, The National Underwriter Co.

The Tools and Techniques of Estate Planning, 10th Ed., Stephan R. Leimberg, Jerry A Kasner, Stephen N. Kandell, Ralph Gano Miller, Morey S. Rosenbloom, and Herbert L. Levy, National Underwriter

U.S. International Estate Planning, William P. Streng, Warren, Gorham & Lamont

WEB SITES

ftp://leginfo.public.ca.gov

www.60plus.org

www.aarp.org

www.aboutlivingtrusts.com

www.aei.org

www.armchairmillionaire.com

www.bankrate.com

www.bartleby.com

www.britannica.com

www.cbpp.org

www.cdc.gov

www.center4debtmanagement.com

www.choices.org

www.cobar.org

www.consumer.pub.findlaw.com

www.courttv.com

www.cpaadvantage.com

www.estate-plan.com

www.familyestate.com

www.fee-only-advisor.com

www.fourmilab.ch

www.freeadvice.com

www.infouse.com

www.johnventura.com

www.law.cornell.edu

www.law.upenn.edu

www.lawbooksusa.com

www.laweasy.com

www.learningco.com

www.legalbills.com

www.mbscott.com

www.michbar.org

www.montana.edu

www.mycounsel.com

www.nccusl.org

www.ncpa.org

www.ncsl.org

www.netplanning.com

www.nolo.com

www.nysscpa.org

www.pcwills.com

www.publicdebt.treas.gov

www.scvpro.com

www.senioralternatives.com

www.toolkit.cch.com

www.uslaw.com

www.wld.com

www.worldbook.com

www.zcalc.com

OTHER PUBLICATIONS

Financial Planning, March 2001

Household Net Worth and Asset Ownership—1995, U.S. Department of Commerce, Economics and Statistics Administration, U.S. Census Bureau

ADDITIONAL SOURCES OF INFORMATION

FINANCIAL

An Estate Planner's Guide to Qualified Retirement Plan Benefits, 2nd Ed., Louis A Mezzullo, American Bar Association

Life and Death Planning for Retirement Benefits—The Essential Handbook for Estate Planners, 3rd Ed., Natalie B. Choate

Macmillan Teach Yourself Personal Finance in 24 Hours, Janet Bigham Bernstel and Lea Saslav

Tax Economics of Charitable Giving, 11th Ed., Arthur Andersen & Co., S.C.

Tax Facts 1—2001, The National Underwriter Co.

The Motley Fool, www.fool.com

Quicken, www.quicken.com

CHOOSING AN ATTORNEY

National Academy of Elder Law Attorneys, www.naela.com

CHOOSING A FINANCIAL PLANNER

College for Financial Planning Board of Standards, Denver, Colorado, www.cfp-board.org

LEGAL

2000 Multistate Guide to Estate Planning, Jeffrey A. Schoenblum, A Panel Publication

American Bar Association Section on Real Property, Probate and Trust Law, www.abanet.org/rppt/home.html

Financial Planner's Guide to Estate Planning, 3rd Ed., Paul J. Lochray, College for Financial Planning, Denver, Co.

The Tools and Techniques of Estate Planning, Stephan R. Leimberg, Jerry A. Kasner, Stephen N. Kandell, Ralph Gano Miller, Morey S. Rosenbloom And Herbert L. Levy, National Underwriter

Third-Party and Self-Created Trusts, 2nd Ed., Clifton B. Kruse Jr., ABA

APPENDIX E
Glossary

50% Charity   A gift to an organization that allows the donor to deduct up to 50% of a taxpayer's adjusted gross income.

401(k) Plan   A qualified retirement plan available to all companies that gives employees some investment options allowing contributions that may not exceed 25% of gross compensation or $30,000 per individual.

403(b)(7) Plan   A qualified retirement plan designed specifically for employees of a public school or qualified tax-exempt organization, including museums, colleges, and non-profit organizations.

2503(b) Trust   An irrevocable trust created for the benefit of a minor that requires a mandatory distribution of income to the trust beneficiary on at least an annual basis and does not require distribution of the principal to the minor at age 21.

2503(c) Trust   An irrevocable trust created for the benefit of a minor that allows for gifts to the trust to qualify for the annual gift tax exclusion and requires distribution of the principal to the minor at age 21.

Ademption   Refers to a situation in which the intended gift cannot be made because the decedent did not own the described gift at the time of death.

Administrative expenses   Expenses incurred in the administration of a decedent's estate.

Administrator   A person appointed to represent an estate of a decedent who died without a will.

Alien   An individual who cannot hold or is not eligible for a U.S. passport.

Ancestor   Refers to a parent, grandparent, or great grandparent or further up the ancestral line. See also *descendant*.

Ancillary administration   The probate of a decedent's estate other than in the state of residence as a result of real estate holdings outside the state of residence.

Annual gift exclusion   The amount allowed by federal law that can be given to another without the imposition of a gift tax, currently $10,000 per person, per year.

Annuity   An investment contract in which the owner deposits a sum of money, either as a lump sum or in periodic installments, which accumulates tax deferred, and in which the owner agrees to certain restrictions on the right of withdrawal.

Annuity trust   A trust that pays a fixed amount. See also *charitable remainder annuity trust*.

Anti-Lapse   A statute that provides that whenever there is a specific gift made to a child (or sometimes any lineal descendant) there is a presumption that the gift does not lapse; rather it is to be distributed to the heirs of the deceased child (or lineal descendant).

Apportionment of Taxes   An allocation of taxes pro-rata among those who receive the property causing taxation.

Articles of Incorporation   Documents that specify the identity of the individuals who are creating a corporation, the name of the corporation, and its stated purpose.

Ascertainable Standard   A standard established by the Internal Revenue Service allowing access to a trust for the "health, maintenance, support, and education" of the beneficiary.

Assignment   A legal transfer of rights under a contract or other legal document.

Attestation Clause   The portion of the will that is signed by the witnesses and which states that the will was executed in their presence.

Attorney-at-law   A person licensed by the state to practice law.

Attorney-in-fact   The person who is appointed to act on behalf of the principal in a power of attorney document.

Basis   The amount paid for an appreciating asset.

Bequest   A gift of personal property.

By-laws   Documents of a corporation that contain the detailed rules that govern the conduct of the corporation.

By Representation   Refers to a manner of distribution whereby the beneficiaries receive the same share that would have been received by a deceased ancestor.

C Corporation   A corporation that operates completely separately from its shareholders and is taxed separately as such.

Capital Gain   Refers to an income tax on appreciation of an asset that has been sold for more than its cost basis. See also *basis*.

Cash value   The portion of a life insurance policy that represents accumulated premiums remaining after policy expenses have been deducted.

Charitable lead trust   A trust that provides for either a unitrust or annuity payment to one or more qualified charities during the term of the trust, with the principal paid to a non-charitable beneficiary at the end of the term.

Charitable remainder annuity trust   A trust designed to permit payment of a fixed amount annually to a non-charitable beneficiary with the remainder going to charity.

Charitable remainder unitrust   A trust designed to permit payment of a fixed percentage of the net fair market value of the trust to a noncharitable beneficiary with the remainder going to charity.

Closely Held Business   A business whose shares are held within a family unit and which has no publicly traded stock.

Codicil   An amendment to a will.

Community property   A form of ownership between husband and wife in which each spouse has a separate, undivided interest in property acquired during marriage.

Conservatorship   A guardianship over a person's property.

Contingent interests   An interest that might cause property to revert back to the original owner upon the occurrence of some specified condition.

Contractual assets   An asset that contains written instructions for the disposition of the asset by beneficiary designation.

Corporation   A legal entity separate from the owners.

Credit shelter trust   A trust used to hold sufficient assets to apply against the unified credit of a deceased spouse and provide for the surviving spouse.

Crummey power   A written notice pursuant to the terms of a trust that notifies beneficiaries of an unrestricted right to demand and receive their proportionate share of the contribution to the trust within a specified period of time.

Death Benefit   That portion of a life insurance policy that the company is obligated to pay upon the death of the insured. See *cash value*.

Decedent   An individual who is deceased.

Deed   A document conveying title to real estate.

Descendant   Refers to a child, grandchild, great-grandchild, or further down the ancestral line. See also *ancestor*.

Devise   A gift of real property.

Devisee   A person who is gifted real property under a will or trust.

Disclaimer   An irrevocable and unqualified refusal to accept an interest in property created in the person disclaiming.

Durable power of attorney   A power of attorney that will continue to be effective even if the principal should later become incapacitated.

Education IRA   A trust authorized by the IRS that is created to help pay for qualified educational expenses of another.

Escheat   A term used to indicate a passing of title from a decedent to the government.

Estate   The sum total of everything owned by a person.

Estate planning   A goal-oriented activity designed to provide the greatest possible financial security for both an individual and his or her beneficiaries during lifetime and to provide for distribution of assets at death in the most efficient and least costly manner possible.

Estate tax   A federal tax assessed on the total value of a decedent's taxable estate.

Execution   The formal signing of a legal document.

Executor   A person appointed to represent an estate of a decedent who died with a will.

Exemption equivalent amount   The dollar amount of property that will incur a federal estate tax equal to the unified credit.

Family limited partnership   A limited partnership organized under applicable statutes used to provide tax and non-tax benefits for family-operated businesses.

Fiduciary   A person (or entity) holding a position of trust and confidence with regard to another's assets.

Fiduciary taxes   Taxes incurred by a trust or estate during administration.

First-to-die insurance   A life insurance policy that insures two or more people and pays the death benefit upon the death of the first insured to die.

Five and five power   Refers to a power vested in a beneficiary of a trust authorizing the right to withdraw the greater of five thousand dollars or five percent of the value of the trust on an annual basis.

Form 56   When the estate is terminated, the personal representative must notify the IRS by filing Form 56, Notice Concerning Fiduciary Relationship.

Form 706   United States Estate Tax Return.

Form 709   United States Gift Tax Return.

Form 1041   The fiduciary tax return used by partnerships, estates and trusts.

Form 1310   An IRS form used to claim a refund on behalf of a deceased taxpayer.

Form K-1   The form used to distribute income from a partnership, estate, or trust to the beneficiaries during the taxable year.

Form SS-4   The application for employer identification number.

Funding a Trust   The process of transferring title to the name of a trust and designating the trust as beneficiary of certain contractual accounts.

Future interest gifts   A gift of property that cannot be enjoyed by the donee until a future date.

Future value   The projected value of assets based on anticipated growth over a period of time.

General partnership   A form of business in which all partners participate in the management of the business and share the profits and losses from the business.

General power of appointment   An unrestricted grant of authority to transfer a property interest owned by another to anyone, including the person having this power.

General power of attorney   A power of attorney that gives someone broad powers to act on behalf of the principal.

Gift   A transfer of money or property for less than full consideration where there is a complete loss of use, possession, and control over the property by the donor.

Gift splitting   A gift by one spouse with the consent of the other spouse allowing for a nontaxable gift of $20,000 to a donee.

Grantor   The designation of a person who creates a trust.

Grantor trust   The term applied to a trust in which the grantor has any of the powers specified at I.R.C. Secs. 671–679, causing trust income to be taxed to the grantor. Those categories are reversionary interest, power to control beneficial enjoyment, administrative powers, power to revoke, and income for benefit of the grantor.

Gross probate estate   The total value of all assets passing through a decedent's probate estate.

Gross taxable estate   The total value of all assets subject to tax.

Guardian ad litem   An attorney or other representative appointed by the court to protect the interests of an incapacitated person.

Guardians   Individuals (or institutions) appointed by the court and given the responsibility of caring for an incapacitated person.

Guardianship   A process of determining the mental and physical capacity of an individual to care for him- or herself.

Health care representative appointment   A legal document authorizing an individual to make health care decisions on behalf of the principal.

Heirs   Those entitled to a decedent's property by operation of law.

Holographic wills   A will prepared in longhand by the testator.

In Kind   Refers to the distribution of specific assets to a beneficiary, as opposed to an equivalent cash value.

In terrorem   A provision that invokes a penalty against anyone contesting the document; usually found in trusts.

Incapacitated Person   Term used to describe a person under legal disability, including minor children as well as those disabled by accident or illness.

Incident of ownership   A term used in reference to life insurance that will result in the inclusion of the policy in the taxable estate of the individual found to have a necessary degree of control over the policy as defined by the Internal Revenue Service.

Income in Respect of a Decedent   Refers to amounts of income earned by a decedent, but not included in the decedent's taxable income in the year of his or her death.

Income tax   Tax imposed on income of a taxpayer.

Individual retirement account (IRA)   A qualified retirement account for individuals and their spouses, with limits on deductible contributions of $2,000 per year.

Inherit   A term used to describe the transfer of ownership from a decedent to a beneficiary.

Inheritance tax   A state tax accessed by the state against an heir based upon the value of the property transferred to the heir and the relationship of the heir to the decedent.

Institutional Trustees   Refers to banks, brokerage firms, and other corporate trust companies that are authorized by state law to serve in the capacity of a trustee.

Insurable interest   Refers to a financial interest in the continued life of another individual.

Intangible property   An item of personal property that has no intrinsic value but represent something of value.

Intestate   Refers to when an individual dies without a will or trust.

Intestate succession   The process of determining heirship when the decedent leaves no valid will or trust containing instructions on who shall inherit his or her property.

Intrinsic Value   The actual, universally recognized, value of some thing.

Inventory   A list all of the decedent's assets.

IRA   A qualified retirement account. See also *individual retirement account.*

Issue   Refers to the children of the decedent.

Joint tenancy with right to survivorship   This type of ownership specifies that upon the death of one co-owner, the surviving named co-owners shall become full owners of the asset.

Joint will   A single will created by two individuals governing the distribution of their separate property.

Judgment creditor   A creditor who has obtained a court judgment against the debtor.

Kiddie tax   Refers to the tax on children under the age of 14 who have at least one living parent and who have over $1,500 (2001) of unearned income. The first $750 of a dependent child's unearned income (in 2001) is exempt from taxation due to the child's standard deduction, and the next $750 of unearned income is taxed at the child's (usually lower) tax bracket.

Lapse   Refers to a situation in which the intended beneficiary is unable to receive a specific gift, usually as a result of his or her death.

Lead trust   See *charitable lead trust.*

Letters testamentary   The court papers appointing the personal representative and authorizing the personal representative to act on behalf of the estate.

Life estate   A retained right of the original owner to live on and enjoy real estate that has been deeded to another owner.

Life insurance   A contract under which the insurer agrees to pay to the insured, in return for a premium, a defined amount upon the occurrence of the death of the insured.

Limited liability company (LLC)   A form of business entity managed by members, who are much like general partners. The members are not personally liable for liabilities of the LLC.

Limited liability partnership (LLP)   A form of business entity similar to a general partnership with limited liability protection; also called registered limited liability partnerships.

Limited partnership   A form of business entity similar to a general partnership except that some partners in a limited partnership do not participate in management of the partnership business and have limited liability for the activities of the partnership.

Limited power of appointment   A grant of authority to transfer a property interest owned by another to anyone except the one with the power, the estate of the one holding the power, or the creditors of either of the above.

Living trust   A trust created during one's lifetime in which you place property held there until you die; then direct the disposition of those assets at your death.

Living will   A document that sets forth wishes for the provision of artificial life support and artificially supplied nutrition and hydration.

Marital deduction   Total tax relief for transfers between a deceased spouse and the surviving spouse.

Marital trust   A trust created to benefit a surviving spouse.

Minimum distribution requirements   Rules issued by the Internal Revenue Service governing the amount and timing of mandatory distributions from qualified retirement accounts.

Minutes   Documents summarizing meetings of directors and shareholders of a corporation.

Mutual will   Separate wills prepared pursuant to an agreement between two parties with mutually binding provisions.

Noncupative wills   A verbal will.

Non-probate assets   Assets that do not require probate to pass to the intended beneficiary.

Non-qualified retirement account   A retirement account that is not subject to minimum distribution rules and in which the contribution receives no special tax treatment.

Officers   Individuals who manage the day-to-day operations of a corporation.

Partnership   A form of business entity between two or more individuals engaged in a business where the individuals agree to share the profits and losses of the business.

Payable on death accounts   An account that designates a beneficiary who will receive the balance in the account upon the death of the owner.

Per capita   To take by head count.

Per stirpes   To take by representation.

Personal property   Objects that are not permanently affixed to the land or to improvements on the land.

Personal representative   An individual who is in charge of a decedent's estate, regardless of whether there is a will to administer.

Pick-up tax   A tax owing to the state of the decedent's domicile based on the use of the credit for state death taxes on the federal estate tax return.

Pooled income fund   A trust established to provide income for the benefit of more than one individual, with the remainder passing to a qualified charity, where the property is commingled with property transferred to the fund by other donors.

Power of appointment trust   A trust established for the benefit of the surviving spouse that qualifies for the marital deduction and over which the surviving spouse has a "general power of appointment."

Power of attorney   A document prepared by an individual granting to another specified powers to act on his or her behalf. See also *general power of attorney,* and *springing power of attorney.*

Power of appointment   A grant of authority to transfer or dispose of a property interest owned by another. See also *general power of appointment* and *springing power of attorney.*

Present-interest gifts   A transfer of ownership giving the donee the immediate right to possession and enjoyment of the gift.

Present value   The current value of assets without regard to future growth.

Principal   The person executing a power of attorney.

Probate   A process created by state law that determines heirship, provides a means for paying creditors, and provides for an orderly distribution of assets.

Probate assets   Property in single name or tenancy in common and contractual property payable to the estate of the owner such as life insurance, annuities and retirement plans.

Probate estate   The sum total of assets owned by a deceased person that must pass through the court system to determine ownership and eventually reach the heirs.

Property   A general term applied to personal and real property, tangible and intangible property.

Pro-rata   A distribution in undivided interests.

Prudent Person Rule   A rule that dictates that a trustee invest in safe and low-risk investments.

QDOT   A qualified domestic trust used for transfers to alien spouses that allows the spouse to benefit from the unlimited marital deduction.

QTIP trust   A qualified terminable interest trust that allows for transfers to the trust to qualify for the marital deduction, with the spouse receiving all income from the trust for life, and the remainder to beneficiaries designated by the spouse who created the trust.

Qualified charity   An organization that allows the donor of the trust to gain either an income, gift, or estate tax deduction.

Qualified disclaimer   A disclaimer that is sufficient to keep the disclaimed asset out of the taxable estate of the beneficiary. See also *disclaimer*.

Qualified domestic trust   See *QDOT*.

Qualified Retirement Account   An account that allows for special tax treatment of contributions, deferral of taxes on income and capital gains, and which is subject to minimum distribution rules.

Qualified state tuition program   State programs created in accordance with Internal Revenue Code 529 that allow for tax-deferred savings for the education of the named beneficiary and provides for other tax benefits.

Qualified terminable interest trust   See *QTIP*.

Real property   Land or permanent improvements on the land.

Remainder Trust   See *charitable remainder unitrust*.

Resident agent   An individual or an entity (such as a financial institution or trust department) that resides (or has a principal place of business) within the state of probate administration that agrees to accept notices from the probate court and notify the personal representative of all such notices.

Residuary estate   The remainder of an estate after debts, taxes, and specific gifts have all been made.

Retained interests   A donor's interest in property that still attach to the property titled in another's name.

Reversionary interests   An interest in property that will cause the property to revert back to the original owner at a specified time.

Revocable transfer   A transfer of property in which the original owner reserves the right to amend, alter, revoke, or terminate the transfer at a later date.

Revocable trust   A trust created during lifetime that owns property and contains instructions for the disposition of property at death. See also *grantor trust* and *living trust*.

Rollover   The transfer of a deceased spouse's qualified retirement account to an IRA established by the surviving spouse that allows for continued deferral.

Roth IRA   An individual retirement account that allows for tax-free growth of assets, but no tax benefits for contributions. Savings incentive match plan for Employees. See also *SIMPLE IRA*.

S Corporation   A corporation which has opted under subchapter S of the Internal Revenue Code to be taxed as a partnership.

Savings Incentive Match Plan for Employees   See *SIMPLE IRA*.

Scrivener   A person who prepares a document.

Second-to-die insurance   Insurance that insures the lives of two individuals, usually spouses, and which pays a death benefit upon the death of the second spouse to die.

Section 170(b)(1)(A)   Organizations that will qualify the donor to receive an income tax charitable deduction.

Section 2055(a)   Organizations that will qualify the donor's estate to obtain an estate tax deduction.

Section 2522(a)   Organizations that will qualify the donor for the gift tax charitable deduction.

SEP   A qualified retirement account, simplified employee pension plan, designed for self-employed individuals or owners of a small business.

Settlor   An individual who creates a trust. See also *grantor*.

Shareholders   Individual owners of a corporation.

SIMPLE IRA   A qualified retirement account for businesses with fewer than 100 employees that allows for pre-tax contributions by employees and matching contributions by employers.

Simple will   A will that leaves all of a decedent's property outright to a select few beneficiaries, typically to a surviving spouse.

Simplified employee pension   See *SEP*.

Sole proprietorship   A form of doing business individually without establishing a separate legal entity.

Special power of attorney   A power of attorney conveying very specific, limited powers to the attorney-in-fact.

Special valuation rules   Special rules regarding the valuation of qualified farms and other trades and businesses.

Spendthrift provision   A provision that makes trust assets unavailable to creditors of a beneficiary and others who might make a claim against the beneficiary's share of the trust.

Split-interest trust   A trust that has both charitable and non-charitable beneficiaries.

Spousal Allowance   A right provided by state law allowing a surviving spouse a minimum guaranteed percentage of probate property at the death of the first spouse to die.

Springing power of attorney   A power of attorney that only conveys authority to an attorney-in-fact if at some later time the principal becomes incompetent.

State death tax credit   A credit authorized against federal estate taxes due. See also *pick-up tax*.

Stepped-up basis   A provision in the tax code that substitutes the date of death value of an appreciated asset as the basis for that asset instead of the decedent's original cost basis.

Stock   A certificate of ownership in a corporation.

Stretch IRA An IRA with a designated beneficiary allowing post-death required distributions to be deferred over the beneficiary's lifetime.

Successor Trustee A trustee that assumes the responsibilities of trustee only after a prior trustee resigns or is no longer able to serve as trustee.

Survivorship insurance See *second-to-die insurance*.

Take Means to acquire or to inherit something.

Tangible property Items of personal property that can be touched or physically possessed.

Tax apportionment Refers to the allocation of taxes to the recipient of property causing the tax.

Tax Deferral Refers to a period of time where taxable income or capital gains are not taxed until the occurrence of an event in the future.

Taxable estate Includes all assets over which the person has a specified degree of control.

Tenancy by the entirety Property held by husband and wife, similar to joint tenancy with rights to survivorship.

Tenancy in common Property held by two or more owners, without survivorship rights.

Term insurance Term insurance provides a death benefit without any accumulation of cash value. See also *cash value*.

Testamentary disposition A disposition of assets made after death according to the terms of a valid will or trust.

Testamentary trust A trust created within an individual's last will and testament.

Title A document that evidences ownership of an asset.

Transfer on death accounts See *payable on death accounts*.

Transfer Tax Taxes imposed as a result of the transfer of ownership of property, either by gift during lifetime or by testamentary transfer at death. See also *estate tax, income tax,* and *inheritance tax*.

Trust funding The process of re-titling assets to the name of a trust.

Trustee The person that controls property held in trust.

UGMA accounts   See *uniform gift to minors account.*

Umbrella Insurance   A form of liability insurance that covers potential liability in excess of your existing homeowners and automobile coverage, typically sold in multiples of millions of dollars in coverage.

Undivided Interest   Refers to a form of ownership in which all owners share equally in the whole property. There are no separate interests that can be identified as belonging to any particular owner.

Unified credit   A specific amount that is allocated to each taxpayer that can be applied against the gift tax or the estate tax.

Uniform gift to minors account   An account created under state law for the benefit of a minor child, in which the child is entitled to the account at age 18. These accounts can include only bank deposits, securities, and insurance policies.

Uniform laws   A proposed statute recommended and available for adoption and modification by any state.

Uniform transfers to minors account   An account created under state law for the benefit of a minor child, where the child is entitled to the account at age 21. There are no restrictions on the property that can be placed into one of these accounts.

Unitrust   A trust that pays a fixed percentage of the trust assets to a beneficiary. See also *charitable remainder unitrust.*

Universal life insurance   A life insurance policy with three separate components: investment, expense, and mortality. The cash value earns interest at rates based on current investment earnings.

Unlimited Marital Deduction   Refers to a tax deduction available for federal estate tax and inheritance tax for the value of any asset transferred from a decedent directly to a surviving spouse.

UTMA accounts   See *uniform transfers to minors account.*

Valuation date   The date on which assets are valued for tax purposes.

Variable life insurance   A life insurance policy without a guaranteed death benefit or surrender value. The cash value can be invested in equities and the policy owner manages the investment decisions.

Variable-universal life insurance A combination of universal life insurance and variable life insurance. It has flexible premiums, adjustable death benefits, and policy loan and partial withdrawal privileges. The owner of the life contract decides where the premiums are invested. The typical variable universal life policy carries a guaranteed minimum death benefit in the event the underlying investments are not profitable. This policy actually is a combination insurance policy and securities investment.

Ward A person over whom a guardianship or conservatorship is established. See also *conservatorship* and *guardianship*.

Will A legal document made in anticipation of death in which a person directs the disposition of his or her property at death and contains instructions for payment of debts and taxes and nominates guardians for minor children and a personal representative for the estate.

Whole life insurance A policy of insurance with a fixed return on cash value dictated by the insurance contract.

Index

Symbols

50% charities, 294
401(k) plans, 213
403(b)(7) plans, 212

A

ABA (American Bar Association),
  Uniform Probate Code, 20
administrative expenses, tax
  deductions, 63, 86
administrators
  ancillary administration, 120
  probate, 114-121
advantages
  charitable trusts, 295-296
  corporations, 234-235
  general partnerships, 225
  gifting, 313
  ILITs, 260
  life insurance, 202
  limited partnerships, 228
  power of attorney, 186
  sole proprietorships, 222
affidavits, estate transfers, 114
aliens
  estate planning, 327
  gifting, 329-330
  marital deductions, 328
  QDOTs (Qualified Domestic
    Trusts), 330-331
  unified credit, 329
  United States treaties, 328
allowable credits, 89-90
allowable deductions, taxes, 63-65
alternate valuation, gifts, 313
amendments, wills, 132-133
  provisions, 154-155
American Bar Association (ABA),
  Uniform Probate Code, 20
ancillary administration, 120
annual gift exclusions, 74, 316
annuities, 49, 208
  estate taxes, 80

anti-lapse statutes, 131
appointing
  executors, 105
  health care representatives,
    186-188
appraisals, property, 77
articles of incorporation, corporations, 229
ascertainable standard, credit shelter trusts, 247
assessing properties, 8
assets
  contractual assets, 48-50
  determining, 5
  documents of title, importance
    of, 31-32
  gifting, 311-312
  growth projecting, 340, 343
  joint assets, 9
  liquid assets, 8
  ownership, 39-48
    bank accounts, 42-43
  sales, probate, 109-110
  see also estates; property
attestation clauses, wills, 127-128
attorneys
  advantages, 186
  attorneys-in-fact, 181
  compensation, 185
  consulting, 14
  durable power of attorney,
    182-183
  fees, 6, 116
  finding, 6
  general power of attorney, 181
  recordation requirements, 185
  reimbursement, 185
  requirements for execution,
    185
  revocation, 185-186
  special power of attorney, 182
  springing durable power of
    attorney, 183-184
  termination at death, 184
attorneys-in-fact, 181
authorized signers, 40

B

bank accounts
  estate taxes, 78
  ownership, 42-43
basis, gifting, 323
beneficiaries
  competency, considerations, 9
  designating
    life insurance, 166
    trusts, 139, 141
  identification, 173
bonds, posting, 109
books, suggested reading, 383
brokerage accounts, estate taxes,
  80
Bureau of Public Debt, Web site,
  79
business entities
  corporations, 228
    advantages, 234-235
    articles of incorporation,
      229
    by-laws, 229-230
    disadvantages, 235
    legal documents, 229
    taxation, 230-233
  FLPs (family limited partner-
    ships), 236
  general partnerships, 223
    advantages, 225
    disadvantages, 227
    legal documents,
      223-224
    liability, 224-225
    taxation, 225
  limited partnerships, 227
    advantages, 228
    disadvantages, 228
    legal documents, 227
    tax requirments, 227
  LLCs (limited liability compa-
    nies), 235
  qualified retirement accounts,
    211-213

sole proprietorships, 221
  advantages, 222
  disadvantages, 222-223
  legal documents, 222
  liability issues, 222
  taxation, 222
by representation, distribution, 176
by-laws, corporations, 229-230

C

"C" corporations, 230
calculating
  estate values, 7
  tax rates, 87-88
capital gains, 281, 323
cash, estate taxes, 78
cash values, life insurance, 193
CDs (certificates of deposit), estate taxes, 78
Certified Financial Planner Board of Standards, 6
charging orders, 236
charitable deductions, 87
charitable lead trusts, 285-286
  annuity trusts, 290
charitable remainder trusts, 275
  annuity trusts, 280-281
  makeup provisions, 285
  unitrusts, 276-280
charitable trusts, 275
  advantages, 295-296
  charitable lead trusts, 285-286
    annuity trusts, 290
  charitable remainder trusts, 275
    annuity trusts, 280-281
    makeup provisions, 285
    unitrusts, 276-277, 279-280
  disadvantages, 295-296
  types, 294-295
charities
  qualified charities, 277
  types, 294-295
children
  disinheritance, 172
  guardianships, 97-98
  issues, 20

minor's trusts, 263
  Education IRA (Education Individual Retirement Account), 267-271
  educational trusts, 267-272
  Section 2503(b) trusts, 266-267
  Section 2503(c) trusts, 263-265
  property transfers, 33
claims, wills, 120
co-trustees, designating, 150
codicils, 132
community property, 20, 50-51
  gifting, 315
compensation, attorneys, 185
competency, beneficiaries, considerations, 9
conservatorships, 97
contests, wills, 109, 120
contingency fees, 117
contingent interest, 33-34
contracts
  annuities, 49
  life insurance, 48
  payable on death accounts, 49-50
  retirement accounts, 49
contractual assets, 48-50
controls, trusts, 139
corporations, 228
  advantages, 234-235
  articles of incorporation, 229
  by-laws, 229-230
  "C" corporations, 230
  disadvantages, 235
  legal documents, 229
  minutes of meetings, 230
  "S" corporations, 232
  stocks, 230
  taxation, 230-233
credit, unified, 72
credit shelter trusts, 241-242
  ascertainable standard, 247
  five and five power, 246
  limited power of appointment, 247
  marital deductions, formula, 244-245
  setting up, 243

spouses, providing for, 245-246
  trustees, choosing, 248-249
creditors, protecting, 115
crummey power, 256

D

death benefits (life insurance, taxation), 200-201
deathbed wills, 126
debt, repaying, 167-169
decedents, 18
deductions (taxes)
  allowable deductions, 63-65
  estate taxes, 86-87
  unlimited marital deductions, 30
deferrals, taxes, 56-57, 212
  qualified retirement accounts, 56-57
  savings bonds, 57
delays, probate, 120
descendants, 18, 23
designating
  personal represenatives, 129-130
  wills, 131
destroying wills, 132
Diana, Princess of Wales, last will and testament, 359-364
disability
  gauardianships
    bypassing, 100-101
    problems with, 99-100
    types, 97-99
  legal considerations, 96-97
  planning for, 95-96
disadvantages
  charitable trusts, 295-296
  corporations, 235
  general partnerships, 227
  limited partnerships, 228
  sole proprietorships, 222-223
disclaimer trusts, 307
disclaimers
  disclaimer trusts, 307
  effects, 305
  non-qualified disclaimers, 307
  qualified disclaimers, 305
    forms, 306

reasons for, 306
trusts, 304-308
wills, 304-308
discretionary distributions, trustees, 148
disinheritance, wills, 170-172
disputes, resolving, 116
distribution
by representation, 176
in kind distribution, 176
per capita, 176
per stirpes, 176
percentage distribution, 177
personal representatives, 111
residue, wills, 166-167
distribution provisions
trusts, 175-177
wills, 175-177
documents of title
importance of, 31-32
rights of survivorship, 40
durable power of attorney, 182-183

E

E-Bonds, estate taxes, 79
Economic Recovery Act of 1981, 73-75
Education IRAs (Education Individual Retirement Accounts), 267-271
educational trusts, 267-272
Education IRA (Education Individual Retirement Account), 267-271
prepaid tuition programs, 272
qualified educational expenses, 268
qualified state tuition programs, 269
Roth IRAs, 272
EE-Bonds, estate taxes, 79
escheating, 18
estate planning
aliens, 327-328
analysis and implementation, 344-345
evolution of, 3
failure to, 12-13
future value, 8
individual case study, 335-345

married couple case study, 346-351
needs, determining, 13-14
process, 5
reasons, 4
reviewing, 6
titles, 8
estate taxes
annuities, 80
bank accounts, 78
brokerage accounts, 80
cash, 78
CDs (certificates of deposit), 78
deductions, 86-87
family-owned businesses, 82-83
filing, preparation, 76
gift taxes, compared, 321-322
gifting, 315
history of, 71-74
inheritance taxes, compared, 64-66, 75
joint interests, 84
life insurance death benefits, 200
life insurance proceeds, 80-82
money market accounts, 78
personal property, 77-78
powers of appointment, 84
probate, 112
property appraisals, 77
retained life estates, 83
retirement accounts, 80, 206
revocable transfers, 84
securities, 82
stocks, 82
transfers, 83
Treasury bills, notes, and bonds, 79
U.S. savings bonds, 78-79
valuation dates, 84
valuations, qualifying for, 85
see also taxes
estate values, calculating, 7
estates, 26
life estates, 32
non-probate estates, probate estates comparisons, 28-29
non-taxable estates, 29
personal representatives, 60
distribution, 111

probate estates, 28
non-probate estate comparisons, 28-29
property, types, 25-28
residuary estates, 163
taxable estates, 30
transfers, affidavits, 114
see also assets; property
execution requirements, wills, 10, 127-128
health care representative appointments, 11
living wills, 10, 188
power of attorney, 10
trusts, 10, 140-142
executors, wills, appointing, 105
executrix, appointing, 105
exemptions, state property taxes, 11
exemptions, trusts, 242

F

f/b/o (for the benefit of), trusts, 145
family dynamics, trustees, 147
family limited partnerships (FLPs), 236
family-owned businesses, estate taxes, 82-83
federal estate taxes, history of, 71-74
fees, 116-117
fiduciaries, 106
fiduciary taxes, 60-62, 106
probate, 112-113
figuring
estate values, 7
tax rates, 87-88
filing
estate taxes, preparation, 76
tax returns, 64
final say, wills, 127
financial needs, understanding, 7-8
financial planners
Certified Financial Planner Board of Standards, 6
finding, 6
financial references, 385
first to die life insurance, 200

five and five power, credit shelter trusts, 246
FLPs (family limited partnerships), 236
forms, qualified disclaimers, 306
funding trusts, 143
funeral expenses, tax deductions, 63, 86
future value, 8
fututre interest gifts, 316

G

general partnerships, 223
  advantages, 225
  disadvantages, 227
  jointly and severally liable, 224
  legal documents, 223-224
  liability, 224-225
  taxation, 225
general power of attorney, 181
general powers of appointment, 35
gift taxes, 74-75
  estate taxes, compared, 321-322
  history of, 71-74
  life insurance death benefits, 201
gifting
  aliens, 329-330
  annual gift exclusions, 316
  assets, 311-312
  basis, 323
  community property, 315
  estate tax benefits, 315
  future interest gifts, 316
  income tax benefits, 313-314
  non-tax advantages, 313
  qualified transfers, 324-325
  taxes, 321-325
  timing, 322
  unlimited marital deductions, 321
  UTMAs (Uniform Transfers to Minors Accounts), 317-319
gifts, 173-175
  splitting, 319-320
  valuation, 312-313
    alternate valuation, 313
  wills, 130-131
    lapses, 130
goals, prioritizing, 5

government assistance programs, joint ownership, 42
grantor trusts, 138
  rules, 34
growth, projecting, 340, 343
guardian *ad litem,* 97
guardianships, 96
  adults, 98-99
  bypassing, 100-101
  designating, wills, 131
  disability
    problems with, 99-100
    types, 97-99
  minors, 97-98
  problems with, 99-100

H

H-Bonds, estate taxes, 79
health care representative appointments, 186-188
  execution requirements, 11
health, maintenance, support and education (HEMS), trusts, 247
heirs
  determining, 116
  identifying, legal history, 18-19
  intestate succession, 19
  protecting, 115
HH-Bonds, estate taxes, 79
history
  legal, 17
    heir identification, 18-19
    property ownership, 17-18
  modern inheritance, 19-21
holographic wills, 125
homes, trusts, transferring to, 157

I

I-Bonds, estate taxes, 78
I.R.C. Section 170(b)(1)(A) organizations, 294
I.R.C. Section 2055(a) organizations, 294
I.R.C. Section 2522(a) organizations, 295
I.R.C. Section 509(a) private foundations, 295
I.R.S. tax tables, marginal income tax brackets, 9
identifications, beneficiaries, 173

ILITs (irrevocable life insurance trusts), 251-260
  advantages, 260
  alternatives to, 258
  beneficiary tax implications, 257
  choosing, 252-253
  premiums, paying, 255-256
  taxable income, 255
  three-year inclusionary rules, 252
  trustees, 254
in kind distribution, 167, 176
in terrorem provisions, trusts, 157
incapacity
  planning for, 95-96
  wills, 155-156
income, 112
income distributions, taxes, 63
income exemptions, taxes, 64
income taxes
  gifting, 313-314
  life insurance death benefits, 200
  probate, 111
  retirement accounts, 206
  rules, trusts, 138
Indiana Inheritance Tax code, 66-68
Individual Retirement Accounts. *See* IRAs (Individual Retirement Accounts)
inheritance, 18
  legal history, 19-21
  per capita, 21, 23
  per stirpes, 21-22
inheritance taxes, 64
  allowable credits, 89
  avoiding, 68
  estate taxes, compared, 64-66, 75
  Indiana Inheritance Tax, 66-68
  life insurance death benefits, 201
  probate, 112
  retirement accounts, 207
  state, 11
institutional trustees, 145, 148-149
  replacing, 149
insurance, life insurance, 193-194
  advantages, 202
  cash values, 193

death benefit taxation, 200-201

first to die life insurance, 200

ILITs (irrevocable life insurance trusts), 252-260

leveraging, 201

surrender value, 199

survivorship life insurance, 199-200

term life insurance, 194-196

universal life insurance, 198

values, 201-202

variable life insurance, 198-199

variable universal life insurance, 199

whole life insurance, 196, 198

intangible personal property, 27, 329

intentions, wills, expressing, 141

interest earnings, taxes, 79

Internal Revenue Code, establishment of, 72, 74

interpolated terminal reserves, 257

intestate law, 11

intestate succession, 19

intrinsic value, 27

inventory, probate, 107

IRAs (Individual Retirement Accounts), 210

Roth IRAs, 210

irrevocable life insurance trust. *See* ILITs (irrevocable life insurance trusts)

issues (children), 20

J–K

joint assets, 9

joint interests, estate taxes, 84

joint ownership, 40-42

joint tenancy with right of survivorship (JTWROS), 40-45

joint wills, 126

jointly and severally liable, general partnerships, 224

JTWROS (joint tenancy with right of survivorship), 40-45

judgment creditors, 27

L

lapses, wills, 130

last wills and testaments

Diana, Princess of Wales, 359-364

Nixon, Richard M., 367-381

see also wills

laws

anti-lapse statutes, 131

disability, 96-97

probate, history, 103-104

state laws, understanding, 10-11

uniform law, 20-21

Uniform Probate Code, 20-21

Uniform Transfers to Minors Act, 314

legal age, wills, 127

legal documents

corporations, 229

general partnerships, 223-224

limited partnerships, 227

sole proprietorships, 222

legal history, 17

heir identification, 18-19

modern inheritance, 19-21

property ownership, 17-18

legal interest, property, removing, 33

legal references, 385

letters, testamentary, 107

leveraging life insurance, 201

liability

general partnerships, 224-225

sole proprietorships, 222

taxes, determining, 7

life estates, 32

estate taxes, 83

life insurance, 193-194

advantages, 202

beneficiary designations, 166

cash values, 193

death benefits, taxation, 200-201

first to die life insurance, 200

ILITs (irrevocable life insurance trusts), 252-260

leveraging, 201

proceeds, estate taxes, 80-82

second-to-die life insurance, 200

surrender value, 199

survivorship life insurance, 199-200

term life insurance, 194-196

universal life insurance, 198

values, 201-202

variable life insurance, 198-199, 209

variable universal life insurance, 199

whole life insurance, 196, 198

life insurance contracts, 48

lifetime financial needs, understanding, 7-8

limited liability companies. *See* LLCs (limited liability companies)

limited partnerships, 227

advantages, 228

disadvantages, 228

legal documents, 227

tax requirements, 227

limited powers of appointment, 36

credit shelter trusts, 247

lineal descendants, 23

liquid assets, 8

living trusts, 138

common myths, 157-159

living wills, 10, 188

LLCs (limited liability companies), 235

M

mandatory distribution, Section 2503(b) trusts, 266

marital deductions, 86

aliens, 328

credit shelter deductions, 244-245

gifting, 321

marital trusts, 301

power of appointment trusts, 301-303

QTIPs (qualified terminable interest trusts), 303-304

unlimited marital deductions, 301

marketability, 82
members of the family, 271
minimum distribution requirements
  non-qualified retirement
    accounts, 207
  qualified retirement accounts,
    214-217
minor's trusts, 263
  Education IRA (Education
    Individual Retirement
    Account), 267-271
  educational trusts, 267-272
  prepaid tuition programs, 272
  Section 2503(b) trusts, 266
    tax implications, 266-267
  Section 2503(c) trusts, 263-264
    advantages, 265
    disadvantages, 265
    tax implications, 264-265
minors, guardianships, 97-98
minutes of meetings, corporations,
  230
money market accounts, estate
  taxes, 78
mutual wills, 126

N

names, trusts, 145
National Conference of
  Commissioners on Uniform State
  Laws, Uniform Probate Code, 20
needs, determining, 13-14
net worth statements, 335-336
Nixon, Richard M., last will and
  testament, 367-381
non-probate estates, probate
  estates, compared, 28-29
non-qualified disclaimers, 307
non-qualified retirement accounts,
  207-209
  minimum distribution require-
    ments, 207
  retirement accounts, 205
non-residents
  estate planning, 327
    taxes, 327-328
  gifting, 329-330
  marital deductions, 328

QDOTs (Qualified Domestic
  Trusts), 330-331
  unified credits, 329
  United States treaties, 328
non-taxable estates, 29
noncupative wills, 126
notice to creditors, 107-108

O

OBRA (Omnibus Budget
  Reconciliation Act), 73
ordinary life insurance, 197
ownership
  authorized signers, 40
  bank accounts, 42-43
  contractual assets, 48-50
  documents of title, 31-32
  joint ownership, 40-42
  JTWROS (joint tenancy with
    right of survivorship), 40-45
  property, 39-48
  risks, 41
  single ownership, 39-40
  tenancy by the entirety, 45-48
  tenancy in common, 43-45

P

payable on death accounts, 49-50
paying premiums, ILITs, 255-256
penalties, taxes, 209
penalty-free distributions, qualified
  retirement accounts, 213
per capita, 21-23, 176
per stirpes, 21-23, 176
percentage distribution, 177
personal property, 26-28
  estate taxes, 77-78
  intangible personal property,
    27
  tangible personal property, 27
personal representatives, 60
  designating, 129-130
  duties, 109
  estates, distribution of, 111
  fees, 116
  protecting, 115
pooled income funds, 295
posting bonds, 109
power of appointment trusts,
  301-303

power of attorney, 11, 181
  advantages, 186
  execution requirements, 10
  granting immediate, 186
  requirements for execution,
    185
  revocation, 185-186
  termination at death, 184
  see also attorneys
powers of appointment, 34-36
  estate taxes, 84
  general powers of appointment,
    35
  limited powers of appointment,
    36
premiums, paying, ILITs, 255-256
prepaid tuition programs, 272
Princess Diana, Princess of Wales,
  last will and testament, 359-364
pro-rata distribution, 167
probate, 103
  administration, 114-116
    disadvantages, 116-121
  bond postings, 109
  delays, 120
  estate taxes, 112
  executors, appointing, 105
  fiduciary taxes, 112-113
  functions, 104-113
  history, 103-104
  income taxes, 111
  inheritance taxes, 112
  inventory, 107
  letters, testamentary, 107
  notice to creditors, 107-108
  personal representatives, duties,
    109
  property, 104
  property insurance, 111
  public proceedings, 121
  sale of assets, 109-110
  simplified administration, 114
  taxes, 111
  valuations, 120
  wills
    contests, 109
    lack of, 105
    validity, 105

probate estates, 4, 28
    non-probate estates, compared,
        28-29
proceeds, life insurance, estate
    taxes, 80-82
projecting asset growth, 340, 343
property
    assessing, 8
    changes, 28
    children, transferring to, 33
    community property, 50-51
    contingent interest, 33-34
    documents of title, importance
        of, 31-32
    estates, 26
    legal interest, removing, 33
    marketability, 82
    non-probate estates, 29
    non-taxable property, 29
    ownership, 39-48
        JTWROS (joint tenancy
            with right of survivorship),
            40-45
        single ownership, 39-40
        tenancy by the entirety,
            45-48
        tenancy in common, 43-45
    personal property, 26-28
    powers of appointment, 34-36
    probate, 104
    probate estates, 29
    real property, 26
    reversionary interest, 34
    revocable transfers, 34
    taxable property, 30, 32-33
    types, 25-28
    see also assets; estates
property appraisals, 77
property assignments, trusts, 143
property identifications, trusts, 142
property insurance, 111
property taxes, state property taxes,
    exemptions, 11
protecting trusts, 156-160
Protective Proceedings Act, 97
provisions
    charitable remainder trusts,
        makeup provisions, 285
    trustees, 150-154
        simultaneous death, 165-166
        survivorship provisions, 164

trusts, 142-148
    distribution provisions,
        175-177
    gifts, 173-175
    in terrorem provisions, 157
    repayment provisions,
        167-170
    spendthrift provisions, 156
wills, 129, 154-155
    disinheritance, 170-172
    distribution provisions,
        175-177
    gifts, 173-175
    repayment provisions,
        167-170
    simultaneous death,
        165-166
    survivorship provisions, 164
public proceedings, 121

Q

QDOTs (Qualified Domestic
    Trusts), 330-331
QTIPs (qualified terminable interest
    trusts), 303-304
qualified charities, 277
qualified disclaimers, 305
    forms, 306
Qualified Domestic Trusts. See
    QDOTs (Qualified Domestic
    Trusts)
qualified educational expenses, 268
qualified retirement accounts, 4,
    205, 210-211
    businesses, 211-213
    minimum required distributions,
        214-217
    penalty-free distributions, 213
qualified state tuition programs, 269
qualified terminable interest trusts.
    See QTIPs (qualified terminable
    interest trusts)
qualified transfers, gifting, 324-325

R

rates, taxes, figuring, 87-88
real property, 26
receipts, ownership, 31
recordation requirements, attorneys,
    185

references
    books, 383
    financial, 385
    legal, 385
    Web sites, 384
reimbursement, attorneys, 185
repayment, debt, 167-169
repayment provisions
    trusts, 167-170
    wills, 167-170
requirements for execution, power
    of attorney, 185
residency, trustees, 147
resident agents, 106, 130
residuary estates, 163
residue, wills, distributing, 166-167
resolving disputes, 116
retained interest, 34
retained life estates, estate taxes, 83
retirement accounts, 49
    annuities, 208
    estate taxes, 80
    IRAs (Individual Retirement
        Accounts), 210
    non-qualified retirement
        accounts, 205-209
    qualified retirement accounts,
        56-57, 205, 210-211
        businesses, 211-213
            minimum required distribu-
                tions, 214-217
            penalty-free distributions,
                213
    Roth IRAs, 210
    spousal rollovers, 218
    taxes, 206-207
Retirement Equity Act, 73
retirement plans, 205
returns, taxes, filing, 64
Revenue Act of 1926, 71
Revenue Act of 1942, 74
Revenue Reconciliation Act, 74
reversionary interest, 34, 86
reviewing wills, 133
revocable living trusts, 138
revocable transfers, 34
    estate taxes, 84
revocable trusts, 104, 138
revocations
    power of attorney, 185-186
    wills, 131-132
        provisions, 154-155

risks, ownership, 41
Roth IRA accounts, educational trusts, 272
Roth IRAs, 210

S

"S" corporations, 232
sale of assets, probate, 109-110
sales receipts, ownership, 31
savings bonds, 57
    estate taxes, 78-79
savings incentive match plan for employees. *See* SIMPLE (savings incentive match plan for employees)
second-to-die life insurance, 200
Section 2503(b) trusts, 266
    mandatory distribution, 266
    tax implications, 266-267
Section 2503(c) trusts, 263-264
    advantages, 265
    disadvantages, 265
    tax implications, 264-265
securities, estate taxes, 82
self-proving declarations, wills, 127-128
SEPs (simplified employee pensions), 211
shorthand, trusts, 145
SIMPLE (savings incentive match plan for employees), 212
simple wills, 126
simplified employee pensions. *See* SEPs (simplified employee pensions)
simultaneous death
    trusts, 165-166
    wills, 165-166
single ownership, 39-40
sole proprietorships, 221-223
sound mind, wills, 127
special power of attorney, 182
spendthrift provisions, trusts, 156
split-interest trusts, 275
splitting gifts, 319-320
spousal allowances, 171
spousal rollovers, retirement accounts, 218
spouses, providing for, credit shelter trusts, 245-246

springing durable power of attorney, 183-184
state inheritance taxes, 11
    life insurance death benefits, 201
state laws, understanding, 10-11
state property taxes, exemptions, 11
states, community property, 51
stepped-up basis, tax code, 207
stocks
    corporations, 230
    estate taxes, 82
straight life insurance, 197
subsidiary trusts, 307
succession trustees, 60, 150
    selecting, 145-148
suggested reading
    books, 383
    financial references, 385
    legal references, 385
surrender value, life insurance, 199
surviving spouse rights, inheritance, 11
survivorship life insurance, 199-200
survivorship provisions, 164

T

tangible personal property, 27
tax apportionments, 163
tax deferrals, 56-57
    qualified retirement accounts, 56-57
    savings bonds, 57
tax liabilities, determining, 7
Tax Reform Act of 1976, 72
Tax Reform Act of 1980, 73
taxable estates, 7, 30
    less obvious assets, 32-33
taxes, 55
    aliens, 327-328
    allowable credits, 89-90
    allowable deductions, 63-65
    capital gains, 281
    corporations, 230-233
    death benefits, 200-201
    deductions, unlimited marital deductions, 30
    estate taxes, 71-74, 321-322
        deductions, 86-87

filing preparation, 76
    inheritance tax comparisons, 64, 66
    inheritance taxe comparisons, 75
fiduciary taxes, 60-62
general partnerships, 225
gift taxes, 71-75, 321-322
gifting, 313-315, 322-325
    annual gift exclusions, 316
    unlimited marital deductions, 321
ILITs, 257
inheritance taxes, 64
    avoiding, 68
    estate tax comparisons, 64, 66, 75
    Indiana Inheritance Tax code, 66-68
    state inheritance taxes, 11
liabilities, determining, 7
limited partnerships, 227
non-taxable estates, 29
penalties, 209
post-mortem filings, 58-59
probate, 111
property taxes, exemptions, 11
rates, figuring, 87-88
retirement accounts, 206-207
returns, filing, 64
sole proprietorships, 222
stepped-up basis, 207
tax deferrals, 56-57
    qualified retirement accounts, 56-57
    savings bonds, 57
taxable assets, 32-33
taxable estates, 30
transfer taxes, 55
trusts
    exemptions, 242
    Section 2503(b) trusts, 266-267
unified credits, 88-89
tenancy by the entirety, 45-48
tenancy in common, 43-45
term life insurance, 194-196
termination at death, power of attorney, 184
testamentary disposition, 125

testators, wills, 128-129
testatrixes, wills, 129
three-year inclusionary rules, ILITs, 252
timing, gifts, 322
titles, 8
    importance of, 31-32
    rights to survivorship, 40
transfer taxes, 55
transferring
    homes to trusts, 157
    property, powers of appointment, 34-36
transfers
    estate taxes, 83
    estates, affidavits, 114
    wills, provisions, 154-155
Treasury bills, notes, and bonds (estate taxes), 79
treaties (United States), aliens, 328
trustees
    choosing, 248-249
    co-trustees, designating, 150
    discretionary distribution, 148
    family dynamics, 147
    identification of, 145
    ILITs, 254
    institutional trustees, 145, 148-149
    provisions, 150-154
    residency, 147
    succession, 150
    successor trustees, 60
        selecting, 145-148
trusts, 137-138, 256
    assets, 144
    beneficiaries
        designating, 139-141
        identification, 173
    charitable trusts, 275
        advantages, 295-296
        charitable lead trusts, 285-286, 290
        charitable remainder trusts, 275-281, 285
        disadvantages, 295-296
        types, 294-295
    co-trustees, designating, 150
    controls, 139

credit shelter trusts, 241-242
        ascertainable standard, 247
        limited power of appointment, 247
        marital deductions, 244-245
        setting up, 243
        spouses, 245-246
    debt, repaying, 167-169
    disclaimer trusts, 307
    disclaimers, 304-308
    educational trusts, prepaid tuition programs, 272
    execution requirements, 10, 140-142
    exemptions, 242
    funding, 143
    grantor trust rules, 34
    homes, transferring, 157
    ILITs (irrevocable life insurance trusts), 251-260
    in terrorem provisions, 157
    income tax rules, 138
    institutional trustees, 145
    living trusts, 138
        common myths, 157-159
    marital trusts, 301
        power of appointment trusts, 301-303
        QTIPs (qualified terminable interest trusts), 303-304
        unlimited marital deductions, 301
    minor's trusts, 263
        Education IRA (Education Individual Retirement Account), 267-271
        educational trusts, 267-272
        Section 2503(b) trusts, 266-267
        Section 2503(c) trusts, 263-265
    names, 145
    property assignments, 143
    property identifications, 142
    protecting, 156-160
    provisions, 142-148
        distribution provisions, 175-177
        gifts, 173-175

    repayment provisions, 167-170
        simultaneous death, 165-166
        survivorship provisions, 164
    purposes, 142
    QDOTs (Qualified Domestic Trusts), 330-331
    revocable trusts, 104
    shorthand, 145
    spendthrift provisions, 156
    split-interest trusts, 275
    subsidiary trusts, 307
    trustees
        choosing, 248-249
        discretionary distribution, 148
        family dynamics, 147
        indentification, 145
        institutional trustees, 148-149
        provisions, 150-154
        residency, 147
        succession, 150
    untitled property, 144
    wills, compared, 139-140

U
U.S. savings bonds, estate taxes, 78-79
u/a/d (under agreement dated), trusts, 145
u/t/d (under trust dated), trusts, 145
UGMA (Uniform Transfers to Minors Act; was the Uniform Gifts to Minors Act), 317
unearned income, 314
unified credit, 72
    aliens, 329
unified credits, 88-89
Uniform Guardianship Act, 97
uniform law, 20-21
Uniform Probate Code, 20-21
Uniform Transfers to Minors Accounts. See UTMAs (Uniform Transfers to Minors Accounts)
Uniform Transfers to Minors Act, 314, 317
universal life insurance, 198

unlimited marital deductions, taxes, 30, 73, 301
  gifts, 321
untitled property, trusts, 144
updating wills, 133
UTMAs (Uniform Transfers to Minors Accounts), 317-319

V

validity, wills, 132
valuation dates, estate taxes, 84
valuations, 120
  gifts, 312-313
  qualifying for, 85
values
  intrinsic, 27
  life insurance, 201-202
variable life insurance, 198-199, 209
variable universal life insurance, 199
Visual Estate Plus, tax liability calculations, 7
voluntary signatures, wills, 127

W–X–Y–Z

Web sites, 384
  Bureau of Public Debt, 79
whole life insurance, 196, 198
wills, 10, 125-126
  amending, 132-133
  amendments, provisions, 154-155
  attestation clauses, 127
  beneficiaries, identification, 173
  claims, 120
  codicils, 132
  contests, 109, 120
  debt, repaying, 167-169
  destroying, 132
  Diana, Princess of Wales, 359-364
  disclaimers, 304-308
  disinheritance, 170-172
  execution requirements, 10, 127-128
  final say, 127

gifts, 130-131
  lapses, 130
guardians, designating, 131
holographic wills, 125
incapacity, 155-156
intentions, expressing, 141
joint wills, 126
lack of, 105
legal age, 127
limitations, 133-134
living wills, 10, 188
  execution requirements, 188
mutual wills, 126
Nixon, Richard M., 367-381
noncupative wills, 126
noted personalities, 134-135
personal represenatives, designating, 129-130
provisions, 129
  disinheritance, 170-172
  distribution provisions, 175-177
  gifts, 173-175
  repayment provisions, 167-170
  simultaneous death, 165-166
  survivorship provisions, 164
resident agents, 130
residue, distributing, 166-167
reviewing, 133
revocation, provisions, 154-155
revocations, 131-132
self-proving declarations, 127-128
simple wills, 126
sound mind, 127
spousal allowances, 171
testamentary, 125
testators, 128-129
testatrixes, 129
transfers, provisions, 154-155
trusts, compared, 139-140
types, 125-126
updating, 133
validity, 105, 132
voluntary signatures, 127

witnesses, wills, 129
written declarations, wills, 131

ZCALC software, tax liability calcualtions, 7